FAULKNER'S FAMILIES
A Southern Saga

Gwendolyn Chabrier

THE GORDIAN PRESS NEW YORK

FAULKNER'S FAMILIES; A Southern Saga. Copyright 1993 Gwendolyn Chabrier. All rights reserved. Printed in the United States of America. No part of this book may be used or reproduced in any manner whatsoever without written permission except in case of brief quotations embodied in critical articles and reviews. For information address The Gordian Press, 85 Tompkins Street, Staten Island NY USA 10304.

First Edition, 1993.   ISBN 0-87752-241-3

Library of Congress Catalogue Card Number: 93-49606

Library of Congress Cataloging in Publication Data

Chabrier, Gwendolyne, 1948-

Faulkner's families : a southern saga / Gwendolyn Chabrier. -- 1st ed.
p.   cm.
Includes bibliographical references.

1. Faulkner, William, 1897-1962 -- Criticism and interpretation.
2. Domestic fiction, American -- History and criticism. 3. Faulkner, William, 1897-1962--Characters. 4. Southern States--In literature. 5. Family--Southern States. 6. Family in literature. I. Title.

PS3511.A86Z7545 1993
813' .52--dc20   93-49606
CIP

TABLE OF CONTENTS

PREFACE

"Faulkner's Families: A Southern Saga" is a study of the Faulknerian family in the author's novels and short stories viewed from the perspective of literary criticism. Any analysis of this Nobel Prize winner's work also needs to take into consideration the sociological and biographical context, while weighing the extent to which Faulkner depends upon projection rather than reality. Faulkner is, first, a Southerner, and his conception of family can be understood only within this very specific framework.

The preponderant role played by the family in Faulkner's work is well synthesized in a recent article by Donald M. Kartiganer:

> More perhaps than the chronicler of a mythic corner of Mississippi, Faulkner is the premier American novelist of family. His people, however uniquely and memorably portrayed, invariably trail behind them clouds of familial qualifiers: the grandparents, parents and siblings whose cumulative identity is the indispensable context of individual character. The bulk of Faulkner's people are not so much single, separate persons as collective enterprises, the products and processes of family dramas apart from which the individual actor is scarcely intelligible.[1]

For Faulkner and his Southern compatriots, from long before the Civil War until the present, the family specifically has been the dominant institution in the South. The family can be seen as a reflection of Southern society at large. In this declining patriarchal and vanishing world, Faulkner's fictional families are in part based on their historical or actual counterparts, on biographical projection, and finally on a vivid and restless imagination which tends often to exaggerate reality.

Faulkner was barely recognized in the United States, except by the literati, until the publication of *Sanctuary* in 1933, which was poorly received by the puritanical audience comprising most of the American reading public. Ironically, as early as 1931 Faulkner was already appreciated abroad. The French were definitely the author's most avid readers. During the winter of 1932, Maurice Coindreau launched Faulkner on a career in France that was subsequently promoted by André Malraux, Valéry Larbaud, Jean-Paul Sartre, and Albert Camus. Later success in America was due in great part to the support he received from what Malcolm, his stepson, described as "Pappy's beloved France." [2]

Until the publication of the Viking *Portable Faulkner* in 1946, he was periodically out of print in the United States. Americans prior to this time had misjudged his work as too regional and had also found him unreadable and immoral. In fact, although Faulkner is a regionalist and the South, particularly the Southern family, is central to his work, his novels constantly transcend his local environment and address themselves to universal verities, a factor overlooked by the provincial middle-class American audience. In other ways he was considered personally too antisocial and withdrawn, and the American reader was overly sensitive to his apparent detachment. Actually, in this regard, the national criticism of Faulkner was certainly justified. His unwillingness to accommodate himself to his public can in great part be explained by an almost paranoid fear of intrusion. He is probably the only author who, once he became famous, took an axe and made holes in his driveway in order to ward off visitors.[3] More overtly according to his housesitter Lamar Stevens, Faulkner urinated systematically in the flower beds of the front porch when he was menaced by tourists.[4] Despite the uneasiness with which fellow Mississippians, including most of his family, viewed the author, the fictional families inhabiting his mythical Yoknapatawpha County are modeled to a great extent on those he knew in Oxford. Some are modeled specifically on his own family, such as the older, upper-class Compsons, Sartorises, and Priests. Until his later work, Yoknapatawpha's dynasties, not dissimilar to his own, show a systematic decline from generation to generation and his characters a consistent evasion of the present while taking refuge in a glamorized past.

The traditional Southerner, like the author himself, regrets the passing of the pre-Civil War South of *Absalom, Absalom!:* "the house

Negroes (who carried) the parasols and flywhisks," [5] ("the ladies moving in hoops among the miniature broadcloths of little boys and the pantalettes of little girls ..."),[6] and, finally, "the big house with candles and silk dresses and champagne." [7] The nostalgic Southerner has difficulty adapting to the vulgarity and amorality of the New South. In fact, Robert Penn Warren comments that the nineteenth-century Southern gentleman is *dépassé* in this twentieth-century society:

> Most of the descendants of the old order are in various ways incompetent: they are prevented by their code from competing with the codeless Snopeses, they cling to the letter and forget the spirit of their tradition, they lose contact with the realities of the present and escape into a dream world of alcohol or rhetoric or gentility or madness, they fall in love with defeat or death [8]

Yoknapatawpha is not, however, inhabited solely by an upper-class elite but also by a middle class such as the Coldfields or Hightowers, who have the proclivity to mingle and identify with the upper class, thus tending often to have similar problems within their own family structures. Another type of middle-class family detested by Faulkner is exemplified by the Snopeses, who have ascended very rapidly in the upwardly mobile twentieth-century Southern society and whose branches are fragmented, especially by the materialistic values characteristic of the parvenu. Faulkner focuses mainly on the upper-class, the poor-white, and the black families. This is not surprising because the South has been a very stratified society with sharp class distinctions in which the middle class either denied their social identity and amalgamated with the upper class or remained a very conservative group apart. It is therefore comprehensible that Faulkner's attention is focused on the few remaining classes and, specifically, on the poor-white families such as the Bundrens or on the black ones such as the Gibsons. In Faulkner's works his poor-white families are fraught with a familial disharmony very similar to that of their social superiors but with added financial pressures. Since the author is also white, he can identify with the lower-class white, but he also continues to project, although to a lesser degree, his own family problems upon this social group.

Faulkner's treatment of the black is totally different. Not able to identify with his black compatriots, who in this society are a caste and class apart, he generally idealizes the black and the mulatto families since as a liberal Southerner he carries the guilt of their exploitation. Simultaneously, Faulkner always creates unthreatening black rural families such as the Beauchamps or the Gibsons who, although they can periodically rebel against their masters, would never imagine being really equal to them or, worse, dethroning them. Finally, and ironically, it is the black family in his fiction, as well as in the South itself, who seem obligated to care for certain of the decadent, *fin de race*, debilitated white families; here is one of the telling reversals of the initial master-slave relationship.

By observing the relationships within the white families, specifically the interaction of the married couples and the parents and children, and their incestuous or miscegenetic involvements, one recognizes that the Faulknerian universe is a puritan hell in which families are doomed to incomprehension, isolation, rejection, ambivalence, domination, rebellion, and guilt. The author's fictional families, like his own and other Southern families, were the offspring of a patriarchical society in which the woman was relegated to a ceremonial pedestal, while the male profited from his superior position over both the female and most especially the black.

With the advent of the Civil War, the South underwent tremendous upheaval, and the power of the white male was questioned particularly by blacks, but also by the women. The impact was subsequently very great on the South's most important institution, the family. Although the South had remained ostensibly male-dominated, the old family structures and relationships were confronted by change, despite the Southerner's limited capacity and fundamental lack of desire for adaptation. At the same time, Faulkner is aware of the woman's ameliorated but still tangential position in the South of his time.

Despite his declaration to the contrary, Faulkner's work reflects a pronounced misogyny rooted, if not in a latently homosexual tendency, then certainly in a mother fixation that was never resolved. With the exception of *The Reivers*, the domineering, overly possessive mother is constantly present in his work, the incarnation of his own overpowering mother whom, if only subconsciously, he projects in the form of a female castrater to whom the male is victim. At the same time, the male's gradually diminishing position is well embodied by Faulkner's own Compson-like father. Finally, the archetype of the dominant Southern male is particularly personified by his grandfather Faulkner, whom he projects vividly into the Sartorises.

The Southern family can be understood by outsiders only in its socio-historical context. The Southerner, like the author, loves the South but is equivocal about his Dixie: emotionally loving it, intellectually hating it. Faulkner confronts the South's contrition over slavery, also with a sense of remorse: this is a state from which the modern Southerner can often not escape because he is still a participant in the region's racism, de facto segregation, and exploitation of the black race. The Southerner's sentiments of guilt are further reinforced by his puritan (that is, excessive and morally rigid) background, which is constantly fortifying his sense of damnation. The traditional, perceptive Southerner, burdened by equivocation and culpability, must also face the dehumanized South of the mercantile Snopeses; filled with a consequent sense of failure, of impotence, he turns inward and toward his family. This introversion is his ultimate means of self-protection in a world that is alien and incomprehensible to him. He must function in a universe in which both he and his accompanying value system are outmoded. With the inevitable loss of his frame of reference, he frequently finds himself without an identity. His turning inward upon himself is at the expense of interaction with his family, as well as with society at large. In the final analysis, the frustration, guilt, ambivalence, rejection, and loss of identity that the Southerner must feel translate to the familial level and reproduce themselves in the marital and parent-child exchange, as well as in incestuous and miscegenetic relationships. Similarly, the author's portrayal of the black family is affected, and the guilt Faulkner feels toward the race in general is a determinant factor, this time in a positive depiction of the rural black family to whom he also offers tribute—though he does so from a distance.

Interestingly, Faulkner's portrait of the white family becomes more moderated, in fact even very optimistic, at the end of his life when he comes more to terms with his own family problems. Families such as the Mallisons or the Priests, especially the latter, are biographical, and *The Reivers* is reflective of the writer's euphoric frame of mind as a grandfather. While his major work is a negative exaggeration of the Southern family, Faulkner's later writing is the opposite. One needs therefore to establish a realistic terrain between these two extremes.

Finally, the depiction of the Faulknerian family may be better understood when compared with that of other major Southern writers such as Robert Penn Warren, Thomas Wolfe, Katherine Anne Porter, Caroline Gordon, James Agee, Carson McCullers, Erskine Caldwell, William Styron, Truman Capote, and Flannery O'Connor. While the critics and historians view the Southern family analytically, these authors, like Faulkner, approach it with great subjectivity. Consequently, they react more passionately, finding themselves, like Faulkner in his major work, captivated mainly by the overpowering, and restrictive dimension of the Southern family, though still aware that it has also been the backbone of Southern life.

CHAPTER 1

The Southern Family Viewed by Faulkner and his Contemporaries

In 1949 William Faulkner won the Nobel Prize, but barely three years before that, in 1946, his work was essentially out of print in the country of his nativity. Although well-liked and received among the younger American writers and critics, his general popularity was less than explosive. In Europe, on the other hand, critics had given him a warm reception. This was particularly true in France where Maurice Edgar Coindreau said in 1931 that Faulkner was "one of the most interesting figures in recent American letters."[1] While his fiction was always set in the American South, his themes (particularly pertinent for that nineteenth- and early twentieth-century South) were also universal, and this explains to a large extent their immediate recognition and appreciation by his foreign audiences.

It is important to have an overview of Faulkner's South that takes into account the major preoccupations of the Southerner: guilt, ambivalence, the past, identity, religion (patricularly Puritanism), and determinism. Only by understanding the author in relation to his puritanical audience and to this Southern context in general is it possible to grasp the intricacies involved in his vision of family, as well as to evaluate its authenticity. Since the family is the major focal point of Southern life, it is possible to penetrate its dynamics once one has understood the psychological, philosophical, religious and historical forces influencing its structure.

There are great historical forces at work in Faulkner's novels and stories. The Old South is dead, or at least dying, but the New South has barely begun to breathe, and Faulkner's families are caught between these two worlds just as Faulkner himself was caught. Phil Stone, with whom Faulkner had a mentor relationship for many years, says of the poems in *The Marble Faun:*

> The author of these poems is a man steeped in the soil of his native land, a Southerner by every instinct, and, more than that, a Mississippian. George Moore said that all universal art became great by first being provincial, and the sunlight and mocking birds and blue hills of North Mississippi are a part of the young man's very being.[2]

But if Faulkner is of the Old South, he also has his reservations with that which she is becoming. As he says: he was at home again in Oxford, Mississippi, yet at the same time . . . not at home.[3]

Faulkner's ambivalence is shared by other contemporary Southern writers and lies at the very heart of the Southern psyche. The aware Southerner, who instinctively loves the South, must simultaneously accomodate himself to its historical responsability for slavery and to the loss in the Civil War of everything that that pre-war society held dear. So Faulkner and many of his heroes and literary contemporaries are often faced with frustration and self-hatred when confronted by their history. It is as Wilbur Cash says in *The Mind of the South:*

> the price for having erected its economic edifice not on the rock of stern morality but on the shifting sands of opportunism and brigandage.[4]

Faulkner's work is a mirror of Southern society, which is a traditional, homogeneous world unwilling and unable to adapt to change. It is a society whose inhabitants try to continue their uniform perception of the world from a commonly held view of life and morality, as indicated by Gavin Stevens in *Intruder in the* Dust:

> We are defending not actually our politics or even our way of life, but simply our homogeneity . . . only from homogeneity comes anything of a people or for a people of durable or lasting value.[5]

Faulkner, like many of his Southern compatriots, is aware of the South's rapid modernization and its consequences: he is distressed by the "doomed wilderness whose edges were constantly and punily gnawed at . . . hacked at in a fury of abhorrence." [6] He is conscious of, and equally averse to, the rise of the New South and to the urban nouveau riche he so detested, as he states in his introduction to *The Sound and the Fury*:

> . . . the South (I speak in the sense of the indigenous dream of any given collection of men having something in common, be it only geography or climate, which shape [sic] their economic and spiritual aspirations into cities, into a pattern of houses or behavior) is all since dead. . . . There is a thing known whimsically as the New South to be sure, but it is not the South. It is a land of immigrants who are rebuilding the towns and cities into replicas of towns and cities in Kansas and Iowa and Illinois, with skyscrapers and striped canvas awnings instead of balconies, and teaching the young men who sell the gasoline and the waitresses in the restaurant to say O yeah? and to speak with hard r's, and hanging over the intersections of quiet and shaped streets where no one save Northern tourists in Cadillacs and Lincolns ever pass at a gait faster than horse trots, changing red-and-green lights and savage and peremptory bells.[7]

The writer and his heroes ultimately resemble Eugene Gant in *Look Homeward, Angel:*

> He was the haunter of himself, trying to recover what he had been part of. He did not understand change, he did not understand growth.[8]

On the other hand, Faulkner's rejection of the New South is characterized by Thomas Wolfe in negative terms in *Look Homeward, Angel* as a "hostile and murderous entrenchment against all new life . . . their cheap mythology, their legend of the charm of their manner, the aristocratic culture of their lives, the quaint sweetness of their drawl." [9] Wilbur Cash views the Southerner's rejection of the present and consequent retreat into the past as a defense mechanism. He understands it as a means of justification to self and to the world, and an attempt to soothe and hide feelings of defeat, shame, and guilt." [10] In fact, the Southerner's escape into a frequently illusory past is a tendency as pivotal as his ambivalence or guilt.

The importance of the past in Faulkner's work was keenly observed, once again by the French, as in Jean-Paul Sartre's article, "Time in Faulkner: The Sound and the Fury," and in Jean Pouillon's "Time and Destiny in Faulkner." Sartre believes that Faulkner's characters often lack a sense of freedom, potentiality, futurity. They are paralyzed by the past. He continues: "Beyond this present time there is nothing, since the future does not exist." For Sartre "the present is nothing but a chaotic din, a future that is past. Faulkner's vision of the world can be compared to that of a man sitting in an open car and looking backward." [11] Jean Pouillon considers that the past conceived by Faulkner "was but is and will be." [12] Pouillon feels that Faulkner and Proust treat time in a different manner. While both chronological and recaptured time exist for the French author, for Faulkner "the past is constantly present."[13]

Faulkner himself on numerous occasions confirmed the importance of the past and its constant reality in the present and in the future. In an interview he stated that "there is no such thing as *was*—only *is*." [14] He also believed that ". . . no man is himself, he is the sum of his past. There is no such thing really as was because the past is." [15] He also affirmed that "there is only the present moment, in which I include both the past and the future, and that is eternity." [16] His heroes are, moreover, the spokesmen for his notions regarding an everpresent past; Gavin Stevens in *Requiem for a Nun* claims, "The past is never dead. It's not even past." [17] In *Intruder in the Dust* Stevens concludes that "yesterday today and tomorrow are Is: Indivisible: One" [18]; or Quentin Compson in *Absalom, Absalom!* sees himself as "a barracks filled with stubborn backlooking ghosts still recovering, even forty-three years afterward . . . ." [19]

The continuing obsession with the past reflects the Southerner's desire to transcend his sense of defeat and impotence from the Civil War. In *Absalom, Absalom!* Faulkner refers to a South free from slavery, "free of the disease and not even aware that the freedom was that of impotence."[20] According to Andrew Lytle, "the Southerner's defeat has also resulted in self-contemplation and self-consciousness." [21] This self-cognizance also engendered a deep introversion, a fear of the unfamiliar and an apprehension—specifically of the outsider. The Southerner's insecurity made him turn inwards on his family and himself and react vehemently toward the outsider who threatened him. This proclivity frequently resulted in a form of xenophobia that can be seen in the reflection of Clarence Sartoris, who the author devalues in *Sanctuary*: "But the lowest, cheapest thing on this earth ain't a nigger: it's a jew." [22]

A South beset by both insecurity and a bad conscience after the Civil War turned its frustration and guilt into aggression, destruction, and lawbreaking; violence became rampant throughout the South. Violence, concluded C. Dwight Dorough, is "a legacy of slavery." [23] In fact, the Ku Klux Klan, the incarnation of Southern violence, was a terrorist organization formed by six ex-Confederate soldiers in Tennessee in 1866. It flourished in the Reconstruction era following the Civil War and was exclusively Southern in its membership and its concerns. The original Klan, with which Faulkner concerns himself, dressed as ghosts and were night riders who went through the countryside dragging people from their homes, whipping, and shooting or otherwise assaulting them. Frequently, they drove their victims away or destroyed their property. The motivation of this original Klan was a desire to perpetuate white supremacy and to keep the blacks in their place economically and socially. Klansmen further dedicated themselves to defeating the Republican Party. The early Klan probably committed more crimes than did their successors and most of their victims were black, though white Republicans did not go unspared.

The Ku Klux Klan is alluded to in *Light in August*: they take away Hightower's Negro cook as well as whipping the reverend himself. They leave Hightower, commanding him to leave town, but when the minister does not comply, he is taken into the woods by the Klan, tied to a tree and beaten unconscious. Faulkner thus affirms the fact of pervasive violence in the South:

> The spirit that moves a man to put on a sheet and burn sticks
> in your yard is pretty prevalent in Mississippi, but not all
> Mississippians wear the sheet and burn the sticks. They hate
> and scorn and look with contempt on people that do, but the
> same spirit, the same impulse is in them too, but they are
> going to use a different method from wearing a nightshirt and
> burning sticks.[24]

Nevertheless, while Faulkner thus strongly condemns violence and the
Ku Klux Klan, other less liberal Southerners such as Thomas Dixon, in
The Klansman: An Historical Romance (1905), not only condoned the Ku
Klux Klan and its activities but even venerated them as an instrument
of justice. Even though Dixon, like Faulkner, is against slavery, he is
also vehemently against equality.

Even more crucial to an overview of Faulkner's South is an understanding of the importance of religion, specifically Southern Protestantism. It is a subject integrally related to that of violence, since
through this vehicle the Southerner could consider himself upholding
his religion or his principles. On the other hand, and possibly more frequently, he also used violence as a means of rebelling against the rigidity of the Southern church: against what E. Callaway saw as the
"straight jacket of the church."[25] While the Northern Protestant
churches were concerned with labor conditions, racial injustice, and fair
civil procedure, the Southern Protestant church involved itself with
what it judged were moral issues such as the evils of tobacco, liquor,
cardplaying, dancing, theater-going, fighting, dueling, brawling, quar-
reling, gossiping, Sabbbath-breaking, excessive luxuries, unethical legal practices, and divorce. The influence of the church was so strong
that state legislatures passed bills prohibiting blasphemy, atheism,
Sabbath-breaking, polygamy, and similar violations of this brand
orthodox Christian morality. The repressive nature of Southern Protestantism and the consequent violence it engendered are well expressed by
Julius in *Mosquitoes*:

> It seems to me that the Protestant faith was invented for the
> sole purpose of filling our jails and morgues and houses of
> detention . . . How do young Protestant boys in small towns
> spend Sunday afternoons, with baseball and all such natural
> muscular vents denied them? They kill, they slay and steal
> and burn.[26]

Furthermore, the preoccupation with sin and guilt characteristic at
least of the Presbyterian and Baptist churches in the South makes the
Southerner, according to Peter Swiggart, unable to accept the antithetical feelings of pleasure.[27] According to Faulkner in *Light in August*, the
Southerner responds through violence: "Pleasure, ecstasy, they cannot

seem to bear: their escape from it is in violence, in drinking and fighting and praying." [28]

Faulkner characteristically treats the Baptists and Presbyterians more harshly than he does the Methodists. He states in an interview in Virginia that "it may be a debatable question" whether the Baptists "believe in religion or not." [29] Most people in Yoknapatawpha are Baptists, and the author's villains are affiliated with the Baptist Church: Flem Snopes, the embodiment of nouveau riche amorality; his sadistic cousin Clarence, a corrupt judge; the townspeople in *Sanctuary*, who lynch the innocent Lee Goodwin; and Mr. Stovall, the deacon who uses Nancy as a prostitute and refuses to pay her, then knocks her down and kicks her teeth in. Presbyterians, too, are derogated by the author, as exemplified by Doc Hines and Simon McEachern, both destructive religious fanatics. The Methodists, however, are depicted more favorably. Although the Methodist merchant Goodhue Coldfield does starve himself in an attic, an act indicative of the excesses of Protestantism, his daughters Rosa and Ellen are sympathetically depicted as the helpless victims of Thomas Sutpen's ruthless opportunism. Will Varner, who is Methodist, is considered the leading citizen of Frenchman's Bend, while the Methodist Mallisons in *Intruder in the Dust* are among Faulkner's most respectable families.

After the family, religion was and is the dominant institution in the South; the extent of its importance is well measured by Lillian Smith in *Killers of the Dream*, in which she affirms that "God was not someone we met on Sunday but a permanent member of our household." [30] In the Southern states, Methodists and Baptists constitute at least two-thirds of the reported Protestant membership; in Georgia, Tennessee, Alabama, Mississippi, Arkansas, and Louisiana, these two denominations account for more than eighty percent of the Protestant population.[31] In *The Town*, for example, Jefferson is founded by a "small inflexible unreconstructed Puritan group, both Baptist and Methodist." [32] There were more Baptist than Methodist churchgoers in the South. Almost half of Southern church members were in the Southern Baptist Church; they comprised more than 12.4 million people and 35,000 congregations in 1973.[33] However, the difference between the Methodists and the Baptists, or even the Presbyterians, concerns not only their belief in man's guilt and depravity but also their belief in predestination versus the Methodists' emphasis on free will. Nevertheless, as remarked by Alwyn Berland, the Calvinist conception of predestination coincides with Faulkner's view that all of time, past and future, lies in the present moment.[34] Calvinists, as notoriously described by George Santayana, feel a fierce pleasure in the existence of misery, especially one's own.[35] Until his later work Faulkner seems himself to be firmly immersed in this tradition. Robert Barthe would concur with this position when he describes the author as being "in the Calvinist Protestant tradition." However, his work in the fifties and his statement in an interview with Jean Stern in 1956 to the effect "that man is indestructible because of his will to freedom," [36] shows that, despite the contradiction found in the greater part of his work, Faulkner is still to some extent under the influence of his Methodist upbringing.

In fact, the author's earlier religious position wavered between agnosticism and atheism. One can certainly question whether Faulkner, like Reverend Mahon in *Soldiers' Pay*, does not equate God with arbitrariness; like Mahon, he seems also to define God as "circumstance." [37] Similarly, as late as *Requiem for a Nun* (1951) one may wonder if Temple is not the author's spokesman when she asks: "What kind of God is it that has to blackmail His customers with the whole world's grief and ruin?" [38]

Faulkner has no allegiance to orthodox religion at all. In an interview in 1952, he does not believe in the mechanical or personal God, the favorite deity of Southern Protestantism, but instead in "a God who is the most complete expression of mankind, a God who rests both in eternity and in the now . . . a deity very close to Bergson's." [39] His later religious position is best described in *A Fable* by Reverend Tobe Sutterfield, who states that he bears witness "to man. God don't need me. I bears witness to Him of course, but my main witness is to man." [40] This later commentary is imbued with overtones of agnosticism.

Finally, it is necessary to consider the puritanical element in Southern Protestantism and its crucial effect on Faulkner's work. The movement known as the Great Awakening, which emerged in the South around 1740, was to have major importance, not only in the South's religious history but also in its considerable influence on Faulkner's thinking. From the beginning this movement was especially attractive to Southerners because it offered as one of its major innovations the practice of "family religion"; it encouraged family devotion. Furthermore, the Great Awakening was a movement against the formalism of the

Episcopal Church. It had a strong appeal for the common man and resulted in tremendous growth in the Baptist, Methodist, and Presbyterian Churches. H.L. Mencken refers to the South as "the bunghole of the United States, a cesspool of Baptists, a miasma of Methodists, snakecharmers, phony realestate operators and syphilitic evangelists" and describes the South as the "last great bulwark of Christianity . . . defender of the ark, its people . . . the chosen people." [41] Although Faulkner does not subscribe to the "orgiastic" [42] element of this evangelical movement or its anthropomorphic God, this "passionate, whimsical tyrant," [43] the God to whom both Doc Hines and Joanna Burden speak "as if he were a man in this room," [44] the author is still very much influenced by the Calvinist repression of sex that was incorporated in the movement.

The strongest puritan influence initially came into the South with the Great Awakening. The equation of sex and sin, man's sexuality being regarded as the dominant symbol of his fallen nature, the image of woman as temptress, an Eve doomed to destroy him, certainly underlies the major part of Faulkner's work and is exemplified by the Charlotte Rittenmeyers, the Temple Drakes, the Joanna Burdens, and the Eula Varners.

Both American and foreign critics remarked frequently on Faulkner's puritanism. Faulkner himself early commented on its consequences in a 1932 letter to Maurice Coindreau. He acknowledges to Coindreau that he has "a quite decided strain of puritanism (in its proper sense, of course; not our American one) regarding sex." [45]

Even though Hermann Hesse denounced "the degenerate, furtive, dreary, indeed almost infernal Puritan theology haunting Faulkner's novels," [46] it is the French who have been especially aware of this puritanical strain marking Faulkner's work. That the French seem to be more conscious of Faulkner's puritanism in connection with women and sex may reflect the fact that their society has historically been more liberal; consequently, the French are much more aware of the conservatism, not to say the misogyny, inherent in the author's views.

Also significant within the Faulknerian universe is the notion of determinism or fate, a theme completely interconnected with Southern religion and Puritanism. Throughout the greater part of his canon, and until his very late work, the author portrays mankind, and more specifically the Southerner and his family, as fate's victim. When interviewed in Virginia, Faulkner himself affirmed the importance of determinism, saying, "I think that man's free will functions against a Greek background." [47] Nevertheless, like the writer himself, his characters have been primarily influenced by the Calvinist strain fundamental to Southern Protestantism. They are repeatedly the helpless victims of fate, destiny, the cosmic joker, the dark dicemen, the opponent, chance, retribution, irony, the stage manager, . . . "this Arbiter, the Architect, the Umpire . . . perverse, impotent or blind." [48] Until nearly the end of his work when the author himself is feeling less fragile, his heroes are propelled by the "hopeless juggernaut of circumstance." [49] Vann Woodward remarked of Faulkner's region that "nothing he asserts about [its] history is conducive to the theory that the South was the darling of divine providence." [50]

This deterministic element in Calvinism was probably appealing to many Southerners. At the turn of the century, many traditional Southerners, like the author, believed that "the South . . . is dead, killed by the Civil War," [51] a notion implied by Thomas Wolfe when he says, "America went off the track somewhere—back around the time of the Civil War, or pretty soon afterward." [52] Considering themselves and their society the hopeless victims of this defeat, Southerners could permit themselves to retreat from society into themselves and their families and justify their withdrawal as a necessary flight from the destructiveness inherent in "the old primal faithless Manipulator of all the lust and folly." [53] They could otherwise warrant their escape by rationalizing that they were helpless against the omnipotence of fate.

In the last analysis, Faulkner's theories of destiny or the Calvinist's notions of determinism were the Southerners' ultimate substantiation of paralysis and ineffectuality; here they found both a religion and a philosophy which permitted them to feel guiltless in their apathy and inaction. Mr. Compson, his son Quentin, young Bayard Sartoris, Horace Benbow and Reverend Hightower are content to wallow in the passivity and ineffectuality permitted by the deterministic thought predominant in the South. Mr. Compson indoctrinates Quentin: "'No battle is ever won,' he said. 'They are not even fought. The field only reveals to man his folly and despair, and victory is an illusion of philosophers and fools.'" [54]

Against this background of Southern Protestantism, Puritanism, and determinism are the spiritual, psychological, and philosophical forces influencing Faulkner's work and Southern thought generally, but the dominant family-centered issues such as ambivalence, guilt, the relevance of the past, and identity, also need to be addressed. Most critics and historians stress that the family was probably the most constructive force in Southern life. Yet Faulkner's major work, like that of his literary contemporaries, portrays a contradictory image and with the exception of his late work, Faulkner never denies the perniciousness of the family.

The historian Arthur Calhoun shows that "the dominance of familism in the colonial South was promoted by rural isolation, and living on a plantation far from towns made the home the central institution." [55] Francis Simkins affirms that in the decades after the Civil War "the family was the core of Southern society; within its bounds everything worthwhile took place." [56] Additionally, he believes that after 1910, when there were certain transformations in Southern domestic life, "there was no significant uprooting of family life." [57] Eugene D. Genovese also maintains that Southern society was, almost from the outset, family-centered.

The old patriarchal family exemplified to a large degree the relations between ruler and ruled; in this respect, it served as model for social organization and political government. In Genovese's analysis of Southern slave society, this sense of extended family came to influence the whole network of race and class relations.[58] Hodding Carter likewise stresses the strong loyalty which arises among family members: "I was raised to believe that whoever harmed any kinsman was also my enemy and whoever befriended him was my friend." [59] For George Fitzhugh, the society-as-family is the ideal toward which Southern society should strive. Individual and regional identity, self-esteem, and status are also determined by family relationships. The region was conceived and organically connected by (pseudo) ties of blood. Fitzhugh even equates the family with destiny.[60] William Stadiem, too, comments on the family's primacy referring not only to the immediate family but also to its past: "The cult of ancestry is Dixie's favorite obsession." [61] Other critics, however, such as Stark Young in "I'll Take My Stand" are conscious of the Southern family's limitations, stating that they are "often onerous to aliens and not seldom one of our own domestic burdens," but he still regards the family as "a good trait." Finally, Clement Eaton views the Southern family more broadly and alludes to "an intense local attachment or patriotism that was supported by a strong feeling for family." [62] He, unlike the others except for Genovese, alludes to the family's white members as well as its black ones. Genovese, in fact, claims that the strong kinship ties felt between blacks and whites connected to the same family have their origins in slavery, in which the owner was the patriarch and master not only to the slaves but also to his own family.[63]

In the South the eminence of the family can also be measured by the fact that families were larger, the extended family was consequential, and divorce rates were lower. The family remains paramount in the South even today, as indicated by former President Carter during his campaign, when he frequently said, "I come from a good family and I want you all to be part of my family." [64] He added in his Inaugural Address that he wanted his service in the Presidency to be remembered for having "strengthened the American family, which is the basis of our society." [65]

Still, in the major part of Faulkner's work, as well as in that of other eminent Southern writers, the family is seen to be deleterious in the manner set forth by Mary Boykin Chesnut:

> It is your own family she calls the familiars of the Inquisition.
> She declares that they set upon you: fall foul of you, watch
> and harass you from morn to dewy eve. They have a perfect
> right to your life, night and day, into the fourth and fifth gen-
> eration. No locks or bolts can keep them out![66]

The strength and support it thus offers to some becomes, for others, a destructive force which is restrictive, authoritarian, and ultimately, completely overwhelming.

Many American and French critics point out Faulkner's negative vision of the family, especially in his most distinguished work. Until his latest novels, Faulkner seemed to focus on the negative aspects of family life to the exclusion of the positive ones; furthermore, he is disposed to exaggerate the former. Although his depiction of the family, especially of parent-child relations, marital relations, incest in the white family, and miscegenation, tends to cast the South's primary institution in a pejorative light, the portrait retains only a limited reality. His treatment of the black family, however, is more indulgent and results in an overview which is also more accurate. His precision here can in great part be explained by the fact that the author is not identifying with the blacks and is consequently capable of greater objectivity, thus, he is able to avoid projecting many of the negative aspects that mark his own family life. By the time of his later work Faulkner had transcended his own familial problems and is inclined, as in *The Reivers*, to depict his families free of any of the problems habitually plaguing the Southern family. In this later work he magnifies, instead, the family's positive attributes, the Mallisons and the Priests being exemplary. Ultimately, in order to really understand his Southern family, it is necessary to take into consideration the writer's work as a whole, making a synthesis of both his major work and his later work.

The despairing vision of family dominating Faulkner's major work is very consistent with the one offered by many of his literary contemporaries. This similarity of viewpoint tends to validate the authenticity of his depiction. Thomas Wolfe, through his hero Eugene Gant in *Look Homeward, Angel*, views the family quite simply as a form of slavery:

> He thought of his own family almost with hatred. My God! Am I never to be free? he thought. What have I done to deserve this slavery?[67]

In *The Hills Beyond*, Wolfe writes of the Joyners that, even though they have a strong sense of family identity, "of 'affection,' 'love,' 'devotion,' even clannishness—as these terms are generally accepted—the family seems to have little." [68] Katherine Anne Porter using Cousin Eva as her spokesman in "Old Morality," bitterly condemns the Southern family as a "hideous institution," one that is the "root of all human wrongs" and that ought to be "wiped from the face of the earth." [69] This view is reiterated by Steven in Porter's "The Downward Path to Wisdom":

> I hate Papa, I hate Mama, I hate Grandma, I hate Uncle David, I hate Old Janet, I hate Marjory, I hate Papa. I hate Mama.[70]

Similiarly, Robert Penn Warren in *All the King's Men* condemns the family; he alludes to parent-child relationships as a "blood greed" stating that:

> ... this thing itself is not love. It is something in the blood. It is
> a kind of blood greed, and it is the fate of man. It is the thing
> which man has which distinguishes him from the happy
> brute. When you get born your father and mother lost some-
> thing out of themselves, and they are going to bust a hame
> trying to get it back, and you are it. They know they can't get it
> all back but they will get as big a chunk out of you as they
> can.[71]

Alienation, especially in relation to the family, is of great concern
to these Southern authors. While Penn Warren's families often suffer
because the parent-child relationship is stifling, the loneliness en-
dured by James Agee's, Carson McCullers', and Eudora Welty's protagonists is of a more personal nature. James Agee explores the bereavement
and solitude caused by death in *A Death in the Family* as well as these
same emotions caused by enforced separation, in this instance with the
mother in *The Morning Watch*. Carson McCullers, too, in *A Member of
the Wedding* and *Reflections in a Golden Eye* focuses on the aloneness
created by estrangement from a family member. Futhermore in *Clock
without Hands*, she portrays family love as narcissistic as demonstrated by Judge Clane, who loves passionately both his family's past
and his dead wife because they were *his*. Family isolationism is characterized by Eudora Welty's Dabney in *Delta Wedding*:

> all together we have a wall, we are self-sufficient against peo-
> ple that come up knocking, we are solid to the outside. Does
> the world suspect that we are very private people? I think one
> by one we're all more lonely than private and more lonely
> than self-sufficient.[72]

According to Welty, the family prison is filled with sequestered cap-
tives. Welty also considers the family suffocating but at least offers a
solution to this problem. For her, temporary separation results in a re-
newed relationship that can keep the family together. Welty's *The
Robber Bridegroom, Delta Wedding,* and "The Bride of the Innisfallen"
are among the many examples. For Wolfe, families can afford sepa-
rateness because they are held together through their sentiments of
family identity. In each case, however, the author's focus is on, and the
protaganist's option is interestingly for, family disjunction.

Meanwhile, identity is also fundamental to Robert Penn Warren's vision of the family. With the exception of Jack Burden at the end of *All the King's Men*, the protagonists of Robert Penn Warren, such as Percy Munn in *Night Rider* or Bogan Murdock in *Heaven's Gate*, are generally incapable of achieving gratifying familial relations because they are unable to transcend the dichotomy of good and evil which would enable them to achieve maturity. Erskine Caldwell's characters are by contrast less hermetic since they lose themselves in a world of promiscuity; sex, including miscegenation, becomes the disruptive force in the poor-white and black families inhabiting Caldwell's South.

The Southerner was deeply affected by the problem of change and decline and the accompanying sentiments of isolation in a modernized world which he considered corrupt and empty and to which he had difficulty adapting. Accordingly, in order to escape this "new" South, he created and escaped into a glamorized past, and since the family is a microcosm of society, it is not surprising that this tendency surfaces first at the level of the family. The decline depicted by Faulkner or the family solitariness insisted upon by McCullers, Agee, or Welty is merely a reflection of the Southerner's societal estrangement.

In a comparable manner, the magnitude of the past and of religion affects certain Southern protagonists, such as William Styron's, who are incapable of accepting adult family responsibilities because they are unable to outgrow adolescence. In *Set this House on Fire*, Mason's behavior towards his family is that of an egocentric child. Likewise, Milton Loftis in *Lie Down in Darkness* longs for his youth, while his wife Helen escapes into the memories of her girlhood. Truman Capote's characters are prisoners of their childhood and of infantile fears, as typified by Kay in "A Tree of Night," Walter in "Shut a Final Door," or Sylvia in "Masterly Misery."

Flannery O'Connor, too, draws a discomforting portrait of the Southerner's relationship to his family. Like the Southerner generally, O'Connor's heroes are faced with the problem of self-definition, of finding a sense of identity in a balanced and moral universe, many needing to free themselves from parental religious control. In her work, the protagonist may be a scapegoat for his family's religious fanaticism or inverse nihilism. O'Connor, a Catholic herself, is particularly sensitive to the excesses of Southern Protestantism as demonstrated by her characters' complete adherence to or total denial of religion. In *The Vi-*

olent Bear it Away, Rufus must escape from the influence of his surrogate father, Sheppard, who is a militant atheist and scientific objectivist; by contrast, Hazel Motes in *Wise Blood* must remove himself from an incestuous relationship with a mother who is a religious fanatic.

It is also necessary when looking at the Southern family to examine the social and economic framework of the particular families populating Faulkner's work. First, he is preoccupied with aristocratic families: the Sartorises, McCaslins, Compsons, and Sutpens in opposition to the nouveau riche families typified by the Snopeses. Unlike in Europe, where generations of family lineage were required to reach aristocratic status, in the colonial South, and even as late as the early part of the nineteenth century, rough frontiersmen through their own industry were able to become aristocrats in the Southern sense of the term by accumulating vast amounts of land and slaves. The importance of landholding is succinctly stated by Thomas Nelson Page, for example, in *Red Rock: A Chronicle of Reconstruction,* when Jacquelin sets out to retrieve his family house remembering his father's last words:

> Keep the old place. Make any sacrifice to do that. Landholding is one of the safeguards of a gentry. Our people for six generations have never sold an acre, and I never knew a man who sold land that throve.[73]

Thomas Sutpen arrives in Jefferson in 1833 having been born in West Virginia of a Scottish mountain woman and a father who was an ex-prisoner. He maneuvers to obtain one hundred square miles from the Chickasaws and manages to join the ranks of the Southern aristocracy, despite the fact that he lacks the social attributes of dynasties like the Sartorises who, being part of the Carolinean aristocracy, come to Yoknapatawpha a few years later not only "with slaves and gear and money,"[74] but also with breeding, refinement, and education, assuming a position of leadership in the community. In fact, according to Frederick J. Hoffman, "the story of Sutpen is a model version of the rise of families."[75] Yet, other families such as the Compsons or the McCaslins are also to obtain their "aristocratic status" only upon entry into Jefferson. Jason Lycurgus Compson is the grandson of a Quentin MacLachan Compson who emigrates from Scotland as a political fugitive and comes to America destitute. Jason obtains his land in Jefferson in 1820 by exchanging a mare with the Indians. Similarly, Lucius Quintus Carothers McCaslin arrives in Mississippi in 1787 and begins as a frontiersman; he "bought the land, took the land no matter how." [76] McCaslin purchases land and slaves from Ikkemotubbe, the Indian chief.

With the exception of the Sartorises, probably all the founders of the ruling dynasties in Yoknapatawpha are self-made men. Furthermore, as William Stadiem verifies, contrary to the image one may have of the South, even in its aristocratic pockets such as Charleston, New Orleans, and Virginia, this aristocracy from which the Sartorises descend is one whose origins are mercantile. One should at no time forget that, despite the delusions that many of these Southerners may have regarding themselves as being "royal houses akin to the Hanoverians and the Bourbons," [77] the family founders were of the lower gentry or the upper bourgeosie in Europe. Actually, almost no members of the Cavalier aristocracy ever left England for the United States.[78] As Wilbur Cash affirms, most settlers of the South were descended from English of humble origins and "the half-wild Scotch and Irish clansmen of the seventeenth and eighteenth centuries." [79] Georgia began as a debtors' colony; North Carolina was a plebian colony peopled by small farmers, not great planters. Tennessee, Alabama, and inland South Carolina were comprised of a wilderness filled with mountain men and Indians, and Faulkner's Mississippi was simply an uncharted malarial swamp. Thus, when alluding to the Faulknerian families in general, one concurs with Cleanth Brooks that "it would be safer to refer, not to the aristocratic tradition, but to the tradition of the Big House." [80]

In Faulkner's work one witnesses the decline of these families. The Sutpens, the Sartorises, the Compsons, and even to some extent the McCaslins are dynasties all subject to the deterioration faced in common by the traditional Southerner. These aristocratic families (in the broad sense of the term) wield the power in Yoknapatawpha County at the time of the Civil War, like many equivalent families throughout the South. By the early part of the twentieth century the Sutpens destroy each other or are destroyed by violating the aristocratic code; the Sartorises are debilitated because they are unable to function in mechanized twentieth-century society; the Compsons fall into decay and become impotent, paralyzed by the New South. The McCaslins' decline, as described by Joe Carl Buice, occurs on a moral level when attempts at expiation of the family's transgressions fail to achieve the brotherhood of men which they seek.[81] The McCaslins descent is provisional because direct descent through a male ceases in the third generation and the dynasty is continued only through the distaff and Negro lines. Finally, in the last generation, Faulkner's predominant families are made up symbolically of idiots like Jim Bond, nymphomaniacs like young Quentin, or weaklings like young Bayard's infant son, who dies at birth. These families, who had often become aristocrats in one generation, relinquished their power in the early part of the twentieth century not to individuals or society but, significantly, to other families—to mercantile families exemplified by the Snopeses: "a family, a clan, a race, maybe even a species, of pure sons of bitches." [82]

Faulkner's work, at least initially, was almost completely rejected by his regional compatriots. Even though he was repudiated at the beginning of his career, he was still clearly appreciated by other writers in his own country and, more importantly, by foreigners, the French in particular, who were really responsible for the author's literary renown in the United States. Despite the initial American reaction, Faulkner is an author very representative of the South. His work comprises a statement of the Southerner's misogyny and Puritanism operating out of a doom-ridden Protestant context with the family existing at its center. His writing, until his latest work, illustrates the predominance of the family. Yet he, like the other major Southern writers of his period, focuses on its destructive aspects rather than its positive ones, demonstrating that generally the family as a unit tends to overpower its individual members, who in turn become the victims of its strength. Finally, Faulkner concentrates on the aristocratic families who serve as models of the Southern family; simultaneously, the descent of these families reflects the Southerner's personal sense of decline when confronted with a world in which he feels totally overcome by modernization and its accompanying antitraditional values. Faulkner's vision of the Southern family becomes one of optimism only at the end of his life, when he is capable of projecting his own familial happiness brought about by the birth of his grandchildren.

CHAPTER 2

Faulkner's Family and the Southern Milieu

Besides the sociological factors that influence Faulkner's work, biographical factors are of great importance: as the author told Phil Stone, "Character came out of family." [1] In his major work this observation is especially true of the Sartorises, but the Compsons, too, are to a great extent projections of the author's own family. Faulkner states that "it is himself that the Southerner is writing about. . ." and that he has "figuratively speaking, taken the artist in him in one hand and his milieu in the other and thrust the one into the other like a clawing and spitting cat into a croker [sic] sack." [2] By exploring the marital, the parent-child, the sibling, the quasi-incestuous, and even the alleged miscegenetive relationships in his own family, it is possible to see a definite correspondence between these complex and often disharmonious intrafamilial relationships and the ones that he created in his fiction. Concomitantly, by the time of his latest work, the decadent and unstable families are replaced by the balanced, harmonious ones of the Mallisons and the Priests, the latter being a positive projection of his own family. Once he has resolved his own family difficulties, Faulkner's fictional families are portrayed very differently.

Faulkner's fictional families, and in particular the Sartorises, are modeled in great part on his own family. Like the Falkner family, and many other Southern and nominally aristocratic families, the Sartorises are faced with a sense of family degeneration. However, the major difference between the Falkners and Sartorises (one, in fact, that

the author seems not to insist upon) is that the origins of the two families differ quite radically. W.C. Falkner, like Thomas Sutpen, was a
penniless man of simple origin who, born in Tennessee of Welsh descent,
was purported to have fought with a younger brother and to have been
punished so severely by his family that he ran away from home, arriv-
ing in Mississippi in 1842. By contrast, John Sartoris arrived in Mississippi in 1833, not only with money and his Carolinean lineage, but also
accompanied by slaves.

Like many Southern aristocrats Colonel W.C. Falkner, the "Old
Colonel," quickly compensated for his initial status; he became a
lawyer, planter, railroad builder, and Confederate officer. Faulkner is,
indeed, proud of the fact that the Old Colonel was "part of Stonewall
Jackson's left at 1st Manassas."[3] He also founded a college and wrote
best-selling books. J.W.T. Falkner, the Young Colonel, was a lawyer, a
banker, and an Assistant United States Attorney. Even though J.W.T.
was less influential than his father, the major family decline was witnessed in the personage of Murry Cuthbert Falkner, William Faulkner's
father. He drifted from job to job working as a conductor on the family
railroad, in a livery stable, in the hardware business, and finally as
secretary and business manager of the University of Mississippi.

The reverence that Faulkner feels toward his great-grandfather is
projected onto his fictional persona. John Sartoris, too, fights in the
Civil War, builds a railroad, and runs for a seat in the legislature; and,
like J.W.T. Falkner, he is killed by his former partner in the railroad.
Like W.C. Falkner, John Sartoris is "the virus, the inspiration and example . . . which dominated them all."[4] Of John Sartoris, in relation
to his son, Bayard, and Will Falls, the author says in *Flags in the Dust*
that,

> freed as he was of time, he was a far more definite presence
> in the room than the two of them cemented by deafness to a
> dead time and drawn thin by the slow attenuation of days. He
> seemed to stand above them, with the bearded, hawklike face
> and the bold glamor of his dream.[5]

Bayard Sartoris, like J.W.T. Falkner, is also the head of a bank; and
like his historical counterpart, Old Bayard lives only in the ethics and
traditions of the past and thus loses control of the bank to Flem Snopes

in the same way the Young Colonel was superseded by a shrewd back-country financier named Joe Parks.

In the Sartoris family, the second John Sartoris, the fictional twin of Faulkner's father, degenerates to such a level of insignificance that he is alluded to in *Flags in the Dust* and *Sartoris* only as having died in 1901 of yellow fever. Such a very brief reference to John Sartoris is demonstrative of the family's decline and, most importantly, is indicative of the author's disparaging attitude toward his own father. Faulkner projects onto his male characters his father Murry's weakness, as well as manifesting his own desire to rid himself entirely of this paternal figure.

However, Faulkner worships his ancestors and like the Sartorises deeply regrets the family downfall—one which for Faulkner (like his own family) personifies the South:

> Sartoris is the name of the game itself—a game outmoded and played with pawns shaped too late and to an old pattern, and of which the Player Himself is a little wearied. For there is death in the sound of it, and a glamourous fatality, like silver pennons downrushing at sunset, or a dying fall of horns along the road to Roncevaux.[6]

The manners, morals, values, beliefs, and traditions belonging to the Old South, as described by Edmond Volpe, represent to the Sartorises, as they did to the Falkners, "the golden age, the apex of human glory and life, the Garden of Eden from which man was driven." [7]

The twentieth-century heirs to the legend are the victims of a conflict between the myth of the past and the reality of the present. The opposing forces either maim or destroy them. Volpe notes that their "lost Eden" can become "a psychological crippler." [8] Olga Vickery asserts that "at its most extreme, devotion to the dead and their design can mean a complete denial of one's own life." [9] This proclivity is exemplified by Hightower in *Light in August*:

> But the town said that if Hightower had just been a more dependable kind of man, the kind a minister should be instead of being born about thirty years after the one day he seemed to have ever lived in the day when his grandfather was shot from the galloping horse —[10]

The author also says of Hightower:

> If he cared or not, with his religion and his grandfather being
> shot from the galloping horse all mixed up, as though the
> seed which his grandfather had transmitted to him had been
> on the horse too that night and had been killed too and time
> had stopped there and then for the seed and nothing had
> happened in time since, not even him.[11]

This tendency toward nostalgia recreates itself at the family
level, marking the Sartorises and the Falkners as well as many of their
regional compatriots. Too often, these Southerners prefer to romanticize
the past and insinuate themselves among the magnolia myths, rather
than face the realities of the mechanical, industrial present. In the
same way that young John Sartoris and Bayard court their own deaths
in their respective plane accidents, Faulkner's alcoholism is an act of
self-destruction finally resulting in the same fate. Each individual ac-
tively participates in what he considers to be the family's doom. Regarding John Sartoris, "the dark shadow of fatality and doom" [12]
shows on his brows. In a similar way, Old Bayard in *Flags in the Dust*
is seen "struggling against the curse of his name" [13] or in *Sartoris* against
the "perverse necessity of his family doom." [14] Bayard, like his fore-
bearer, is an embodiment of thwarted destiny. When Narcissa takes
his face between her hands and draws it down, "his lips were cold and
upon them she tasted fatality and doom." [15] Finally, even Bayard's
very young son, Benbow, is not spared and must similarly incarnate the
family fate. Faulkner, speaking of Narcissa in reference to Benbow,
says, "It was as though already she could discern the dark silver shape
of that doom which she had incurred, standing beside her chair, waiting and biding its time." [16]

The importance of the author's relationship with his grandfather
and particularly his great-grandfather needs to be stressed. The Old
Colonel was himself a writer of romance and realism. He wrote a short
story, "The Spanish Heroine," and a poem, "The Siege of Monterey,"
about his experiences in the Civil War; a play entitled *The Lost Diamond*; and a best-selling novel, *The White Rose of Memphis*, which
sold 150,000 copies before it went out of print. He also wrote an historical novel, *The Little Brick Church*, called *Lady Olivia* in a later edi-

tion. Additionally, Falkner also wrote a book about his travels, which he entitled *Rapid Ramblings in Europe.*

As a young boy in the third grade, Faulkner had already identified mainly with his great-grandfather, having decided, "I want to be a writer like my great-granddaddy." [17] Robert Coughlan proposes that Colonel Falkner "had been enshrined . . . as a household deity, and on the evidence of the books and stories was among the strongest influences of William Faulkner's life." [18] Yet, although Faulkner tended to identify with the Old Colonel more than with his grandfather, he was still very fond of J.W.T. Falkner. Minnie Ruth Little recalls that Bill talked much more about his grandfather and his greatgrandfather than about his own father.[19] His daughter, Jill, concurred with this obervation saying that he seemed, in fact, completely interested in his great-grandfather to the total exclusion of his father.[20] Faulkner probably responded to W.C. Falkner because he already admired him as a writer, but also because he spent much cherished time with his grandfather, who regularly told him stories about the Civil War, glorifying at all times the young author's great-grandfather. After having heard stories about "Kunnel Falkner" and about the fighting in Virginia in the first years of the war, Faulkner and his brothers rode their horses pretending to be J.E.B. Stuart and W.C. Falkner galloping in the Shenandoah Valley. At other times their grandfather would show Faulkner and his younger brothers the mementos of the Old Colonel— his cane, the machete he brought back from the Mexican War, his books, his silver watch, the pipe he was smoking the day he was shot—all souvenirs which the novelist later transmits to Old Bayard Sartoris in *Flags in the Dust* and *Sartoris*—after John Sartoris' death.

As described in an interview with Malcolm Franklin, Faulkner's stepson, the author's identification with his great-grandfather was to continue through adulthood, when the earlier anecdotes and memorabilia belonging to the Old Colonel were replaced by a new ritual: Faulkner's journeys to the spring in order to return with uncontaminated water for the bourbon he would share with his grandfather.[21] It is not surprising that Gloria Franklin, Malcolm's first wife, should also mention in an interview that even as an adult Faulkner long kept the portrait of the Young Colonel hanging in the library in order to separate himself as little as possible from his beloved grandfather and surrogate father.[22]

Faulkner was, in fact, very much like the young hero in "Sepulture South: Gaslight" who is the oldest son, aware of the significance of his own role within the family, of the relevance of his family's past, and of the continued presence not only of his dead grandparents but also of his ancestors. Some day he, as the oldest male, will, like his father at his grandfather's death, ride to the cemetery on horseback, and even now those earlier generations maintain their impact on them:

> three or four times a year I would come back. I would not know why, alone to look at them, not just at Grandfather and Grandmother but all of them looming among the lush green of summer and the regal blaze of fall and the rain and ruin of winter before spring would bloom again, stained now, a little darkened by time and weather and endurance but still serene, impervious, remote, gazing at nothing, not like sentinels, not defending the living from the dead by means of their vast ton-measured weight and mass, but rather the dead from the living; shielding instead the vacant and dissolving bones, the harmless and defenseless dust, from the anguish and grief and inhumanity of mankind.[23]

The psychological pattern of the son identifying with the grandfather rather than the father is one well documented by Ernest Jones in his *Papers on Psycho-Analysis*. According to Jones, the grandfather can serve as a heroic substitute for the demoted father.[24] Considering Faulkner's indifference, if not animosity toward his father, this pattern certainly becomes applicable. For Faulkner, both W.C. Falkner and J.W.T. Falkner can be taken to represent the grandfather figure. Jones further points out that there is a fantasy common among small children that, when they grow up and their parents grow old, the children "will become the parents and their parents the children." Jones writes of "the phantasy of the reversal of generations."[25]

> The logical consequence of the phantasy, which the imagination at times does not fail to draw, is that the relative positions are so completely reversed that the child becomes the actual parent of his parents. Another way of stating this conclusion is that the child becomes identified with his grandfather, and there are many indications of this unconscious identification in mythology, folklore, and custom . . . The custom of naming their children after their grand-parents is extremely widespread in both civilized and uncivilized races; among

many it is not merely a common habit, but an invariable
rule.[26]

Furthermore, according to Jones, there are people who believe "that the
grandfather has returned in the person of the child."[27] In the last
analysis, however, Jones suggests that the principal origin of the reversal fantasy is the belief in personal immortality.[28]

While Faulkner wanted avidly to follow in his grandfather's
footsteps, as he grew up he revised his initial position, wanting above
all to create a literary identity of his own. The very young William,
who wanted to be a writer like his great-grandfather, later as a young
novelist did not want to take advantage of W.C. Falkner's name. In a
letter to Malcolm Cowley on December 8, 1945, he explains how his
parents saw his willingness to change the spelling of his name:

> My first recollection of the name [Falkner] was, no outsider
> seemed able to pronounce it from reading it, and when he
> did once pronounce it, he always wrote the "u" into it. Maybe
> when I began to write, even though I thought that I was writ-
> ing for fun, I was secretly ambitious and did not want to ride
> on grandfather's coattails, and so accepted the "u," was glad
> of such an easy way to strike out for myself.[29]

Later, Faulkner concedes W.C. Falkner's influence but denies his great-
grandfather's talent. This refusal is probably in part the author's subconscious attempt to affirm himself as a writer. Notwithstanding, John
Faulkner, in *My Brother Bill: An Affectionate Reminiscence*, says that
"Bill's writing ability probably came from our great-grandfather."[30] In
his letter to Malcolm Cowley in 1945, Faulkner also asserts that "my
greatgrandfather whose name I bear, was a considerable figure in his
time and provincial milieu. He was a prototype of John Sartoris . . . "[31]
Yet, nine years later in an interview with Anne Brierre, William shows
his reticence regarding his grandfather's talent as a writer:

> Your great-grandfather was a colonel during the Civil War
> and the author of a book which sold fifty thousand copies. Is
> this which motivated you to write? No. It is a bad book. He did
> everything in his life and so he had to try to be a writer.[32]

There are thus three phases in Faulkner's evolving attitude toward his great-grandfather as an author. This evolution underlines
Faulkner's innate problem of identity, a problem which is especially

pronounced in the South. He wishes first to pattern himself after W.C. Falkner as a writer, afterwards he rejects the name in order to establish himself independently, and finally he accedes to his ancestor's influence, but then denounces the quality of his writing. This final position is indicative of a certain ambivalence, probably resulting from a fear of finding himself in his grandfather's shadow, an attitude that is accentuated by his Southernness. Faulkner's ultimate stance might also explain why John Sartoris is different from Faulkner's great-grandfather in only one significant way: John Sartoris, unlike W.C. Falkner, is not a writer. Young William was reserving this characteristic for himself alone.

Even though his great-grandfather was probably the author's greatest literary inspiration within his own family, other members were also artistically endowed. His grandmother on his mother's side, Lelia Swift Butler, was an amateur sculptress. Meanwhile, his mother Maud, as well as having "an abiding love for literature" [33] which she transmitted to her sons, was also known for her paintings. Faulkner inherited her drawing talent, as exemplified by the ten drawings included in *Marionettes*. His younger brother John also painted and exhibited pictures. John, more importantly, also wrote numerous novels—*Men Working, Dollar Cotton, Chooky, Uncle Good's Weekend Party, The Sin Shouter of Cabin Road - Cabin Road, Ain't Gonna Rain No More, Uncle Good's Girls* and a biography entitled *My Brother Bill: An Affectionate Reminiscence*. In fact, according to Joseph Blotner both Maud and John found so many similarities in Faulkner's short story "A Point of Law" to John's work, that they were convinced he had purloined the plot.[34] When Miss Maud first read *Go Down, Moses*, much to her dismay she recognized many likenesses, again, with one of John's stories.[35]

Faulkner even as a young child had all the earmarks of a creator. In his early youth, he was already prone to extremes. His early behavior is well summarized by Phil Stone, who describes him as "a child that for three weeks in the month . . . was an angel and the fourth week . . . a devil." [36] As a young man, the author had already sensed his talent. When, in 1924, *The Saturday Evening Post* rejected one of his stories, with great foresight he announced to his mother that "the day will come when they'll be glad to buy anything I write, and there too, without changing a word." [37] Much later he told Gloria Franklin, Malcolm's first wife, that he believed himself as great as Shakespeare.[38]

Initially, however, he was a highly controversial figure not only in Oxford, but even among his own family. His Uncle John Falkner's attitude toward his nephew's literary career was evident when he told Phil Stone:

> that damn Billy is not worth a Mississippi goddam—and never will be . . . He's a Falkner and I hate to say it about my own nephew, but hell, there's a black sheep in everybody's family and Billy's ours. Not worth a cent.[39]

When Stone took his protégé's part, Faulkner's uncle only reaffirmed his earlier statement, "Ah hell!" and continued, "that goddam tripe Billy writes!" [40] His Uncle John's sentiment was one very much shared by Faulkner's father, who disapproved of what he considered his son's rather degenerate, vagabond existence. When this young writer explained to his father, for example, that he was going to Hollywood for screenwriting, Murry very curtly answered that "he was confounded that mere scribbling, could earn five hundred dollars a week." [41] The author later recalled that, "when I showed him the check, he asked if it was legal." [42] His father, like his fellow Oxfordians, was furthermore completely outraged by *Sanctuary*, a reaction which was shared by most of the family, according to Faulkner's aunt, Mrs. John Falkner, when interviewed in 1977.[43] His cousin Sally Murry even asked him quite directly, "Do you think up that material when you are drunk?" [44] On the other hand, his mother, who thought he was "a genius," [45] avidly gave her support, as did his youngest brother Dean. When one afternoon a member of Maud Faulkner's bridge foursome asked why Bill had written a book like *Sanctuary*, Maud answered: "My Billy writes what he has to write." [46] She never spoke to Billy's detractor again. Dean, too, defended his brother's work and said that Bill would write "the great American novel." [47]

Freud had said, "A man who has been the indisputable favorite of his mother keeps for life the feeling of a conqueror, that confidence of success that often induces real success." [48] Despite Faulkner's definite conviction about himself as an author and his proven capability as the family's head, he still had feelings of inferiority that stemmed from his childhood. Although he was his mother's favorite, he had been

rejected by his father. He also felt subordinate to all his brothers. Jack
was taller, John was better-looking, and Dean was the gregarious child
adored by all. According to his brother Jack, Bill tended to belittle
himself and, when disparaged by others, was inclined not to defend
himself.[49] This concurrent sense of inferiority is significant because it
propelled Faulkner to become a writer. When, for example, his brother
Jack complimented him on his work, William referred to his height
and implied to his brother that writing was his principal form of compensation. He told Jack that "as big as you are, you can march anywhere you want, but when you're little you have to push." [50] He reiterates this notion when he says that as a young man he used his writing
to further his precarious relationship with Estelle as well as to make
himself noticed in Oxford:

> I read and employed verse, firstly for the purpose of further-
> ing various philanderings in which I was engaged, secondly,
> to complete a youthful gesture I was making of being
> 'different' in a small town.[51]

In *Mosquitoes*, he also states that writing is a means of attracting a
woman. Implicit in this statement are Faulkner's sentiments of inferiority for which he attempted to compensate through his work:

> I believe that every word a writing man writes is put down with
> the ultimate intention of impressing some woman that prob-
> ably don't care anything at all for literature, as is the nature of
> women.[52]

Similarly, writing can also act as a substitute for action and, more
importantly, for involvement, as expressed by the author in *Mosquitoes*.
In this respect, it is a form of emotional escape:

> Well, it is a kind of sterility—Words . . . You begin to substi-
> tute words for things and deeds, like the withered cuckold
> husband that took the Decameron to bed with him every
> night.[53]

At the same time, he makes it clear that writing is also a source of emotional evasion, when in *Mosquitoes* he says, "You don't commit suicide
when you are disappointed in love. You write a book." [54] Faulkner told

Joan Williams that he wrote *The Wild Palms* specifically "to stave off heartbreak." [55] In all probability the author was referring to his brother Dean's fatal plane crash.

Ultimately, although writing is undoubtedly therapeutic for Faulkner, it must still not be viewed as only a form of compensation or as a source of solace. Writing, for the author as for many another artist, is also the visceral need to express himself, as he insisted to Joan Williams in 1951:

> You have to have something burning your very entrails to be said . . . writing is important only when you want to do it, and nothing nothing nothing else but writing will suffice, give you peace.[56]

Psychologists agree that the eldest among brothers is the leader and becomes the authority figure among the siblings;[57] yet Faulkner often felt that his familial responsibilities came to intrude upon his art. Also according to psychologists, the eldest brother, like Faulkner, identifies with some authority figure, as the writer did with both his grandfather and his great-grandfather. Contrarily, the son belittles and/or overthrows the father figure[58] as, in fact, the author simultaneously did with his father, Murry. Eventually he assumed financial responsibility for his family. By the time he was forty-two years old, he took care of an inept brother and his wife, two sons, another brother's widow and child, a wife of his own and two stepchildren, plus his own daughter. He inherited, for that matter, his father's debts and his dependents, both white and black, without inheriting any money or property. Dean Wells, when interviewed, accurately referred to the artist's family as an albatross needing to be fed.[59] This ancient mariner, in fact, told Joan Williams in 1950:

> You can begin to see now how it is almost impossible for a middleclass Southerner to be anything but a middleclass Southerner; how you have to fight your family for every inch of art you ever gain—at the very time when the whole tribe of them are hanging around like so many buzzards over every penny you earn by it.[60]

Throughout such trials, according to Joan Williams, Faulkner was all the more antagonized by Estelle's attempts to burn at least one of his manuscripts.[61] Despite the obligations he undertook, Faulkner, according to Joseph Blotner, his biographer, wasn't "a father or a husband or a companion first, he was a writer." [62] His daughter Jill would have agreed with Blotner: "Pappy would become so involved in his writing that his nearest, his dearest, weren't accepted." [63] Much later Jill would think that, "given his independent personality, he shouldn't have burdened himself with a family." [64] His surrogate daughters such as the younger Meta Doherty, with whom he was having an extramarital affair, also noticed his "lack of attention to [her] when his characters possessed his mind." [65] Not surprisingly, he expressed himself to her much more by poems and letters than he did face-to-face.

Faulkner's generally disharmonious family life surfaces in the white families populating his work. Their relationships are generally destructive and bear a correspondence to the author's own personal and family life where there was a lack of personal comprehension one for the other between spouses. Late in the author's life the situation improved.

Despite the considerable influence his grandfather was to have on Faulkner, the Young Colonel's marriage certainly did not serve as a model for his grandson's. In fact, Faulkner's marriage to Estelle showed more similarities to his parents' marriage, for J.W.T. Falkner and his wife Sallie Murry had an idyllic marriage, her death leaving the Colonel grief-stricken. John Falkner was to write as his wife's epitaph: *"The heart of her husband doth safely trust in her. Her children arise and call her Blessed. Her husband also, and he praiseth her."* [66]

His daughter-in-law, by contrast, at the end of her life dreaded any possible encounter with her husband in an afterlife. When William assured her that she would not be obliged to meet Murry unless she chose to, Maud was very relieved. Her reaction summarizes her attitude toward her husband: "That's good," she said, "I never did like him." [67] In fact, their marriage was initially not supported by either family. While Leila Swift Butler did not favor the marriage because of Murry's alcoholism as well as the intrusion into her relationship with her daughter, the Falkners, according to Faulkner's aunt, Mrs. John Falkner, considered Maud socially inferior.[68]

However, more important factors were to separate the couple, for their interests were completely opposite. While Maud was artistic and intellectual, Murry was athletic and earthy. Relevant, too, was

Murry's heavy drinking, which he inherited from both his grandfather and his great-grandfather and to which Maud was violently opposed. Maud, according to David Minter, came to think that Murry increased his drinking to punish her since he was aware of her total disapproval of his vice.[69] She, on the other hand, dramatized his weakness and intensified his guilt by taking him to the Keeley Institute, with which the earlier Falkners were well-acquainted. Although Maud made her young sons accompany their father to the institute in order to discourage their future drinking, the pattern was nevertheless set, and William was to follow in the paternal footsteps.

Even though Faulkner's marriage to Estelle likewise did not meet with their parents' approval, the young couple were not intrinsically incompatible. Both were artistic. They had, furthermore, grown up together and since their early youth were actually infatuated with one another. During their childhood they had even decided that they would later marry and live on a chicken farm. When Estelle, age seven, witnessed a family procession of Falkners on the way to their grandparents, she pointed to William Faulkner and said to her mammy, Noila: "See that little boy? I'm going to marry him when I grow up."[70] Even though Noila tried to discourage her by attempting to convince her, albeit mistakenly, that "Folks what say they goin' to get married while they little, is sho to grow up to be ol' maids;"[71] Estelle obviously wasn't to be so easily dissuaded.

According to Jack, William even as a young adult seemed to share Estelle's childhood sentiments. Apropos of his brother and Estelle, Jack says, "I don't think Bill ever stopped thinking of her during the years she was gone or ever had an idea of someday marrying anyone else."[72] Faulkner, himself, in the typed version of *Vision of Spring*—a collection of poetry he completed in 1921—had originally entitled Section XI "Marriage." The poem is autobiographical and describes a man sitting by firelight watching a beautiful woman at the piano (as Estelle would often be), while her admirer is tortured by emotions:

> Laxly reclining, he sees her sitting there
> With firelight like a hand laid on her hair,
> With firelight like a hand upon the keys
> Playing a music of lustrous silent gold . . .
> The firelight steadily hums, steadily wheeling
> Until his brain, stretched and tautened, suddenly cracks.[73]

The ambivalence that must have beset Faulkner because of Estelle's marriage to the established Cornell Franklin is projected instead onto his pianist heroine:

> At the turn she stops, and shivers there,
> And hates him as he steadily mounts the stair.[74]

Faulkner, though always drawn to his siren was aware, even before their marriage, of Estelle's limitations. As he writes his Aunt Bama,

> I have something—someone, I mean,—to show you. . . Of course it's a woman. I would like to see you taken with her utter charm, and intrigued by her utter shallowness. Like a lovely vase. It isn't even empty, but it is filled with something—well, a yeast cake in water is the nearest simile that occurs to me. She gets the days past for me, though.[75]

The marriage of Estelle and Faulkner was fraught with one problem that seemed to supersede all other—alcoholism. Unlike the situation with the older Falkners, this time it was not one-sided. Richard McCool, a Memphis psychiatrist whom Faulkner consulted, concluded simply that "alcoholism was to be Faulkner's main problem."[76] Marion Hall, the local blacksmith in Oxford, concurs with McCool's diagnosis. When questioned about Faulkner, Hall claimed, "Mostly we would talk about huntin', fishin', ridin', and drinkin'." "Drinkin," Hall, replied without hesitation, when he was asked what Faulkner liked best.[77] Although Estelle finally gave up drinking toward the end of their marriage, her alcoholism was even more detrimental than his in that it accentuated a suicidal streak. In the same way that Estelle had returned home from Shanghai with bandages on both wrists, she later attempted on her honeymoon with Bill to kill herself. Although drunk, she tried to drown herself but was saved. Her addictions were not limited to alcohol, since she also had a particular weakness for codeine, as described by Joan Williams in *The Wintering*.[78] Mrs. Ross Brown in an interview concurred that Estelle took drugs.[79] It was probably because of the drugs and alcohol that Estelle had what Marc Connelly describes as "some kind of slips of mental processes, of thinking and so on." Faulkner, inured and without any reproach in his action, would reach out and slap her face very hard; she would then return to a state of normal conduct.[80]

Other problems that divided the couple were the classic ones of money and sex. Estelle's tastes surpassed her pocketbook. She was a compulsive shopper who habitually did not pay her bills. This negligence enraged Faulkner, and finally his only recourse was to place an announcement in the classified section of the local paper to the effect that he could not be responsible for his wife's debts.

Sex was probably a more complex problem. According to Meta Doherty, Faulkner's mistress, in *The Loving Gentleman* (her autobiographical account of her affair with Faulkner), the author had told her that from the time Jill was born, all sexual relations had ceased between himself and his wife.[81] His stepson, Malcolm, considered that Faulkner was sexually afraid of his mother.[82] Malcolm's opinion seems defensible given the inherent misogyny evident in the major part of Faulkner's work, and because others who knew Faulkner well agree with his stepson's commentary. Emily Stone (Phil Stone's wife) spoke generally of "the Faulkner women as being hot and the Faulkner men as being cold." [83] She averred that Faulkner disliked women and that much of the explanation was that he feared that they could do something better than he could,[84] an attitude indicative of his profound sense of subordination.

Faulkner, moreover, like Mr. Compson in *Absalom, Absalom!* divided women into three categories:

> Ladies, women, females—the virgins whom gentlemen someday married, the courtesans to whom they went while on sabbaticals to the cities, the slave girls and women upon whom that first caste rested and to whom in certain cases it doubtless owed the very fact of its virginity."[85]

When interviewed, Malcolm claimed that the Faulkner men would marry only "ladies." [86] As a young man, Malcolm was advised by his stepfather, in his chauvinistic manner, to "keep several young ladies on the string at one time." [87] In fact, Faulkner followed closely the advice he gave his stepson, as demonstrated by the author's three major extramarital affairs with Meta Doherty, Joan Williams, and Jean Stein. Many years later Estelle would say that some people thought her husband "hated women by the way he wrote about them. When someone asked me why he disliked them so, I said I wasn't aware that he did. I was so scared that he liked women a little too much." [88] However, in 1944 in a far more serious tone, she asked Buzz Bezzerides if Bill had ever told him anything about their relationship. "Something went wrong," she told him and began to cry, saying, "I don't know what went wrong. We used to go fishing together." [89] Her husband also felt alienation. This reaction is exemplified in his treatment of marriage throughout the major part of his work and is expressed in *The Wintering* through his fictional persona, Jeffery Almoner: "It is sad, Amy, that people can live in an isolation which blood ties, and even marriage, can't break, sometimes." [90]

Of the author's extramarital relationships, Faulkner's affair with Meta was probably the most revealing, not only because it was the longest, lasting over a twenty year period, but also because it appears on the sexual level to have been the most intense and reciprocal. In this relationship, he can be considered truly Southern, having responded to the contradictory philosophy that has been an integral part of Southern religion. He associated his wife Estelle, symbolically, with light and with its corresponding maternal role, while he identified Meta, his mistress, metaphorically, with darkness and the inverse role of prostitute, equating her with the illicit. Given the rigorous sexual attitudes of Southern Puritanism, the mother-whore syndrome described by Lillian Smith in *Killers of the Dream*[91] is particularly applicable. It also explains the writer's attraction to the excitement of the forbidden. Meta, for example, was "his love's long girl's body sweet to fuck;" [92] entering the darkness with her, he, like a true Southern Puritan felt free to "clip and kiss. For her, at least for a time, he became something like the high-bouncing, irresistible, and insatiable lover he had always wanted to be." [93]

Mrs. Ross Brown described Estelle as a nymphomaniac who, when on drugs or alcohol, allegedly propositioned even her doctors, much to Faulkner's embarrassment.[94] Yet Estelle was not known to have illicit affairs. Faulkner's extramarital relationships, by contrast, persisted until almost the end of his life, creating contention for the couple and engendering violent fighting on numerous occasions. However, as odious as his affairs may have been to Estelle, there was an added element of sadism to them which made them injurious. Gloria Franklin, consulted about Faulkner's marriage, said that the author deliberately left compromising letters on the hall table for Estelle to find.[95] This anecdote appears consistent with the incident in which Faulkner brought Meta to his house in Oxford as Bill Wasson's date. When Meta was questioned many years later in her Beverly Hills apartment, her conclusion was that "it was perversity." [96] The author's cruelty toward his wife can probably be understood best as a projection of his ambivalence as a Southerner, the embodiment of his equivocal attitude toward women comprehensively and toward Estelle specifically because of her first marriage to Cornell Franklin and her concomitant prior rejection of him.

Significantly, his relationship with Meta nearly caused a divorce.[97] Despite their mutual ardor, the writer's feelings of guilt toward his stepdaughter, as well as an unstable wife, came to be the sword between man and mistress. Also, he knew that he would lose custody of Jill since the Mississippi courts awarded the child to the mother. Particularly as a Southerner, he must have been overwhelmed with contrition when confronted with prospective divorce. Considering his origins, he must have recoiled equally from the specter of uprooting his family life. What he says about marriage in regard to Ike in *Go Down, Moses* certainly applies to his own marriage: "He would marry someday and they too would own for their brief while that brief unsubstanced glory which inherently of itself cannot last and hence why glory . . . " [98] Finally, however, with Estelle no longer drinking and with the birth of his grandsons near the end of his life, their marriage did improve. Faulkner ultimately followed his own philosophy. Apropos of Hemingway he said:

> Poor bloke, to have to marry three times to find out that marriage is a failure, and the only way to get any peace out of it is (if you are fool enough to marry at all) keep the first one and stay as far away from her as much as you can, with the hope of someday outliving her. At least you will be safe then from any other one marrying you—which is bound to happen if you ever divorce her. Apparently man can be cured of drugs, drink, gambling, biting his nails and picking his nose, but not of marrying.[99]

The discord characteristic of both Murry's and William's marriage was to recreate itself at the level of the parent-child relationships. Within the Falkner family the preferential treatment of one child at the expense of another was later to be portrayed by the author in his work. J.W.T. Falkner, like many of the writer's parental figures, had a definite preference for his son John, referred to as "John, honey" even as a young boy. John, much to his father's contentment later, became a lawyer like the Young Colonel as well as a powerful figure in politics. Murry was, by contrast, unmotivated. At least for a period he created a niche for himself in his family's railroad; however, J.W.T., weary of the railroad and unwilling to turn it over to his son, sold it without any provision to maintain a job for his eldest son. Although J.W.T. offered his assistance in finding other jobs for Murry, his son's career became a very checkered one, and most of his professional endeavors were doomed to failure. The attitude of the Colonel towards his two sons was moreover probably best summarized by Mrs. Heron Roland. The Colonel, she said, was very partial to John and wanted him to come and live on Front Street with him, meanwhile Murry was living on Back Street where his father intended him to stay.[100]

The prejudice which Murry experienced as a child was repeated when he had his own children, at least with regard to young William. Although Dean was incontestably his father's favorite, he also had great affection for John and Jack. While Murry went hunting with Dean, who seemed to enjoy a privileged relationship with him, he also had an avid interest in sports which he shared not only with Dean but also with John. Much to his pleasure, they both excelled in athletics, permitting him to give them unstinting support on the high school and college sport fields. Although Jack was not as athletically inclined, there was still affection between them.

Murry's attitude toward William, who most resembled Maud and least resembled his father, was reminiscent of the Colonel's attitude toward Murry as a son: one of rejection. He may have even rebuffed William more overtly, given Murry's unsupportive and condescending attitude toward William's literary pursuits. Murry was not for the most part remembered by his sons as "an easy man to know."[101] With them, as with people generally, he usually remained distant and cautious. Looking back, his sons thought of him as a cold man "whose capacity for affection was limited."[102] His uncommunicativeness is probably best illustrated by the fact that he did not allow any conversation at meals until their conclusion, when he would put down his napkin. This ritual, of course, as pointed out by Cornell Franklin, was contingent on the fact that Murry should grace the family with his presence at all; if meals were not served on time, he simply left for town.[103]

Although Faulkner told his stepson Malcolm (as he quotes in *Bitterweeds*) that "Mr. Murry was a kind gentleman who always made sure I had two feet under the table,"[104] one can deduce from other statements the author made that he was probably trying to reinforce the family image and, more importantly, to subtly buttress his own position of authority with his stepson. Phil Stone described Faulkner as respectful but finding his father dull and conservative.[105] Emily Stone, however, contended that Faulkner judged his father too harshly.[106] The author was undeniably merciless on the subject of his father's ability to succeed.

His inability to reconcile himself to his father's professional failure is apparent in an autobiographical piece of fiction in *A Faulkner Miscellany* about a boy who grows up, like himself, in his father's livery stable and who was not self-conscious as he

> had gone through grammar school and one year in high school with girls and boys . . . whose fathers were lawyers and doctors and merchants—all genteel professions, with starched collars.[107]

This changed with burgeoning sexuality as he looked at the blossoming of his classmates with "a feeling of inferiority."[108] He, in fact, felt not even the most minimal respect for his father; looking over fifty years of his life, he could say of Murry that "mentally he was about ten years old."[109]

Yet, Faulkner's attitude toward his father does not seem limited only to disdain: implicit are additional elements of animosity, as indicated by his characterization of young Jason Compson. Jason, whom Faulkner significantly alluded to at the Nagano Conference as representing complete evil and as being the most vicious character he ever created,[110] bears a close external resemblance to Murry Falkner. This identification was made by Miss Maud when she noted that they spoke the same way, with similar words and style. Both also owned a hardware store uptown and both had a Negro servant called Jobus.[111]

Faulkner's dislike of his father is also connected to Murry's nihilism, which Faulkner despised. The pessimism that Murry consistently voiced is that which the author later projects onto Mr. Compson in *The Sound and the Fury*. Like the older Jason Compson, Murry was persuaded that "Man was a sum of his misfortunes,"[112] a philosophy that he attempted to transmit to young William—as does Mr. Compson to Quentin. Faulkner identified with Quentin. He initially told Joan Williams to send her letters to Quentin Compson, General Delivery, in Oxford, but then he decided that the name might be too well known, and suggested another name in its place.[113] He also told Jean Stein that he equated himself with Quentin. Furthermore, what he thought of the Falkners, he also believes of the Compsons: beginning with General Compson, "a Compson was doomed," he says in the appendix to *The Sound and the Fury*, "to fail at everything he touched save longevity or suicide."[114] Likewise, at the University of Virginia in 1957, he stated "that the basic failure Quentin inherited through his father, or beyond proclivity for his father."[115] Murry is thus portrayed in both of the degenerated Compsons.

Faulkner's unfulfilling relationship both emotionally and intellectually with Murry led him to seek surrogate fathers, the two important ones being Phil Stone and Sherwood Anderson. Although they were unquestionably of great assistance to Faulkner, like his father, they distanced themselves to varying degrees, much to the chagrin of the ascendant author. Ultimately, neither could accept the classic stuation of the pupil superseding the master, of the son supplanting the father.

Phil Stone, the first to assume the surrogate's role, came into Faulkner's life in 1914 when Faulkner was in the eleventh grade. Stone was a lawyer-to-be who had a passion for literature. He was immediately aware of Faulkner's genius and later would recall, "Anybody would have seen that he had real talent." For Stone, "It was perfectly obvious."[116] Not only was William talented, but he was also committed. As Stone told the incredulous Murry in 1921, "I'm not a writer, I will never be a writer, but I know one when I see one."[117] Both reading Balzac, Stone and William formed a type of literary partnership which was to last through the publication of *Sanctuary* in 1931. Faulkner wrote poems and later short stories and novels which were edited by Stone, typed by his secretary, and then mailed to the publisher. In addition, Stone punctiliously read proofs and made corrections on the galley sheets. He and his protégé arrived at their first success with the publication of Faulkner's poem "L'Après-midi d'un

Faune" in the *New Republic* of August, 1919. Although Stone financed William's early literary vocation, he refused to take credit, insisting that "it was a partnership. The idea was to use whatever money was realized from the sale of Bill's literature to keep things moving." [118] In the meantime, Faulkner helped support himself by working at odd jobs, among them carpentry, house-painting, and sign-painting.

His first book, *The Marble Faun*, a collection of poetry containing nineteen poems, a prologue, and an epilogue, as well as a preface written by Phil Stone, was published in 1924. Faulkner's mentor subsequently claimed that he had been responsible for both its title and the money for its initial publication. The possessive nature of Bill's Pygmalion is clearly revealed at this time when Phil writes the *Yale Alumni Magazine* that "this poet is my personal property and I urge all my friends and classmates to buy this book." [119] By 1927 Faulkner had already begun to rebel against his surrogate father's proprietary attitude, as he made explicit when he told Tom Kell that "nobody dictates to me what I can write and what I can't write." [120] However, Phil's assistance was still instrumental to the young author at the time of the publication of *Sartoris*, Stone later stating that he contributed more to *Sartoris* than he had to any of the other books.

Nevertheless, by the early 1930's the mentor relationship had degenerated, and by 1937 Phil was no longer reading William's manuscripts. By the spring of 1945 he had written a prejudicial letter to Malcolm Cowley regarding Faulkner's work, telling him, "I quite disagree with you about the merit of his later books. The trouble is that he keeps on rewriting *Sanctuary*. Except in a few books and a few places the characters all talk like William Faulkner." [121] He also criticizes his style, stating that it "is really not a style in the proper sense but merely a personal mannerism." [122] Stone, not surprisingly, had chosen to criticize his protégé's work when the young author was beginning to assume his true independence as a writer. By 1952, after Faulkner won the Nobel Prize, Phil showed jealousy and resentment, bitterly claiming that his student had "Nobelitis in the Head." [123] He also claimed that "Faulkner is a great writer but sometimes he is like a Negro preacher, using big words he doesn't know the meaning of, and if the dictionary disagrees, it's wrong." [124] The more famous his ward became, the more he chose to criticize his work; yet, Stone's attitude about Faulkner, personally, was less judgmental. Instead, it was fraught with both paternal and Southern ambivalence, exhibiting two contradictory positions. In 1950 he wrote:

> A lot of us talk about decency, about honor, about loyalty, about gratitude. Bill doesn't talk about these things; he lives them. Other people may desert you but not Bill if he's your friend. People may persecute you and revile you but this would only bring Bill quickly to your side if you are his friend. If you are his friend and if the mob should choose to crucify you, Bill would be there without summons. He would carry your cross up the hill for you.[125]

In 1953, by contrast, while criticizing his work at length, he bitterly told Robert Coughlan: "Give a Faulkner success, and he'll ride you down with boots and spurs." [126]

Stone's wife, Emily, when interviewed in Montgomery, Alabama in 1977, describes Faulkner's friendship with her husband as "a succubus-incubus relationship," in that Faulkner was sucking his mentor's essence and then rejecting him.[127] Emily's attitude seems biased considering that, on a professional level, Faulkner continues through the fifties to show his gratitude to Phil by dedicating the Snopes trilogy to him. He at one juncture even borrowed money in order to help Phil monetarily after he had inherited his father's debts.

With Faulkner's development as an established writer, he freed himself from his early dependence on Stone. He still cared greatly for his friend however, despite Phil's frequent personal or professional rebuffs. He made him executor of his will and often made visits to him at his office, although he was not always received. On the other hand, Phil's emotional distance can be understood: Pygmalion had difficulty accepting his protégé's success at a time when he was beset with emotional and financial problems.

A subsequent, Faulkner relationship with Sherwood Anderson is in many ways reminiscent of his friendship with Phil, the major difference being that he contests more overtly his mentor's judgments and authority. Consequently, after scarcely two intense years, Anderson breaks entirely with him. Faulkner and Anderson had met at the end of 1924. As was the case with Phil, Faulkner deeply respected Anderson, a feeling he had never had for his own father. Like Faulkner's earlier intellectual mentor, Anderson was also conscious of his protégé's gifts:

"You've got too much talent. You can do it too easy, in too many different ways. If you're not careful, you'll never write anything." [128]

Like Phil Stone, Anderson stressed to Faulkner the importance of place, of creating out of one's own environment:

> You're a country boy, all you know is that little patch up there in Mississippi where you started from. But that's all right too. It's America too; pull it out, as little and unknown as it is, and the whole thing will collapse, like when you prize [sic]a brick out of a wall. [129]

Anderson urged Faulkner to write and assisted him with the publication of *Soldiers' Pay*, recommending his manuscript for publication in 1925. On the other hand, indicative of his ambivalence, Anderson wrote an article entitled "A Meeting South" in which he caricatures Faulkner's speech and Southern background. This article was probably the catalyst that, soon after, terminated their friendship. Anderson's article was answered by one Faulkner wrote for the *Dallas Morning News*, when the young author was asked to write an essay on Anderson. He depicts Anderson "as a lusty cornfield in his native Ohio," [130] compares him to Harding, renowned as a dishonest president, and refers to his "elephantine kind of humor." [131] In early 1926 he calls Anderson "a giant," the "father of all my generation," but claims that he made only "two or perhaps three gestures commensurate with gianthood." [132] Anderson's prose style was criticized for its simplicity.[133] Besides, his work—his whole output, finally—was that of "only a one- or two-book man." [134] Apart from sincere critical opinions, many of Faulkner's judgments on his surrogate father seem to be a reaction to Anderson's satire of him in "A Meeting South." He told Ben Wasson, "I think that when a writer reaches the point when he's got to write about people he knows, his friends, then he has reached the tragic point." [135] Faulkner was equally offended that Anderson had recommended his "damn manuscript," [136] referring to *Soldiers' Pay*, only on condition that he would not have to read it.

Although Anderson explains their separation to Horace Liveright as owing to Faulkner's nastiness to him, to Ben Wasson he justifies it by the fact that Faulkner had lied to him about his war injuries. Beyond the rivalry Anderson necessarily felt with his young protégé, the rupture in their friendship was probably the result of Faulkner's satire of his master. Anderson also broke with Hemingway during the same year and openly admitted that their disunion was because of his discontent with Hemingway's satire of *Dark Laughter* in *Torrents of Spring.*

Ironically, *Sherwood Anderson and Other Famous Creoles,* published at the end of 1926, and *Mosquitoes,* published in 1927, were more widely recognized satires of Anderson. A 500-word "Foreward" signed "W.F." is a subtle but unmistakable parody of the styles and opinions of Anderson. Meanwhile, through the persona of Dawson Fairchild, Faulkner again burlesques his mentor in *Mosquitoes.* He speaks of him as "an American of a provincial midwestern lower middle class family," [137]standing in awe of education. "His writing seems fumbling, not because life is unclear to him, but because of his innate humorless belief that, though it bewilder him at times, life at bottom is sound and admirable and fine." [138] If he can get "himself and his own bewilderment and inhibitions out of the way by describing . . . American life as American life is, it will become eternal and timeless despite him." [139] Faulkner undoubtedly came to regret that he responded to his master's criticism. In 1929, he dedicated *Sartoris* to him, a man "through whose kindness I was first published, with the belief that this book will give him no reason to regret that fact." [140]

After he received a bad burn in a 1937 accident, he asked to see Anderson. His mentor consented to visit, but it would be for the last time until they met years later, accidentally, at a literary cocktail party. It is interesting to note that Faulkner, inspite of "breaks" with both Stone and Anderson, gives each a dedication in his books. Here is a way, perhaps, of placating and asking for a "father's" blessing while at the same time asserting Selfhood. Interestingly, neither Anderson nor Stone ever gave real blessing to Faulkner without taking some credit from him at the same time.

Nonetheless, Faulkner always regretted Anderson's rejection and made efforts to pay tribute to him. At the University of Mississippi in April, 1947, he told students that he thought James Joyce was the father of modern literature and Sherwood Anderson the father of modern American literature.[141] In his Nobel Speech, he deprecated himself as a literary man; the only "literary people" whose work he knew were Hemingway, Dos Passos, Wolfe, and Caldwell "all of us children of Sherwood Anderson." [142] As a tribute to Anderson in 1953, he published a colorful reminiscence of his association with him in New Orleans in the 1920's, believing that his mentor had not received the critical attention he deserved. In it he gave a flattering portrait of Anderson, recognizing his influence as both writer and friend upon his work. At Nagano, he asserted that ". . . he was one of the finest, sweetest people I ever knew." [143]

Just as Faulkner suffered from his father's rejection as well as the separation from both his surrogate fathers, his own child was destined to bear the cross of her parents' relationship. In her case, Jill found herself the victim of her father's extreme self-absorption. Despite the fact that in his way he cared deeply for her, he saw her more as a prized possession than as a sensitive, maturing woman. Obviously the atmosphere at Rowan Oak, one of alcoholism, drugs, and violent fighting was not a reassuring one for William and Estelle's child. Neither parent was sufficiently concerned to improve this atmosphere for young Jill's sake. She also became the scapegoat for Oxford's rejection of her father. Psychologically , and inspite of himself, Faulkner shunned his daughter. She thus found herself with few friends, a social outcast. Her sense of repudiation increased when according to Cornell Franklin, Faulkner, intoxicated, appeared naked at one of Jill's birthday parties.[144] Additionally, it was a social handicap that her parents did not take her to church; for a young girl growing up in the South of the 1930s and 1940s, Protestant churchgoing was one of the major activities in any small town. Faulkner's reticence regarding religion is, however, comprehensible considering the inflexibility of his great-grandfather, Dr. John Young Murry, a Presbyterian patriarch; the Baptist fanaticism of his grandmother, Leila Swift Butler, who came to live with them; and Murry's abjuring profanity of Sunday. Given her family's uncooperativeness, Jill was obliged to find girls who would take her to their churches.

Faulkner, as well as Estelle, was at all times oblivious to her needs: she only "ached for mediocrity." [145] Even though Faulkner and Estelle in their own manner felt affection for their daughter, they also rejected her. Jill, if only subconsciously, felt them to be indifferent, as reflected in a recurring dream. She dreamt that in twenty-four hours her legs were going to give out, or be cut off. She would never be able to walk again, and she had to determine how she would spend the time with her parents. She suddenly realized that neither of them cared.[146] In 1978, when questioned about her father's attitude toward her and her problems, Jill replied that he was "largely oblivious." [147] Later, she added that "he didn't really care about people. I think he cared about me. But, I also think I could have gotten in his way and he could have walked on me." [148] It is not surprising that Jill was very pleased to go away to college and free herself from two emotionally inadequate parents.

Apart from the author's other limitations as a father, he was very possessive and consequently had difficulty accepting Jill's growing independence. Faulkner's neurotic need to cling "to the symbolic vestiges of her childhood" [149] is well illustrated by an anecdote told by Joseph Blotner. At Easter, when Jill was nearly fourteen, Faulkner insisted on maintaining her childhood ritual of hiding jelly beans and colored eggs.[150] Faulkner's difficulty in reconciling himself to Jill's maturing is also demonstrated by a comment he made in the summer of 1943 to his friend Buzz Bezzerides when Buzz gave Bill a picture of Jill. "It's very soon. This is the end of it. She'll grow into a woman," the author reflected with sadness.[151] However, according to Jeanne Franklin, Faulkner, jealous and threatened by Jill's boyfriends, would appear naked when she had a date at home, saying, "Excuse me, please, it's hot." [152] By the time that she was twenty-one, he resigned himself to her adulthood; he dedicated *The Fable* to her, writing a letter of accompaniment that "this was just a gesture toward her when she became of age and no longer under my thumb. It was just a way of saying 'Goodbye to your childhood, you are grown now and you are on your own.'" [153] Years later, he would look at six-year-old Nancy Blotner and with great nostalgia tell her "I had a little girl like you once, but she grew up on me." [154]

Linked, too, with his possessiveness was Faulkner's profound conservatism, which revealed itself especially in his reactions to his daughter, but also to his niece, Dean Wells, and his step-granddaughter, Vicki Black. Faulkner expected "his girls" at all times to fulfill Mr. Compson's definition of being "ladies." One day when Jill was still a teenager, he ran into her in Oxford in a pair of shorts and deliberately ignored her. At her wedding he prudishly remarked: "Isn't Jill the perfect virgin?" [155] Similarly, Faulkner offered to go over her writing and even help to get it published, yet Jill felt he was ambivalent: he deeply believed that domesticity was well suited to her as it was to all women, especially his Southern girls.[156] His basically traditional attitude toward women and purity was evident when he made the statement to his nineteen-year-old niece, Dean, that he liked "girls in white muslin dresses." [157] Though he told his step-granddaughter, Vicki Black, that he viewed the women in her generation with a new respect mainly because they went to college and were well-educated, Faulkner's behavior still suggested his conservatism, his puritanical thinking. Vicki Black recounts that when she was well into her twenties and Pappy, as they called Faulkner, tried to reach her one Friday night to no avail, Sunday morning she found herself confronted with the following telegram: "10, 4, 7, in the morning, no answer—You know what I'll have to tell your mother and father." [158]

Faulkner's relationship with his stepson, Malcolm, was marked by an even greater equivocation than that with Jill. Although Malcolm liked to think that Faulkner felt the same about Jill and him, Jean Stein and both of Malcolm's wives argued, probably quite justly, that Faulkner's attitude toward his son was one of rejection[159] reminiscent of Murry's neglect of Faulkner himself. Malcom's second wife, Jeanne, characterized the author's sentiments toward Malcolm as inconsistent, the poles being acceptance and refusal.[160] In their support, it is certainly significant that the author should leave both Malcolm and his sister, Victoria, out of his will.

Faulkner's negative attitude is explicable for numerous reasons. First, and probably most important, Malcolm was the product of Estelle's first marriage, a source of extreme sensitivity for Faulkner. Malcolm is thus, if only subconsciously, the statement to Faulkner of Estelle's rejection and betrayal. Secondly, Faulkner lacked respect for Malcolm because he found him weak and ineffectual. Faulkner said to Victoria, as reported by Dean Wells, "You're lucky, sister, you took after your father, not your mother, you're the strong one, Malcolm is the weak one." [161] As pointed out by Arthur Guyton, Faulkner preferred Malcolm as a child when Malcolm's lack of ambition was still not evident. Faulkner, recognizing Malcolm's superior intelligence, came to view him as a failure.[162]

On the other hand, his nephew Jimmy felt that Faulkner made "an honest effort" as a stepfather to Malcolm.[163] The author tried, according even to Malcolm, to instill in him a set of values. Faulkner and Malcolm felt great camaraderie as woodsmen. One day when young Malcolm shot a hawk, Faulkner made him climb up a tree to wring the baby chicken hawks' necks so that they would not starve. Even as an older man, Malcolm was always grateful for this lesson.[164] Faulkner would also "beat the hell out of him with a switch" when his stepson misbehaved, reported Ashton Holly.[165] Faulkner was a firm disciplinarian: his stepson, "Buddy" as Faulkner called him, was subject to the same sternness his mother and half-sister were forced to endure. Faulkner's perversity, evidenced by his deliberate exposition of Meta's letters to Estelle, or his promenading naked when Jill was at home with a date, also made him intentionally distract his stepson before his exams.[166] It was the author's sadistic side which also explains an incident that was to occur later during a time of great strain for Malcolm, after his wife Gloria had left him. Pappy had feigned that he needed Malcolm to take him to Tucker's Hospital in Richmond, Virginia. When they arrived, Faulkner registered Malcolm in his own place, where he was to stay six or eight weeks in order to dry out.[167]

Notwithstanding, Malcolm was very much in awe of Pappy and strove for his love. As reported by Arthur Guyton, Malcolm tried above all to emulate Faulkner's image: he dressed like him, took on the same mannerisms, and even smoked a pipe in an identical way. Most troublesome, Buddy too became an alcoholic.[168] Malcolm was probably responding instinctively to the author's deeply equivocal attitude toward him, a response implicit in his choice of *The Bitterweeds*, as title for the book he wrote describing their close association. It is interesting that Faulkner should have been obsessed with bitterweeds so that he kept a hoe leaning against the side of the house, and that, when he had a hangover or when he was meeting with obstacles in his writing, he would go out to the pasture and attack them.[169] A case could be made that Faulkner recapitulated with Malcolm some of his own emotionally destructive relationship with *his father*, and that this may be the source of his own ambivalence. On the deepest level, Malcolm must have seen their relationship as one of anger and frustration.

A related family issue is the sibling relationships of Faulkner and his brothers. While in his work he focuses on incestuous brother-sister relationships, Faulkner also depicts complex fraternal relationships. Among the most prominent sibling rivalries are those between Quentin and his brother Jason in *The Sound and the Fury*, between Charles Bon and Henry Sutpen in *Absalom, Absalom!*, and between Darl and his brother Jewel in *As I Lay Dying*—all reflections of the author's competitiveness with his own brother, John. Jason is jealous that Mr. Compson has sold family land to send Quentin to Harvard; Charles Bon feels similar emotions regarding his father's decision to recognize only his white son, Henry, and Darl is jealous of Addie's preference for Jewel. Similarly, Faulkner was most envious of the camaraderie that John and their father shared, as opposed to Murry's emotional denial of his oldest son. Fraternal rivalry was reawakened when they both found themselves authors. Meanwhile, the admiration felt by the young narrator in "Two Soldiers" for his older brother, Pete Grier, is reminiscent of Dean's admiration for his older brother William. And the narrator's desire to follow Pete to war recalls Faulkner's desire, when he was in the RAF in Toronto, to join his brother Jack on the French Front. Similar combinations of closeness and guilt are depicted in *Flags in the Dust*, the original version of *Sartoris*, as well as in *Sartoris* itself, published six years before Dean's death.

Faulkner had little in common with his brother John. He found him dull and lacking in personality and did not consider him very capable. According to rumor, when John needed money from William, it was refused. Allegedly, when John tried to reach a particular publisher through his brother, he was denied access.[170] After word reached Pappy that John had changed the spelling of his surname, he was enraged. Then a few weeks later, Pappy philosophically decided: "If putting a 'u' in his name would get a leech off my back I am happy." [171] After the contretemps over his short story "A Point of Law," albeit upon his mother's request, he did this time put his brother in touch with Bennett Cerf at Random House regarding the publication of *Dollar Cotton*. Yet he introduced his brother in an ambiguous way, taking a position that was much more equivocal than the one taken by Sherwood Anderson with regard to *Soldiers' Pay*. He appended the following postscript to Cerf: "My brother has written a novel. I have not read it, am too busy to intend to. Do you want to look at it?" [172] In 1940, when John received an advance of five hundred dollars for his book, payment greater than any that William had ever received, it must have rubbed salt in his older brother's wounds.

While Bill's attitude was very antagonistic toward John, he felt great affection for his brother Jack. Although Jack spent much time out of Oxford working for the FBI, Faulkner always spoke of him with great pride. Dean was, however, the author's favorite. When his youngest brother, who idealized William, grew a mustache and also changed his name to Faulkner, the author was flattered. It was his encouragement and financing that spurred his younger brother's interest in flying and which led eventually to his death in a 1935 plane crash, much to Bill's lasting remorse.

The closeness enjoyed by Bill and Dean is projected, whether consciously or unconsciously, onto the Sartoris twins, Bayard and John, in *Flags in the Dust* and *Sartoris*. Faulkner, like his hero Bayard, felt deeper affection for his brother than he did for his wife. These same feelings were reciprocal, as noted by Dean's wife Louise, who realized after she had married Dean that "Mother and Bill always come first." [173] The privileged relationship between Bill and Dean is similar to the one in both versions of the novel. Bayard, lying beside his wife the last night of his leave before he goes back to England, is thinking about his brother:

> But he was not thinking of her then. When he thought of her who lay rigid in the dark beside him, holding his arm tightly between her breasts, it was only to be a little savagely ashamed of the needless thing which he had done to her. He was thinking of his brother whom he had not seen in over a year, thinking in a month they would see one another again. [174]

Again, when he returns he is not thinking of his dead wife and child but of his brother. After John's death Bayard burns his brother's canvas hunting coat and all the other old clothes and possessions, in order to distance himself as much as possible from his brother's death. Narcissa, Bayard's second wife, feels that despite John's death he still takes precedence for her husband: Narcissa views him as a "ghost between them." [175] Bayard's sentiments toward his brother are distilled by Aunt Jenny: "He never cared a snap of his fingers for anybody in his life except Johnny." [176]

Six years after the novel's publication, Dean, like John Sartoris, was dead, killed in a plane crash. One is entitled to ask if, as early as 1929, *Flags in the Dust* and *Sartoris* were not a prescience of the author's deepest fear, his brother's death. Dean's passing triggered William's guilt. Bayard Sartoris, Faulkner's fictional persona, feels culpability intensified by his Southern origins. Bayard feels great responsibility for his brother's accident, associating Old Bayard's decease with Johnny's death:

> Well, damn it, suppose it had: was he to blame? had he insisted that his grandfather ride with him? had he given the old fellow a bum heart? And then coldly: You were scared to go home. You made a nigger sneak your horse out for you. You, who deliberately do things your judgment tells you may not be successful, even possible, are afraid to face the consequences of your own acts. Then again something bitter and deep and sleepless in him blazed out in vindication and justification; what he knew not, blazing out at what. Whom, he did not know: You did! You caused it all: you killed Johnny.[177]

Bayard's feelings of remorse are accentuated more in *Sartoris* than in *Flags in the Dust*. In *Sartoris*, for example, when Bayard wakes up anguished in the middle of the night, "the old terror" that he must confront is specifically identified with the terror of the imagined death of a pilot, implicitly John's accident. The "old terror" he confronts in the earlier *Flags* is unspecific. Also, in the MacCallum section, after reliving Johnny's death, it is only in *Sartoris* that Bayard has a momentary suicidal impulse. Walter M. Brylowski questions whether Bayard's guilt might not be explained by an unconscious wish, because Johnny had been considered generally superior in a way similar to young Dean.[178] Interestingly, the epitaph that Faulkner gave John Sartoris is the same one he would later give to his brother Dean:

> I bear him on eagles'
> wings and brought him
> unto me.[179]

Maud, however, disapproved of it; one family member said that she considered it "a monument to William's grief and guilt."[180] Faulkner's guilt remained with him throughout his life, as remarked by both Louise Meadow and Meta Carpenter. When Louise told him one morning at breakfast "I can't eat. I dreamed the whole accident last night."[181] He replied, "You're lucky to have dreamed it only once. I dream it every night."[182] Meta observed that Faulkner had mentally reconstructed the death scene down to the last graphic detail and that it would leap into his mind at odd times during the day with the force of guilt.[183]

Though experiencing no brother-sister relationship with emotionally incestuous overtones, Faulkner was involved in two incestuous relationships: one with his mother and the other with his stepdaughter Victoria Franklin. Both are incestuous in the sense that they are mutual adorations superseding the banal or normal attitudes of mother-son or father-daughter relationships characteristic of most families. Maud's extremely possessive relationship with her sons, particularly with her older son, William, resembles Caroline Compson's with Jason in *The Sound and the Fury*, Addie Bundren's with Jewel in *As I Lay Dying*, Mrs. Bland's comportment toward Gerald in *The Sound and the Fury*, or Mrs. Boyd's behavior toward Howard in "The Brooch." Miss Maud called the Falkner boys, according to Dean Wells, "her Johncy, Deanie, Billie, and Jackie." [184]

Erik Erikson observes that American mothers often hold up their sons as figures of power and integrity while rejecting their husbands.[185] This behavior is certainly true in the case of the Falkner boys to the point that the parents' fighting made Faulkner feel guilty since he could not find an acceptable response. According to Dolly Faulkner, John Faulkner's wife, Maud, resented the boys' marriages, in fact not wanting any of them to marry.[186] Faulkner's mother actually said herself, "I don't see how my sons get along with those women they married!" [187] All of Maud's daughters-in-law were to have difficulty with her. Dolly Faulkner asserted that her mother-in-law was "the most possessive person I've ever known." [188] Phil Stone felt that all of the Falkner boys were tied to their mother and resented it. Most important, he believed that this trait was in part the explanation of Faulkner's animosity toward women.[189]

Walter Toman in *Family Constellation* states that oldest brothers like William tend always to be looking for a mother-figure and prefer, like the author, androgynous women.[190] All the women Faulkner deeply cared about: Helen Baird, Estelle Franklin, Meta Carpenter, Joan Williams, and Jean Stein, were physically of the epicene type. In fact, most women Faulkner loved resembled his mother either physically or temperamentally. Miss Maud, like all the Falkner women, was strong and domineering, resembling in many ways Lizzie Vance,[191] Faulkner's great-grandfather's wife. This is also true of Sally Murry, his maternal grandmother; Leila Swift Butler, his maternal grandmother; his Aunt Bama, the Colonel's sister; and his Aunt Holland, his father's sister. They were among the unvanquished and all women on whom he modeled his older heroines such as: Virginia Du Pre in *Flags in the Dust, Sartoris,* and "There Was a Queen;" Rosa Millard in *The Unvanquished;* or Eunice Habersham in *Intruder in the Dust* and *The Town.* According to Vicki Black, they were "indomitable types and they were on a pedestal." [192] Faulkner's daughter said that her grandmother had such an influence on him that no other woman was able to replace her:

> I think that probably Pappy's idea of women—ladies—always revolved a great deal around Granny. She was just a very determined tiny old lady that Pappy adored. Pappy admired that so much in Granny and he didn't find it in my mother and I don't think he ever found it in anybody. I think that maybe all these [women] including my mother were, just second place. [193]

Jill added that for her father there was "no grey, either ladies or women, and that he was probably looking for his mother in all the others." [194] Malcolm, too, believed that for Faulkner "Maud was on a pedestal." [195] Faulkner's attitude toward his mother is summarized by the critic Irving Malin, who speaks of it as "latently homosexual or, if this is too extreme, Oedipal." [196]

Maud required frequent visits from her sons and a letter once a week throughout her life should they be on a trip. It was William who was the most dutiful: he visited her daily in Oxford, and when he was traveling he not only addressed his letters "Dear Moms" and signed them "Billy," but mailed them—for example, when he was in Paris—regularly every Wednesday and Sunday. Not surprisingly, it was to his mother that he dedicated his first book, *The Marble Faun.* In the debilitating relationships Maud fostered with her sons and grandsons, "Billy," as she referred to him, was her favorite, "the light of my life." [197] Maud's possessiveness was not limited to her behavior with her sons but extended to her grandsons. When her grandson Jimmy was in the Marine Corps, each time he received a promotion she proudly altered the insignia on his portrait in order to make the news public. [198]

To a lesser degree, Maud had a weakness for her son Dean. He, like his oldest brother, was an example of what Faulkner describes in his short story, "Hair," as the male incapability of cutting the umbilical cord:

> Girls are different from boys. Girls are born weaned and boys don't ever get weaned. You see one sixty years old, and be damned if he won't go back to the perambulator at the bat of an eye.[199]

When Murry died, Dean became his mother's mainstay. As described by Dean Wells,

> He was a grown man . . . twenty-five years old, without employment, as dependent on his mother for his livelihood as she was on him for emotional security. He loved her and he was caught.[200]

Finally, when Maud was much older, long after Dean's death, Jack being away, Johncy and Billie continued to take care of her. The same capriciousness which made her change the hair on her grandmother's portrait and then quixotically change it back[201] marked her attitude toward her remaining sons. This quality, combined with pronounced egotism, explains in great part her refusal of a servant or nurse and her insistence, instead, that her sons bring her all her meals cooked by their respective spouses; this was, in fact, the last obligation that she imposed on her family.

The privileged, yet ambiguous bond Faulkner shared with his mother was one that he also shared in a different way with his stepdaughter, Victoria Franklin. His feelings became evident even when she was a very young girl, and in 1921 he inscribed her copy of *Marionettes*, a one act play, "To 'Cho-Cho,' / A Tiny Flower of the Flame / The Eternal Gesture Chrystallized; / This, A Shadowy Fumbling / In Windy Darkness Is Most Re- / Spectfully Tendered." [202] Further, he dedicated a novella, *The Wishing Tree*, to her and gave her a copy for her eighth birthday in 1927. The dedication reads as follows:

> . . . I have seen music, heard
> Grave and mindless bells; mine air
> Hath verities of vernal leaf and bird,
> Ah, let this fade: it doth and must; nor grieve,
> Dream ever, thou; she ever young and fair.[203]

He also inscribed her copy as follows: "For his dear friend / Victoria / on her eighth birthday / Bill he made / this book." [204]

Faulkner had great confidence in Victoria. When Jill and Estelle left California in May, 1937, to go to Oxford, he fully entrusted Jill to Victoria's supervision. Faulkner wrote Cho-Cho with this plea:

> take care of my little baby for me, Sister . . . I know I don't even have to ask this, I just need to repeat, because she is little and helpless and wants little save to be happy and looked after. Take care of my little baby. [205]

The deep affection he had for Victoria, whom he referred to very symbolically in Freudian terms as "Sister," was clear; when at sixteen or seventeen, for example, she was having her tonsils taken out, Faulkner stayed with her in the operating room, refusing to leave until the end of the operation. [206]

The rapport between Victoria and her stepfather was one of such closeness that it was even rumored that Victoria was Faulkner's mistress. [207] Though to the best of anyone's knowledge there was no validity in this gossip, it underlines the degree to which their intimacy was evident. Lewis Dollarhide considered that "next to her own husband, she loved William Faulkner." [208] Her daughter, Vicki Black, even stated that her mother "had loved him more than any other man." [209] Finally, Cho-Cho said herself that he was "the best friend I've ever had." [210] Faulkner's relationship with his stepdaughter closely parallels the kind of emotional relationship he himself experienced with his own mother.

The quasi-incestuous relationship that Faulkner had with his stepdaughter lacked only the sexual dimension of his relations with his three mistresses: Meta Doherty, Joan Williams and Jean Stein, all of whom he regarded not just as women but also as daughters. Despite the very passionate relationship Faulkner enjoyed with Meta, he felt the need and the desire to regard her, like his own daughter, as a young girl who had not grown up. Meta in *The Loving Gentleman* describes his need to turn her "into a sweet tremulous girl." [211] Also, he gave her presents a father might normally give his daughter: a puppy dog, a hair ribbon, or rubber ducks for her bath. Meta, however, did not reciprocate these feelings; instead, she thought of him as "not father so much" but "as older mate."[212]

Faulkner's paternal attitude is particularly true with the latter two women: he was easily old enough to be their father, almost their grandfather. Additionally, he assumed the role of literary mentor with Joan, in particular, but also with Jean. In *The Town* Faulkner duplicates this role using Gavin Stevens in his relationships with Melisandre Backus and especially Linda Snopes; the added role of educator only reinforced the paternal one.

Possibly because Faulkner was aging and increasingly aware that Jill was reaching adulthood, by 1949 he seemed in need of reassuming the role of father. Now in his fifties, he chose two girls of college age to be the serial objects of his affection. He had evidently reached a stage of great loneliness, which he described to Joan:

> He had come to a point where he just simply was lonesome. And he needed somebody. He said, "I have to have somebody suddenly for the first time in my life that I feel I am doing the writing for. I've got to be doing it for somebody." He said that he'd always been the cat who walked by himself and that this didn't exist any longer.[213]

The father role which Faulkner filled with Joan is well demonstrated by a letter he wrote her in December, 1953: "I think I was— am—the father you never had—the one who never raised his hand against you, who desired, tried to put always first your hopes and dreams and happiness."[214] The author's paternal sentiment is further revealed in *The Wintering* (written by Joan), when, in the persona of Jeffery Almoner, he tells Joan's literary surrogate, Amy Howard, "you wanted to escape your background and since I had done it, I thought I could help you. I wanted to save you some of the knocks I knew."[215] In fact, the fatherly element was so dominant in Faulkner's attitude toward Joan that her psychiatrist seriously asked if Faulkner had children of his own.[216] In *The Wintering* Jeffery Almoner describes the relationship as an incestuous one:

> There's a bond that nothing can break. There's been love between us, but sin. No, I'm not talking about morality. I know I was the father you wanted. We've committed incest, then. That alone will always hold us together.[217]

This excerpt, admitted Joan Williams, was based on a very similar statement made to her by Faulkner.[218] Simultaneously, Faulkner felt frustrated because his role as lover was a very limited one. Although the author initially told Joan that he would try to be "whatever you want me to be to you," [219] he was sexually interested in her from the beginning, while Joan was drawn to him mainly as an intellectual mentor. Their relationship took three years to be consummated. Once they became lovers, very much as a result of Faulkner's insistence, the sexual dimension of their relationship was a very limited one. Faulkner's frustration and consequent hostility are demonstrated in what he wrote to her at the end of 1953:

> You take too much, and are willing to give too little. . . . People have attributes like animals; you are a mixture of cat and mule and possum—the cat's secretiveness and self-centeredness, the mule's stubborness to get what it wants no matter who or what suffers, the possum's nature of playing dead-running into sleep or its pretence—whenever it is faced with a situation it is not going to like.[220]

At the same time, despite the break in their affair, Faulkner wrote to Joan telling her, "I believe you know that until I die, I will be the best friend you ever had." [221]

Like Gavin Stevens in *The Town*, the author played a very important part in Joan's literary development. Gavin brings Melisandre Backus, his younger protégé, flowers and books and claims to be forming her mind, while with Linda he eats ice cream, reads poetry, and later concerns himself with her choice of colleges. As Faulkner was with Joan, Gavin too is infatuated with both his intellectual wards. Yet, unlike Gavin, who desires only a platonic relationship, Faulkner, as he would often reflect sadly, felt instead like Cyrano de Bergerac, the unsuccessful lover who was a master at words. Joan said, when interviewed, that Faulkner had constantly alluded to himself as Pygmalion.[222] Otherwise, the author told her that he was "creating not a cold and beautiful statue, in order to fall in love with it, but Pygmalion taking his love and creating a poet out of her . . . will you risk it?" [223] He told her also:

It may have been partly that, belief which drew me to begin
with or maybe its vanity: Lucifer's own pride: I don't, refuse to,
believe that I can take you—a young woman—into my life
(spirit) and not have her make something new under the sun
whether she wills it or not.[224]

Faulkner further suggested partnership in assisting Joan's literary endeavors: "All right: Here is the idea: let's try if I can get the Joan W.
written quicker. I don't mean, collaborate or rewrite it . . . but the two
of us together . . . to get the good stuff out of Joan Williams . . . "[225]

By 1952, he continued to offer criticism and encouragement, and
they published together the television script "The Graduation Dress"
on which, however, Faulkner did most of the work. At the end of 1952,
Joan's short story "The Morning and the Evening" was accepted for publication; by 1960 it had been enlarged and accepted for publication as a
novel. At this time, Faulkner had written her, "Splendid news" and
continued to tell her, "That not only justifies us but maybe absolves me
of what harm and hurt I might have done you; maybe annoyance and
exasperation are better words." [226] Joan is now a telented and established writer, thanks in great part to Faulkner's counsel and support.
Among many novels, Joan wrote *The Wintering*, published in 1971,
which was the young author's literary tribute to her mentor, a fictional
account of their relationship.

Faulkner's affair with Jean Stein is one which, in contrast to the
others, has been kept very private. For Faulkner, Jean was unquestionably a daughter figure as well as a mistress, as suggested by their difference in age alone. When interviewed, Jean made it apparent that
she considered him both a spiritual and an intellectual mentor and that
she was particularly impressed, . . . by his sense of values.[227] She
added that she felt remorse regarding her relationship and considered
herself too young to appreciate it fully.[228] He occupied a very sacred
place in her life, and when Meta and Joan were alluded to she immediately retorted, "Don't mention the others." [229]

On a professional level also, Faulkner tried to assist her, playing
her 'Gavin Stevens,' though he was a literary mentor to a more limited
degree than with Joan Williams. Jean was one of the editors of *The
Paris Review*, in which capacity she conducted an interview with
Faulkner about his life and his work. It is an outstanding, if not actu-

ally his most brilliant interview. Faulkner certainly may have even helped his protégé with its construction.

Finally, of the family themes marking Faulkner's work, the miscegenative one also seems to have its biographical corollary. Virginia Hines McKinney of Amory, Mississippi, mentions the rumor that Aunt Bama, Colonel Falkner's favorite daughter, had a mulatto maid reputed to be the Colonel's daughter like Elnora in "There Was A Queen" or Clytemnestra in *Absalom, Absalom!* One day when Bama was exercising her authority, the maid seems to have told her that "she was as good as she was and the daughter of the same father." [230]

The family themes in the bulk of Faulkner's work as well as in that of the other Southern writers are an indication of the potentially destructive nature of the close family relationships in the South. In addition to the sociological factors of the larger community, there are also biographical factors important in determining the extent to which Faulkner's fiction is a projection of his family's experience. With the birth of four grandchildren in the 1950s, and after Estelle stopped drinking, Faulkner became better balanced. *The Reivers,* which he dedicates to the five children of Victoria, Malcolm and Jill, is an idyllic account of his family, who assume the personae of the Priests. Jill said, "Pappy really changed." She continued, "He became so much easier for everyone to live with—not just family, but everybody . . . he was a different man. . . . He was enjoying life." [231] Nevertheless, his late work loses the early force, and upon it alone he could never have gained the literary renown that he has achieved. Historically, contentment and art have generally been incompatible and Faulkner is yet another example.

CHAPTER 3

Women and Marital Relationships

Faulkner's concern with women and marriage is a central theme throughout his work. His writing reflects the woman's subordinate social role in the South. The critics almost unanimously concur that his early and middle work portrays an uncontestable misogyny. Yet, taking into account the author's puritanical and matriarchal Southern background one can understand the underlying reasons for his attitude. The disharmonious family relations in his work involve ambivalent emotions, illusion, evasion, isolation, guilt—all preoccupations that are endemic to the South. Furthermore, the poor white families of Yoknapatawpha, as well as their non-fictional counterparts, suffer from marital conflicts that are based to a great extent on material problems: financial burdens inevitably engender almost all the others. With regard to the woman, marriage, and the family, Faulkner only really begins to view them differently with his creation of the Mallison family who appear initially in 1948 with the publication of *Intruder in the Dust* and later in *The Town* in 1957. Women and marriage are once again portrayed favorably in *The Reivers* at a time when the author, not uncoincidentally, has resolved most of his own familial problems.

Women, beginning in the pre-Civil War South, while trained to be the ideals of perfection and submission, were unmistakably given a social position inferior to that of men. Slavery and religion were major institutions that reinforced women's inferior role. The Pauline doctrine in the Episcopal church and the paternalistic system of slavery reinforced the male's dominance. Women were indoctrinated by schools, parents, magazines and, as Ann Firor Scott points out, all were promulgating the same message "be a lady and you will be loved, respected, supported." [1] There was also a unilateral emphasis upon education for men. Women were denied any right to mental cultivation to the extent that they were equally untrained even for what were considered womanly responsibilities. It is not surprising that Colonel Byrd, in his account of his visits to Virginia as early as the eighteenth century, writes that "Our conversation with the ladies was like whip-syllabub, very pretty but nothing in it." [2] A woman was trained solely to be a man's appendage, as Faulkner says in the first edition of *Sanctuary*:

> As though whatever women had dwelled there had been no
> more than a part of the vanished pageantry of a dream; in
> their hoops and crinoline but the lost puppets of someone's
> pomp and pride.[3]

In *Flags in the Dust* and *Sartoris* he also states that they were only a man's reflection:

> It didn't make much difference what women rode in, their
> menfolks permitting of course. They only showed off a
> gentleman's equipage anyhow; they were but the barometers
> of a gentleman's establishment, the glass of his gentility.[4]

A woman was thus destined only for marriage and children. Once she married, her status did improve, albeit within limits, according to Keith F. McKean in his article, "Southern Patriarch: A Portrait." While still occupying a woman's place, she became:

> the served and prolific queen, the mother of the line, loved
> and obeyed by her children—for she is, after all, the precious
> vessel that contains the prized blood that continues the fam-
> ily line.[5]

As described by Louise Blackwell, Faulkner's women characters live in relation to somebody or something. They are individuals who live primarily as a function of men, society, or religion; yet, almost without exception they exist in relationship to men.[6] Harold Douglas believes that the radical difference between a man and a woman in the

Faulknerian universe, as well as in the South, is that a woman is described to a greater degree through her sexuality while a man is defined through his profession, a notion which is not unsimilar to Blackwell's. Douglas concludes that while a woman is a virgin, a mistress, a wife, a mother, an old maid, a widow, a prostitute, men are identified instead as farmers, soldiers, pilots, bankers, lawyers, merchants, or bootleggers. A woman's identity is determined by her relationship to men, while the man's identity is an entity in and unto itself. It is a pattern pointed out by Douglas that Faulkner's women have an identity that is only sexual. Mrs. Littlejohn, who runs a boarding house; Drusilla, who fights in the Confederate Army; and Charlotte Rittenmeyer, an artist are among the exceptions. Even evil in women is generally a function of her sexuality. Faulkner's men, though not paragons of perfection, have vices which are not a function of their sexuality. The weakness and ineffectuality of Mr. Compson, the pride and self-absorption of Thomas Sutpen, the cruelty of Henry Armstid, the rapacity of Flem Snopes, the obsessiveness of Gail Hightower, the self-promotion of Anse Bundren and, finally, the evil natures of Popeye and Jason Compson are characteristics unrelated to sexuality.[7]

It is thus not surprising that women often married for the sake of marriage itself. In *The Wild Palms* Wilbourne reflects, that:

> It's not the romance of illicit love which draws them (women),
> not the passionate idea of two damned and doomed and iso-
> lated forever against the world and God and the irrevocable
> which draws men; it's because the idea of illicit love is a chal-
> lenge to them, because they have an irresistible desire to ...
> take the illicit love and make it respectable ... [8]

In *Intruder in the Dust*, Gavin says "My experience was that few of them [women] were interested in love or sex either. They wanted to be married." [9] Eula also tells Gavin in *The Town*: "marriage is the only fact. The rest of it is still the poet's romantic dream." [10] Thus, in Yoknapatawpha County as well as in the South generally there are many contractual marriages. It is usually the woman who considered marriage for practical reasons. Melisandre Backus, Addie Bundren, Ike's unnamed wife, Belle Mitchell, Caroline Compson, Elly, Drusilla Hawk and Candace Compson are among the women who could directly or indirectly be classified in this category. Meanwhile, Eula's marriage to

Flem, or Sutpen's marriage to either his Haitian wife or to Ellen Cold-field, or the eventual marriage between Judith and Bon are all marriages of convenience that are profitable for both parties. Hightower's marriage to his wife is, by contrast, one which is solely advantageous to himself, the male.

Melisandre Backus is certainly an example of a woman who does not marry for love. When her fiancé disappears after World War I, she marries the wealthy Harriss to save the family plantation. Addie Bundren also considers the material advantage involved in matrimony to Anse. Addie, for instance, asks Anse: "But they tell me you've got a house and a good farm. And you live there alone doing for yourself, do you?" Aware of his interest in her, she continues to ask him if he is going to marry, concluding: "So I took Anse." [11] Furthermore, Faulkner himself speculates that Addie Bundren probably "married Anse because of her pressure from her people ... she was ambitious probably and she married against her inclination." [12] Since she is not emotionally involved with Anse, she deems that her children are hers alone. Consequently, she becomes Whitfield's mistress. In a similar way, Ike's wife decides to marry him once she is certain that the McCaslin farm belongs to him. When Ike refuses to accept his inheritance, his wife immediately refuses to have sexual relations. This denies him the McCaslin scions who might also be forced by Ike to share their one room cubicle. Belle Mitchell similarly marries Horace because he has money. She frees herself while kissing him and asks quite pointedly: "Have you plenty of money, Horace?" [13] When he answers in the affirmative, she begins again to embrace him. Belle, who is by definition completely *interessée*, chooses their new home, in a prestigious neighborhood. Horace remarks that the money there was:

> like that afflatus of rank fecundity above a foul and stagnant
> pool on which bugs dart spawning, die, are replaced in mid-
> darting; in the air, in men's voices and gestures, seemingly to
> be had for the taking. That is why Belle has chosen it. [14]

Finally, and a point which is made in *Flags in the Dust* but not in *Sartoris*, Belle is disappointed in her marriage with Horace because he does not have enough money and he has lied to her by pretending to have more than he has; Belle even accuses him of taking her away from her husband. Interestingly, these women are all active agents on their own behalf in the only endeavor in which real choice is available to them.

Other Faulkner women are motivated by social advancement or status rather than financial gain. Caroline Compson, for instance, marries Jason Compson for the social position of a prestigious name and an ancestral mansion. Elly is only attracted to the Louisianian, Paul de Montigny, who refuses to marry her. She plans instead to marry Frank in whom she is completely uninterested because she is aware that her social posture would be enhanced through marriage to this young man in line to be bank president. Elly thinks of her marriage as Addie does hers "with quiet despair and resignation"[15] and persuades herself that, "'Anyway I can live quietly now.... At least I can live out the rest of my dead life as quietly as if I were already dead.'"[16]

Again for social reasons, but this time on account of their mothers, Drusilla Hawk and Candace Compson are forced into marriages which are supposed to protect both of them socially. Louisa Hawk insists that Drusilla and her distant cousin, John Sartoris, marry because they have been living and traveling together during the war, albeit as brother and sister. The attitude of Louisa Hawk is parodied by the author in a letter she writes to her sister. Faulkner's burlesque of the Southern myth of chivalric gyneolatry is revealed when Louisa Hawk claims that:

> when I think of my husband who laid down his life to protect a heritage of courageous men and spotless women looking down from heaven upon a daughter who had deliberately cast away that for which he died, and when I think of my half-orphan son who will one day ask of me why his martyred father's sacrifice was not enough to preserve his sister's good name— [17]

Furthermore, when Mrs. Hawk sees Drusilla in brogans and overalls, after her daughter had been working in the sawmill, she also exclaims, "'Lost, lost. Thank God in His mercy that Dennison Hawk was taken before he lived to see what I see.'"[18] Candace's marriage to Herbert Head occurs because Caroline Compson insists upon it since her daughter is pregnant and needs the social protection of a husband.

The marriage of convenience so frequently practiced in the South can operate in Yoknapatawpha to the woman's and the man's mutual advantage. Eula is pregnant, for instance, and like Caddy needs a husband. This time, Flem is basically bought by her father. Will Varner,

Eula's father, not only pays for the license and wedding trip, but also gives Flem the title to the Old Frenchman's place. Thomas Sutpen is another example of a Faulkner hero, or anti-hero, who enters into a marriage that is not only to the woman's advantage but also to his own. When he marries Eulalia Bon, whom he barely knows, he receives property from her father as her dowry. In exchange, she marries a white man. When Bon learns at the time of the birth of their son that Eulalia is part black, he annuls their marriage and leaves Haiti. Although his sentiments are uninvolved, he does show a business-like sincerity toward "the deal" he originally undertook: he provides his spouse and son with fair compensation, giving them all the property he received from Eulalia's father as well as all he had earned since his arrival. The contract, however, becomes null and void because misrepresentation is involved. According to Quentin in *Absalom, Absalom!*, Sutpen concluded the following: "I found that she was not and could never be, through no fault of her own, adjunctive or incremental to the design which I had in mind, so I provided for her and put her aside." [19] Later, while Ellen's marriage to Sutpen helps her to realize her social ambition, she marries this *arriviste* to obey her father who derives some implicit benefit from their matrimony. She weeps, however, at her magnificent marriage which has only ten guests including the wedding party but Mr. Compson says that later, "She seemed not only to acquiesce, to be reconciled to her life and marriage, but to be actually proud of it." [20] Ellen's marriage comes to be "a fairy tale written for and acted by a fashionable ladies' club." [21] The wealthy Sutpen needed, on the other hand, "respectability, the shield of a virtuous woman, to make his position impregnable." [22] "All he would need would be Ellen's and our father's name on a wedding license (or any other patent of respectability);" [23] ultimately, "To accomplish [the design, Sutpen] should require money, a house, a plantation, slaves, a family incidentally of course, a wife." [24] Likewise, after Ellen's death, Sutpen proposes marriage to her sister, Rosa, on condition that she will provide him with a male heir. Again, marriage for Sutpen is necessarily contractual.

Similarly, Judith's forthcoming marriage to Charles Bon is one which is at least intended to be expedient for both of them. Judith's marriage, before knowledge of Bon's identity, is regarded by her father and especially her mother as a vehicle for bringing her the social posture of a married woman. Bon, himself, is probably not unconscious of the advantages of marriage to his half-sister. Mr. Compson, for instance, supposes with regard to Bon that "perhaps it was even more than Judith or Henry either: perhaps the life, the existence, which they represented." [25] Lastly, Hightower is a rare example of a man being the sole benefactor materially or socially through marriage. Hightower marries his wife because, as he quite accurately calculates, being a minister's daughter her family has sufficient influence to obtain for him a minister's job in Jefferson where he wishes to be.

Apropos of the woman's status generally in the South, Thomas Nelson Page in *Social Life in Old Virginia* concludes that "Her life was one long act of devotion, — devotion to God, devotion to her husband, devotion to her children, devotion to her servants, to the poor, to humanity." [26] Despite the improved status women obtained through marriage, they were still in great part equated with slaves. Mary Chesnut in *A Diary from Dixie* believed that "All married women, all children and girls who live in their fathers' houses are slaves." [27] She also stated, "There is no slave, after all, like a wife" [28] or "You know how women sell themselves and are sold in marriage, from queens downward . . . Poor women, poor slaves." [29] Angelina Grimké in *Letters to Catherine Beecher* views a woman as being converted to "a mere drudge to suit the convenience of her lord and master." [30] Susan Dabney Smedes in *Memorials of a Southern Planter* also alludes to this saying "that the mistress of a plantation was the most complete slave on it." [31] Arthur Calhoun in *A Social History of the American Family* further observes that:

> Gallantry to women was the gallantry of the harem. Nowhere in the world were women shown more surface respect than in the South, yet degradation of the sex was obvious.[32]

In fact, the gallantry shown to women was an element of utmost importance in the South. White men, remorseful for their own sexual desires toward black women as well as consciously or unconsciously fearful that their spouses might come to share this attraction, glorified or idealized their wives, placing them on pedestals in theory, if conveniently not in practice. The white Southerner's concurrent veneration and culpability is well defined by Gunnar Myrdal in *An American Dilemma*:

> The fixation of the purity of white womanhood, and also part
> of the intensity of emotion surrounding the whole sphere of
> segregation and discrimination, are to be understood as the
> backwashes of the sore conscience on the part of the white
> men for their compeers' relations with, or desires for, Negro
> women.[33]

On the other hand, and as remarked upon by Lillian Smith, the
Southern woman's last and only recourse was to establish a police state
in order to attempt to control her husband's philanderings, leading the
men in turn to further alcoholism.[34] In *Killers of the Dream* she also describes the "culturally stunted" women, on their "lonely pedestals"
with their men elsewhere. They were made to equate "innocence,
virtue, ignorance, silence," and forced into lives of "sexual blankness"
which was "God's way" of pushing sex "out through the back door as a
shameful thing never to be mentioned." [35] Wilbur Cash in *The Mind of
the South* emphasizes once again the importance of the Negro threat
which made the woman, at least in theory, the object of the Southerner's chivalry:

> The upshot, in this land of spreading notions of chivalry, was
> downright gyneolatry. She was the South's Palladium, this
> Southern woman—the shield-bearing Athena gleaming
> whitely in the clouds, the standard for its rallying, the mystic
> symbol of its nationality in face of the foe. She was the lily-
> pure maid of Astolat and the hunting goddess of the Bœ-
> tian.[36]

Carl Rowan refers to this preponderant "mocked venery" [37] described
by Calhoun as "the white goddess complex." [38] It placed white women
on a pedestal before and after marriage and hedged them around with
taboos to insure the purity of the white blood and the husbands paternity of the offspring.

Some of the sense of gallantry toward women comes out of the pecu-
liarly Southern tradition of plantation owners viewing themselves as
American "royalty," even to the point of acting out medieval
pageantry. The importance that the cult of womanhood was to assume
was well demonstrated by the annual jousting march at Faquier Springs,
a Virginia resort in 1845. The jousting was for the hand of a "queen" of

the tournament. Lists, replicas possibly of those at Ashby-de-la-Zouche, were constructed. Liveried heralds were also provided in order to announce the arrival in medieval array of the opposing champions. Unlike Ivanhoe and his enemies, the combatants rode at rings, rather than at each other, but the recompense was the same. The victor received laurels from the queen as well as her presence at the Grand Ball.

The paradox, as noted by Howard Odum, is that the culture which placed woman on "the highest pedestal," [39] honoring her through the ritual of medieval-like tournaments, was the same one that did not permit her the basic rights and privileges such as education or in fact any form of social equality. However, it was a Southern woman who voiced the earliest protest in America against the female condition. In 1838, Sarah Moore Grimké wrote a book, *Letters on the Equality of the Sexes and the Condition of Women, Addressed to Mary S. Parker* in which she developed her position on "woman's rights." Believing that men demanded it, women came to consider themselves as "pretty toys" or "mere instruments of pleasure." She was one of the first American social critics to expose the fact that women were being paid less well than their male counterparts. Grimké added that their belief in their own inferiority was a significant element weakening their bargaining position.[40] Although the Southern woman until very recently was pushed away on the lonely pedestal of Sacred Womanhood, the Civil War marked the beginning of improvement in her status.

While the prewar South was traditionally a patriarchy, at the time of the war and particularly afterwards, that paternal system was undermined. At the outbreak of the war women were almost immediately called into new kinds of activity. They acted as hospital matrons or superintendents, or became managers, planters, millers, merchants, or manufacturers. Male supremacy no longer reinforced the slave system. Defeat and postwar conditions in the South were deleterious to the patriarchy and to marital relations. Faulkner, himself, summed up the position of the Southern male after the war when interviewed at the University of Virginia:

> they were obsolete, that the men, the Southern men, were the ones that couldn't bear it because they never had surrendered. The men were dead and even generations later were seeking death.[41]

Generations later many of Faulkner's heroes could also be considered *fin de race* and seeking death, the best example being Quentin Compson who is the typical offspring of his heredity.

The impotence of the Southern male commencing at the time of the Civil War could also explain the hermaphroditus dimension of many of Faulkner's characters, one of which is exemplified by Fairchild in *Mosquitoes*:

> men nowadays are not masculine and lusty enough to tamper with something that borders so close to the unnatural. A kind of sterile race: women too masculine to conceive, men too feminine to be - get ... [42]

More precisely, the Southern males' weakened position explains at least in part the effeminate characterization of certain of Faulkner's heroes. He refers to Januarius Jones in *Soldiers' Pay* and Charles Bon, Valery Bon and Shreve in *Absalom, Absalom!* in totally feminine terms. Januarius Jones in *Soldiers' Pay* is described by the author as cat-like and on several occasions he alludes to Jones as feminine. Of Jones he also says that "the feminine predominant so in him, and the rest of him was feline: a woman with a man's body and a cat's nature." [43] Charles Bon, Valery Bon, and Shreve in *Absalom, Absalom!* are also examples of the androgyny to which the Southern male was potentially receptive. Charles Bon is handsome, elegant and even catlike and wears "a flowered, almost feminized gown." [44] The author continues to describe his "outlandish and almost feminine garments" [45] and states that Bon acts "as an elegant and indolent esoteric hothouse bloom." [46] Valery Bon, his son, is depicted in a similar feminine way. Valery is portrayed as "—a thin delicate child with a smooth ivory sexless face," [47] as having "light bones," [48] "womanish hands," [49] and finally as a " 'man with body and limbs almost as light and delicate as a girl's.'" [50] Shreve, too, is far from a paragon of virility. He is described as having a "naked torso pink-gleaming and baby-smooth, cherubic, almost hairless." [51]

The Reconstruction also foreshadowed a new type of woman, one who was more independent, at least financially and intellectually. During this period, teaching and writing, for example, absorbed the largest number of women, many being newspaper editors. For married women, in particular, church work was the first step toward their emancipation in the South. This was, in one way, quite ironic since the church itself, at the doctrinal level, maintained its position with respect to male superiority. The Methodist Episcopal church in the South stood firmly with St. Paul and forbade women to preach. The Baptists concurred and their opinions did not alter much with the passing decades. In 1868 the Baptist *Religious Herald* asserted that:

> As the rival of man, in the struggle for place, power and prominence, she, as 'the weaker' vessel, is doomed to defeat. From such a contest, she must inevitably come forth, not with modesty, delicacy and loveliness which impart a charmed influence to her sex, but soiled, dishonored and disappointed.[52]

At the turn of the century the same paper was saying:

> When... woman becomes *emancipated* from the care of the young and the making of the home, she has entered into the worst of all bondage, which comes always to every one who disregards the law of his own life.[53]

While many women became involved in teaching, writing, and church work, by the end of the nineteenth century women in the lower classes often worked in the dairies and laundries. They also found jobs as seamstresses. The more promising ones sought employment at clerking, dressmaking, textiles, and in box and cigarette factories.

The female's subordinate position was apparent even in the laws of the fourteen Southern states[55] as opposed to the laws in the rest of the country during the period of Faulkner's greatest works. The pervasive Southern attitude toward women is reflected in the laws pertaining to women's public, private, and property rights during this period. In 1929, for instance, thirteen states permitted women to serve as jurors; only one, Arkansas, was Southern.[56] As late as 1945, of the seventeen states that still excluded women from jury duty, eleven were Southern:

Despite the increase in womens' jobs at the end of the century and the continuing improvement generally of the woman's status in the twentieth century the Southern woman was never, throughout all of Faulkner's life, on an even footing with her masculine counterpart. In the author's time, she was not expected to get a college education or to earn her own living. Marriage still remained the only serious option that satisfied both her family and society.[54]

Alabama, Georgia, Florida, Mississippi, North Carolina, South Carolina, Texas, Tennessee, Virginia, Maryland and Oklahoma.[57] In 1929, eighteen states had laws regulating a woman's work schedule and wages, only one, South Carolina, was Southern.[58] In 1945, of the twenty-one states that granted divorce to the woman for the husband's failure to support her, only three, Alabama, Kentucky, and Tennessee were in the South.[59] Yet, seven of the fourteen states that granted the husband divorce for the wife's unchaste character were Southern: Alabama, Georgia, Kentucky, Tennessee, Mississippi, North Carolina, and Virginia.[60] It is noteworthy, however, that the only two states that granted the woman a divorce for the husband's dangerously violent conduct towards his spouse were also in this region: Alabama and Tennessee.[61] These laws imply that Southern men behave with greater brutality towards their wives than men in other parts of the country. In 1945, of the twenty-two states that did not require a contribution from the father for the mother's expenses relating to childbirth, nine were Southern: Alabama, Kentucky, Louisiana, Mississippi, Oklahoma, South Carolina, Tennessee, Texas, and Virginia.[62]

With regard to property, in 1945 five states still made the wife's conveyance of her separate real estate void unless her husband was present. Of the five states, where this law existed four of the states were Southern: Alabama, Florida, North Carolina, and Texas.[63] At this time, no Southern state had any legal provisions to assure that a wife's personal earnings were her separate property when cohabitating with her husband.[64] Otherwise, the only three states that had not fully emancipated married women with respect to litigation by 1945 were also all Southern: Florida, North Carolina, and Texas.[65] Finally, the two states that still favored the husband over the wife in one of the provisions for the forfeiture of marital property rights in 1945 were both Southern, being Arkansas and North Carolina.[66]

In a society so restrictive, many women, and particularly Faulkner's heroines, reacted to the constraints imposed upon them through an act of sedition, one which seemed often and inevitably to involve a man who is in some way alien to the society. While Narcissa Sartoris' rebellion in "There Was a Queen" is secretive, reflecting her hypocrisy, the protest of many of the author's other belles is quite overt. Temple Drake, Elly, Emily Grierson, Linda Snopes, Candace Compson, her daughter, Quentin, are all illustrations of this second category. The seemingly righteous Narcissa, symbolically clad in white, is both fascinated and disgusted by the anonymous letters sent by Byron Snopes in *Flags in the Dust* and *Sartoris*. Her ambivalence toward the letters as well as the fact that she gives herself to the Jewish FBI agent in "There Was a Queen" is indicative of her revolt against the Southern system restricting her womanhood. Her weekend in Memphis as pointed out by Elizabeth Kerr is "atoned for by baptismal immersion, white clothes and all, in the pasture creek at Sartoris." [67] Narcissa, unlike many of the author's other heroines, feels the need to mask her actions in order at least to pretend to live up to the standards of the Southern code. Many of Faulkner's other heroines also rebel by choosing a man who is by Southern standards ineligible—an outsider because of race, class, and/or geography. The woman's frequent attraction to a man who is not of her social milieu is another way in which Faulkner accentuates the extent to which a woman feels the need to subvert the status quo.

Temple Drake, alluding to her past, immediately implies the seditious aspect of her enjoyment of her sojourn at the Memphis whorehouse: "all she had to do was, do the one thing which she knew they [her father and brothers] would forbid her to do if they had the chance." [68] Furthermore, her respective lovers, Red and Pete, are representative of the lower class men who are not suitable for a woman of her upbringing. Regarding Pete, Gavin Stevens speculates in *Requiem for a Nun* that he must have been "a man . . . so single, . . . so hard and ruthless, . . . so impeccable in amorality." [69] Similarly, Elly's desire to have an affair with Paul de Montigny, a Louisianian alleged to be part Negro, is another example of the dissatisfaction of the young Southern woman abandoned on her lofty pedestal. Before she makes love with Paul, her obsession to enrage her grandmother underlines this heroine's utterance of protestation: "I wish she were here to see! I wish she were here to see!" [70] Additionally, Emily Grierson, who engages in necrophilia particularly with a Yankee day laborer, is certainly one of the Faulknerian heroines, or perhaps an antiheroine, who voices most loudly her unwillingness to conform to the dictates of Southern decorum. Yet, while Temple, Elly, and Emily remain within the confines of Yoknapatawpha, Linda Snopes, Candace Compson and her daughter, Quentin, choose men who are not only of different backgrounds but who, furthermore, offer them the possibility of an escape that is geographic as well as psychological. Linda, for instance, marries the Communist Jewish sculptor, Barton Kohl, who is also a New Yorker. Candace first marries the Indianian, Herbert Head, and, afterwards, a minor moving picture magnate from Hollywood, while her third marriage is to a German staff general. Meanwhile, Quentin leaves Yoknapatawpha with a pitchman.

Although the author makes a few significant statements to the effect that he views women positively, his generally negative attitude throughout the major part of his work as well as his more subtle statements, show that the author is, if anything, most ambivalent, if not actually hostile to women. However, Elizabeth Kerr in her article "William Faulkner and the Southern Concept of Women," or in her later article, "Women in Yoknapatawpha," maintains the opposite position, believing instead, that Faulkner depicts women sympathetically. She, along with David Williams in his critical work, *Faulkner's Women: The Myth and the Muse,* is one of the few critics to consider Faulkner indulgent toward the weaker sex. Nevertheless, most critics, on the contrary, consider the author a misogynist. Ultimately, the views toward women and marriage held by the Southerner, attitudes so strongly entrenched that even the laws pertaining to womens' rights reflect them, are beliefs which Faulkner definitely shares. Faulkner's position toward women and marriage only begins to change with the first appearance of the Mallison family in *Intruder in the Dust,* published in 1948. Charles and Margaret Mallison reappear in *The Town* and are ultimately replaced by the Priests in *The Reivers.* They are the author's last testimonial that he has come to envision woman and the married couple as a harmonious unity.

Faulkner tried perhaps to denounce his seemingly reprobatory stance with regard to women. At the Nagano Conference he states:

> No. I think there's no difference between women anywhere. Just as I think there's no difference between men anywhere. The women that have been unpleasant characters in my books were not created to be unpleasant characters, let alone unpleasant women. They were used as implements, instruments, to tell a story . . . [71]

Again at Nagano he takes another affirmative stand regarding women when he declares "I don't think I would make any generalization about

an opinion of women—some of the best people are women." [72] Joseph
Blotner also records the author as voicing his admiration of the opposite sex, declaring that "I think women are wonderful, they're much
stronger than men, I admire them tremendously" [73] At the University
of Virginia he again alludes to his "admiration for women, for the
courage and endurance of women." [74] This statement cannot be contested
when taking into account Faulkner's attitude especially toward his
mother.

Even though the author had an indisputable attachment for
Maud, one cannot take for granted that these sentiments extended to
women in general. Although we have just alluded to a few of the exceptionally favorable statements, largely in self-defense, that the author
made with respect to women, one must now consider other comments
that act as evidence of the author's deep ambivalence. In the interview
with Jean Stein in *The Paris Review*, Faulkner voices his opinion that
the relationship between men and women is basically reduced to a *rapport de force* created by the woman:

> Success is feminine and like a woman; if you cringe before
> her, she will override you. So the way to treat her is to show
> her the back of your hand. Then maybe she will do the
> crawling. [75]

Faulkner also questions his friend, Ben Wasson, if Ben had understood
what he was saying in *Sanctuary*. He tells Ben, "I was saying that
women are impervious to evil." [76] Faulkner's reply to Wasson is indicative of his negative judgment with regard to women. Even war and the
accompanying threat of death are more constructive for Faulkner because they free men without justification from women's enslavement.
During another interview, the author simply states, "The only good I
know of that comes from a war is that it allows men to be free of their
womenfolks without being blacklisted by it." [77]

In addition to these isolated statements that certainly contradict
the affirmative ones, Faulkner's ambivalence, if not animosity, toward
women during the period of his major work can be seen by looking at the
texts themselves. In an overview of the author's work, there are a few
commentaries which occasionally are not deleterious to the woman.
These are usually analytical statements which are related to her will-
fulness, pragmatism, and ingenuity. These potentially positive quali-

ties assume at other times very destructive overtones. Her tenacity is commented on by Faulkner in "Delta Autumn" when he says:

> But women hope for so much. They never live too long to still believe that anything within the scope of their passionate wanting is likewise within the range of their passionate hope.[78]

In *Mosquitoes*, Dawson Fairchild comments on their practicality saying that women "ain't interested in what you're going to say: they are interested in what you're going to do." [79] Jenny Du Pre in *Sanctuary* also believes that women, although idealized by men, are themselves intransigent realists: "Fiddlesticks. You don't wonder. You just do things and then stop, until the next time to do something comes around." [80] A woman's cleverness is not independent of her strength, her determination and her practicality. Ephraim advises in *Intruder in the Dust*, "If you ever needs anything done outside the common run, don't waste your time on the menfolks; get the womens and children to working at it." [81]

However, fortitude and cleverness can also manifest themselves as noxious feminine forces which debilitate the male. Charles Bon in *Absalom, Absalom!* learns: "you can't beat women anyhow and that if you are wise or dislike trouble and uproar you don't even try to." [82] The female not only suppresses men but destroys them in *Mosquitoes* when Fairchild says:

> There is a kind of spider or something. The female is the larger, and when the male goes to her as he goes to death: she devours him during the act of conception.[83]

Men like Wilbourne in *Wild Palms* are also *"throttled and sapped of strength by the old weary Lilith of the year...."* [84] In mythology Lilith is the demon of the night, the mother of the empusae who in the form of bewitching maidens suck the juices of men until they die. It is probably not surprising that many of Faulkner's heroes like the fat convict in "Old Man" prefer one hundred and ninety-nine years of prison to facing the female whom he transported across the state line; the sole desire of the tall convict is to rid himself of the pregnant woman. This is an opinion Faulkner shares with his colleague, Shelby Foote, who also views woman as noxious to the male. Foote declares "I agree that woman is a destroyer ... If she's allowed to destroy, I think she will." [85] Women viewed as annihilators through their sexuality are also alluded to in "And Now What's To Do" as "traps" [86] or "spider webs" [87] or in "Nympholepsy" as "importune sirens." [88]

Faulkner's ambivalance, if not repulsion, is rooted in his inability to accept female sexuality. Even Eula, Faulkner's venerated heroine, who is goddess of the hamlet, is the incarnation of both the sacred and the bestial. "Fecund and foul," [89] "unchaste and inviolable," [90] she is the "unawares bitch" [91] and the eternal goddess. Faulkner pays tribute to her as "some symbology out of the old Dionysic times—honey in sunlight and bursting grapes, the writhen bleeding of the crushed fecundated vine beneath the hard rapacious trampling goat-hoof." [92] However, he demonstrates his contradictory feelings and derides her simultaneously, claiming: "She's just like a dog! Soon as she passes anything in long pants she begins to give off something. You can smell it! You can smell it ten feet away!" [93] For him, as for Labove in *The Hamlet* love is a perpetual battle, a physical manifestation of the battle of the sexes described by the author to Jean Stein. Labove states the following:

> Fight it. Fight it. That's what it is: a man and a woman fighting each other. The hating. To kill, only to do it in such a way that the other will have to know forever afterward he or she is dead.[94]

Women and sex are associated with death in "Nympholepsy," where death is "like a woman shining and drowned and waiting." [95] His misogyny is also revealed in his attitude toward menstruation, which is illustrated by the disgust of Mr. Compson in *The Sound and the Fury*. He describes menstruation to Quentin as a "Delicate equilibrium of periodical filth between two moons balanced." [96] In *Light in August*, the author expresses the same revulsion when Bobbie Allen explains to Christmas that she is menstruating, and he runs from her seeking refuge in the woods. Faulkner describes the hero's repulsion as follows:

> In the notseeing and hardknowing as though in a cave he seemed to see a diminishing row of suavely shaped urns in moonlight, blanched. And not one was perfect. Each one was cracked and from each crack there issued something liquid, deathcolored, and foul. He touched a tree, leaning his

propped arms against it, seeing the ranked and moonlit urns. He vomited.[97]

The author's obsessive rejection of menstruation is really made explicit in a statement he makes to Malcolm Franklin's first wife, Rita, when she tells him that her fantasy is to be a game warden. Faulkner tells her, "You couldn't be a game warden you're a woman so you menstruate and would be incapacitated."[98] The author shows an equal apprehension and unacceptance toward pregnancy as demonstrated by the tall convict who in *The Wild Palms* compares the pregnant woman he accompanies to "the living timber in a barn which had to be burned to rid itself of vermin."[99] Considering Faulkner's deeply puritanical fear and rejection of sex it is not surprising that the only sexual state which is not menacing, but instead comforting to him, is the one of virginity described in *Mosquitoes*:

> It was kind of nice, wasn't it? Young people, young men and girls caught in that strange hushed magic of sex and the mystery of intimate clothing and functions and all, and of lying side by side in the darkness, telling each other things ... that's the dream of virginity: telling each other things. Virginity don't make any difference as far as the body is concerned.[100]

In *The Wild Palms*, loss of virginity, this state of negative change is described by Wilbourne as a "dark precipice,"[101] one which the hero confronts for the first time when he is twenty-seven years old:

> the dark precipice; all mankind before you went over it and lived and all you went over it and lived and after all you will, but that means nothing to you because they can't tell you, forewarn you, what to do in order to survive. It's the solitude, you see. You must do it in solitude and you can bear just so much solitude and still live ... you surrender volition, hope, all—the darkness, the falling, the thunder of solitude, the shock, the death, the moment when, stopped physically by the ponderable day, you yet feel all your life rush out of you into the pervading immemorial blind receptive matrix, the hot fluid blind foundation-grave-womb or womb-grave, it's all one.[102]

By contrast, Mr. Compson associates the state of virginity itself
with death, as in the following passage: "Father said it's like death:
only a state in which the others are left." [103] Thus, while death in *The
Wild Palms* is connected with the loss of virginity, in *The Sound and
the Fury* it is connected to virginity, itself. It is important to underline
not the fact that the two statements made by Harry Wilbourne and Jason Compson are apparently contradictory, but to stress instead their
similarity; sex and death are inextricably equated. Faulkner's eulogy
of virginity can also be understood as a reflection of the Southerner's
desire to preserve himself and his family from violation from the outsider, as well as a profound need to reassure himself by safeguarding
the status quo. The changing and reordered world of the New South dis-
tresses the traditional Southerner creating for him feelings of imbal-
ance and uncertainty.

Lastly, and again with respect to womens' sexuality, Faulkner considers that men are the intellectual and creative force while women
demean art through their sexuality. Fairchild states of the male as
creator in *Mosquitoes* :

> But in art, a man creates without any assistance at all: what he
> does is his. A perversion, I grant you, but a perversion that
> builds Chartres and invents Lear is a pretty good thing.[104]

Meanwhile, the satiric portrait of Miss Jameson is more than a cruel
vindication of his belief that women are subordinate to the purposes of
art. Miss Jameson uses painting as an ineffective vehicle for seducing
artistic men. She commits the ultimate blasphemy, not of prostituting
herself, which becomes almost incidental, but of debasing creativity,
one of the principal Faulknerian gods.

Faulkner's hostility toward women extends beyond their sexuality. Besides their tendency toward dissatisfaction which he alludes to,
the female's dominant characteristic according to the author is her absolute adherence to evil—a proclivity that he makes explicit in his
earlier statement to Ben Wasson. Harry Mitchell in both *Flags in the
Dust* and *Sartoris* comments on the feminine inability for contentment:

> You've got to make allowance for women anyhow. Different
> from men. Born contrary; complain when you don't please
> 'em and complain when you do.[105]

The fact that women are seen as the incarnation of evil is made clear as early as *Mosquitoes* in the following statement made by Mr. Talliafero: "Yes, Fairchild was right, he knew women, the feminine soul—? No, not soul: they have no souls."[106] In "Hair," the narrator states:

> There's not any such thing as a woman born bad, because they are all bad, born with the badness in them. The thing is to get them married before the badness comes to a natural head.[107]

Faulkner interprets the actions of the dietician in *Light in August* who persecutes Christmas in the Memphis orphanage as follows: "her natural female infallibility for the spontaneous comprehension of evil."[108] Mr. Compson also tells Quentin that:

> Women are like that they are just born with a practical fertility of suspicion that makes a crop every so often and usually right they have an affinity for evil for supplying whatever the evil lacks in itself for drawing it about them instinctively as you do bed-clothing.[109]

Ultimately, the Reverend Hightower when he urges Byron Bunch not to marry Lena Grove in *Light in August* also makes explicit this evil:

> No woman who has a child is ever betrayed; the husband of a mother, whether he be the father or not, is already a cuckhold ... There have been good women who were martyrs to brutes ... But what woman, good or bad, has ever suffered from any brute as men have suffered from good women?[110]

Horace, too, in the first version of *Sanctuary* reflects on the intrinsic evil of women:

> I thank God that no bone and flesh of mine has taken that form which, rife with its inherent folly, knells and bequeaths its own disaster ... That's what hurts. Not that there is evil in the world; evil belong [sic] in the world: it is the mortar in which the bricks are set. It's that they can be so impervious to the mire which they reveal and teach us to abhor.[111]

Even though most critics, quite justly, are aware of Faukner's disparaging attitude toward women throughout the major part of his work, Elizabeth Kerr or David Williams are the author's most vocal spokesmen to the contrary. In her article, "William Faulkner and the Southern Concept of Women," Kerr argues that what the author dislikes in women has its origins in the Southerner's glorification of woman. The unnatural ideals and conventions fostered by this gyneolatry are conducive, for instance, to the frustration of Rosa Coldfield, the perversion of Emily Grierson and the destruction of women such as Elly, Temple Drake, or Caroline Compson. Thus, Faulkner's women are not themselves at the source of feminine evil but are instead the victims of codes and standards of behavior which are deleterious to them. According to Kerr, the author tends to respect lower-class women who react spontaneously and instinctively like Lena Grove, or more upper-class women who have the courage to rebel against convention, like Eula Varner and Caddy Compson. Kerr also feels that women who are totally marginal to society such as Ruby Lamar who prostitutes herself in an attempt to save Lee Goodwin, her common-law husband; or Reba Rivers, the keeper of the whorehouse in which Temple stays in Memphis and who incarnates kindness and love, earn the author's compassion. Furthermore, she believes that Faulkner has undying admiration for certain older women such as Granny Millard, Miss Habersham, or Jenny Du Pre who represent integrity as well as gentility. They are symbolic of Southern womanhood at its most genuine.[112]

In "Women in Yoknapatawpha," Kerr once again takes a stand against the critics traditional opinion about Faulkner as a misogynist, reiterating that the author regarded women at the mercy of the stronger sex. In this article, Kerr mentions Cora Tull and Addie Bundren as two exceptions to women falling under male domination. These women do not obtain the reader's sympathy.[113] The critic implies that the Faulknerian antiheroine is granted mercy only when she is portrayed as the martyr of the South's Pauline doctrine. Elizabeth Kerr also refers in this later article to the fact that women were oppressed by "the tyranny of men" [114] in marriage and were subjugated to male domination:

> In this male-dominated society woman was on a pedestal
> from which she fell to her own ruin, regardless of who or what

caused her fall. Men made the rules of the sex-marriage game, umpired it, and called fouls on women but not men.[115]

David Williams in *Faulkner's Women: The Myth and the Muse* likewise contradicts the critics who claim Faulkner to be a woman-hater. For Williams, the Faulknerian woman, like Candace Compson, creates, sustains, and increases life; the feminine is regarded negatively only because male consciousness desires permanence not change. The male like Candace's brother, Quentin, seeks eternity not transformation, law not creative spontaneity. Williams refutes Fairchild's theories and considers woman as the incarnation of a deity or as the expression of some magnanimous and inspiring power in the creative act and thus central to Faulkner's work.

Most critics, however, believe that Faulkner is, at best, filled with great reserve in his approach to women. Sally R. Page in her critical work, *Faulkner's Women: Characterization and Meaning,* concurs in part with David Williams' standpoint. Her view is still one which views Faulkner as a misogynist. In the section, "Woman: The Image of Life," Page shows that in both *Light in August* and the Snopes trilogy there exists the continuing dialectic in Faulkner's work of "the life-nourishing female principle versus the life-destructive male principle." Lena Grove and Eula Varner represent a need to comply with the life process, while the men or masculinized women in Faulkner's novels portray instead the desire for self-assertion and personal freedom.[116] However, in the first section, "Woman: The Image of Romantic Ideality," the once again uninnocent woman in Faulkner's work is considered by Page to mock the ideal which the female's beauty seems to represent.[117] In the section, "Woman: The Image of Moral Order," Page states that woman is closer to nature than her male counterpart and although she is able to submit positively to the natural reproductive process, this surrender is often counterpointed by the refusal to submit to the sexual processes, leading to destruction and the denial of life.[118] In part three, "Woman: The Image of Death," she elaborates upon her earlier point and details woman's misuse of her natural purpose: childbearing. Woman can thus negate both the sexual and reproductive acts.[119] In this case, like Addie Bundren or Charlotte Rittenmeyer, she does bear a child, but, according to Page:

attempts to use sexuality as a means of escaping the reality of
life's limitations rather than as a means of reproducing life,
she aligns herself with the forces which destroy life, and,
ironically, in her search for life's vitality she embraces de-
cayed death.[120]

While Sally R. Page finds Faulkner's view of women predomi-
nantly negative, other critics find his attitude wholly condemnatory.
Irving Malin alludes to Faulkner's "brutal treatment of sex" which in
the biographical chapter, he considers as having homosexual overtones.[121] Malin furthermore concludes that men in Faulkner's work:

> disregard or fear emotions for healthy women. Faulkner spe-
> cializes in twisted creatures such as Temple Drake and
> Joanna Burden and Miss Habersham, who are willful and
> masculine.[122]

Leslie Fiedler in *Love and Death in the American Novel* describes
the author's misogyny when he declares the following:

> In no other writer in the world do pejorative stereotypes of
> woman appear with greater frequency and on more levels,
> from the most trivial to the most profound; had Faulkner
> dared treat in such terms any racial minority, his books would
> have been banned in every enlightened school in the coun-
> try.[123]

Fiedler also declares emphatically:

> In the work of William Faulkner, the fear of the castrating
> woman and the disease present in the novels of his contem-
> poraries, Fitzgerald and Hemingway, attain their fullest and
> shrillest expression. Not content with merely projecting im-
> ages of the anti-virgin, he insists upon editorializing against
> the woman he travesties in character and situation. No Jiggs
> and Maggie cliché of popular anti-feminism is too banal for
> him to use; he reminds us (again and again!) that men are
> helpless in the hands of their mothers, wives, and sisters; that
> females do think but proceed from evidence to conclusions
> by paths too devious for males to follow; that they possess nei-
> ther morality nor honor; ... they use their sexuality with cold
> calcuation to achieve their ends.[124]

Women's sexuality in Faulkner's work, specifically in *Sanctuary*, is also criticized by Cleanth Brooks in *William Faulkner: The Yoknapatawpha County*. This critic, however, sees female sexuality as detrimental to idealism:

> Women are particularly mammals, creatures that give suck, and to Horace, the appalled and outraged idealist, these human beings whose function is so invincibly animal, are nowhere more so than in their unwillingness to believe in ideals.[125]

While Kenneth E. Richardson in his critical work, *Force and Faith in the Novels of Faulkner*, claims that Faulkner, "invariably uses women to display the destructive power of sexual irresponsibility," [126] Samuel A. Yorks in his article, "Faulkner's Women: The Peril of Mankind" depicts female sexuality as a source of male despoliation. A woman may be seductive and thus morally malevolent such as Caroline Compson, Charlotte Rittenmeyer, or Joanna Burden. She may be a mindless and amoral force and also a source of peril as exemplified by Eula Varner Snopes or Lena Groves. The role of the male is to protect his realm, to flee feminine involvement. Yorks describes Faulkner's view of women as Pauline in severity:

> ... if not better be castrated than seduced. It is not the fate of the flesh but the fate of the spirit that so concerns this descendant of Puritans. The devil in female shape is precisely most to be feared when attractive. The Southern author's Old Testament view makes men into Adams fleeing the perennial serpent, declining the apple. ... [127]

Faulkner's puritanism with regard to women and sex is also discussed by Ilse Dusoir Lind in her article, "Faulkner's Women." She explicitly notes that Faulkner is the only major American fiction writer of the twenties and thirties who incorporates into his depiction of women the functioning of the organs of reproduction. She gives as illustrations his reference to menstruation when Mr. Compson counsels Quentin in *The Sound and the Fury* or when Joe Christmas educates himself about sex in *Light in August;* his reference to the menopause, in Joanna's missed menses in *Light in August;* his account of the process of childbirth in Hightower's midwifery and in the convict's impromptu delivery in *The*

Wild Palms; or his use of such medically exact words such as "uterus" and "tumescence" in the Snopes trilogy.[128] Faulkner's clinical involvement with women and sex can imply at best a detachment resulting from his profound fear of the opposite sex and consequent rejection of women.

Women's perniciousness, this time outside a puritanical context, is also the subject of Thomas Lorch's article, "Thomas Sutpen and the Female Principle." Throughout Faulkner's work even though it is the female principle that sustains men, providing the male, like Thomas Sutpen, with the material for him to shape and elevate, allowing him also transcendent flights toward the ideal, it is ultimately, however, the female principle that also destroys him.[129] Karl E. Zink in "Faulkner's Garden: Women and the Immemorial Earth" alludes to the author's ambivalence toward women. According to Zink, Faulkner often links the earth, nature, and woman. This critic speculates that Faulkner's ambivalent attitude toward women might reflect his fear, hatred, and love of the earth.[130]

In addition, the critics rather unanimously agree regarding the choice of his heroines. His habitual preference for young girls before the age of puberty, older women beyond the menopause or earthmothers—these types of women indicate that the author has safely removed from his literary universe any women who might be simultaneously sexually threatening and potential mates, and in doing so he has once again revealed his underlying fear of the opposite sex. Albert J. Guerard in the chapter entitled "Forbidden Games III: Faulkner's Misogyny" in *The Triumph of the Novel* concludes that "the ultimate and repugnantly forbidden game to the Faulknerian imagination was normal intercourse with a woman of marriageable age."[131] This critic also adds that "young girls before the age of puberty are not sources of anxiety... Eccentric or benign old ladies also represent no menace."[132] Meanwhile, Richard King in *The Southern Renaissance* classifies Faulkner's women as "feisty, yet asexual older women" or aside from these figures as "mindless, mysterious or often destructively sexual."[133] The only positive women figures being the black women, it is probably not completely fortuitous that the only category which is worthy of approbation is the one that for both social and racial reasons does not place in question the author's masculinity.

David Miller in his article, "Faulkner's Women," divides Faulkner's feminine universe into two subdivisions; the ghosts and the earthmothers; the ghosts consist of spinster-like women such as Emily Grierson, Aunt Jenny, Narcissa, Drusilla or Mrs. McEachern while the earthmothers are distinguished by their animality like innocent Lena Grove or the debased Joanna Burden or as the self-seeking Belle Mitchell.[134] It is probably not completely coincidental that as soon as an earthmother such as Joanna Burden or Belle Mitchell can be equated with a woman of Faulkner's own social strata, her sexuality instantly takes on a noxious aspect. Not only does she defy the codes of her class, but she once again awakens the Southern male's and Faulkner's fear of impotency.

Guerard, King and Miller have alluded to the importance of Faulkner's older women. While Guerard and King have cited them directly as a category, Miller has included these elderly ladies, such as Aunt Jenny, among his spinster portraits. For the other critics, too, Faulkner's older women reassure the author because he can create them without concerning himself with their potential sexual demands. Faulkner himself, however, does not choose to acknowledge the reason for his preference for these Southern dowagers but comments at Nagano:

> I'm inclined to think that every young man should know one old woman, that they talk more sense—they'd be good for any young man—well, an old aunt, or an old school teacher, just to listen to.[135]

Leslie Fiedler, Sally Page, Irving Howe and Ruel E. Foster, as did earlier critics, also take note of the author's esteem for these Southern matriarchs. Fiedler remarks that until his latest books:

> Faulkner has treated with respect only females, white ladies or colored women, past the menopause. The elderly maiden or widowed aunt is the sole feminine figure in his fiction exempt from travesty and contempt.[136]

Sally Page in *Faulkner's Women: Characterization and Meaning* agrees with Leslie Fiedler that the most appealing of Faulkner's women characters are of the older generation, such as Miss Jenny Du Pre, Miss Habersham, and Rosa Millard, these women being the stabilizing and life-sustaining forces in the homes and communities they inhabit.[137] Ruel E. Foster in his article, "Social Order and Disorder in Faulkner's Fiction," also concludes that:

> The women Faulkner seems to admire most in his novels are
> older women, women past the menopause, no longer con-
> cerned with the madness of sex and able to devote them-
> selves to enduring the evils which life thrusts upon them.[138]

Dilsey, the great Negro matriarch of *The Sound and the Fury*, Old Miss
Habersham of *Intruder in the Dust* and Aunt Jenny Du Pre of *Sartoris* are
among the examples he gives. What is implied by Ruel Foster concerning Faulkner's women is made explicit by Irving Howe. Howe explains
that since the author's women are "no longer concerned with the madness of sex," they remove themselves as a threat to the author:

> Such splendid old ladies as Rosa Millard, Aunt Jenny Du Pre
> and Dilsey, all conspicuously beyond the age of sexual dis-
> traction, gain Faulkner's admiration. They neither threaten
> nor attract; they are beyond the magical powers of sexual-
> ity.[139]

However, Howe does place Faulkner's matrons in a classification apart
because with the exception of Linda Snopes in *The Mansion* he feels the
author treats women with total disgust:

> But there is hardly a young woman in Faulkner's novels —
> one notable exception is Linda Snopes in *The Mansion*—
> who does not provoke quantities of bitterness and bile; and so
> persistent is this distaste of the doings of "woman-flesh" that
> it cannot be dismissed as vagary of either Faulkner or the
> characters who convey it.[140]

The epicene quality of so many of Faulkner's heroines can be regarded as yet another sign of his misogyny, once again rooted in his personal fear of the opposite sex. The author himself was not attracted to
the voluptuous Rubens-like woman, probably because subconsciously she
seemed to evoke in him a greater sexual appetite. Because of his deep-
rooted fearfulness of women, Faulkner's feminine ideal could to some
degree be situated closely to Gordon's. Gordon describes her in
Mosquitoes as follows: "my feminine ideal: a virgin with no legs to
leave me, no arms to hold me, no head to talk to me."[141] The
hermaphroditic women such as Patricia Robyn, Cecily Saunders, Charlotte Rittenmeyer, Temple Drake, or Joanna Bundren are among the

many heroïnes of Faulkner's early and middle work who are described by Ilse Dusoir Lind as being of "dubious sexuality." [142] They are

> those darlings of his heart, his charming boy-girls, the slim-hipped Venuses who had been erotically idealized for him—fatefully, it would appear—by his early poetic mentors, Verlaine and Swinburne.[143]

Even though Sally Page is also aware that Faulkner has masculinized many of his heroines such as Drusilla Hawk, she joins to some degree Elizabeth Kerr and believes that these women are still products of their circumstance. This viewpoint could be regarded as a simplification. It is, moreover, Irving Malin who appears to have grasped the problem at its more fundamental level when he states that Faulkner "never gives them the chance to flower into feminity," once again due to his own subconscious fear of women.[144]

Finally, other critics also view Faulkner as completely antipathetic to women believing that the author takes a similarly negative position to both the Negro and the woman. Geismar first summarizes Faulkner's position toward women as follows: he sees him as having "suspicion of woman when it is not contempt, and contempt when it is not hatred." [145] Geismar additionally sees the Negro and the woman as the destructive elements in Faulkner's work, referring to them as "the twin furies." [146] Barbara Giles in her article, "The South of William Faulkner," maintains a similar viewpoint. The Negro and the female are both a corrupting power of flesh and seduction; they are the dangerous potential of the dark, the unknown, the "irrational" and the "instinctual." [147]

The author's attitude toward women in his major work is one which he also holds toward the relationship of marriage and the couple. The critics have also pointed out the negativeness he projects onto the couple. Even though, for instance, Malcolm Cowley feels that a strong fidelity can exist in the Faulknerian universe, he still qualifies this view: "With few exceptions, the relationship of husband and wife is one of mutual conflict." [148] Ilse Dusoir Lind also comments that one of the most striking recurring patterns in the novel is the "problem of legal marriage." [149] Faulkner's own stance on marriage is probably well summarized when he says: "It was marriage they were trying to quit, since any woman makes a better mistress than she does wife." [150] Apropos of the couple Faulkner states in *Absalom, Absalom!*:

> Because you can't beat them ... You just flee (and thank
> God you can flee, you escape from that massy five-foot thick
> maggot-cheesy solidarity which overlaps the earth, in which
> men and women in couples are ranked and racked like
> ninepins: thanks to whatever Gods for that masculine hipless
> tapering peg which fit light and glib to move where the car-
> tridge-chambered hips of women hold them fast)"[151]

This is escape into a kind of masculine sexuality, but it is devoid of any true emotional intimacy.

The negative potential of this institution is taken to its extreme by the author in his creation as early as *Pylon* of an antimarriage: the menage à trois of Jack Holmes, Laverne and Roger Shumann. Furthermore, Faulkner's early and middle work show that the difficulties within the couple are often the very problems also faced on a broader psychological and philosophical level by the traditional Southerner: identity and ambivalence of feeling.

Ambivalence toward marriage, certainly one of the dominant Southern attitudes, is demonstrated by Margaret Powers in *Soldiers' Pay* or Narcissa Sartoris in the first edition of *Sartoris, Flags in the Dust*. Margaret remembers Dick her husband as beautiful but ugly. She desired him but sex was a violation, "Dick your ugly body breaking into mine like a burglar;" [152] he was her lover whom she did not love: "Dear dead Dick." [153] Narcissa's sentiments towards her husband, Bayard, are also marked by contradiction:

> All her instincts were antipathetic toward him, toward his vio-
> lence and his brutally obtuse disregard of all the qualities
> which composed her being. His idea was like a trampling of
> those heavy feet in these corridors of hers, in that grave
> serenity in which her days accompanied themselves; at the
> very syllables of his name her instincts brought her upstand-
> ing and under arms against him, thus increasing, doubling
> the sense of violation by the wound ... And yet, despite her
> armed sentinels, he still crashed with hot violence of his
> through the bastions and thundered at the very most citadel
> of her being.[154]

In both cases, Margaret and Narcissa are anguished victims of violation.

Fear itself is another motivating force for the Southerner in connection to marriage. Cecily Saunders marries George Farr in *Soldiers' Pay* because she fears Januarius Jones will expose her affair with George to the dying Mahon. Destruction, feared by Southerners since the time of the Civil War, propels certain of Faulkner's heroes in their decision to choose a wife in Yoknaptawpha. Horace's marriage to Belle is:

> Not any subconscious stirring after what we believed will be happiness, contentment; but a sort of gadfly urge after the petty ignoble impulses which man has tried to conjure with words out of himself.[155]

The attraction toward "the abyss" can also be seen as a self-destructive proclivity in the Southerner, who feels impotent in the face of the decadence of the South's current social reality and thus chooses on the deepest level to annihilate himself. However, matrimony can also be attractive to some Southerners as a means of escaping what is to them the hideous reality of the New South. Faulkner shows that marriage can give them the illusion of emotional security or can be a form of vicarious life —if not escapism. Wedlock for Margaret Powers, for instance, is her means of reassuring herself in the period of particular uncertainty when World War I breaks out.

The illusory aspect of marriage is also portrayed in *Light in August* when the author says that Hightower's marriage is

> a dead state carried over into and existing still among the living like two shadows chained together with the shadow of a chain. He was used to that; he had grown up with a ghost.[156]

In *Absalom, Absalom!* Rosa Coldfield lives by proxy through her niece, Judith, by making garments for her trousseau. In "Zilphia Gant" when Zilphia's husband leaves her for another woman and she realizes that he will no longer return she continues to exist in a similar way:

> Sometimes at night she would become one of the two of them, entering their bodies in turn and crucified anew by her

ubiquity, particularly in ecstasies the more racking for being
vicarious and transcendent of the actual flesh.[157]

Ellen's marriage to Sutpen is itself an example of evasion: "she escaped
at last into a world of pure illusion in which she moved, lived, from attitude to attitude ... " [158] Furthermore, illusion through marriage can
take the form, as it does for Narcissa, of an attempted flight from the
incestuous-like emotions she has for her brother, Horace. Her younger
brother's marriage is, as described by Aunt Jenny, her means of liberation:

> That man is making an old maid out of you. It isn't too late
> now, but if he'd waited five years later to play the fool, there
> wouldn't be anything left for you except to give music
> lessons.[159]

Marriage in the Faulknerian world is also considered by some a
prison, still worse a monotonous one. Wedlock in Yoknapatawpha and
the surrounding Southern regions is, according to the author, punctuated
by sentiments of loneliness and alienation as well as egotism. The
Faulknerian male, such as Houston, associates marriage with the loss
of his independence and both Lucy as well as his mother with
"proferred slavedom." [160] Houston views matrimony as a *rapport de
force* which is very similar to the one described by Faulkner to Jean
Stein:

> ... a feud, a gage, wordless, uncapitulating, between that
> unflagging will not for love or passion but for the married
> state, and that furious and as unbending one for solitariness
> and freedom.[161]

When he marries, he instantly buys a stallion, as a vestige of the sexual freedom, power and masculinity he still wishes to retain. Houston
intends to make Lucy Pate aware that despite the fact that he has
agreed to marry her, he refuses complete imprisonment.

This question of independence is also related to the problem of
monotony. Since many women in Yoknapatawpha, as well as in the
South in general, married for pragmatic reasons rather than for sentiment, it is not totally surprising that faced with a husband such as Anse

or Frank, women like Addie Bundren or Elly are overwhelmed with boredom and consequently choose lovers with whom they attempt to fill the void. This is the reason Charlotte Rittenmeyer in *The Wild Palms* leaves her husband, Rat, for Henry Wilbourne. She, like her Southern compatriots, elects to denounce the rigidity of the social system and chooses adventure over security. With a lack of realism, once again characteristic of many Southerners, she expects her affair with Harry Wilbourne "to be all honeymoon, always. Forever and ever, until one of us dies." [162] Yet, the ultimate danger to their love is Charlotte's accidental pregnancy, which would restrict the bohemian life that they seek. Charlotte's insistence on an abortion and the death of both her and her child is in many ways illustrative of the effect of change on the South and its consequences as viewed by the traditional Southerner: transformation quickly becomes synonymous with death. Ultimately, however, even change, itself, is illusory in Faulkner's South: Rat, who is representative of the conservative force, proves himself more liberal than Wilbourne. While Harry, as Rat says, has become a spouse: "I had turned into a husband." [163] Rat has not only helped finance their departure, but because he loves his wife, offers Wilbourne cyanide and tries later to have him released. The reversals within this triangle recall the male-female reversals as well as the societal ones where the aristocracy was replaced by the mercantile Southern parvenu. Again, and for very similar reasons, the feelings of alienation held by the twentieth-century Southerner were emotions felt within the couple itself.

Besides the solitude felt by characters such as Addie Bundren, division within a couple can often be explained by social differences. Addie, alluding to her estrangement with her husband, says in *As I Lay Dying*:

> He had a word, too. Love, he called it. But I had been used to words for a long time. I knew that that word was like the others: just a shape to fill a lack; that when the right time came, you wouldn't need for that anymore than for pride or fear.[164]

The alienation felt by Addie as well as by Caroline Compson in her marriage is, in great part, accountable to the marriage of convenience so widely practiced in the South. As both Addie and Caroline married men who were socially superior to themselves, they are consequently aware of the social dissimilarities which bring a greater division between them and their husbands. While Caroline is obsessed with being a Bascomb, Addie is likewise fixated with being buried with *her* family. In the Bundren marriage egotism is an element that plays a part; Anse is only interested in interring his wife so that he can go himself to Jefferson and get new teeth: "But now I can get them teeth." [165]

The emotional isolation and selfishness exhibited in certain marriages in Yoknapatawpha is manifested at the level of Southern society as on a broader horizon. The traditional Southerner views himself as alien, an isolated entity amid the twentieth-century world—he turns inward and becomes inaccessible even to his family.

The widespread influence of Puritanism in the South is another aspect of marital relationships which can be potentially destructive to the couple. The McEacherns, the Hightowers, and the Hines are the prototypes of the puritan couple: punctuated by frustration, impotence and fanaticism. Mrs. McEachern is depicted, for instance, as a "beaten creature without sex demarcation" [166] and as "an attenuation of dumb hopes and frustrated desires." [167] Reverend Hightower's wife also is the victim of his spiritual and sexual impotence which is manifested in his characteristically Southern flight into the past. The author says of Hightower "[It was] as though the seed which his grandfather has transmitted to him had been on the horse too that night and had been killed too." [168] Hightower is also drawn to Tennyson's poetry which for him is "like listening in a cathedral to an eunuch chanting in a language which he does not even understand." [169] Consequently, he completely neglects his wife. Thus in the middle of one of his sermons she begins to scream out of frustration. Later, she even jumps or falls out of a window in a Memphis hotel where she has spent the weekend with another man in an attempt to alleviate her feelings of rejection. It is only at the time that Lena gives birth that Hightower becomes aware that man's first duty is to propagate the race. He learns that he, as his Southern compatriots on a larger scale, needs to transcend his self-enclosed personal and societal prison. Hines' wife, too is a product of nonfulfilment, and both she and Hines have come to incorporate the rigidity of their religion which acts as a barrier between them. Hines' wife becomes "a puppet, a ventriloquist in the next room," [170] "a stonefaced woman," [171] and they are both described as puppets "operated by clumsy springwork." [172] The author focuses on the fanatical element in Protestantism which acts as another obstacle in their relationship. Hines, although a far more extreme version of Hightower, his eyes being "blind, wide open, ice cold, fanatical," [173] is also so obsessed by what he deems his mission that he, too, overlooks his wife.

Hypocrisy is yet another noxious element portrayed in Yoknapatawpha marriages. The obsequious Reverend Whitfield, for example, has an affair with Addie Bundren, while Flem Snopes, the new bastion of Protestant Yoknapatawpha, has a monument built in honor of his dead wife on which he inscribes the following: "A Virtuous Wife Is a Crown to Her Husband Her Children Rise and Call Her Blessed." [174] Not only was Eula unfaithful, like many of Faulkner's other heroines, but Flem himself behaves disingenuously when he spits out the car window on her grave.

The sense of guilt is as much a problem for the couple as it is for the Southerner in general, and it is also a function of his religious background. As early as *Soldiers' Pay*, Margaret Powers marries Donald Mahon on account of the remorse she feels toward her deceased husband, who had never received her letter terminating their relationship before his death. Similarly, Bayard Sartoris is overwhelmed by culpability in connection with his brother's death in *Flags in the Dust*, and on an emotional level, in *Sartoris*, he has little left to give to his wife Narcissa. Gowan Stevens and Temple Drake are also brought together by their sense of mutual guilt in *Requiem for a Nun*. Gowan marries Temple as compensation for leaving her at the Old Frenchman's place in *Sanctuary*. He forgives all that requires forgiveness but continually demands gratitude in return. Ironically, Temple (who also marries Gowan as a means of rectifying her past) is attracted in part to Pete because according to Gavin Stevens she welcomes a "man . . . after six years of that sort of forgiving debased not only the forgiven but the forgiven's gratitude. . . . " [175] Thus blameworthiness engenders even more sinfulness. Parsimony, also related to puritanism, is another divisive trait for the couple. In "The Brooch," for example, Mrs. Boyd is left by her husband because he can no longer stand her rolling onto empty spools the string saved from parcels from the stores.

All these are problems that historically, as well as in Faulkner's work, pertain specifically to poor whites and to their marriages. When interviewed, Faulkner, alluding to the family, states:

> ... there are certain similarities in family relationships be-
> tween a family of planters and a family of tenant farmers. The
> superficial differences could be vast and varied, but basically
> the same relationship is there because it's based on the need
> for solidarity in a country which not too long ago was still fron-
> tier.[176]

Despite the similarity that exists between these families belonging to
different social classes, there are also major differences, the most important differences being the greater marital instability found in lower
class families. There were more instances of separation and divorce
here—usually for nonsupport, cruelty, or infidelity. In Faulkner's work
one observes that desertion, for example, is a phenomenon that exists in
the lower classes. Both Goodwin's father and stepfather, for instance,
leave his mother in *Sanctuary*. Mrs. Gant's husband, the street trader,
also deserts her. In each case the desertion occurs very spontaneously,
which underlines the male's irresponsibility. Popeye's father is completely unconscious and one day when the strike is over leaves town
without even telling his wife, sending her a nonchalant card at
Christmas. Her second husband simply disappears one day carrying a
blank check to pay the butcher. Mrs. Gant's husband also vanishes
without notification, sending his half-wit partner to break the news to
his wife and two-year-old daughter.

   Although Faulkner accurately portrays the impermanence typifying the marriages in this lower strata, he tends to depict the husband
deserting the family, when historically it was almost always the wife
who left the husband. The dominant role already assumed by the
Southern male is more prevalent in the lower classes. James Agee, after
spending two months interviewing three families in Hale County, Alabama, concludes in *Let Us Now Praise Famous Men* that "the husband
was running this show, and a wife does as she is told and keeps quiet
about it." [177]

   The image of the poor white, in the literary tradition from
William Byrd to Erskine Caldwell and analyzed by Shields McIl-
waine in his critical study *The Southern Poor White from Lubberland to
Tobacco Road*, is one of moral and physical depravity.[178] Although the
poor white, as depicted by Merrel Macguire Skaggs in her work *The
Folk of Southern Fiction* or Sylvia Jenkins Cook in her later *From To-*

bacco Road to Route 66, The Southern Poor White in Fiction, falls into this pattern,[179] others contest this viewpoint, such as Herbert Weaver in *Mississippi Farmers 1850-1960* and W.H. Peck in *The M'Donalds or The Ashes of Southern Homes.*[180] Yet, as justly pointed out by Jean Rouberol, this stereotype is not a true portrayal of the reality.[181], Historians and sociologists are almost unanimous that the woman was the industrious one. Margaret Jarman Hagood in *Mothers of the South; Portraiture of the White Tenant Farm Woman* explains that the woman had not only the responsibility of the home and the children but for about half the year was also obliged to help with the field work.[182] Faulkner, alludes, for instance, in "Adolescence" to Joe Bundren's "rank laziness." [183] Anse in *As I Lay Dying* refers to his mother in the following terms:

> It's a hard life on women, for a fact. Some women. I mind my mammy lived to be seventy and more. Worked every day, rain or shine; never a sick day since her chap was born until one day she kind of looked around her and then went and taken that lace-trimmed night gown she had forty-five years and never wore out of the chest and put it on and laid down on the bed and pulled the covers up and shut her eyes.[184]

Of Martha Armstid, in *Light in August,* the author declares that she "bore five children in six years and raised them to man- and woman-hood. She is not idle." [185]

The woman's diligence can be explained by the economic problems that are at the root of the other difficulties confronting the couple in this social stratum. Since the male feels even weaker than his upper-class equivalent, his need to dominate so as to prove himself is more pronounced. Thus, the pressure placed on the women is all the greater. Since the horse in Faulkner's work is representative, according to Melvin Backman, of "an untamed masculine violence or freedom," [186] it is not surprising that Henry Armstid in *The Hamlet* so covets one of Flem's ponies that he deprives his children of food so that he can purchase it. His neighbor Ab Snopes, equally obsessed with owning a horse, buys one with the money his wife has saved for a cream separator. Later, he mortgages all his property and purchases an interest in the Old Frenchman's place, where he goes crazy looking for non-existent buried treasure.

Also, much of the apathy characteristic of the poor-white male can be attributed to his profound sense of financial hopelessness. His despair and frustration are vented in his physical cruelty. When Martha Armstid fails to capture his cherished pony, Henry cruelly strikes her. Likewise, in *The Hamlet*, Mink Snopes beats his wife after he has killed Houston. Because the lower classes in white society were less influenced by the morality of Protestantism, this cruelty is understandable.

Infidelity has historically also been another source of friction in such marriages. Owing to their relative amorality, the poor whites indulged quite freely in a hedonistic sexuality, behavior which Erskine Caldwell highlights in his fiction. In lower class unions the tendency toward infidelity was, thus, all the greater. Addie Bundren is probably Faulkner's most obvious offender. Even though it was the male who historically was the most habitual adulterer, in this case it was a woman's sexuality and potential infidelity that is the threat to a lower-class male's masculinity.

In addition to the economic, psychological, and physical factors acting as impediments in poor-white marriages, social considerations also played a role in reducing the self-esteem of the lower-class white. Wash expresses the view that he inhabits a:

> world in which Negroes, whom the Bible told him had been
> created and cursed by God to be brute and vassal to all men
> of white skin, were found better and housed and even clothed
> than he and his.[187]

Poverty, then, was fundamental in the strife of the poor-white couple, more than other sources of affliction that the partners must face.

With few exceptions, women and marriage are portrayed by Faulkner as systematically destructive; it is only at the time of his creation of the Mallisons and the Priests that his view changes. In his earlier work, disparately, he creates a couple who are compatible: Miss Reba, although widowed, in *Sanctuary*; Cora and Vernon Tull in *As I Lay Dying*; and Mr. and Mrs. Grier in "Two Soldiers" are examples. Yet, it is not until the appearance of the Mallisons in 1948 that two central families in succession are depicted positively. It is also during this time frame that Faulkner is capable of creating an anomalous marriage within the Snopes family, as exemplified by Wallstreet Snopes' marriage in *The Town*. The isolated reverberations of Faulkner's earlier misogyny are thus very infrequent.

Despite the fact that Chick Mallison as late as *The Mansion* still echoes Faulkner's earlier philosophy, by the time of his later work Faulkner views both women and marriage more optimistically. Thus, Mallison's comment about marriage seems cynical in a new context:

> (... a condition of constant discomfort of course but mainly of unflagging mutual suspicion and mutual distrust and in a time which is probably the best of all training for successful matrimony).[188]

Faulkner's reappraisal of women is well represented in *The Reivers* where their strength and determination are viewed positively, no longer as a potential source of male destruction. Lucius Priest concludes in *The Reivers*:

> It's not men who cope with death; they resist, try to fight back and get their brains trampled out in consequence; where women just flank it, envelop it one soft and instaneous confederation of unresistance like cotton batting or cobwebs.[189]

A woman's ability to withstand difficulty is later reiterated by Lucius:

> Because women are wonderful. They can bear anything because they are wise enough to know that all you have to do with grief and trouble is just go through them and come out on the other side.[190]

Faulkner's evident resolution of his ambivalence toward women and marriage seems additionally reflected by the fact that the author comes closer to transcending his earlier manichæism. Women are no longer either mothers or prostitutes. Although whores have become mothers, women like Everbe Corinthia, despite this transformation, are not of the upper classes and thus could not be equated with a serious feminine menace. She would never be among the women who were hypothetically eligible partners for him. Leslie Fiedler concurs that Faulkner, who had earlier divided women "into the viable (to him) categories of mothers and whores," had succeeded in *The Reivers* in "proving to his own satisfaction that the whores are mothers too." [191]

Although Ruby Goodwin, "the one-time whore" [192] is also the madonna in *Sanctuary*, she, unlike her later incarnation Everbe Corinthia, never legalizes her status nor even really stabilizes her relationship with the ex-convict, Lee Goodwin. Everbe Corinithia in *The Reivers* renounces prostitution and marries Boon, with whom she has a son.

Faulkner's evolution in overcoming his equivocation is probably best exemplified by his presentation of the Mallisons and the Priests. Although in *Intruder in the Dust* and especially *The Town* Margaret's brother has a strong emotional hold on his sister, one which at times seems more dominant than that of her husband, there is still a sense of stability, trust, and complete acceptance of each other. The author also implies that Charles Mallison is a devoted and faithful husband, having no interest in Eula, who is the sexual magnet of Yoknapatawpha County. Yet, despite his virtues, Mr. Mallison, as indicated by Elizabeth Kerr, is still "colorless." [193] This can be attributed in great part to the fact that in creating even a balanced family the ghost of Murry Faulkner appears; the author himself has a certain difficulty in producing a dominant male figure at the level of the parental generation. The author's familial universe in *The Reivers*, a novel in large part biographical, follows very much the same pattern. This time, however, the Priest family resembles even more closely Faulkner's own family. Grandfather and Grandmother Priest, modeled after the Falkner grandparents have enjoyed thirty-five years of marital happiness. Maury and Alison Priest, like the Mallisons, are again portrayed as a couple who live in harmony. In both cases, the Mallisons' and the Priests' respective marriages are the one major deviation from the biographical reality. On the other hand, Maury Priest, named after Faulkner's father, seems to be his biographical counterpart. He is also reminiscent of Charles Mallison, Chick's father, though the author does not give him the same stature or presence that he gives to Gavin Stevens in *Intruder in the Dust* and in *The Town*. Otherwise, the Priests like the Mallisons are reinforced by the strength in their respective families, who this time live in adjacent houses rather than cohabitate.

In the last novel, the couple seems all strengthened by the compatibility of Alison and her mother-in-law, Sarah. Furthermore, Alison and Maury's parents are also intimate college friends, which accentuates once again the family solidarity surrounding the couple. According to young Charles this could

> possibly have had a little something to do with why Mother
> and Father chose one another out of all the earth to look into
> his eyes forevermore (I understand you call it going
> steady).[194]

So, despite the fact that much of Faulkner's work indicates a real ambivalence toward women and marriage, his later work shows a favorable change in his attitude. Faulkner's "rather strong disgust of women"[195] described by members of his own family, is in part clearly personal prejudice; yet, it is consonant with the values upheld in the South, where a woman was worshipped in theory but disregarded in practice in a way similar to the Negro. In this puritanical and paternalistic region of America, reflected in the laws themselves, a woman was relegated, regardless of class, to a position of inferiority both socially and materially. Faulkner's misogynistic attitude is probably well summed up in the manuscript of *The Wild Palms* when the convict declares: " 'Woman, Shit.' " [196] But Faulkner's attitude improves, radically, during the period of his late work when he is both a Nobel Prize winner and the grandfather of five grandchildren to whom he dedicates his last novel, *The Reivers*.

CHAPTER 4

Parent-Child Relationships

Faulkner's portrayal of parent-child relations shares many similarities with his portrayal of the marital relationships. In his early and middle work, Faulkner again strongly projects his personal unhappiness into his fiction. In general, children are presented as helpless victims at the mercy of their parents. They are, furthermore and to an exaggerated degree, unable to extricate themselves from their inevitable destinies. The Faulknerian parents, when not absent, are often egotistical and domineering, the overstated products (almost parodies) of the negative aspects of the caste system of Southern society.

The power relationships that existed historically within the South's paternalistic system are repeated at the parent-child level in Faulkner's work. These vertical relationships are based primarily on rank and self-preservation. In 1942, the author begins to make a more accurate and more affirmative statement with regard to the bond between parent and child, a development that continues until the end of his life. The Mallisons, and particularly the Priests, are the dominant family units through whom Faulkner shows his growing faith in the possibility of a harmonious and productive relationship between parent and child.

The parent-child relationship in the white family described by Faulkner in his major work is subject to a greater degree of negative distortion than many of the other familial relationships. This greater distortion in certain of the parent-child relationships can be explained by the fact that these relationships from a sociological standpoint often tended to be more positive emotionally than the marital, incestuous-like, or miscegenous ones within the white family.

Although some of the parent-child configurations are extremely realistic, Faulkner's work fails to convey the close bond that actually existed—at least between the middle class Southern mother and her children, for example. Zilphia Gant and her daughter, Zilphia, in the short story, "Miss Zilphia Gant," are certainly an unrepresentative caricature of their middle class socio-historial counterpart described by D. R. Hundley in *Social Relations in Our Southern States:*

> Such a Southern matron is ever idolized almost worshiped by
> her dependents, and beloved by her children, to whom no
> word ever sounds half so sweet as *mother,* and for whom no
> place possesses one half the charm of *home.*[1]

According to Burleigh B. Gardner, the poor-white mother was renowned for her concordant relationship with her children, particularly with her daughter.[2] Her children were, in fact, regarded as compensation for a lack of tangible possessions.[3] Addie Bundren, the maternal anti-heroine of the South's lower class, is an example of Faulkner's negative incarnations of her socio-historic predecessor. Not only does she favor her son, Jewel, to the exclusion of her other children, but she totally rejects her daughter, Dewel Dell, as she states herself in *As I Lay Dying:*

> I gave Anse Dewey Dell to negative Jewel. Then I gave him
> Vardaman to replace the child I had robbed him of. And now
> he has three children that are his and not mine.[4]

By contrast, Faulkner depicts very accurately the poor-white father who, according to Gardner in *Deep South: A Social Anthropological Study of Caste and Class,* is systematically indifferent and frequently deserted his children. The lower-class Southern father was also known to physically abuse his children.[5] Thus, we see that Popeye's father in *Sanctuary* deserts him and his mother as does his stepfather. I.O. Snopes, although risen now to the middle class in the Snopes trilogy, deserts his wife and child. Other fathers, such as Anse Bundren in *As I Lay Dying* or Will Varner in *The Hamlet,* both of very simple origins, are also completely uninvolved with their children.

The physical violence that often characterizes the poor-white father is a factor that reoccurs frequently in Yoknapatawpha. Mink Snopes in *The Hamlet*, Ab Snopes in "Barn Burning," or Will Varner in *The Hamlet* are all examples of fathers who are gratuitously brutal to their sons.

André Bleikasten in his article, "Fathers in Faulkner," stresses the importance of the Faulkner "fathers" whom he views as a guilty incarnation of the Freudian father. He states that:

> Faulkner's father figures range from such well-meaning weaklings as Reverend Mr. Mahon (*Soldiers' Pay*) or Mr. Compson (*The Sound and the Fury*) to comic villains like the blandly predacious Anse Bundren (*As I Lay Dying*), from dour disciplinarians McEachern (*Light in August*) and arrogant despots like Thomas Sutpen (*Absalom, Absalom!*) to venerable patriarchs like Virginius MacCallum (*Sartoris/Flags in the Dust*); and whether living or dead, present or absent, domineering or feckless, malevolent or benign, they loom large in most of his novels.[6]

Bleikasten also refers to the frequent lack of paternity in the Faulknerian universe.[7] Januarius Jones, the womanizer of *Soldiers' Pay*, "might have claimed any number of possible fathers,"[8] while Miss Quentin, Caddy's illegitimate daughter, is "fatherless nine months before her birth."[9] Joe Christmas' birth causes the murder of his father by Doc Hines; it is never known whether his father was Mexican or Negro. In *As I Lay Dying* Darl taunts his half-brother Jewel, who is Addie's adulterous son, by questioning him, " ' Your mother was a horse, but who was your father, Jewel?' "[10] His sadistic interrogation is reiterated in *Pylon* by Jiggs when he asks young Jack Schumann "Who's your old man today, kid?"[11]

Although Bleikasten's article is limited mainly to Faulkner's fathers, one must add that the maternal figures certainly fare no better in Faulkner's work. They share, in fact, one major similarity with the Faulknerian father in the author's early and middle work. For although Faulkner presents a broad spectrum of mother figures, during this period many tend to be almost inevitably domineering and egocentric. Caroline Compson and Mrs. Bland in *The Sound and the Fury*, Addie Bundren in *As I Lay Dying*, Mrs. Boyd in "The Brooch," Zilphia

Gant, in "Miss Zilphia Gant," Alvina King in "Dr. Martino," or Elly's grandmother, Ailanthia, in "Elly" are among the many prototypes.

Despite the fact that Albert Devlin views the Faulknerian father as almost invariably weak or absent, there are also many paternal figures who resemble the author's standard mother just alluded to. In fact, the Faulknerian father can be just as egocentric and domineering as the mother figure, whether Judge Drake in *Sanctuary*, John Sartoris in *Sartoris* and *Flags in the Dust*, Emmy's father in *Soldiers' Pay*, Miss Emily Grierson's father in "A Rose for Emily," or Harry Wilbourne's or Dr. Richardson's in *The Wild Palms*, to name a few.

One should note that the absence of a paternal figure as noted by Bleikasten is a family pattern that is not limited to the male in Faulkner's work. Among the many motherless heroes and heroines are Joe Christmas and Joanna Burden in *Light in August*, Old Bayard Sartoris in *The Unvanquished*, *Flags in the Dust* and *Sartoris*, the McCallum sons in *Flags in the Dust* and *Sartoris*, Temple Drake in *Sanctuary* and *Requiem for a Nun*, Roth Edmonds in *Go Down, Moses*. Horace and Narcissa Benbow lose their mother at an early age. The author's repeated portrayal of parentless characters is one way that Faulkner shows that the child himself is invariably the victim of parental lovelessness.

Yet, André Bleikasten underlines one fundamental difference between the Faulknerian mothers and fathers. Bleikasten rightfully believes that whether the paternal role is assumed by the actual begetter or a surrogate is of little importance in the sense that all father figures are all more or less outsiders, representing within the family a power that transcends familial bonds and is therefore vested with an authority that, unlike the mother's, is unnatural.[12] As Ike recognizes in "The Bear," "even fathers and sons are no kin." [13] According to Bleikasten, that which supersedes the paternal relationship is the self-enclosed intimacy of the primal, nuclear relationships of mother and child—the father being necessarily more removed from his progeny. Bleikasten observes that at some period during the child's development this feeling of estrangement will evolve into hostility."[14] Gail Hightower in *Light in August*, exemplifies this fundamental difference in the relationship between the child and his mother versus the child and his father in Faulkner's work. As Gail Hightower recalls the fears of his grim childhood, he comes to liken himself and his mother to

> two small, weak beasts in a den, a cavern, into which now and
> then the father entered, that man who was a stranger to them
> both, a foreigner, almost a threat. He was more than a
> stranger: he was an enemy. He smelled differently from
> them. He spoke with a different voice, almost in different
> words, as though he dwelled by ordinary among different sur-
> roundings in a different world....[15]

Many of the defects marking the marital relationship are also
found in the parental bond. The fact that marriages in the South were
often based on social and financial considerations rather than emotional ones reflects an element of opportunism that influences the sentiments between parents and children. In general, this is not alluded to
by sociologists or historians except indirectly, as by Ruth Cavan in reference to farm families in the South. Cavan states that children were
earners among the farm tenants and mill workers and that all earnings
went into the family income and that there was no distribution of this
money to the children themselves.[16]

Although Faulkner portrays this problem as one that occurs
within the poor-white families, he does not limit it to this class. The
poor white, Anse Bundren, tries to profit from his daughter Dewey
Dell; and Jason Compson, although upper class and the surrogate father
of Quentin, tries to exploit his niece. Anse, who is obsessed, for example, with having a new set of teeth, wants Dewey Dell to give him her
abortion money. In order to persuade her, he resorts to sentimental
blackmail:

> God knows, I hate for my blooden children to reproach me.
> But I give them what was mine without stint. Cheerful I give
> them, without stint. And now they deny me, Addie. It was
> lucky for you you died, Addie.[17]

Ultimately, his daughter even accuses Anse of being a thief. Vis à vis
Jason in *The Sound and the Fury* he is unquestionably dishonest and
steals monthly the two hundred dollars sent by Caddy for Quentin's
support. Quentin, however, vindicates herself against her uncle and
takes not only the money that is due her but also some of her uncle's.

In Faulkner's later work the relationship between Flem Snopes
and his putative daughter Linda is another illustration of the merce-

nary behavior of a man who has risen from this same poor-white class. Like Anse, Flem in the Snopes trilogy is also very hypocritical in his attitude toward Linda, trying always to play on her emotions in order to maintain control over Eula and ultimately over Will Varner's money, half of which Eula will inherit. It is only after Flem manipulates Linda into signing over all she might inherit from her mother that Flem allows her to attend the state university at Oxford. In *The Mansion*, Linda is vengeful and deeply involved in Flem's murder. Linda, as described by Cleanth Brooks, actually becomes a sort of "Medea, an implacable avenging spirit." [18] Similarly, Flem also reasserts his amorality with regard to his idiot cousin, Ike. In *The Hamlet*, Flem again assumes an inverted paternal role toward Ike to whom he is guardian. Rather than protect his helpless relative, he robs him of his ten dollar inheritance. Fundamental to Faulkner is the belief that almost any member of Southern society, irrespective of social class, is to some degree the victim of Snopeism—the materialism characteristic of the "new" South.

The puritanism so predominant in the South also affects the parent-child relationships in the author's work in ways not dissimilar to the manner in which it is a factor in the marital relationships. Generally, the child, or sometimes a grandchild, who is the recipient of a puritanical upbringing is weaned on principles and empty abstractions, not on love. In *Absalom, Absalom!*, Rosa Coldfield is raised by her Methodist father who, through his masochistic death, divorces himself entirely from his life and especially his daugher. It is not surprising that Coldfield's daughter complains of a "warped and spartan solitude which I called my childhood," [19] her early memories being "formal and funeral." [20] Rosa further likens herself to a "crucified child." [21] Rather than establishing a warm and immediate relationship with his daughter, Goodhue Coldfield is "a queer silent man whose only companion and friend seems to have been his conscience." [22]

Gail Hightower in *Light in August* is another of Faulkner's heroes who as a child is subject to a puritanical education. Like Rosa Coldfield, Gail Hightower also feels alienated from his austere father who is both minister and doctor. Hightower's estrangement from his father is another example of Faulkner's children who, in the Calvinist South, is the victim of a father's "spartan sobriety." [23] In *Light in August*, the Burdens are also illustrative of a family whose children are the product of parents more involved with doctrine than affection. Calvin Burden, the son of Nathaniel Burrington, runs away at twelve from his father's biblical prison. In turn, he imposes on his own son, Nathaniel, the "bleak and bloodless logic" [24] of his father's doctrine. At fourteen this son flees the coldness of the familial nest. Although the Burdens are Unitarians rather than members of one of the other more common Southern Protestant sects, the Unitarians, according to George Santayana, share many beliefs with the Calvinists. In his "Genteel Traditions in American Philosophy," Santayana insists that the Unitarians, like the Calvinists, believed that human nature is totally depraved and man must pay for it.[25] Joe Christmas in *Light in August* is confronted by a not dissimilar oppressive religious upbringing. In his case, he is beaten by his adopted father, the Presbyterian minister, Simon McEachern, for failing to learn his Bible lessons. McEachern is described as having a "bearded face as firm as carved stone, his eyes ruthless, cold." [26] Glenn Sanstrom has justly concluded that the influence of Christmas' grandfather and adopted father have ultimately eliminated for him the "viable ideologies, such as love, success, happiness." [27] Like the marital relationships, the parent-child relationship is steeped in guilt.

The question of guilt is part of the puritan heritage of these characters. With respect to the Burden family, the Southerner's culpability is also related directly to slavery, and the sense of remorse is transmitted from parent to child. It is reflected in the fact that the Burdens have imparted to each succeeding generation the abolitionist philosophy that is summed up by Calvin Burden when he tells his son Nathaniel, "I learn you to hate two things . . . hell and slaveholders." [28] Nathaniel, Joanna's father, conveys to her the same abolitionist stand in which is implicit the white man's collective guilt:

> Remember this. Your grandfather and brother are lying there, murdered not by one white man but by the curse which God put on a whole race before your grandfather or your brother or me or you were even thought of. A race doomed and cursed to be forever and ever a part of the white race's doom and curse for its sins. Remember that. His doom and his curse. Forever and ever. Mine. Your mother's. Yours, even though you are a child.[29]

It is Joanna's sense of blameworthiness toward the black man which, as an adult, motivates her to work in order to assist the Negoes.

Yet the culpability ingrained by this Southern puritanism is not only related to the Southerner's responsibility toward the black man. It extends to encompass an Augustinian attitude toward sex. Doc Hines' attitude toward his grandson, Christmas, illustrates the potential guilt projected onto a child by a parent, particularly one who is a religious fanatic; in this instance, race and sex are interlinked. Christmas is rejected by Hines, who regards him as "a pollution and abomination on this earth,"[30] because Christmas is the offspring not only of his mother's lechery but also of her involvement in a miscegenous union. Contrition is directly related to sex itself. The products of puritanical families are consequently unable to enjoy their sexuality. Joe Christmas when caught by his adopted father at a dance with Bobbie is totally condemned by McEachern for his alleged immorality. Similarly, one can deduce that Joanna Burden has also been subject to such a rigorous sexual education that she remains not only a spinster but also a virgin until in middle age when she is deflowered by Christmas. Even Mr. Compson in *The Sound and the Fury* is affected by the South's puritanism: teaching Quentin that sex and sin are equivalent. Meanwhile, Caroline Compson imparts to Caddy a similar moral code. When Caroline catches her daughter kissing a boyfriend she dresses herself in a black veil and dress and claims her daughter is dead.

Besides this very obvious sense of remorse, the fundamental pessimism inherent in Puritanism is also communicated from parent to child. For Faulkner, this is another factor that stunts the child's psychological growth. Mr. Compson, for instance, in *The Sound and The Fury* constantly reiterates to the susceptible young Quentin his negative deterministic philosophy by telling him that, "all men are just accumulations, dolls stuffed with sawdust swept up from the trash heaps where all previous dolls had been thrown away." Addie Bundren's father indoctrinates her with a similar value system when he convinces her "that the reason for living was to get ready to stay dead a long time."[31] It is, thus, not coincidental that both Quentin and Addie as adults are portrayed as preoccupied solely by death.

In fact, the determinism characteristic of Puritanism is something that Faulkner expounded generally in his treatment of parent-child relationships. In his work, many children are so influenced by their upbringing that as adults they become a replica of the parent figure. In Yoknapatawpha their behavior is equally damaging to their own children. Regarding this transfer of personal characteristics, Ernest Jones in his *Papers on Psycho-Analysis* notes that a child's character is

> moulded, or distorted, not only by the effort to imitate its parents', but by the effort to imitate its parents' ideals which are mostly taken from the grandparent of the corresponding sex.[32]

He further adds that

> the reaction of the child . . . which may be either positive or negative; that is, the child may either accept the transference or rebel against it, in the latter case developing character traits of exactly the opposite kind to those it sought to implant.[33]

This transference of characteristics from parent to child is made explicit by Quentin in *Absalom, Absalom!*:

> *Yes, maybe we are both Father. Maybe nothing ever happens once and is finished. Maybe happen is never once but like ripples maybe on water after the pebble sinks, the ripples moving on, spreading, the pool attached by a narrow umbilical water-cord to the next pool which the first pool feeds, has fed, did feed, let this second pool a different temperature of water, a different molecularity of having seen felt remembered, reflect in a different tone the infinitive unchanging sky, it doesn't matter: that pebble's watery echo whose fall it did not even see moves across its surface too at the original ripple-space, to the old ineradicable rhythm thinking. Yes, we are both father.*[34]

This psychological determinism is particularly well illustrated in Faulkner's early and middle work by Charles Bon and Zilphia Gant whose children are, significantly, named after their parents. Henry Sutpen, who is himself a victim of rejection as a young boy, rebuffs his own son Charles Bon, who in turn abandons his own son, Charles Etienne Saint-Valery. In a similar fashion, Zilphia Gant imprisons and isolates her daughter, Zilphia, who likewise repeats the same pattern years later with *her* daughter. Though part of the author's later work,

Faulkner continues to express this destructive element of determinism in the parent-child relationship in the Snopes trilogy. Byron Snopes, for example, is a bank embezzler, liar, and extortionist. His young children are totally amoral and during their stay with Flem Snopes burn Clarence Snopes at the stake. Simultaneously, I. O. Snopes is a bigamist and an insurance swindler; his son Montgomery Ward, a pornographer; St. Elmo, a thief; and Clarence, a corrupt senator and sadist. Similarly, Ab Snopes is a barn burner, his son Flem is impotent and completely immoral. By contrast, his other son, Cernal Sartoris is, as defined by Ernest Jones, the paragon of integrity. Sarty is representative of the child who acquires the opposite personality traits of the parent.

Related to determinism throughout Faulkner's work is the transmission of values or lack of values from parent or grandparent to their children. The transmission of an outmoded code of ethics is a problem particularly plaguing to the twentieth century South's upper class, who have to adapt themselves to a value system based mainly on money rather than on the honor, integrity, loyalty, courage, or other similar virtues which were at the heart of the chivalric code of the pre-Civil War South. These principles had become anachronistic in the New South. As pointed out by Thomas E. Connolly, in *Flags in the Dust* and *Sartoris*, young Bayard Sartoris' shallowness and lack of direction can partially be traced to his incapacitating experiences during the war, particularly the death of his twin brother, John. However, young Bayard is also seriously affected by his family unit which is accursed because it is unable to renounce a demoded way of life.[35] Albert Devlin concurs with this viewpoint and concludes that young Bayard "inherits a tradition of grandiose gestures that is essentially fatalistic." [36] Ironically, even Old Bayard is faced with a not dissimilar conflict of values when as a young man in *The Unvanquished* he is required to avenge his father's death. Unlike his grandson Bayard, who living in the twentieth century seeks a gratuitous death, Old Bayard courageously vindicates his father's death unarmed.

Besides the problem of a nihilistic philosophy, on the one hand, and an obsolete moral code that is conveyed from generation to generation, on the other hand, Faulkner also elucidates the consequences of empty values being transferred from parent to child. Belle Mitchell, as an illustration, imposes her vacuousness on her daughter, Little Belle, in *Flags in the Dust* and *Sartoris*. Belle is a Southern woman of the upper class who, despite her background, manages to assume the values of the New South, more specifically those of the wealthy Southern parvenu of the twentieth century. She transmits this code to her young daughter, Little Belle, whose sole interest is performing at her mother's parties. Meanwhile, Narcissa Sartoris in "There Was a Queen," in spite of her hypocritical stance toward her family and society, is immoral to the point of prostituting herself with the F.B.I. agent. It is evident that a woman who is so lacking in scruples will be unable to impart moral principles to her young son, Bory. Gardner's assessment is that the upper-class Southern mother, unlike the mother of the lower and middle class, was more involved with her maternal *role* than with the emotional or physical reality of motherhood.[37] Both Belle Mitchell and Narcissa, like their socio-historic counterparts, reflect this self-centered tendency of mothers in relation to their children and the moral vacuum that is a concommitant.

With regard to the mother figure generally, she tends, regardless of class, to share the narcissism characteristic of the upper-class mother—at least, in Faulkner's early and middle work. The Faulknerian mother very often tends to be self-involved and also domineering, thus leaving her children with the sense of being unloved. Quentin, in *The Sound and the Fury,* is certainly one of the best examples of this syndrome. Although Joan Williams views Caroline Compson as "warm, loving and supportive, teaching them [her children] to love one another,"[38] in the main, the critics like Cleanth Brooks or Walter Brylowski judge her more accurately. Of Quentin's mother, Brooks perceives that "the basic cause of the breakup of the Compson family . . . is the cold and self-centered mother . . . "[39] Brylowski concurs with Cleanth Brooks and concludes that

> Mrs. Compson, one of Faulkner's most brilliantly realized characters, stands at the core of the novel as she stands at the core of the family, the decay and the disintegration of the Compsons affected largely by her failure.[40]

The maternal renunciation Quentin feels from Caroline Compson is shown when, apropos of Caddy, he says protectively in *The Sound and the Fury:* "*My little sister had no. If I could say Mother. Mother.*"[41] He later continues: "*Done in Mother's mind though. Finished. Finished. Then we were all poisoned.*"[42] Caroline Compson is completely self-involved, a self-pitying hypochondriac unable to give her children the minimal emotion they require except, of course, for Jason whom she favors and even smothers with love at the expense of the others. After the birth of Miss Quentin, Caroline imposes her will on her children to such an extent that she forbids Caddy to see her own daughter. In the case of the sensitive young Quentin, since his father is also unable to respond to his emotional needs, he comes to regard even Mr. Compson's attitude towards him as one of abdication. He recalls a childhood storybook with a picture of "a dark place into which a single ray of light came slanting." He becomes obsessed by the picture

> until the dungeon was Mother herself she and Father upward
> into weak light holding hands and us lost somewhere below
> even them without even a ray of light.[43]

Addie Bundren in *As I Lay Dying* is yet another example of the strong, self-centered mother. Addie is obsessed by her burial, and her energy is spent entirely on ensuring that her children are executing her command. Like Caroline Compson, Addie also rebuffs all her children—in this case, in favor of her son Jewel. Again, like the earlier heroine, Addie is also completely insensitive to the noxious affect her attitude has on her other children, particularly on the most fragile one, her son Darl. John K. Simon regards Darl's "failure as an individual," his psychotic state at the end of the novel as a total consequence of his mother's unqualified abdication.[44] William Handy also holds Addie reponsible for Darl's emotional and mental fragmentation. He finds that Addie is "the one who determined the direction his psychological development would take."[45] The sentiments of repudiation which Darl experiences become coupled with his anxiety about lack of identity.

The flagrant egotism that marks the Faulknerian mother has a parallel in the tendency of the Southerner toward social introversion, but the problem of identity is also a dilemma for the Southerner in the rapidly changing South where the set of parvenu values has overridden the traditional ones. The issues of this dilemma, which affect the Southerner on that societal level, are recreated yet again on the parent-child level. In *As I Lay Dying*, Darl feels as a result of his mother's indifference that he is consequently without a sense of identity, in opposition to his brother, Jewel. Darl's doubts are clarified when he states: "I don't know what I am. I don't know if I am or not. Jewel knows he is."[46] Furthermore, he tells Jewel that the fact that he is Jewel's brother confirms his lack of identity, indicating that their mother's love, in Darl's view, could not be given to both of them.

Addie's relationship to Jewel is still more complex than is expressed by Darl since it is fraught with the element of ambivalence—a factor typifying the Southerner's reaction to society as well as to many of his own family members. Though Addie adores her illegitimate son, she is basically incapable of love. This is demonstrated by the fact that she vacillates between whipping and petting him, a reaction which Jewel himself repeats with his revered horse. Addie's need to hurt her idolized Jewel is also her means of communicating with him, and thus, alienation becomes another problem between parent and child. She compares herself and the children to spiders dangling by their mouths from a beam, "swinging and twisting and never touching."[47] Addie's way of relating to her children, unlike her socio-historical Southern counterparts is, as with her students, through physical cruelty. She herself admits that only through these sadistic lashings can she bridge the gap and make "my blood and their blood flow as one stream."[48]

The equivocation characteristic of Addie Bundren is also true of the children in relationship to their parents. Cernal Sartoris, Ab Snope's son in "Barn Burning," is probably the best illustration. Sarty is torn between his filial love for Ab and his innate honesty and respect for justice. When his father plans to burn Mayor de Spain's barn in revenge for his treatment of him over the rug, Sarty forewarns de Spain. However, Sartoris not only runs away but also grieves for the loss of his father, making a final attempt, despite its unreality, to envision his father as a courageous war hero; Sartoris exemplifies the divided son.

Yet another manifestation of maternal narcissism in Faulkner's early and middle period are the many mothers who are so "self"-centered that they desert their children not only without remorse but also without any feeling of loss. Among the most obvious illustrations are Charlotte Rittenmeyer in *The Wild Palms*, Temple Drake Stevens in *Requiem for a Nun*, and Laverne Shumann in *Pylon*. In *The Wild Palms*, Charlotte leaves her two young children, Ann and Charlotte, in order to live with her lover Harry. Her attitude toward her children she reveals to her lover as follows:

I wasn't thinking of them. I mean, Ihave

already thought of them. So now I don't
need to think of them any more ... [49]

Although Nancy, in *Requiem for a Nun*, acts as Temple's conscience,
like Charlotte, Temple herself is preoccupied with furthering her romance with the immoral Pete and is unaffected by the fact that she
plans to leave her six-year-old son, Bucky, behind. Likewise, Laverne
Shumann and Roger Holmes relinquish their young son, Jack, without
any sense of culpability; they abandon the child to his grandparents so
that they can continue to live their nomadic existence of circus airmen.
Although critics such as George Friend view Jack's family—this menage à trois—as united by a "secure bond," [50] Faulkner himself refutes
this position by implication when he deems the flyers "outside the
range of ... love." [51] Conclusively illustrative of parental egotism,
this desertion is one more example among Faulkner's distortions of the
parent-child relationship in the South. Even assuming the existence of
a certain selfishness, especially on the part of the upper-class Southern
woman in relationship to her children, this frequent abandonment of
her family should be treated as a falsification of the Southern family
reality.

Parental desertion in the Faulknerian universe usually involves
infidelity. Even though the children currently cited are too young to be
distressed by the moral overtones of their mother's desertion, they are
not too young to be emotionally upset by it. Thus, adultery becomes another factor that divides children from parents. In *As I Lay Dying*,
Darl is obsessed by his mother's relationship with Whitfield and constantly taunts Jewel about his father's identity. Equally, Linda in *The
Town* is upset by her mother's adultery and confesses to Gavin:

I hated [my mother] and Manfred both. Oh yes, I knew about
Manfred: I have ... seen them look at each other ... [52]

Not much better than the mothers, Faulkner's fathers are often absent and sometimes, like Jason Compson (modeled on Faulkner's own father), they also expect blind obedience from their children. Although
from the time of the Civil War the Southern male was no longer invested with his former power, many of the Faulknerian fathers still
attempt, at least, to assume it. According to Keith F. McKean in his article, "Southern Patriarch: A Portrait," the Southern father is re-

garded as "a minor king in his own home. In truth, a 'Big Daddy.' " [53]
Florence King says the Southern male perpetually measures himself
against his father, whom he worships. She continues in *Confessions of a
Failed Southern Lady* that "If the Jewish boy's problem is the umbilical cord, the Southern boy's is the tale of the spermatozoon." [54] For the
Southern boy, as she states in *Southern Ladies and Gentlemen*, is convinced that "if you're half the man your daddy was you'll be all
right." [55] Bayard in *The Unvanquished* expresses similar sentiments
when, as a young boy, he makes the following comment regarding his
father John:

> Then we could see him good. I mean, Father. He was not big:
> it was just the things he did, that we knew he was doing, had
> been doing in Virginia and Tennessee, that made him big to
> us. [56]

The relationship between father and daughter is also important
as explained by Stuart A. Queen in *The Family*. The daughter, Stuart
says, is actually viewed by the Southern male as more consequential
than his wife. While the Southern father is intent upon his son affirm-
ing his masculinity, he is equally concerned that his daughter's femi-
ninity be reinforced. [57] Thus, the Southern father is likely to make a
sexual differentiation between his children which is almost Victorian.

But paternal domination is seen as early as Faulkner's first novel,
Soldiers' Pay. Emmy is taken out of school at fourteen when her father
finds that she is enamored of Donald Mahon. Donald comes to get
Emmy later, and her father, like an overly authoritarian Southern father, tries to get rid of him. Once Emmy's father has not only hit her
but also forbidden her to see Donald, she, like many of her Southern sisters, rebels against her father and makes love to Donald.

Judge Drake's importance in his relationship with his daughter,
Temple, is strongly portrayed in *Sanctuary* and is a later and more
evolved adaptation of Emmy's relationship with her father in *Soldiers' Pay*. Like Emmy's father, Temple's father is also totally uncon-
cerned with his daughter's emotional state. He is principally and vehemently intent upon his, as well as the South's, abstract set of morality being upheld. He is resolute that his only daughter be the chaste
vessel of Southern womanhood. In the case of this later heroine, Temple's father's rigid principles are reinforced by her four brothers. In ref-

erence to Gowan, at the time of their courtship, Temple, for example, comments:

> Buddy—that's Hubert, my youngest brother—said that if he ever caught me with a drunk man, he'd beat hell out of me. And now I'm with one that gets drunk three times in one day.[58]

Temple also tells Ruby that while her brother Hubert threatens to kill Frank, a town boy with whom she was involved, her father actually takes his shotgun and shoots him; In addition her father refers to Temple as a whore. The masculine domination to which Temple is subject is particularly well shown at the time of the heroine's exit from the courtroom:

> They stood like soldiers, staring straight ahead until the old man and the girl reached there. Then they moved and surrounded the other two, and in a close body, the girl hidden among them, they moved toward the door ... She appeared to be clinging there, then the five bodies hid her again and again in a close body and disappeared.[59]

Temple must thus answer to an "army" of father and brothers. As pointed out by Walter Brylowski, they are "all bastions of ... society." [60] The father is a judge and two of the brothers are lawyers, another is a newspaper man, and the fourth is a Yale student. In fact, their established positions in society probably act to further incite Temple's sedition. In *Sanctuary*, Faulkner even reveals that

> she just had unbounded faith that her father and brothers would know evil when they saw it, so all she had to do was, do the one thing which she knew they would forbid her to do if she had a chance.[61]

In his very provocative article, "William Faulkner's *Sanctuary*," Lawrence S. Rubie also believes that Temple's rebellion is principally related to her rejection of what she considers to be a fraternal and paternal police state. Rubie speculates

> that this paradoxical and perverted impulse to revenge herself on those who have not harmed her, but who are essen-

tially normal in their masculinity, fits the whole history of her
defiant, rebellious and provocative attitude toward boys and
men. Her career seemed to shape itself out of her hate of her
father and her four stalwart brothers.[62]

Emily Grierson's father in the short story "A Rose for Emily" is
another paternal figure made from the same mold as both Emmy's and
Temple's father. He is a stern and peremptory man who, like the
others, is possessive and drives away his daughter's young suitors.
Faulkner himself, when interviewed in Virginia, describes Miss Emily
as a girl with normal ambitions—love, marriage, a family—"who was
brow-beaten and kept down by her father, a selfish man who didn't
want her to leave home because he wanted a housekeeper."[63] Yet,
Emily's fixation with him is so excessive that the town views her as
having an "upright torso motionless as that of an idol."[64] Her attachment to him is so overpowering that she even denies his death; the
townspeople thus bury him by force.

While Emmy and Temple rebel against their magisterial fathers,
Emily transfers her affections after her father's death to her lover,
Homer Barron. Emily's necrophilia is a statement of her inextricable
bond to her father. According to Irving Malin, necrophilia is, in fact, a
manifestation of repressed sexual needs and an obsession with a dead,
though still overbearing father.[65] It is interesting to note how her
necrophilia is a mirror image of Faulkner's "ideal" woman—"legless,
armless, headles . . . "—lifeless. Although Temple never engages in
necrophilia, Faulkner makes clear that she too has been so over-pow-
ered by her father that she identifies her impotent lover, Popeye, with
Judge Drake when she refers to him as "Daddy."[66] Despite her protest,
Temple cannot completely extricate herself from her father's presence.

The Faulknerian father asserts himself with equal force and
selfishness in relationship to his son. John Sartoris' complete self-absorption, for example, manifests itself in *The Unvanquished* when Bayard seeks him out needing to confess his flirtation with Drusilla. It is
significant that Sartoris does not so much as even hear his son. By the
time Bayard is twenty-four, he clearly perceives his father's "violent
and ruthless dictatorialness and will to dominate."[67] Even as an older
man, John Sartoris' influence is still so strong that in *Flags in the Dust*
and *Sartoris* Bayard is totally overwhelmed by the memories of his
dead father:

> John Sartoris seemed to loom still in the room, above and
> about his son, with the bearded, hawklike face, so that as old
> Bayard sat with his crossed feet propped against the corner of
> the cold hearth, holding the pipe in his hand, it seemed to
> him that he could hear his father's breathing even, as though
> that other were more palpable than mere transiently articu-
> lated clay as to even penetrate into the uttermost citadel of
> silence in which his son lived.[68]

Also in *Flags in the Dust* and *Sartoris*, Virginius MacCallum has
such a strong influence on his sons that, even as grown men, five of them
are unmarried and still living at home. The youngest son, Buddy, in the
short story, "The Tall Men," is the only one to marry and perpetuate
the line. Although certain critics such as Melvin Backman or Cleanth
Brooks surprisingly enough view the MacCallums as the paragons of
normality, this is uncontestably a divergence from social norms. Melvin
Backman considers that "the malaise of Bayard is set in moving counterpoint against the natural idyll of the MacCallum family." [69] He regards the MacCallums as a family "bound in simple affection" and
their home as "a refuge of warmth and light." He also describes "the
absoluteness of their mutual loyalty, the straightness and simplicity of
their code." [70] Cleanth Brooks would agree with Backman since he perceives them as "sane, vigorous, and very much alive." He further remarks that they provide Bayard with a "background of solid values
and purposeful life.[71] However, what these critics fail to realize is
that old Virginius MacCallum is a formidable, imposing man who has
had a crushing impact on all of his sons except Buddy, his namesake,
who endowed with the same stature is capable of resisting him. By contrast, two of Virginius' sons, Henry and Lee, are so debilitated and de-
masculinized that they are described as totally effeminate. There is,
for instance, "something domestic, womanish, about Henry, with his
squat, slightly tubby figure and his mild brown eyes and his capable,
unhurried hands." [72] Lee is described as sitting "brooding over the fire,
his womanish hands moving restlessly on his kness." [73] Ultimately, except for Buddy who is "stamped clearly from the same die," [74] the
MacCallums are paralyzed by their father whom Albert Devlin
rightly compares to a "threatening ogre figure frequently found in children's literature" and whose "treatment of the boys is equally devas-
tating." [75]

Lastly, in *The Wild Palms* although the father-son relationship between Dr. Richardson and Harry Wilbourne and their respective fathers is less developed than the preceding relationship, Faulkner still makes clear that they are both the products of their fathers' authority. Of Dr. Richardson, one learns that his father directed his destiny without any consideration of his son's sentiments. Dr. Richardson is depicted as follows:

> Lee graduated ... and within the year married the wife his father had picked out for him and within four years owned the house which his father had built and assumed the practice which his father had created, losing nothing from it and adding nothing to it.[76]

Harry Wilbourne's father is likewise a determinant influence on his son. He leaves a minimal inheritance for Harry whom he assumes must necessarily pursue the same career as he. This is clearly stated in his will:

> *To my son, Harry Wilbourne, and realizing that conditions as well as the intrinsic value of money has changed and therefore he cannot be expected to obtain his degree in Surgery and Medicine for the same outlay of money which obtained in my day, I hereby bequeath and set aside the sum of two thousand dollars, to be used for the furthering and completing of his college course and the acquiring of his degree and license to practice in Surgery and Medicine, believing that the aforesaid sum will be amply sufficient for that purpose.[77]*

It is thus evident that Faulkner's children as presented in his work of this period are often doomed to be the prisoners of the narrow lives their parents allowed them. Faulkner's young heros and heroines are not faced with an existential dilemma of choice; they are portrayed as puppets, their parents the puppeteers.

However, beginning in 1942, Faulkner depicts the parent-child relationship with far more optimism. In *Go Down, Moses,* even though relations between parents and children are still fraught with major weaknesses, Ike's relationship with his surrogate fathers, Cass and Sam, is marked by the transmission of positive values lacking in most of Faulkner's earlier works. It was also in 1942 that Faulkner published his short story, "Two Soldiers," which, though a minor work, is probably one of his most positive statements with regard to the interrelationship between parents and their children. This was followed by "Shall Not Perish," published a year later, that further extends the author's vision in "Two Soldiers."

Go Down, Moses portrays a more favorable parent-child relationship mainly because both Sam and Cass, each in his own way, care about Ike and are capable, at least to varying degrees, of extending to him a set of values that are mostly constructive. They no longer indoctrinate their progeny with Compson-like defeatism. As described by Walter Brylowski, Sam as father figure acts as a "priest of the cult of the wilderness." [78] He "taught the boy the woods, to hunt, when to shoot and when to kill and when not to kill, and better, what to do afterward."[79] He is also Ike's spiritual father: "who had been his spirits' father if they had, whom he had revered and harkened to and loved and lost and grieved."[80]

Sam is also supportive of Cass in his role of father vis à vis Ike:

> Sam always referred to the boy's cousin as his father, establishing even before the boy's orphanhood did that relationship between not of the ward to his guardian and kinsman and chief and head of his blood, but of the child to the man who sired his flesh and his thinking too.[81]

By contrast, as a father figure, Cass is the societal father who assumes responsibility in the world, as indicated by the fact that he does not repudiate his birthright and runs the plantation. Ike views Cass as "his kinsman—his father;" [82] it is Cass who gives Ike a sense of security. This is best demonstrated when Ike does everything in his power to find Carother's two missing heirs, James and Fonsiba Beauchamp. Cass also conveys to his young cousin the essential Faulknerian values. He tells Ike:

> *Truth is one. It doesn't change. It covers all things which touch the heart—honor and pride and pity and justice and courage and love.*[83]

Faulkner himself made a similar statement when interviewed at the University of Virginia:

> Man will prevail, will endure because he is capable of com-
> passion and honor and pride and endurance.[84]

As pointed out by Michael Millgate, the extent to which Ike actually
incorporates Cass' view becomes apparent during the conversation in
the commissary when Ike repeats almost verbatim several of Cass's
earlier conclusions about the nature of truth.[85]

Despite the salutary influence of his mentors, Ike, having seen
Carothers's ledgers and having been strongly influenced by Sam, repu-
diates his heritage. Sam, as well as being a constructive force, indoctrinates his ward into the world of the past to such an extent that Ike is
unable to adapt himself to the present, a dilemma common to many of
his real Southern contemporaries. Cass is aware that "I could do no
else. I am what I am; I will be always what I was born and have always been." [86] Meanwhile, Ike considers, albeit erroneously, that
"Sam, Father's set me free." [87] It is precisely for this reason that at
twenty-one

> ... he could repudiate the wrong and the shame, at least in
> principle, and at least the land itself in fact, for his son at
> least. Saving and freeing his son lost him.[88]

On the subject of Ike McCaslin, Faulkner (at the University of Virginia) made his position quite clear:

> Well, I think a man ought to do more than just repudiate. He
> should have been more affirmative instead of just shunning
> people.[89]

Ike himself becomes conscious of the futility of his abdication, and he
admits:

> That I revenged, cried calf-rope, sold my birthright, betrayed
> my blood, for what he too calls not peace but obliteration, and
> a little food.[90]

Although Ike's mentors, especially Cass, are representative of a
more optimistic, less destructive parent-child portrayal in Faulkner's
work, Ike himself still proves not only sterile but incapable of having
the same imprint on Roth Edmonds to whom he becomes a surrogate fa-

ther. Roth shows no respect toward his paternal guide, as when he makes the following commentary to Ike:

> "So you've lived almost eighty years", Edmond said. "And that's what you finally learned about the other animals you lived among. I suppose the question to ask you is, where have you been all the time you were dead." [91]

Roth's attitude toward Ike as well as his behavior in the wilderness or with his mistress shows that Ike has not been able to convey to Roth the principles he was given by Cass, or by Sam.

Ike's education by Sam is reminiscent of the education by Mister Ernest of his adopted son in "Race at Morning." In this later short story, Sam's wisdom and set of ethics come to have a constructive effect on Ernest's young son because they are no longer isolated but are integrated into modern, societal life. We see this in the ensuing conversation between father and son:

> "I am," I said. "I'm doing it now. I'm going to be hunter and a farmer like you."
> "No," Mister Ernest said. "That ain't enough any more. Time was when all a man had to do was just farm eleven and a half months, and hunt the other half. But not now. Now just to belong to the farming business and the hunting business ain't enough. You got to belong to the business of mankind."
> "Mankind?" I said
> "Yes," Mister Ernest said. "So you're going to school. Because you got to know why. You can belong to the farming and hunting business and you can learn the difference between what's right and what's wrong, and do right. And that used to be enough—just to do right. But not now. You got to know why it's right and why it's wrong . . ." [92]

In *Go Down, Moses,* Ike is never really capable of achieving a synthesis between the primitive and the societal viewpoint of his two mentors; by contrast, the young Grier boy in "Two Soldiers," like Mister Ernest's adopted son, is never fragmented by two opposing philosophies. While Mister Ernest reconciles for his son the dichotomy between the ideal and the real, the Grier boys are simply raised in a loving home where they are sheltered entirely from conflict. Mrs. Grier, no longer the monster of egotism frequently found in Faulkner's earlier works, is instead a mother emotionally involved with her children. Rather than deserting them, it is she who grieves when her oldest son Pete is sent to war. The Griers also teach their sons consideration for others, especially their parents. When Pete, for instance, leaves to join the military, his father's parting words are, "Goodby, Son. Always remember what your ma told you and write her when you find the time." [93] The strength of the parent-child relationship is actually made explicit by Mrs. Grier herself in "Shall Not Perish." After she learns of Pete's death, she says of her deceased son: "There is nothing in him that I or his father didn't put there." [94] The sentiments that Mrs. Grier feels for Pete are similar to the ones that the Griers have for their own families. Pete's younger brother, also in "Shall Not Perish," clarifies this positive determinism when he comments: "And I remembered how Father used to prove any point he wanted to make to Pete and me, by Grandfather." [95]

The creation of the Mallison family in *Intruder in the Dust* and later in *The Town* and *The Mansion* is another indication that the author is now perceiving parent-child relations with less cynicism. It may be more than coincidental that two years earlier, in 1946, Malcolm Cowley published the Viking Portable edition of Faulkner's work. The author may be seen, at least in part, as projecting the optimism he currently felt now that he was certain to remain in print for a time.

The parent-child relationship is particularly well developed in *Intruder in the Dust*, especially the relationship between young Chick Mallison; his mother, Margaret; and his surrogate father, Gavin Stevens. Although Charles Mallison, the father, is also present in the novel, he is significantly relegated quietly to the background, and Gavin takes his place. Faulkner's need to impose the paternal role on Gavin rather than on Chick's father is probably in great part a projection of his own relationship with his father, Murry. In the same way that Faulkner was forced to seek out foster fathers so too must his young hero. The reason for Chick's option of Gavin is made quite clear in the later novel, *The Mansion*:

> Oh yes, I liked Father too all right but Father just talked to me while Uncle Gavin listened to me, no matter how foolish what I was saying finally began to sound even to me, listening to me until I had finished, then saying, 'Well, I don't know

> whether it will hold together or not, but I know a good way to find out. Let's try it.' Not YOU try it but US try it.[96]

In fact, Gavin's influence on Chick is so inclusive that Charles almost lives vicariously through his uncle. This is well expressed by Chick himself when, again in *The Mansion*, he reflects:

> Ratliff put it, as I had spent the first eleven or twelve years of my existence in the middle of Uncle Gavin, thinking what he thought and seeing what he saw, not because he taught me to but maybe just because he let me, allowed me to.[97]

Charles cares so much for his uncle that, as Ratliff points out also in *The Mansion*, he is even proprietary about him:

> What you want to waste all this good weather being jealous of your uncle for? Somebody's bound to marry him sooner or later. Someday you're going to outgrow him and you'll be too busy yourself just to hang around and protect him.[98]

As previously mentioned, the critics otherwise generally view the Mallisons solid family life as a harmonious backdrop for *Intruder in the Dust* and *The Town*. Although in *The Town* the focus is less on parent-child relations, Faulkner's incorporation of Gowan Stevens, a cousin and, more significantly, a judge, as well as Chick's patriarchical grandfather, solidifies the concept of family as a whole. This is particularly well shown in the respect that each of the family members gives Judge Stevens. Chick opens the novel by stating that, " 'Us' was Grandfather and Mother and Father and Uncle Gavin then." [99]

In *Intruder in the Dust* and in *Go Down, Moses*, Chick undergoes his initiation to manhood. While Ike is not capable of integrating his experience, Chick, owing to Gavin's close guidance, is able to assimilate the evil in his Southern heritage without repudiating it. Chick learns from his Uncle Gavin that

> Some things you must always be unable to bear. Some things you never stop refusing to bear. Injustice and outrage and dishonor and shame. No matter how young you are or old you have got. Not for kudos and not for cash; your picture in the paper nor money in the bank either. Just refuse to bear them.[100]

Gavin also explains to Chick that he cannot escape his heritage:

> ... because you escape nothing, you flee nothing; the pur-
> suer is what is doing the running and tomorrow night is
> nothing, but one sleepless wrestle with yesterday's omissions
> and regrets.[101]

He must assume the South's historical guilt and assist in alleviating injustice.

Despite the fact that Chick learns through his uncle to accept his Southern identity, Faulkner's treatment of Gavin as successful sexual mentor is less convincing. Gavin demonstrates his own sexual immaturity, which is implied by the fact that he is an aging bachelor pursing a young teenage girl, and is, thus, not an appropriate model for his young nephew.

Meanwhile, Margaret Mallison, both loving and supportive of her sons, is a definite improvement over Faulkner's earlier mothers. However, like Maud Falkner (and many of her earlier literary incarnations), Margaret's major defect is her possessiveness. This, as exposed by Lillian Smith, is a classic manifestation of the white mother's sexual and social frustration in the South:

> We know that these women, forced by their culture and their
> heartbreak, did a thorough job of closing the path to mature
> gentility for many of their sons and daughters, and an equally
> good job of leaving little cleared detours that led downhill to
> homosexual and infantile green pastures, and on to alco-
> holism, neuroses, divorce, to race-hate, and brutality, and to a
> tight inflexible mind that could not question itself.[102]

Margaret Mallison is both understanding and proud regarding Chick's sexual initiation though worried in her maternal way about missed school and lack of sleep. She nonetheless encourages Chick to be with his uncle and Hope Hampton when they exhume Vinson Gowrie's body. She is also proud of Chick's courage. Albert Devlin accurately describes her as a "loving mother who does not inhibit but rather supports her son's developing masculinity." [103] Though Chick's sentiments about his mother are, unlike many of the earlier heroes, marked by a definite affection—"that fond constant familiar face which he had known all his life," [104]—he still struggles against her overprotectiveness. In *Intruder in the Dust*, Margaret "would never really forgive him for being able to button his own buttons and wash behind his ears." [105] Despite her sponsorship of Charles, she refuses to cut the unbilical cord. It is thus not entirely astounding that in the same way that Mrs. Bland follows Gerald not only to Harvard but also rowing, Margaret attends her son's football games, cheering; her voice is symbolically, "triumphant and blood-thirsty." [106] Again reminiscent of Mrs. Bland, Chick finds his mother with the other players on the backseat of the car returning from the game. In sum, although the parent-child relationship is definitely portrayed in this later period in a much more favorable light, it is still subject to the limitations the author confronted personally in his own family life. Faulkner could not release his characters from the matriarchal figure anymore than he could escape his own mother who was attempting to dominate his life, even while he was abroad.

In *A Fable*, a later work and a novel apart, the military acts as a substitute family. In this later novel, father and son reach a form of understanding rarely achieved in the author's earlier work. The following conversation makes explicit that the general and his son Stephen come to share the same insight concerning man's future:

> "I don't fear man. I do better: I respect and admire him. And pride: I am ten times prouder of that immorality which he does possess than ever he of that heavenly one of his delusion. Because man and his folly—"
> "Will endure," the corporal said.
> "They will do more," the old general said proudly. "They will prevail.—Shall we return?" [107]

Faulkner made a similar statement in his Nobel speech:

> I believe that man will not merely endure: he will prevail. He is immortal, not because he alone among creatures has an inexhaustible voice, but because he has a soul, a spirit capable of compassion and sacrifice and endurance. [108]

Stephen, the Christ-like corporal, in *A Fable*, represents youth, hope, idealism, freedom and rebellion. His father, the supreme general, incarnates age, loss of hope and faith, realism, constraint, and the status quo with established power, but the conflict between the father and son is, in fact, ideological rather than personal. Their discord is well explained by the supreme general:

> I champion of this mundane earth which, whether I like it or not, is, and to which I did not ask to come, yet since I am here, not only must stop but intend to stop during my alloted while; you champion of an esoteric realm of man's baseless hopes and his infinite capacity—no: passion for unfact. No, they are not inimical really, there is no contest actually; they can exist side by side together in this one restricted arena, and could and would, had yours not interfered with mine.[109]

Although the supreme general is as dominant as many of Faulkner's early fathers, unlike his predecessors, such as Henry Sutpen who rejects his son, he does everything within his power to convince Stephen to save himself. Unlike Sutpen, he offers his illegitimate son acknowledgment and inheritance, but the corporal refuses to betray the men who trust him.

During this period (the late forties and early fifties), despite the fact that Faulkner created a family such as the Snopeses whom he describes as "colonies of rats or termites," [110] he is also capable of creating characters who react against their father's destructiveness, such as Ab's son, Cernal Sartoris. Even in this family he creates characters such as Eck's two sons: Wallstreet Snopes and Admiral Dewey Snopes, "the non-Snopes son of a non-Snopes." [111] Rather than profiting from others, Wallstreet begins as delivery boy in a grocery store to support himself and his brother, Admiral Dewey, through school. This accomplished son of the honest, industrious, and kind Eck, himself the offspring of "some extracurricular night work," [111] opens a wholesale grocery supply house in Jefferson which serves the entire country.

Faulkner's final novel, *The Reivers*, is an even more affirmative statement about parent-child relations with, however, one reservation: the reappearance of the unassuming father figure, already encountered in the Mallison family. While Gavin Stevens has replaced Charles Mallison in the role of father in the Mallison family, grandfather Priest assumes the paternal role toward Lucius in Faulkner's last novel. The Priests are modeled, like the Sartorises, after Faulkner's own family and typify Erik Erikson's "myth of the grandfather":[113] a dynamic masterful figure who begets sons less capable and less vigorous. Lucius himself is aware of this as he says when Maury, his father, is about to administer him a traditional strapping:

> If after all the lying and deceiving and disobeying and conniving I had done, all he could do about it was to whip me, then Father was not good enough for me. And if all that I had done was balanced by no more than that shaving strap, then both of us were debased. You see? it was impasse, until Grandfather knocked.[114]

Grandfather Priest, undermining his son, refuses to have Lucius beaten. Instead, he wishes him to live with the resultant guilt from his adventure. His grandfather also communicates to him the importance of strength, courage, and responsibility:

> You will. A gentleman always does. A gentleman can live through anything. He faces anything. A gentleman accepts the responsibility of his actions and bears the burden of their consequences, even when he did not himself instigate them but only acquiesed to them, didn't say No though he knew he should. Come here.[115]

When, after learning of his punishment, Lucius begins to sob, his grandfather comforts him showing that he is sensitive to his grandson's emotional needs.

Despite Grandfather Priest's domination, it is implicit that in some ways his relationship with Lucius is closer than that between Charles Mallison and his father. While the earlier hero works on Saturdays for his uncle and is paid by Gavin, in the later novel the young Lucius is hired instead by his father. Furthermore, *The Reivers* covers a period of five generations rather than three, thus reinforcing the importance of tradition and line. It is also made apparent in this novel that despite the incident where Lucius is punished, Lucius' values have been imparted to him by both his parents and his grandfather. Lucius' high principles are part of

> that inviolable and inescapable rectitude concomitant with the name [he] bore, patterned on the knightly shapes of my male ancestors as bequeathed—nay, compelled—to [him] by his father's word-of-mouth, further bolstered and made vulnerable to shame [his] mother's doting conviction.[116]

The main transformation in *The Reivers* is Faulkner's presentation of Lucius' relationship with his mother, which becomes quite comprehensible considering the author's personal adoration for his own mother. Alison Priest is the loving, supportive mother who, unlike Faulkner's earlier mothers, is capable of entirely accepting her son's maturation. The reassurance Alison gives Lucius has its effect since after he leaves home he is nostalgic for his mother's protection:

> ... suddenly I wanted my mother; I wanted to return, to relinquish, be secure, safe from the sort of decisions and deciding whose foster twin was this having to steal an automobile.[117]

Lucius makes clear that, unlike Margaret Mallison, his mother is attentive but never overbearing. He alludes to

> the way Mother would watch me and my brothers and whatever neighborhood boys were involved, not missing anything, quite constant and quite dependable, even warmly so, bright and kind but insulate until the moment, the need arrived to abolish the bone and (when necessary) stanch the consequent blood.[118]

His mother also encourages his sense of duty to his younger brothers. Before the Priest adults leave for St. Louis to attend his grandfather's funeral, Miss Alison tells him:

> You're the big boy, the man now. You must help Aunt Callie with the others, so they won't worry about Cousin Louisa.[119]

In the final analysis, as noted by Elizabeth Kerr, in the entire Yoknapatawpha saga the Priest family is the only dynasty in which three generations with several children are not only living but thriving in 1905. A fifth generation is growing up in 1961. The last Compson, Miss Quentin, runs away and only childless Jason remains. Carothers Edmonds spurns his only child as well as its mother; Isaac McCaslin has no children; Benbow, the last of the Sartorises, allegedly did not marry, nor did Charles Mallison; Gavin Stevens had no progeny of his own. The Priest family reversed the trend toward shrinking families.[120] The fertility which marks the Priest family in the last analysis is confirmation that Faulkner has come to view family relations generally and parent-child relations specifically in a more positive way than he had in the beginning of his literary career.

The parent-child relations in Faulkner's work, like his other familial themes, show a definite evolution in his later works. Initially, the young Faulknerian hero, when he is not parentless, is subject to tyrannical, egocentric parents. Although there is a certain correspondence between Faulkner's depiction of this relationship and the sociohistorical reality, there is also a proclivity toward negative distortion—particularly during his early and, to some extent, his middle periods. However, these relationships, like other familial relations in the Faulkner canon, are influenced by problems that confronted the South at large. The bond between parents and children operates, for instance, out of a puritanical background where the issues of identity, guilt, ambivalence, and predestination play an important role. The materialism and the introversion of the South generally are recreated by Faulkner in these parent-child relationships.

Although the Faulkner family relations definitely begin to develop more positive aspects at the time of the publication of *Intruder in the Dust*, as early as *Go Down, Moses* the author began to establish the possibility of a harmonious terrain between parent and child. Yet, it is not until the publication of *The Reivers* in 1962 that a large family unit is portrayed as totally stable and completely compatible. There is, of course, the exception of the ever present ghost of Murry Falkner, who is meekly incarnated by Charles Mallison or totally obliterated in the Stevens family, or completely substituted by a grandfather figure with whom the author was familiar in his own family. Otherwise, the personal contentment which the author had by then found in his own life liberates him from the psychologically insecure hero exemplified by Quentin Compson, or the guilt-ridden Ike McCaslin, or the racially-disquieted Charles Mallison. Young Lucius is no longer faced with the conflicts of the earlier characters since his grandfather's eminent presence is there to protect and direct him as the dominant paternal figure.

CHAPTER 5

Incest and the Family

Incestuous relationships are ubiquitous in Faulkner's work. Brother-sister incest, characteristic of the author's work, appears frequently in twentieth-century literature and historically was common throughout the South. The frequency of its occurrence becomes apparent upon examination of the South's laws in contrast with state laws in other parts of the country. The incestuous bond described in Faulkner's work is especially important because of the Southern context from which it emerges. Broadly, these relationships are punctuated by emotions that surpass normal feelings between family members and often have a sexual overtone, if not a sexual manifestation. Incest is an attempt on the part of both the real-life Southerner and the fictional hero or heroine to escape the pressures of the adult world. It reflects the Southerner's insecurity with regard to a rapidly industrializing society and demonstrates an emotionally abusive as well as a nostalgic vision. The pressures are historical, societal and personal.

The individual's evasion of normal relationships reflects his regressive desire to return to a childhood paradise. Faulkner is unmerciful to his protagonists and allows them only the illusion of escape. Once they engage in illicit emotional or physical intimacy they are forced to assume the guilt, doom and death which are component parts of their Southern heritage and destiny. It is only in the fifties with the publication of *The Town* and *The Mansion* that Faulkner's protagonists who show incestuous proclivities begin to be reprieved from the author's stern sentence. By the time he wrote *The Reivers*, Faulkner himself seemed resigned to being sisterless and had abandoned even the pose of intellectual mentor and surrogate incestuous father in order to focus his energies on his grandchildren.

Intrafamilial marriage was very common in the South as early as the seventeenth century. Since the upper classes were small in number, most marriages took place not only within the social group but often within the same family. Genteel Southerners preferred the dangers of consaguinity to the ones entailed in a marriage which was socially below them. Although incest was usually associated with the upper classes, it also occurred quite frequently according to Wilbur Cash among black and white members of the same family.[1] Such is the case of Carothers McCaslin, who has incestuous relations with his mulatto daughter, Tomasina. This is, in fact, the only example in Faulkner's work of consummated incest, at least where immediate family members are involved. Although sexual or emotional obsessions involving another family member occur frequently, only Drusilla in *The Unvanquished* and Laverne in *Pylon* become sexually entangled within the family, though neither Bayard nor Laverne's stepfather is a blood relation. Paul Conner notes that intermarriage was also habitual among the lower classes, who resorted to it as a means of defending the family financially and as a way of insuring personal property. On the psychological level, they also saw it as a means of protecting themselves against the unfamiliar and the threatening.[2]

"Incest was a constant among the Southern scene," [3] according to Andrew Lytle. In both the Old and the New South it arose frequently in the isolation of Southern families, as in the incestuous feelings between Henry and Judith in *Absalom, Absalom!*

> ... That rapport not like the conventional delusion of that between twins but rather as might exist between two people who, regardless of sex or age or heritage or race or tongue, had been marooned at birth on a desert island: the island here Sutpen's Hundred;[4]

The rural existence to which the Southerner was subject, in which "partial isolation meant an intimacy and constancy of association in work and play which induced excessive jealousy against the outside" [5] conduced also "incest of the spirit," [6] "a spiritual condition which inhered within the family itself." [7] Yet, as Andrew Lytle demonstrates, the attraction was generally so strong between brothers and sisters in the South that their parents became fearful of incest; consequently, the boys' and girls' rooms were far apart, and the back staircase was solidly panelled to deliberately hide the ankles and lower legs of the girls as they came down the stairs.[8] Lytle says that incest was so widespread that the whorehouses were filled with girls who had been "ravished by their fathers and brothers."[9] However, incest in Faulkner's work, as well as in general, occurred more frequently between brothers and sisters than between children and parents.[10] According to sociological studies, brother-sister incest was five times as common as father-daughter incest; mother-son incest was the least common of the three.[11]

Laws were created to curb these incestuous practices since such offenses affronted morality. Furthermore, despite the fact that there is little scientific evidence to support the view, incestuous marriages were regarded as degenerative, as bringing out the worst traits of both the male and the female. Probably the most valid explanation for preclusion of incest, however, is that the consanguineous relationships were believed to create friction among family members. Nonetheless, considering the habitual nature of incest, particularly in the South, it is not surprising that in the Southern states the incest laws were less severe than in other parts of the country.

If one examines the laws regarding incest that were in effect very recently after Faulkner's death, one can conclude that the laws relating to marriage between cousins, for example, as well as the penalties inposed for committing incest, tended generally to be more liberal in the South. In 1965, for instance, of the seventeen states allowing sexual relations and intermarriage between cousins, six were Southern (Florida, Georgia, Kentucky, North Carolina, Texas, Virginia),[12] showing that, proportionally, incest was more generally condoned in the South than elsewhere within America. Additionally, the penalty for incest in the South was from five to twenty-one years in Tennessee, while in states such as California the offender could be imprisoned for up to fifty years.[13] While fines for incest never exceeded a thousand dollars in any of the Southern states, in other parts of the country such as Oregon and Pennsylvania they could be twice as high.[14]

Even today incest laws generally remain more liberal in the South, again reflecting the fact that it is a practice still more acceptable there than in other parts of the country. Although Maryland and the District of Columbia alone prohibit marriage and sexual relations between persons of more distant consaguinity than first cousins, no Southern state prohibits marriage between first cousins, while eight non-Southern states (Arizona, Kansas, Montana, Nevada, South Dakota, North Dakota, Utah, Wisconsin) interdict it.[15] Additionally, a number of states include within the definition of incest, sexual relations between parents and their adopted children; of the eleven states with laws proscribing incestuous relations between an adopted child and a parent, none is Southern.[16] In Minnesota there are laws forbidding incest even between adopted siblings.[17] The least severe penalty for incest today is in Virginia, where there can be six months' imprisonment or a five-hundred-dollar fine.[18]

Despite its freqency in the South, and notwithstanding a greater tolerance for it on the part of Southerners, incest was generally condemned there, as it has been, with certain exceptions, throughout history. In certain primitive tribes, it appears incest was considered a therapeutic practice and was viewed as a panacea for the plague and syphilis, while in other primitive societies incest was practiced on the night before battle because it was considered to imbue the individual with strength. In other communities, by contrast, it was connected with witchcraft and suicide. In Egyptian and Greek society, although it was initially accepted, with time incest came to be condemned. In ancient Egypt incest between the gods was paralleled by the brother-sister marriages of the rulers. Later, although tolerance remained for the marriage of siblings, incestuous marriage was generally condemned by public opinion if not by law. Ancient Greece followed the same pattern. In the Homeric version of the Œdipus myth, neither Œdipus nor his mother Jocasta is punished for having consummated their incestuous marriage. Then in Sophocles, the version used by Freud for developing his theory of the Œdipus complex, disaster follows their incestuous union.

Yet, gradually the Egyptians and the Greeks totally interdicted incest. Christian society, like the Roman, has generally been very severe in its prohibitions against incest; during certain periods in Europe, the Roman Catholic Church prohibited even sixth cousins to marry. Yet, even in Christian society, as in the earlier civilizations, there could be a period of laxity in the restrictions. During the Italian Re-

naissance, for example, the interdictions were overtly ignored, and no-
bles, popes, and many of the church dignitaries became openly involved
in incestuous practices. This anomaly is particularly ironic in that the
Judeo-Christian West, and more specifically the United States and the
South, derived their prohibitions not from taboo but from religious in-
terdiction. Thus, Henry in *Absalom, Absalom!*, very conscious of the
South's religious prohibitions regarding incest, with contrition resorts
to history and to the Italian Renaissance for the ultimate justification
of his "privileged relationship" with his sister Judith:

> But kings have done it! Even dukes! There was that Lorraine
> duke named John something that married his sister. The
> Pope excommunicated him but it didn't hurt! It didn't hurt!
> They were still husband and wife. They were still alive. They
> still loved![19]

In literature incest is first treated by the Greeks in their drama. It
reappears much later during the Christian medieval period and during
the Renaissance. It is present in the sketch of Margaret of Navarre, "A
Tale of Incest," and it seems, according to a note made by Havelock El-
lis, to have been mentioned, if not discussed, in 1615 by de Rosset in a
work entitled *Les Histoires Tragiques de Notre Temps*.[20] However, it
was probably not until the performance of John Ford's drama, *Tis Pity
She's a Whore*, that the theme of incest was really recognized in Western culture in any significant way. With the major exception of the
Marquis de Sade, during the seventeenth and eighteenth centuries the
references to incest are not numerous; the subject was for the most part as
banned as the act itself. However, with the publication of Nathaniel
Hawthorne's "Alice Doane's Appeal," Herman Melville's *Pierre*, and
Edgar Allan Poe's "The Fall of the House of Usher," incest themes began to assume a role of greater importance.

In great part because of the sexual liberation characteristic of the
second half of our century, incest has made a frequent appearance in
novels such as Theodora Keogh's *Gemini*, Harold Robbins' *The Carpet-
baggers*, Grace Metalious' *Peyton Place*, Vladimir Nabokov's *Lolita*,
D.H. Lawrence's *Sons and Lovers*, and Henry Miller's *Tropic of Capri-
corn*. In general, the literary treatment of incest shows a preoccupation
with brother-sister incest, especially with brothers and sisters who
find each other again after a period of separation, rather than with

those who are inextricably bonded since infancy, as is characteristic in Faulkner.

The incest theme personally engaged many of the major writers of the nineteenth and twentieth centuries. Latent incestuous feelings, such as those that Faulkner had for his mother, are expressed much more explicitly by other major writers, among them Stendhal, Proust, and Sartre. Proust states that:

> I was always in love with my mother. I was always kissing my mother and wishing that we had no clothes on . . . I kissed her with such ardor that she felt to a certain degree in duty bound to withdraw. *I detested my father* when he came and interrupted our embraces. I wanted to kiss her breast always.[21]

Jean-Paul Sartre, who in his childhood slept in a double bed with his mother, became aware in 1963, while writing the first part of his autobiography, of the incestuous fantasies which he had transferred from his mother to an imagined sister. This is a process similar to Faulkner's transfer of his own incestuous fantasies to Candace in *The Sound and the Fury*. When Sartre says, "At all events as a brother I would have committed incest," he reminds one of Faulkner's own fantasies: "the only bond of relationship which makes any impression on me." [22] Sartre further claimed:

> What engages me about this family bond is less the erotic temperature than the forbidden love: fire and ice, a mixture of rapture and renunciation. I liked incest, so long as it stayed platonic.[23]

Sartre's notion of forbidden but platonic love is certainly reminiscent of Quentin's affection for Candace in *The Sound and the Fury*.

Crucial to Faulkner's work, as well as to an understanding of incest in general, is Freud's Œdipus complex, which Freud explains as follows: "A little boy may take his sister as love-object in place of his faithless mother.... A little girl takes an older brother as substitute for the father." [24] Otto Rank believed that incest between brother and sister is a substitute for parent-child incest.[25] Throughout Faulkner's work, it is explicit that all his protagonists involved in incestuous attractions are the products of loveless or non-existent families and they seek through a sibling of the opposite sex to find a parent substitute. The sole exception is Laverne in *Pylon* who commits incest with her unnamed brother-in-law, a brother-substitute as described by Freud. Although the author offers no parental background with regard to Charlotte and Rat in *The Wild Palms* or to Pat and Josh in *Mosquitoes*, one can safely conjecture that their family histories were similar to that of the other protagonists.

Faulkner's fictional siblings who become incestuously involved suffer above all from parental neglect. This also follows the family pattern described by psychologists in cases of mother-son incest. The father is absent from, subordinate in, or indifferent to the family; he is incapacitated, old, weak, or overworked. Frequently, he was removed from the family through death or desertion.[26] This parental profile, in fact, fits all of Faulkner's fathers whose children are prone to incestuous attractions. Psychologists add that the mother is also usually detached if not absent from the family.[27] In the author's work if the mother (with the exception of Elmer's mother in *Elmer* and "A Portrait of Elmer") is not physically absent, she is almost inevitably detached on the psychological level. Furthermore, again according to psychological studies, even though the mother is usually respected by her son, she is known to be hostile to her daughter,[28] just as Addie Bundren is toward Dewey Dell in *As I Lay Dying*, the second Mrs. Bundren toward Juliet in "Adolescence," and Caroline toward Candace in *The Sound and the Fury*.

There are numerous examples of incestuous relationships in both Faulkner's major and minor work. In *Absalom, Absalom!*, Judith and Henry are the offspring of a ruthlessly ambitious father and a mother completely detached from reality. The Cassandra-like mother of Henry's son Bon views him as her best means of achieving revenge. In *Elmer* and "A Portrait of Elmer," Addie and Elmer are the progeny of a domineering mother and an apathetic father. Juliet and Lafe in "Adolescence" are the children of Joe Bundren, an earlier and equally selfish version of Anse Bundren, and a mother who dies in childbirth; she is replaced by a stepmother who despises them. In *As I Lay Dying* Darl and Dewey Dell are the son and daughter of a mother who rejects them and a father who is completely indifferent to them. Mr. and Mrs. Compson in *The Sound and The Fury* are equally incapable of creating a loving and stable home life for Quentin, Benjy, or their sister Candace;

Mr. Compson is an alcoholic and a nihilist, while his wife is a self-centered hypochondriac. The Varners in *The Hamlet* are prolific bearers, as demonstrated by their sixteen children, but are completely indifferent to all of them, as evidenced by Faulkner's treatment of Eula and her brother Jody. In *The Unvanquished* Bayard's father, John Sartoris, is power driven and self-absorbed, while his mother is deceased; concomitantly, Drusilla's mother is concerned with "honor" more than with her daughter's happiness. In *Pylon* Laverne is orphaned. And in *Flags in the Dust* and *Sartoris* Horace and Narcissa also are orphans, while Little Belle is the product of a divorced home as well as an immature father and an ambitious, egocentric mother.

Despite the fact that the brother-sister transferral elucidated by Freud is implicit throughout Faulkner's work and is readily comprehensible given the siblings' family context, the transference itself is verbalized only in Horace and Narcissa's relationship in *Flags in the Dust* and *Sartoris*. Horace's very serious attachment to his mother is implied by his preference for being in debt, rather than sell his childhood home. The home is described, in the original edition of *Sanctuary*, in a nightmare from which Horace awakens calling his mother's name. Horace's strong emotions toward his mother are transferred to his sister in the first edition of *Sanctuary*. At the time, he is a middle-aged man who feels in Narcissa "that quality that seemed to take him by the shoulders as though he were a little boy and turn him about to face himself." [29] In *Flags in the Dust* and *Sartoris*, this emotional transferral to Narcissa is made clearer when he returns from war and strokes "his hands on her face as a child would." [30] Narcissa, in turn, makes Horace her own through a "maternal perseverance" [31] that is also implied by the womblike image in *Sartoris* when "his spirit slipped, like a swimmer into a tideless sea, into the serene constancy of her affection," [32] and in *Flags in the Dust*, where the text is slightly altered: "... and he let slip, as into water, into the constant serenity of her affection again." [33] The water is symbolic of the eternal feminine and clearly suggests a return to the womb—Narcissa being the replacement for his mother.

This psychological transference to Narcissa is noticed by Belle (in the original version) who tells Horace, "You're in love with your sister. What do books call it? What sort of complex?" [34] In fact, the mother transfer occurs later, at the time of Horace's courtship and marriage to

Belle, and Belle herself becomes the mother substitute and is now the replacement for Narcissa. Belle's eventual role of wife and mother is implied through the water imagery used in *Flags in the Dust* and *Sartoris*. Belle envelopes him "like a rich and fatal drug, like a motionless and cloying sea in which he watched himself drown." [35] In Horace's case, water and the maternal are specifically linked with sex because, as implied in the orginal edition of the novel, Horace associates sex and security with his mother and his childhood:

> In the center of the lawn, equidistant from either wing of the drives between house and fence, was an oak. It was old and thick and squat, impenetrable to sun or rain. It was circled by a crude wooden bench, onto the planks of which the bole, like breasts of that pneumatic constancy so remote from lungs as to be untroubled by breath, had croached and over-bosomed until supporting trestles were no longer necessary. He sat on the bench, smoking against the tree, remembering how on summer afternoons, all four of them would sit there while the spent summer rain murmured among the leaves and the thick breath of the honeysuckle bore up this slope in rich gusts . . . [36]

The image of overdeveloped breasts, representative of the mother, and honeysuckle, symbolic of sex, indicates the connection he makes between sex and maternal security. This explains why he later chooses a very feminine and sexual woman like Belle, whom he associates with his mother, rather than one of the author's usual epicene women.

When Horace, who fits the classic description of the incestuous father, passive and weak with a wife who represents the strong and severe mother figure,[37] is disappointed with his marriage, his incestuous feelings are transferred to his stepdaughter, Little Belle. Ernest Jones in his *Papers on Psycho-Analysis* states that a man who has an abnormally strong affection for his daughter (in this instance, his stepdaughter) has also, like Horace, a strong infantile fixation on his mother.[38] Max Marcuse adds that a "recognition motive" is invovled, and the man is attracted to the daughter or stepdaughter also because she has a striking resemblance to another object of his affections such as a mother, a sister, or, as in this case, a wife.[39] It is interesting to note how closely Faulkner's own relationships with his mother, daughter and stepdaughter conform to these patterns. In Horace's case, Little

Belle as described by Edmond Volpe is the "carbon copy"[40] of her mother, endowed with the same animal magnetism. At the end, Horace's incestuous attraction nevertheless reverts to its source. When he leaves his marriage with Belle, he returns to Narcissa "with something of the chaotic emotions of a bridegroom of twenty-one."[41] Horace's incestuous feelings toward his sister and then later toward his wife and stepdaughter are all integrally linked with his inability to reconcile himself to his mother's death.

Faulkner demonstrates that incestuous feelings are not usually engaged in to an equal degree or are sometimes unrequited, despite the disjointed familial situation shared by the siblings. In the brother-sister incest depicted by Faulkner, it is almost always the male who seems more involved. This propensity can probably be viewed as a projection on the author's part, and Faulkner can be seen as vulnerable to this potential involvement with and rejection by a sister he never had. Of Candace, he even admits to Maurice Coindreau:

> the same thing happened to me that happens to so many writers—I fell in love with one of my characters, Caddy. I loved her so much I couldn't decide to give her life just for the duration of a short story. She deserved more than that. So my novel was created almost in spite of myself.[42]

In his University of Virginia interviews, Faulkner refers to Candace also as "my heart's darling,"[43] and in his introduction to *The Sound and The Fury* he says of Candace:

> Whereupon I, who had three brothers and no sisters and was destined to lose my first daughter in infancy, began to write about a little girl. I did not realize that I was trying to manufacture the sister which I did not have and the daughter which I was to lose, though the former might have been apparent from the fact that Caddy had three brothers almost before I wrote her name on paper.[44]

Faulkner's search for and his creation of a surrogate sister can be seen in Horace who comes to view Belle and Narcissa as interchangeable:

> He tried to think of his sister, of Belle. But they seemed interchangeable now; two tiny, not distinguishable figures like two china figurines seen backward through a telescope.[45]

Faulkner appears to create many of these other surrogate sisters, like Candace, to replace the one he had never had and always wanted. The only examples of sisters more emotionally involved with brothers than vice versa are Charlotte in *The Wild Palms*, who, because she cannot marry her brother, marries his roommate Rat, instead; and Pat in *Mosquitoes*, who, totally infatuated with her brother Josh, gets into his bed and suggestively nibbles his ear while she makes plans to follow him to Yale. Actually, in the relationships between Horace and either Narcissa or Belle, there seems to be an equal degree of emotional involvement on the part of each. On the other hand, Little Belle appears completely uninterested in her stepfather's sexual attitude toward her.

In the unpublished novel *Elmer* and in "A Portrait of Elmer," although Jo-Addie feels affection for her brother, as illustrated by the box of paints she sends him, it seems that Elmer's incestuous feelings are not reciprocated. It is he who associates her with trees, phallic symbols representative of the life force, and it is Elmer who enjoys being in bed naked with his sister Jo-Addie. In "Adolescence" Juliet is not without sisterly sentiments for her younger brother: she takes pity on him and gives him food and all her savings after their father dies and Lafe does not want to remain with their cruel stepmother. It is, however, Lafe who looks to his older sister for emotional support as a mother substitute as he puts "his arms around her legs burrowing his face into her sharp little hip." [46]

In *As I Lay Dying* Darl has the same telepathic yearning for Dewey Dell that he has for his mother, suggesting the depth of his feelings for his sister. By contrast, Dewey Dell is interested only with her pregnancy. In a fantasy that is the inverse of Quentin's in *The Sound and the Fury*, she thinks about killing her brother; in fact, she becomes instrumental in sending him to the asylum in Jackson in order to prevent his telling their father about her pregnancy. Candace feels much tenderness for Benjy and a certain incestuous attraction to Quentin, as implied by the displeasure she displays when the latter engages in a limited degree of physical contact with Natalie. However, both Benjy and Quentin are completely obsessed with Candace. They have transferred all their libidinal energy onto their sister; they consequently do their utmost to curtail her relationships with other males such as Charley, Dalton Ames, and Herbert Head. In *The Hamlet* Eula seems completely indifferent to her brother, while Jody is fixated on his sister and her sexuality. He daily takes her on horseback to and from a school easily within walking distance in order to avoid male intrusion. In *Pylon*, fifteen-year-old Laverne laconically resigns herself to her brother-in-law's eager advances. Thus, Faulkner's work reflects that brother-sister incest is almost inevitably propagated and is sustained by the male sibling.

In *Absalom, Absalom!*, Faulkner presents one of the more complex treatments of incest because of the added factor of homosexuality. Here Judith and Henry are regarded since childhood as spiritual twins, considered to have a telepathic closeness like Darl and Dewey Dell's; they anticipate "one another's actions as two birds leave a limb at the same instant." [47] Yet, the incestuous intimacy they feel for one another is overriden by the homosexual attraction, particularly strong on Henry's part, involving Bon. Henry seduces his sister in Bon's name, partially because of his incestuous yearning for Judith but mainly because of his homosexual link to Bon:

> She was the blank shape, the empty vessel in which each of them strove to preserve, not the illusion of himself nor his illusion of the other but what each conceived the other to believe him to be—the man and the youth, the seducer and seduced, who had known one another, seduced and been seduced, victimized in turn each by the other, conqueror vanquished by his own strength, vanquished conquering by his own weakness, before Judith came into their joint lives even so much as girlname. [48]

Bon, also attracted to Judith, is still more interested in Henry. Yet, Bon is, above all, concerned with gaining recognition from his father and is using both Judith and Henry to achieve his purpose. Ultimately, both Henry and Bon, each for his own reasons, are more active and entangled in the incestuous relationships.

Faulkner's work contains sibling incest and also mother-son incest, though that variation occurs less frequently than father-daughter incest. According to Freud, mother-son incest arises usually when the mother, neurotic and unsatisfied by her husband, is over-tender and over-anxious in regard to the male child to whom she has transferred her love. [49] The substitution awakens in the son a sexual precocity. [50]

Psychologists observed that mother-son incest occurred in families in which the mother was dominant while the father was either absent or very subordinate. Often the mother was widowed or separated from her husband, or, when present, he was either weak or incapacitated.[51] In examining Drusilla's behavior toward Bayard in *The Unvanquished*; Caroline Compson's comportment toward Jason in *The Sound and the Fury*; Addie Bundren's response to Jewel in *As I Lay Dying*; Mrs. Bland's attitude toward Gerald, also in *The Sound and the Fury*; and Mrs. Boyd's conduct toward Howard in "The Brooch;" one finds that Faulkner's portrayal of these incestuous relationships follows for the most part the patterns described by Freud and other psychologists. In fact, despite the author's protests that he was unfamiliar with Freud, Joseph Blotner demonstrates the contrary in his biography. According to Blotner, Faulkner heard a great deal about Freud during his extended stay in New Orleans in the 1920s.[52]

The first of these mother-son relationships is that of Drusilla and Bayard. Drusilla, Bayard's stepmother in *The Unvanquished*, functions as a mother substitute. She is the only one of the maternal figures cited who is actually infatuated sexually with her stepson, Bayard. After having lost her fiancé, Gavin Breckbridge, she spends a year traveling with her distant cousin John Sartoris in order to fight the Yankees. They marry only because they are forced to by Drusilla's mother Louisa. She insists on their union because of their cohabitation, which she regards as the ultimate infamy against Drusilla and Southern womanhood. Neither is enamored of the other, John Sartoris being substantially older, so it is not surprising that Drusilla should turn to her stepson, only eight years her junior, as a substitute husband. Drusilla is Bayard's temptress, it is Drusilla who, now symbolically, initiates the lovemaking that Bayard refuses when she gives him the pistols to avenge his father's death.

In *The Sound and the Fury* and *As I Lay Dying*, Caroline Compson and Addie Bundren have incestuous feelings for their favorite sons, Jason and Jewel, respectively; yet unlike Drusilla, their sentiments are based on emotions rather than sexual attraction. Both Mrs. Compson and Mrs. Bundren follow the pattern described by psychologists with regard to mother-son incest in that they occupy a more dominant place in the home because they have stronger personalities than their respective spouses, Jason Compson and Anse Bundren. Caroline Compson considers that, unlike her other children, Jason is quite simply her salvation:

> what have I done to have been given children like these ...
> except Jason he has never given me one moment's sorrow
> since I first held him in my arms I knew then he was to be my
> joy and my salvation ... only Jason can do wrong because he
> is more Bascomb than Compson ...[53]

She wants to go away with Jason, to leave the others. Although she tells him she wants him to get married, Jason himself realizes that she is much too possessive and tells her, if "I was to get married you'd go up like a balloon."[54] He adds that, even if she were dead, she would oppose his marriage: "You'd get right up out of your grave, you know you would."[55] Likewise Jewel, Addie's illegitimate son by the Reverend Whitfield, is a favorite child whom Addie considers her redemption:

> He is my cross and he will be my salvation. He will save me
> from the water and from the fire. Even though I have laid
> down my life he will save me.[56]

When she is on her death bed, Addie asks to see Jewel first. She also helps him with his chores when he is tired and prepares special meals which she hides for him. Like Bayard, neither Jason nor Jewel is insensitive to his mother's attentions. While Jason cheats her financially and is frequently impolite to her, he is still emotionally bound to her, as implied by his bachelor status and demonstrated in his consistently taking her wishes strongly into consideration. Furthermore, the sadistic Jason refrains from beating her grandchild, Quentin, and also for his mother's sake does not send Benjy to the asylum in Jackson. In fact, the incestuous feelings that Jason has for his mother even extend to his niece, Quentin. This interest manifests itself perversely in his constant attacks on her sexual looseness for which he calls her a bitch, slut, and whore. He is sexually obsessed with her in a way resembling his brother Quentin's sexual fixation on Caddy.

Both men attempt to repress their feelings, but Jason exhibits his emotions very differently from Jewel. In contrast to the possessiveness, tenderness, and dependency which his brother feels regarding Caddy, Jason treats young Quentin with systematic cruelty and hatred. Jewel, in turn, fantasizes about being away from the others with his mother.

He buys a horse, much to his mother's chagrin, to which he transfers his affections at the time he is faced with Addie's death. Olga Vickery notes that many of Jewel's actions constitute an attempt to make his fantasies "a reality and so to claim exclusive possession of Addie."[57]

Mrs. Bland is another Faulkner mother who is very domineering in her relationship with her son. Mr. Bland, Gerald's father, has so little importance that he is never even alluded to. Mrs. Bland, although she is not sexually desirous of her son, still treats him almost as if he were her husband—Quentin referring to them as the "King and the Queen." [58] When Gerald is at Harvard, his mother takes an apartment in Cambridge. She is constantly with him, to the point that, even when he is boat racing, she rides parallel to him in the motorcar. In the same way that she interferes with his extracurricular activities, she also concerns herself with his roommates: when, as with Shreve, she deems them unsuitable, she quite simply orders that they be changed. She also spoils Gerald materially by giving him his own apartment in town, as well as a room in the dormitory. Gerald himself, however, seems to be content that his mother is present.

Mrs. Boyd in "The Brooch" is even more possessive about her son, Howard, and the consequences are thus more dramatic. In the same way that Mrs. Bland follows Gerald to Harvard, Mrs. Boyd accompanies her son to the University of Virginia, where she, too, resides during his college years. Mrs. Boyd's "vigilant maternity" [59] is noted by Hans H. Skei when he observes that she has abandoned herself to her son. He describes her as "an instance of a deserted and betrayed woman trying to gain control at least over *one male* and never lose him to another female." [60] Even though Howard does marry, he is unable to cut the umbilical cord. Refusing to move out of his mother's home, he tells Amy quite adamantly: "I won't leave her. I will not, until she is dead. Or this house. I won't. I can't." [61] His over-attachment to his mother results in his separation from his wife and ultimately his suicide.

Freud discussed the frequent occurrence of a precocious sexuality developing when the son was subject to incestuous emotions from his mother. Although Faulkner does not present Jason or Gerald as showing signs of premature sexuality, he suggests that their relationships with regard to sex are problematic. The problem translates into Jason's inability to form a serious relationship except with Lorraine, who is a prostitute. While Gerald, despite the numerous girlfriends whom his mother comments on, has a certain effeminacy, indicated in his girlish features.

Jealousy is an important aspect of these incestuous relationships in Faulkner. Jealousy appears either independently or linked with impotence and homosexuality. It is related to the male protagonist's attraction to androgynous women, especially sisters, who often also act as mother substitutes. In a society viewed by the Southerner as both doomed and death-oriented it is perhaps understandable that the individual should possess an instinct for self-preservation not only on the societal level but also on the familial one. The emotions of jealousy and possessiveness may appear in connection with this survival instinct because at the deepest level the individual feels threatened by outside forces that can sever him from family. The menace is particularly clear when the individual is fragile, like many of Faulkner heroes, because emasculate, and turns especially to epicene women who are family members. He is drawn to them because they do not put in question his ambiguous sexuality since they do not seek or expect that he will consummate his incestuous desires.

While mutual jealousy linked to incestuous feelings is well illustrated by Horace and Narcissa in *Flags in the Dust, Sartoris,* and the original version of *Sanctuary,* similar emotions are also felt by Horace for Little Belle, although made explicit only in the first edition of *Sanctuary.* Horace's possessiveness and potential jealousy become evident when he first asks Narcissa not to marry Bayard but to remain at home with him:

> "Nancy," he said, "don't do it, Nancy. We both won't. You haven't gone too far that you can't, and when I think that we ... with this house, and all, and all—it—Don't you see we can't?"[62]

Horace's jealousy is implicit when he does not attend Bayard and Narcissa's wedding, never sees the two together after they are married, and sees her only once before Bayard, whom Horace refers to as a "blackguard," dies.[63] Even then, Horace says to himself, "Damn that brute. Damn that brute." [64] The sexual jealousy that Horace feels is also evident in the original version of the novel when he questions how Narcissa can "lie there with the supreme and placid stupidity of a cow being milked." [65] The incestuous sentiments that Horace has for Narcissa are also understood by Belle, who considers Narcissa competition, at least emotionally. Consequently, in the original version, Belle piques Horace's jealousy by forcing him to imagine his sister with another man. One concurs with Michael Millgate's judgment that Horace's "weak and untidy involvement with every woman he meets" [66] may be explained in part by this over-attachment to his sister. Yet Horace's incestuous involvment is not limited to his sister but extends to Little Belle as well—as do his accompanying sentiments of jealousy, which are well expressed twice in the first edition. Looking at Little Belle's photograph and thinking about her potential suitor, he whispers to himself: "Damn him, damn him," tramping back and forth before the photograph.[67] Also, in a telephone conversation with Little Belle, he reveals his jealousy of a young boyfriend, though this rival is not imaginary but real. Narcissa's jealousy of Belle is less developed, but nevertheless the author makes it implicit when, in the original edition of the novel, he refers to Narcissa as Belle's "enemy," [68] or in *Flags in the Dust* and *Sartoris* when Narcissa weeps over Horace's marriage.

Laverne's brother-in-law in *Pylon* also demonstrates jealousy toward her, as does Darl toward Dewey Dell in *As I Lay Dying*, and Jody toward his sister Eula in *The Hamlet*. Fearing competition from younger men, her brother-in-law takes Laverne only to places where he is sure these younger competitors cannot be found. When Laverne does find a man she is attracted to, her brother-in-law follows her like a betrayed suitor. While Laverne's brother-in-law's jealousy is explicit, the envy to which Darl is subject is implicit. Dewey Dell fears that Darl will tell their father about her pregnancy. One can only deduce that, this being true, Darl must be motivated principally by possessiveness considering his incestuous feelings for his sister. Finally, Jody's envy and accompanying incestuous feelings for Eula are strongly connected to his own impotence. He is described as "the jealous seething eunuch priest," [69] reacting with "raging impotence" [70] to Eula's obliviousness to her own appeal, or as Will Varner's "huge, bull-goated impotent and outraged" [71] son. Jody wants to shoot Eula's seducer because he is jealous of him. The brother is described by Walter Brylowski as wanting to defend the family honor,[72] but this is actually Jody's rationale to justify his incestuous feelings toward his sister. The protagonist's concern with honor is, in fact, rooted in his own sexual impotence and consequent feelings of inadequacy; thus, in the name of honor, he attempts to secure his sister's affections by preventing her escape through an involvement with another man.

Although the jealousy felt by Benjy and Quentin in *The Sound and the Fury* has already been alluded to, one must add that it is finally Quentin's covetousness, not unlike Jody's, and his confrontation with Dalton Ames that end Candace's relationship with the man who really loves her. Ames is probably her only salvation from the wasteland of her family existence. Quentin also justifies his own jealousy in great part by his need to defend the family honor, despite Olga Vickery's accurate observation that Caddy is an "unstable guardian" [73] for that "concept of Compson honor precariously and ... only temporarily supported by the minute fragile membrance of her maidenhead." [74] Quentin's preoccupation, like Jody's, with family honor is his means of avoiding the need to deal with his impotence and, in his case, even latent homosexuality, a predicament suggested both in *The Sound and the Fury* and in *Absalom, Absalom!* In *The Sound and the Fury*, Spoade refers to Shreve as "Quentin's husband," [75] and in *Absalom, Absalom!* his attraction to Shreve is suggested when Quentin associates him with wisteria, which like honeysuckle is used by Faulkner to symbolize sex.

Yoknapatawpha is inhabited by jealous, possessive siblings who are the offspring of disfunctional families in a decadant society. The children, as the society, are riddled with insecurity and grope blindly to protect and to propagate any relationship with those they can.

In *Absalom, Absalom!*, the homosexual attraction between Bon and Henry, for example, is understandable because these two, like Quentin, come from a family background conducive to forming homosexuality. Psychologists have noted that homosexuals usually have domineering mothers[76] who tend to ally with them against their fathers, as does Quentin's or Charles Bon's mother. They also have distant relations with their fathers,[77] like Henry and, especially, Charles with Thomas Sutpen. They are apt also to be very solitary,[78] similar to the three heroes described. Yet, in *The Sound and the Fury* Quentin inclines toward homosexuality, in what would be considered by Freud a flight from incest, as a compensation for the limited incestuous responses of Candace.[79] Both Bon and Henry seem, by contrast, to prefer their homosexual attraction to the incestuous one with Judith.

Elmer Hodge in *Elmer* and "A Portrait of Elmer," is another example of Faulkner's heroes with an overbearing mother. Elmer's mother's
presence is so strong that years after her death, when he meets a hotel
keeper in France who resembles her and who is scolding the man next to
her in a way similar to the way in which his mother habitually re-
proached his father, Elmer imagines himself as his father and regret-
fully thinks, "I might have known she would not stay dead." [80] Mr.
Hodge, like Bon and Henry's father, is more remote from his son than is
his wife. Yet, like Quentin, Elmer appears to have turned away from
incest when Jo-Addie, his beloved sister, leaves home as a young girl.
He transfers the emotions he feels for his sister first to his teacher and
then to a young school boy, who seems as "beautiful to him as a God." [81]
After the boy behaves cruelly to him, he transfers his emotions once
again to his teacher. Later, after being rejected by all the women who
attract him—Velma, Ethel, and Myrtle—he turns his affections once
again to a man, this time an Italian named Angelo who, when Elmer
speaks to him, seems as though he "is making love to him."[82]

Closely related to their incestuous desires and homosexuality is
the frequent attraction of Faulkner's heroes to sisters or to mother substitutes who are androgynous. Certain of these women, Faulkner's female protagonists, are both epicene and are *themselves* attracted to
brother or father substitutes. These incestuous attractions involving androgynous women generally arise by default: as the hero or heroine is
usually incapable of either assuming or sustaining a satisfactory extra-
familial relationship, he or she turns to a family member of the opposite sex to provide the illusion of one. For overt or latent homosexuals
this union ironically encloses them further in the prison of their sexual
ambiguity. An ambivalent Faulkner hero such as Elmer Hodge is particularly reassured by the masculine maternal figure or maternal substitute who can act as both mother and double.

In other cases, Narcissa and Horace Benbow, Drusilla and Bayard
Sartoris, and Laverne and her brother-in-law are all to varying degrees
attracted to each other. Lafe is interested in his sister Juliet, while
Charlotte is infatuated with her brother. As adults these female protagonists will find themselves in marriages which do not fulfill them.
Juliet is the only exception, but the author does not depict her in adulthood. Implicitly, these women cannot accept their roles as females
within the marital framework. Drusilla, for example, is described as

"not tall, not slender as a woman is but a youth, a boy, is motionless," [83] or as having a "boy-hard body, the close implacable head with its savagely cropped hair ... the body not slender as women but as boys are slender." [84] Laverne is also completely defeminized, wearing men's pants or dressing for the street in a sexless trenchcoat. She has a "hard body's face that looks like any one of the four of them might cut her hair for her with a pocket knife when it needs it." [85] While Juliet is described simply as having a "flat body," [86] Charlotte is referred to as "Charley" [87] in New Orleans and wears her overalls or puts on Harry's trousers. She has a yellow cat's stare "with a speculative sobriety like a man," [88] while her grasp on Harry's wrist is "simple, ruthless and firm." [89] Her refusal of her feminine role is suggested in her eyes by a "profound and distracted blaze of objectless hatred" that the doctor senses is directed at "the entire race of men, males."[90]

In the case of Pat Robyn and Jo-Addie Hodge, not only is the sister figure hermaphroditic, but the sibling relationship becomes more complex with the added homosexual dimension. Pat is defeminized by "her flat breast and belly, her boy's body which the poise of it and the thinness of her arms belied. Sexless, yet somehow troubling." [91] Although the incestuous attraction is basically one-sided on Pat's part, there is also the masculine-feminie reversal previously noted, which is shared by both Josh Robyn and his sister. This suggests an ambivalent sexuality on both their parts, as well as an added element of lesbianism, since Pat also has sexual contact with Jenny. Yet, the most explicit example of the commingling of incestuous attraction, androgyny, and homosexuality occurs in the unpublished novel *Elmer*, as Elmer fondles his tubes of paints. In those

> fat portentous tubes ... was yet wombed his heart's desire,
> the word itself — thick bodied and female and at the same
> time phallic hermaphroditic.[92]

In his protagonist Elmer, the author expresses many of the hidden impulses not only within his heroes, but also within many Southerners, including himself.

The themes of incest and guilt, operating out of a puritanical Southern background, are inextricably interwined throughout Faulkner's work. The correlation between sex and guilt is probably best portrayed in *The Sound and the Fury* in Quentin's incestuous feelings for his sister Caddy. Quentin is one of Faulkner's major illustrations of the power of guilt. He is remorseful in part because of his mother's rejection; the contempt she shows her son as well as the other family members, with the exception of Jason and her brother Maury, creates his self-contempt, especially because he is a sensitive young man. His self-hatred becomes tied to sex and, specifically, to incestuous feelings for his sister.

Quentin's guilty sexual feelings also result from the education he has been given by his father. He has been taught to associate sex with revulsion and sin in a manner characteristic of Southern puritanism in general. On the day of his suicide, for example, he remembers his father's description of the female as repugnant because of her menstrual cycle; this depiction is intermingled with Mr. Compson's equally repellent one of sex symbolized by honeysuckle, and by floating contraceptives: "liquid putrefaction like drowned things floating like pale rubber flabbily filled getting the odour of honeysuckle all mixed up." [93] Quentin himself consequently comes to associate sex with bestiality, as demonstrated by his fantasy of Candace and Dalton Ames making love: "*the beast with two backs ... the swine of Euboelus running coupled with how many Caddy.*" [94] Later he envisions "the swine untethered in pairs rushing coupled into the sea."[95]

This negative association of women and sex, is also made by Darl in *As I Lay Dying*. More exactly, Darl has incestuous feelings for his sister, Dewey Dell, and he reacts with the same revulsion characteristic of Quentin and similarly associates women, sex, and incest with pig imagery. When, at the end of the novel, Darl is being taken to the state asylum, one of the two guards accompanying him must ride backwards in the railroad coach so that the guards are facing each other:

> One of them had to ride backward because the state's money had a face to each backside and backside to each face, and they are riding on the state's money which is incest. A nickel has a woman on one side and a buffalo on the other; two faces and no back. I don't know what that is. Darl had a little spyglass he got in France at the war. In it had a woman and a pig with two backs and no face. I know what that is.[96]

This attitude of disgust toward women and sex, a reflection of Faulkner's own misogyny, explains young Quentin's inability to accept a sexual relationship; his aversion is clear when, as a young boy and after sexual contact with Nathalie, he considers her a "dirty girl" [97] and throws himself in the pig trough. It is thus not surprising that Quentin relates women to shadows, to imperfection. He refers to them "walking in the shadows and whispering with their soft girl voices lingering in the shadowy places."[98]

In fact, this image of the shadow is particularly important because it is connected directly to Quentin's feelings of self-accusation. In Jungian terms the shadow is related to an opposing self; it is the shadow self of the archetype and corresponds to "a negative ego-personality and includes all those qualities we find painful or regrettable,"[99] all those characteristics which in this instance signal Quentin's culpability. It is "the dark half of the psyche which we invariably get rid of by means of projection ... with all the faults which we obviously have ourselves by casting our sins upon a divine mediator."[100] Quentin projects much of his self-remorse onto Candace, whom he considers another part of himself. In such terms, according to Otto Rank, the shadow is the double, an evil anti-self,[101] which Quentin attempts to trick or destroy. He succeeds in annihilating his shadow only through suicide, the ultimate self-punishment for sin. John Irwin, applying Freudian concepts to Quentin, concludes that "the bright self, the ego controlled by the superego" is punishing the id, "the dark self, the ego shadowed by the unconscious."[102]

Considering the guilt Quentin attaches to sex, it is understandable that he turns inward and focuses his libidinal energies on his sister, since he realizes subconsciously that he will never be expected to consummate their relationship. Actually, the guilt Quentin feels over sex, as Lawrence E. Bowling points out, is not limited to the act alone but encompasses the desire itself;[103] he even considers self-castration as a means of freeing himself from desire, castration being the traditional punishment for incest.[104] Castration as a punishment is significant because of the contrition Quentin feels regarding both his virginity and his psycho-sexual impotence. With regard to his virginity, his father is again in large part responsible because Mr. Compson has never encouraged him to assume his manhood. On the contrary, he tells Quentin that virginity is unimportant, that "it's like death: only a state in which the others are left."[105] Quentin, nevertheless, realizes that psychologically he is impaired by his condition, so he tries to convince Caddy that he is no longer a virgin: "Yes yes lots of times with lots of girls."[106] His virginity and implied impotence are intermeshed and make him feel both remorseful and helpless when faced with Caddy's suitors; he will be unsuccessful both as avenger and as seducer. When he attempts to take revenge for Caddy's loss of virginity, he fails, as demonstrated by his inability to accept the gun given to him by Dalton Ames. The weapon may be seen as a phallic symbol and thus represents the boy's inability to avenge his sister's honor. His helplessness is further illustrated when Dalton grasps his wrists and Quentin becomes unconscious. Finally, this "half baked Galahad" [107] is not successful as sibling-seducer and is unable to convince his sister not to marry Herbert Head and to leave her brothers.

Quentin's guilty remorse is early projected unto his sister Candace. When they are young children playing and Caddy muddies her dress, taking it off in front of her brothers and Versh, the Negro boy, Quentin slaps her in order to punish her. His puritanical reaction to her sullied underdrawers announces his latent attitude toward sexual sin. Later, he tries to make Caddy ashamed of her schoolgirl flirtations with boys and slaps her and rubs her head in the grass. After she loses her virginity to Dalton Ames, he finds her lying in the creek; he becomes angry particularly because Candace seems incapable, as Peter Swiggart points out, of recognizing her behavior as sinful. For this reason, more than for the act itself, does he attempt to make her feel remorseful.[108] Ultimately, Quentin is only successful at projecting his self-loathing onto his sister: "*There was something terrible in me,*" she tells Quentin. "*Sometimes at night I could see it grinning at me I could see it through them grinning at me through their face ...* " [109] Completely consumed with guilt, Candace even accepts responsibility for her father's excessive drinking: "*Father will be dead in a year they say if he doesnt stop drinking and he wont stop since I since last summer ...* " [110]

Yet, the contrition Caddy comes to feel regarding sex is not only in connection with Quentin's incestuous attitude but also as a consequence of Benjy's incestuous desires and the guilt that he too projects upon his sister. Lawrence Thompson even considers that Benjamin acts for Caddy as a "moral mirror." [111] Benjy moans his disapproval of Caddy's wearing perfume, of her kissing boys and, later, making love with Danton Ames. Feeling blameworthy, Candace responds first by washing off the perfume, then by washing her mouth in the sink after she kisses Charlie on the swing, and finally by going into the bathroom with Benjamin following sexual relations with Dalton Ames. The suggestion is that her idiot brother will assist in this catharsis.

Regarding both Quentin's and Benjy's incestuous sentiments toward their sister, one must stress that, contrary to appearances, their motivation is primarily emotional. Both the younger and the older brother attempt to make their sister feel contrition in relation to sex because they fear it as the vehicle by which she will leave them alone in the lovelessness of the Compson family. They fear her abandonment of them. Consequently, her suitors are threatening to Benjy and Quentin chiefly because they might entice her away permanently from the family prison.

In *Sanctuary*, Horace experiences no guilt in connection with his incestuous feelings for his sister Narcissa, however, he does feel remorseful concerning his incestuous desires for his stepdaughter, Little Belle, whom Michael Millgate refers to as a "disabling obsession." [112] Despite Melvin Backman's contention that Horace feels aversion to his incestuous emotions for both his sister and his stepdaughter,[113] careful scrutiny of both the original and the final version of the text shows that the culpability he feels is limited to his incestuous feelings for Little Belle. These sentiments are particularly evident in the original version of *Sanctuary*. Notwithstanding that, as Edmond L. Volpe and Cleanth Brooks insist, Horace feels no sexual attraction to his stepdaughter,[114] but analysis of the text, particularly the first version of *Sanctuary*, proves their viewpoint inaccurate. In the final version of *Sanctuary*, Horace is certainly not insensitive to the "pale whisper" of Little Belle's:

> white dress, of the delicate and urgent mammalian whisper of that curious small flesh which he had not beget and in which appeared to be vutted delicately some seething sympathy with the blossoming grape.[115]

The sexual element involved in Horace's reaction to Little Belle was clearer still in the first edition:

> Then she cried "No! No! flinging herself upon him in a myriad secret softnesses beneath firm young flesh and thin small bones.[116]

The short hair was straight and smooth, neither light nor dark; the secret eyes darker than light and with a shining quality beneath soft and secret lids; a prim smooth mouth innocently travestied by the painted bow of the period.[117]

In the original version Little Belle is several times likened to Temple Drake, whom Horace is also sexually attracted to:

He would subpoena Temple; he thought in a paroxysm of raging pleasure of flinging her into the courtroom, of stripping her: This is what a man has killed another over. This, the offspring of respectable people: let them blush for shame, since he could never blush for anything again. Stripping her background, environment . . . [118]

The identification of the two heroines further underscores Horace's attraction to Little Belle.

While Quentin's contrition is fundamentally linked to his impotence and his consequent inability to control Candace, Horace's guilt is primarily related to the actual physical desire he feels toward Little Belle. Like the other protagonist, he, too, attempts to absolve himself of his remorse and to project it onto the object of his desires. Little Belle comes to represent the evil and sin he associates with the lust he feels for her. When he looks at her photograph he sees

the image blurred into the highlight, like something familiar seen beneath disturbed though clear water; he looked at the familiar image with a kind of horror and despair, at a face suddenly older in sin than he would ever be, a face more blurred than sweet, at eyes more secret than soft.[119]

In the original edition, Horace's sexual guilt extends even to Belle herself, who, also is involved with him in a form of psychological incest in that she is not only his wife but simultaneously a mother replacement for him. In a dream he merges his mother with his wife as well as with the women he had met and desired at Old Frenchman's place. He conjures an image of evil which is so appalling that he associates it with the blackness he smells in Popeye:

[His mother] sat on the side of the bed, talking to him. With her hands, her touch, because he realized that she had not opened her mouth. Then he saw that she wore a shapeless garment of faded calico and that Belle's rich, full mouth burned suddenly out of the half light, and he knew that she was about to open her mouth and tried to scream at her, to clap his hand to her mouth. But it was too late. He saw her mouth open; a thick, black liquid welled in a bursting bubble that splayed out upon her fading chin and the sun was shining on his face and he was thinking He smells black. He smells like that black stuff that ran out of Bovary's mouth when they raised her head.[120]

If Horace's remorse in *Sanctuary* is related to his incestuous sexual attraction to his stepdaughter, young Bayard's culpability in *The Unvanquished* is, by contrast, connected to his realization of these desires. Bayard's contrition is felt to a more limited degree for his attraction to his stepmother Drusilla, who discharges into him a shock "like electricity that dark and passionate voracity." [121] Bayard feels blameworthy for having responded to her allure, for having kissed her. Wiliam E. Walker justly refers to Bayard as the "Second Adam," [122] tempted by his Eve, and Drusilla is a heroine who Faulkner describes in a way reminiscent of Balzac's seductive *femme de trente ans*:

I thought then of the woman of thirty, the symbol of the ancient and eternal Snake and of the men who have written of her ...the eternal and symbolical thirty to a young man, a youth, each time both cumulative and retroactive, immitigably unrepetitive, each wherein remembering; the skill without weariness, the knowledge virginal to surfeit, the cunning secret muscles to guide and control just as within the wrists and elbows lay slumbering the mastery of horses:[123]

John Irwin aptly describes Bayard's willingness to endanger himself in order to avenge his father's life as an effort on the son's part to face the punishment for his own sin of desiring his father's death.[124] Unlike the other heroes, Bayard assumes responsibility for both his desires and his deeds without making his stepmother a scapegoat.

Finally, the culpability normally associated with incest is in *Absalom, Absalom!* caught up in *vicarious* incest. Henry, who feels desire for his sister, Judith, makes her fall in love with Bon through himself, "as though it actually were the brother who had put the spell on the sister." [125] By means of this vicarious seduction, Henry absolves himself of the guilt he associates with his incestuous feelings because Bon is a legitimate suitor, at least until the discovery of his blood relationship. As Mr. Compson points out, the act is probably an exemplar of

> the pure and perfect incest: the brother realizing that the sister's virginity must be destroyed in order to have existed at all, taking that virginity in the person of the brother-in-law, the man whom he would be if he could become, metamorphose into, the lover, the husband.[126]

Notwithstanding that in *Absalom, Absalom!* Faulkner manages to relieve Henry of contrition for incestuous feelings, in the Calvinist world of the South, where guilt, sex and punishment are inextricably linked, certain Faulkner characters such as Quentin Compson are necessarily still preoccupied with punishment and damnation for incestuous desires or actions. Quentin manages to transform the Puritan hell into an absolute refuge for both him and his sister. For the young hero it becomes, ultimately, analogous to the longed-for security of a childhood recaptured.

Young Quentin looks vainly to his father for chastisement. He tells Mr. Compson that he has committed incest with Caddy, partially in order to be absolved through punishment. In this way, he hopes to confirm his masculinity, which he considers would be achieved through Mr. Compson's condemnation even though he hasn't actually committed the incest but only desired it. By accomplishing this end, Quentin would no longer be forced to view himself or to be seen by others as a powerless virgin. He would be ridding himself of the self-disdain attached to virginity and implicit impotence. Instead of punishing him, however, Mr. Compson tells him that incest is not evil and is, furthermore, commonplace. His father's denying him punishment leads him to assume his own punishment and consequent self-absolution through suicide.

Bayard, who likewise looks to a father for chastisement for his having kissed Drusilla, also gets a reaction of indifference. Yet, since Bayard is much stronger in his masculinity, he is able to transcend his need for punishment by instead avenging his father's death.

Still, like many Puritans and especially Southern ones, Quentin in *The Sound and the Fury* associates incest not only with sin, guilt and punishment but also with a certain allurement, the attraction of the forbidden. Quentin, a twentieth-century version of Dante's Paolo, is attracted to "some presbyterian concept of . . . eternal punishment." [127] He tells Caddy, "*It was a crime we did a terrible crime it cannot be hid . . . we'll have to go away amid the pointing and the horror of the clean flame.*" [128] Despite Marion George O'Donnell's opinion that "Quentin is really striving toward the condition of tragedy for his family; he is trying to transform meaningless degeneracy into significant doom," [129] close examination of the text shows that his motives are, in fact, more humble, or at least more immediate. Even Quentin's inclination to damnation is related mainly to his compulsion to isolate Candace, with himself away from the others — an aspiration like Jewel's as a result of his incestuous feelings for his mother in *As I Lay Dying*. In the same way that Jewel fantasizes that "it would just be me and her on a high hill," [130] Quentin contemplates his confinement with Candace in hell:

> Because it were just to hell; if that were all of it. Finished. If things just finished themselves. Nobody else there but her and me. If we could just have done something so dreadful that they too would have fled hell except us.[131]

Damnation is evidently Quentin's means of eternalizing his relationship with Candace, lifting it outside of time. As Faulkner makes explicit in the appendix, it is the way to "guard her forever and keep her forevermore intact amid the eternal flames." [132] These notions of exile and death associated with incest are reiterated by Shreve in *Absalom, Absalom!* when, after discussing Bon's relationship with Judith, he also supposes that damnation for incest would result in the couple's eternal sentence:

> . . . but maybe if there were sin too. Maybe you would not be permitted to escape, uncouple, return — Ain't that right?[133]

Finally, for Quentin it is implicit that damnation would allow him his desired regression into the world of childhood, where he can move his sister "out of the loud world" [134] of adulthood. In eternity, he can relive with Candace that time which Michael Millgate describes as "lost innocence;" [135] he can return to a sexless universe in which anything sex related is considered "Chinese" [136] and the protagonist can reassure himself and the others "that that's Chinese I don't know Chinese." [137] There, he is no longer expected to perform sexually, nor will his sister be able to escape their familial bond through sex. In the same way that in "That Evening Sun," by narrating the story, Quentin is able to return to events and to relive his nine-year-old persona, in *The Sound and the Fury* his damnation fantasy involving incest allows him to retreat to his cherished childhood haven, to what Irving Malin would describe as his "childhood paradise." [138]

Finally, incest related to damnation is not restricted only to a couple; in *Absalom, Absalom!*, it becomes a family's doom:

> It isn't yours nor his nor the Pope's hell that we are all going to: it's my mother's and her mother's and father's and their mother's and father's hell, and it isn't you who are going there, but we, the three — no: four of us. And so at least we will be together where we belong, since even if only he went there we would still have to be there too since the three of us are just illusions that he begot, and your illusions are a part of you like your bones and flesh and memory. And we will all be together in torment and so we will not need to remember love and fornication, and maybe in torment you cannot even remember why you are. And if we cannot remember all this, it can't be much torment. [139]

Unlike the hell chosen by Quentin as the refuge for him and his sister alone in *Absalom, Absalom!*, the damnation described by Henry is extended into a family hell. It is no longer a choice but an inevitability, self-engendered, and at least he is not alone without her.

In Faulkner's treatment of incest, death is frequently linked to guilt, punishment and damnation. In *Sanctuary* death becomes the inevitable punishment of a guilt-ridden Horace for the sexual attraction he feels toward Little Belle. After Horace binds Little Belle's image with that of Temple Drake, associating evil with death, he remembers

> the expression he had once seen in the eyes of a dead child, and the other dead: the cooling indignation, the shocked despair fading, leaving two empty globes in which the motionless linked profoundly in miniature. [140]

Horace projects his feeling of despair onto the death of the universe, as if the world were

> approaching the moment when it must decide to turn on or to
> remain forever still: a motionless ball in cooling space, across
> which a thick smell of honeysuckle writhed like old smoke.[141]

Horace is so overpowered by remorse and revulsion that he comes to
fear impotence as part of the death sentence executed by his Puritan
gods. Faulkner's hero also undergoes a sudden and unexpected identity
change, signaled by the use of "she," referring to Horace, in the lava-
tory scene in which he vomits:

> she watched something black and furious go roaring out of
> her pale body. She was bound naked on her back on a flat car
> moving at speed through a black tunnel ... Far beneath her
> she could hear the faint, furious uproar of the shucks.[142]

This image of passivity and self-distancing shows Horace's fear of im-
pending impotence.

According to Irwin, death is important in Faulkner's work because
it can be equated with the symbolic consummation of incest.[143] Henry's
killing of Bon in *Absalom, Absalom!* can be viewed as incest on a symbolic level, since he kills Bon to avoid the incestuous union between Bon
and Judith; thus, the brother and half-brother of Judith can be considered to consummate incest on a metaphorical level. Henry's murder of
Bon can be viewed as a symbolic bonding in homosexuality.

By contrast, when Quentin is first given the opportunity of symbolically committing incest, he is unable to consummate his desire, is unable to kill Caddy with a knife—only points it at her throat. Likewise, when Bayard is given pistols by Drusilla in *The Unvanquished* so
as to avenge his father's death, he refuses to take vengeance through
violence. In this case, to his stepmother's disappointment, Bayard also
rejects, on a symbolic level, the act of love. The incest desired by
Drusilla is made apparent in the following scene:

> She faced me, she was quite near; again the scent of the ver-
> bena in her hair seemed to have increased a hundred times
> as she stood holding out to me, one in either hand, the two
> duelling pistols. "Take them, Bayard," she said, in the same
> tone in which she had said "Kiss me" last summer, already
> pressing them into my hands, watching me with that passion-
> ate and voracious exaltation, speaking in a voice fainting and

> passionate with promise: "Take them. I have kept them for
> you. I give them to you. Oh you will thank me, you will re-
> member me who put into your hands what they say is an at-
> tribute only of God's, who took what belongs to heaven and
> gave it to you. Do you feel them? The long true barrels true as
> justice, the triggers (you have fired them) quick as retribution,
> the two of them slender and invisible and fatal as the physical
> shape of love?[144]

Although Bayard's decision is based on choice and is an act of courage,
Quentin's is related to his impotence. However, through his suicide,
almost in spite of himself, Quentin does later finally perform a symbolic act of incest. According to Freud, suicide is linked with the killing
of an object or a person with whom the victim identified, since he is di-
recting toward himself a death wish which is aimed against another
person.[145] In Quentin's case, he is subconsciously also killing Candace,
which is his ultimate means of preventing her from leaving their family world and of joining with her forever. According to Jung, death by
drowning is specifically indicative of the male's desire to return to the
safety of the womb.[146] Since the sister in Freudian terms can also be a
mother substitute, Freud's theories connecting the death-wish to a surrogate are consonant in Quentin's case with Jung's belief of the male
seeking refuge in the primordial feminine. Candace and his mother become synonymous. As described by David Williams, Quentin is finally
"overwhelmed by the mother archetype of the unconscious; its fascina-
tion leads him to the uroboric incest of madness and the urge for
death." [147] Quentin seeks "the caverns and the grottos of the sea tum-
bling peacefully to the wavering tides." [148] As described by John Earl
Basset, Quentin's desire to return to a primitive fusion with the mother
is also a desire to return to a self-enclosed world, significantly free of
competition.[149] Quentin's desire for a place of safety and emotional security is justifiable, considering Mrs. Compson's preference for Jason and
her complete rejection of Quentin. These forces in combination help to
explain Faulkner's claim that Quentin "loved death above all who
loved only death loved and lived in a deliberate and almost perverted
anticipation of death." [150] In the same way that Quentin expects to find
refuge in damnation, he also aspires to find permanency in the eternal
feminine which represents, ironically, the opposed forces of creativity
and change, thus reinforcing his need for unification with his mother.

As viewed by André Bleikasten, his death becomes "the last of his fictions." [151]

Death, like the other morbid themes of guilt, punishment and damnation, is inextricably linked to Faulkner's treatment of incest. Yet death related to incest, unlike death related to the other themes, must not be seen only as a concept that fetters the hero or heroine. Instead, the idea of death for certain protagonists is so overwhelming that they are ironically pulled toward life; thus, incest is both death inspiring and life enhancing in Faulkner's work. Confronted by death and decay, a hero such as Darl in *As I Lay Dying* or Drusilla in *The Unvanquished* forms an incestuous attraction to a sister or stepson, respectively because both are representative of life and youth. As Darl feels rootless and unloved since he considers himself motherless, he is attracted to his sister, Dewey Dell, who is by contrast a life force in her young sensuality. Darl sees Dewey Dell's leg as she climbs into the wagon as "that lever which moves the world; one of that caliper which measures the length and breadth of life." [152] Later, Darl pictures Dewey Dell's wet dress as revealing "those mammalian ludicrosities which are the horizons and valleys of the earth." [153] Likewise, Drusilla, who has lived through the bleakness of war and through the death of her fiancé, her father and her husband, turns to Bayard for what he represents of youth and regeneracy. Drusilla, who is "dark, passionate and damned forever of all peace," [154] is attracted to her stepson because he is simply "beautiful! young." [155] Certain of Faulkner's characters not only hope through incest to preserve their family prison, but aspire to eventually revitalize themselves within it.

However, Faulkner's work in the 1950s and 1960s shows a change regarding the theme of incest. In his 1950s work, as a theme, it is treated only in *The Town*, and by his last novel, *The Reivers*, he no longer alludes to it at all. Furthermore, by the time of the publication of *The Town* brother-sister incest is no longer presented in the dramatic form in which it was expressed in the author's earlier works; instead, it is now replaced by a very close brother-sister relationship with overtones of spiritual incest, as between Gavin and his twin sister Margaret. Also, the overtly incestuous relationships depicted by Faulkner in his work from the 1920s through the 1940s are now replaced by a surrogate incest. In Galvin's relationship with Linda in both *The Town* and *The Mansion*, for example, he becomes incestuously involved with a surro-

gate daughter, rather than with his own child. The shift indicates
that Faulkner's treatment of the family in his later work again reflects
the author's more optimistic outlook in the sense that these relationships are no longer directed toward family members themselves.

That Gavin and Margaret have a telepathic relationship, one
similar to that of Judith and Henry as children in *Absalom, Absalom!*,
is well illustrated in *The Town*:

> Maybe it was because Mother and Uncle Gavin were twins
> that Mother knew what Uncle Gavin's trouble was just as
> soon as Ratliff did.[156]

In addition, they react identically to the same situation, being virtu-
ally the same person. Charles Mallison puts it this way:

> I was only twelve, yet it was because you didn't have to notice
> Uncle Gavin because you could always tell from Mother
> since she was his twin; it was like when you said "What's the
> matter?" to Mother, you and she and everybody else knew
> you were saying What's wrong with Uncle Gavin?[157]

Their closeness is also implicit in Margaret's deep understanding of her
brother, which is reflected when Charles suggests that Gavin is not yet
ready to marry and accurately foresees his making a marital commit-
ment much later in life to a widow with grown children. Margaret is
his confidante and protectress. It is with her that he discusses his in-
fatuations with Eula and Linda, respectively. After he has fought
with Manfred de Spain over Eula, it is Margaret, knowing that he is
upset, who tries to reassure him by giving him a red rose that she tells
him, though untruthfully, has been sent by Eula. She also feels great
pity for Gavin because she believes that none of the women are worthy
of him:

> You fool! You fool! They don't deserve you! They aren't good
> enough for you! None of them are, no matter how much they
> look and act like a—like a—like a god damn whorehouse!
> None of them! None of them![158]

At thirty-five, Gavin lives in the same house with his father, his
sister Margaret, his brother-in-law, Charles Mallison, his nephew

Chick Mallison, and Chick's cousin, Gowan Stevens. Not only is he still living at home, but he is also treated by Margaret as if he were her elder son. The sister, as Freudian psychology observes, has once again become the mother figure. In fact, as expressed by Gavin himself in *The Town* he has a definite tendency to "run home to Maggie who has tried to be my mother ever since ours died and some day may succeed." [159] Although their relationship is certainly a supportive one for both Margaret and, particularly, Gavin, one can deduce from an observation made by Chick that the brother-sister relationship, because of its strength, might detract from Margaret's marriage with Charles' father:

> even if Mother and Uncle Gavin were brother and sister one was a woman and the other was a man and Freud wasn't any kin to either one of them. [160]

In "Knight's Gambit" Gavin does not marry Melisandre Backus, a woman he has known all his life, until he is in his fifties. The relationship seems accurately described by Michael Millgate as a "sadly middle-aged affair." [161] The bond between Gavin and Linda in his later work *The Town* and *The Mansion* is best described as surrogate incest in the sense that Gavin fantasizes that he is Linda's father:

> So that girl-child was not Flem Snopes's at all, but mine; my child and my grandchild both since the McCarron boy who begot her (oh yes, I can even believe Ratliff when it suits me) in that lost time, was Gavin Stevens in that lost time; and since remaining must remain or quit being remaining, Gavin Stevens is fixed by her own child forever at that one age in that one moment. [162]

This incestuous surrogate relationship replacing an incestuous sibling may reflect Faulkner's own greater detachment from both his daughter and his stepdaughter. The sexual overtones of the relationship are made explicit when Faulkner depicts Gavin's physical closeness to Linda in *The Mansion*:

> he holding her, his hand moving down her back while the dividing incleft outswell of the buttocks rose under the harsh khaki . . . [163]

The critics generally allude to Gavin's romanticism. Cleanth Brooks describes Gavin as "a countrified descendent of Sir Tristian" [164] and states that "he does not dare tamper with a romantic dream." [165] John Lewis Longley, Jr., and James B. Watson refer to Gavin's "romantic idealism," [166] while Edmond Volpe describes Gavin's idealism as "unquestionably his dominant character trait." [167] Even his very practical and perspicacious sister observes, apropos of Linda and her brother, that one does not "marry Semiramis." [168]

Despite the critics' and his family's attitude toward him, honor or romanticism is really Gavin's rationalization for his inability to perform sexually. In his empty romanticism he is like Jody or, particularly, "that young Lochinvar," [169] Quentin; as Charles Mallison says in *The Town*:

> What he was doing was simply defending forever with his blood the principle that chastity and virtue in women shall be defended whether they exist or not.[170]

Although Gavin is very much in love with Eula and later transfers these affections to her daughter Linda, he rejects both of them sexually because he is virginal and afraid of sex. This thirty-five year old virgin is depicted as follows in *The Town*:

> It was adolescence in reverse, turned upside down: the youth, himself virgin and—who knew?—maybe even more so, at once drawn and terrified of what draws him, contriving by clumsy and timorous artifice the accidental encounters in which he still would not and never quite touch, would not even hope to touch, really want to touch, too terrified in fact to touch; but only to breathe the same air, be loved by the same circumambience which laved the mistress's moving limbs ...[171]

Gavin, even later in life, likes to consider Linda a virgin; it is his way of imagining that she will make no sexual demands on him:

> the bride of silence more immaculate in that chastity than even Caesar's wife because she was invulnerable too, forever safe, in that chastity forever pure ...[172]

The relationship between Gavin and Eula, described by Cleanth Brooks as "an ice-cream parlor courtship," [173] is justified by Gavin to Linda in *The Mansion* by his telling her that they, unlike others, do not need sex to express their mutual affection: "we are the two in all the world who can love each other without having to." [174] But Linda, not a crippled puritan enclosed in Gavin's family world of sister and nephew, is capable and desirous of expressing the emotions she feels for Gavin as both a daughter surrogate and a woman.

Finally, Gavin assumes the position of intellectual mentor of both Linda and Melisandre, whom he later marries. It is the same role that Faulkner took with regard to Joan Williams and Jean Stein. In his way, Gavin establishes an emotional and intellectual closeness with both Linda and Melisandre while avoiding sexual intimacy. Faulkner at the University of Virginia said of Gavin that he "was probably afraid to be married." [175] When Gavin finally does marry, it is to a woman whom he has known all his life. Warren Beck describes their marriage as "a sound reality taken for granted by its partners." [176] In *The Mansion* Charles suggests the passionlessness of Gavin's marriage when he questions whether at any point Melisandre and Gavin have been involved sexually.

Thus, although incestuous relationships do exist in Faulkner's later work until *The Reivers*, they are less pronounced than in his earlier writing. In a decadent society, such as that of the nineteenth-century South, it is understandable that the Southerner wishes to preserve himself against the change which threatens him. Even if the motivation is only subconcious, the Southerner often attempts to preserve himself through a family member for whom he feels an attraction and with whom he simultaneously feels secure. If the attraction does not manifest itself on the physical level, it is revealed on the spiritual one. The protagonist in this way avoids an intimate relationship with some outsider because he feels that everything external to him calls him into question and confronts his spiritual, if not his sexual impotence. The outside world also acts as a mirror reflecting his individual responsibility in the societal guilt, his share in the damnation and spiritual death inflicted upon the South.

When like Faulkner's heroes the sensitive, tormented Southerner is forced to evaluate himself, he turns inward and tries to find solace in an incestuous relationship, usually with a brother or sister but sometimes with some other blood tie. This anguished pattern marks Faulkner's work until the 1950s, when incest becomes limited to its least destructive form of spiritual incest in *The Town*, or is replaced by a surrogate incest in *The Town* and *The Mansion*. This change and the complete absence of incestuous relationships in the author's last novel, *The Reivers*, reflect Faulkner's diminishing portrayal of radically problematic family relationships, which is coincident with a time in which his own personal life had stabilized.

CHAPTER 6

Miscegenation and the Family

Miscegenation, or the blending of the races, is another family theme that dominates Faulkner's work. To understand the extent of its importance it is necessary to see the author's literary treatment against its broad social-historical background. By comparing Faulkner's literary portrayal with both historical and contemporary reality, it is possible to grasp to what degree the author is actually aware that miscegenetic relations, particularly between white men and Negro women during slavery, are noxious to the Southern family in the post-slavery and modern period.

Faulkner is preoccupied with the destruction of the black home as well as with the negative effects on black and particularly mulatto family members. Contrary to most of the critics who believe that he is a spokesman against miscegenation, Faulkner depicts the mulatto with compassion and presents him almost inevitably as the victim of his mixed heritage. The mulatto is especially visible in such major works as *Light in August; Go Down, Moses;* and *Absalom, Absalom!;* in which he is an isolated racial and family prisoner. Not until the publication of *The Reivers*—when Faulkner is more at peace with life—does the author seem capable of successfully integrating a mulatto family member into his fictional white family. However, even when Faulkner reduces the racial and family tension, he is unable, because of his own Southern education, to allow the mulatto totally equal family status. With great respect and in spite of himself, he relegates the mulatto to the servant class, where he feels this coffee-colored family member necessarily belongs.

As late as 1962, the year of Faulkner's death, all the Southern states had miscegenation laws. The definition of "Negro" in the Southern miscegenation laws ranged from "one-fourth or more Negro blood" to "Persons with any trace of Negro blood whatsoever." [1] As John T. Irwin points out, this latter formulation could apply to someone with only one-sixty-fourth Negro blood.[2] In Mississippi, a marriage was void when a white person had one-eighth or more Negro blood.[3] The result is clearly recognized in *Absalom, Absalom!* by Charles Bon, who says that in Mississippi "we even made the laws which declare that one eighth of a specified kind of blood shall outweigh seven eighths of another kind." [4] The laws of Mississippi also prohibited marriages of whites with Mongolians but allowed marriages with Indians. The prohibition was originally based on the belief that significant differences existed between races and that marriage across color lines would result in a "weakening of the dominant race." [5] The first legislation against black and white marriages was passed in Maryland as early as 1691 and was aimed at limiting the amorous activities of the freeborn. As late as the 1960's, punishment for miscegenation was thirty days in jail or a hundred dollar fine in Delaware, Florida, Indiana, Maryland, Mississippi, and North Carolina.[6] Davis K. of Ellisville, Mississippi, for example, was sentenced to five years in jail in 1949 for his marriage to a white girl, although he had lived his whole life as a white in the white section of town and he and his family had for seventy years been considered white. Although he had no Negroid features, owing to rumors of his black identity, he was tried and convicted.[7] In 1967, the bans against miscegenation in the South were finally lifted, Faulkner's Mississippi being their last bastion.

Mississippi celebrated its first legal mixed marriage in 1970 when a civil rights worker married a black woman in Jackson. If Faulkner had lived a few years longer, it is doubtful that he would have changed the very definite stand against racial assimilation he took at the University of Virginia in 1958:

> No sir, I don't think that would solve many problems. The same amount of bickering would go on and they would find another subject for it. I think that the only thing that that will solve that problem is not integration but equality.[8]

Faulkner, like his hero Ike, who is also a liberal Southerner with regard to race, is tolerant—but only to certain limits. When Roth's unnamed black mistress arrives with their mulatto son Ike, in "Delta Autumn," he supplicates her to go North and marry a black man. Unable to face the possibility of racial assimilation, Ike accepts its eventuality only at a time when he is sure to no longer be alive: *"Maybe in a thousand or two thousand years in America,"* he thought. *"But not now! Not now!"* [9] Faulkner's own position is very similar to his hero's when he envisions this possibility only in a very distant future in which he, too, is sure not to take part. Speaking to a group at the Tokyo American Cultural Center, Faulkner said "in a few hundred years the Negro in my country will vanish away. He will be assimilated into the white race simply because there are more white people." [10] In his interview with Russel Howe in 1956, he said despite its controversiality: "In the long view, the Negro race will vanish in three hundred years by intermarriage. It has happened to every racial minority everywhere, and it will happen here." [11]

Despite the author's reluctance to acknowledge outwardly the Southerner's responsibility, one is aware of the degree to which Faulkner condemns the white Southerner's destructive role in the miscegenetic relationship. In his writings Faulkner condemns it primarily because he considers it pernicious to the mulatto offspring. Although historians and sociologists alike have discussed at length the harmful effects of miscegenation on the white family, Faulkner, interestingly enough, makes no direct allusion to this very crucial historical factor. This failure can probably be best explained, at least in part, by his inherent misogyny. Faulkner was not sympathetic to the plight of the Southern white woman nor to the noxious consequences that her husband's wanderings had on his wife and his family. Rather, his sympathy toward the mulatto and his preoccupation with the disintegration of the slave (and particularly the black) family, can to a great extent be attributed once again to the guilt he may feel as an awakened Southerner.

Miscegenation among white men and Negro women frequently occurred in the cities of the Old and New South. The Negro population in the urban communities contained numerous mulattoes, partly as a result of race mixture there and partly because the Southern slave-holding fathers of mulatto children sometimes freed their offspring and sent them to the cities, if not to the North. Sexual relations between Negro men and white women were very infrequent and seriously discouraged. Such unions became the subject of special legislation. The abhorrence of the legislators toward these unions is noticeable from the language employed in the formation of these laws. The Virginia law of 1691 forbidding miscegenetive relationships reads as follows:

> ... and for the prevention of that abominable mixture and spurious issue which may hereafter increase in this dominion with English, or white women, as well as by their unlawful accompanying one another.[12]

In Southern society both white and the black women were relegated to second class citizenship. While the white male enjoyed a position of superiority, he assuaged his guilt-ridden dalliances with darker skinned women by isolating his wife on an illusory pedestal. The psychological dynamics of miscegenation within the white family are well expressed by Lillian Smith:

> The more trails the white man made to backyard cabins, the higher he raised his white wife on her pedestal when he returned to the big house. The higher the pedestal, the less he enjoyed her whom he had put there, for statues after all are only nice things to look at.[13]

Ellen's marriage to Sutpen in *Absalom, Absalom!* is one resembling this pattern. Ellen is socially, rather than morally or psychologically, placed on a pedestal by Sutpen; she is then also ignored. Ellen is described as "the stainless wife,"[14] "the epicene objet d'art"[15] who is likened to

> Niobe without tears who had conceived to the demon in a kind of nightmare, who even while alive had moved but without life and grieved but without weeping, who now had an air of tranquil and unwitting desolation, not as if she had either outlived the others or had died first, but as if she had never lived at all.[16]

However, the crucial difference between the Sutpen marriage and many other Southern marriages of the period is that Sutpen's journeys to backyard cabins occurred before, not during, his marriage to Ellen and had resulted in his prior marriage to the daughter of a Haitian sugar planter whom he had divorced upon learning of her Negro blood. Although Ellen is unhappy in her marriage, this unhappiness is due to the fact that it is a marriage of convenience, not that it is a marriage based on infidelity.

Ellen's great state of aggrievement was not uncommon during the pre-Civil War period. Her sister Southerners were almost systematically the victims of infidelity—often with a particular slave woman. Although miscegenation was seldom mentioned, it was widely practiced. One woman of the pre-Civil War period wrote bitterly, "under slavery we live surrounded by prostitutes." She continues, "any lady is ready to tell you who is the father of all the mulatto children in everybody's household but her own ... my disgust sometimes is boiling over." [17]

The divorce records of this period show that the treatment of women could at times be despicable. They show that the planters were capable of removing their wives momentarily from their pedestals and sometimes even brought their Negro slaves into the bedrooms, where they forced their wives to witness illicit copulation. One distressed North Carolinean wife sued for alimony in 1849 on the ground that her husband had not only "abandoned her bed" in order to bed "with Negro Lucy," but had also placed Lucy in full possession of the house, giving her authority over his wife while behaving towards Lucy as if she were his spouse.[18] Women sometimes retaliated by selling the slave or, in rare instances, by divorcing the husband. In other circumstances, the white woman sometimes sought vengeance on the slave mother's children, rather than directly on the slave. A few women avenged themselves by having sexual relations with black men. Although this form of vengeance was very rare, black men are mentioned in a number of nineteenth-century divorce cases, and some white men accused their wives of committing adultery with blacks. Two 1832 divorces in North Carolina even involved the birth of a mulatto child.[19] If the planter managed to placate his wife, it was only by giving her compensation of a material kind.

Despite the fact that in "The Bear" Hubert and Sophonsiba are only brother and sister, a similar situation arises in which the white female is placated in some material fashion for her brother's dalliance with a cook. Hubert has a weakness for a very light mulatto cook, who, consequently, takes advantage of the situation and dresses up in Sophonsiba's silk gown and jewelry until Sophonsiba insists that Hubert dismiss the cook. Elmer's father in "Elmer," once a widower, is also smitten by his mulatto cook. The fact that Faulkner limits this kind of situation to a brother-sister relationship and to a widower, instead of a marriage, demonstrates once again the degree to which the author seems indifferent to the plight of the white female. Additionally, Faulkner seems impervious to the fact that the white male was jeopardizing the white home and family by frequenting slave women.

By contrast, even though the author does not focus on the harm done to the slave couple by miscegenation, in "The Bear" he does show sympathy for Eunice, a slave purchased by Carothers and who is portrayed unquestionably as Carothers' victim. Her consequent suicide inevitably destroys both herself and her family.

The potentially explosive and debasing nature of these miscegenetic relationships within the context of slavery is additionally well demonstrated in *Absalom, Absalom!*, when Sutpen's choice of Clytemnestra's mother is compared to his choosing livestock. Speaking of Clytemnestra and another slave, Faulkner says that Sutpen "brought the two women deliberately; he probably chose them with the same care and shrewdness with which he chose the other livestock—the horses and mules and cattle—which he brought later on." [20] Faulkner's description of a young man riding up to beckon the watching overseer and to tell him to "Send me Juno or Missylena or Chlory," [21] as if the slaves were animals, reenforces the dehumanizing nature that relations between master and slave could assume.

The behavior of the whites toward the mulattoes broke up the white homes and the black homes. Yet, the deleterious consequences of miscegenetic relations were not limited only to whites and their Negro slaves. Miscegenation between Indians and the Negro slaves was also very frequent, and those families were equally disrupted, as exemplified in "A Justice" when Crawford takes a fancy to the wife of one of Doom's slaves. Although Doom later maneuvers to reunite the couple, the inhumane nature of these relations is underlined when Crawford takes the Negress slave, much to her husband's complete dismay, as if she were livestock or property and, furthermore, impregnates her.

In his treatment of slavery in relationship to miscegenation, Faulkner focuses mainly on the effects of these relationships on the mulatto offpsring. He would agree with Frederick Douglass that a mulatto child was disadvantaged in front of his white father because the child's presence alone activated the guilt which the white father wished to avoid, thus, according to Douglass:

> Men do not love those who remind them of their sins unless they have a mind to repent—and the mulatto child's face is a standing accusation against him who is the master and father to the child.[22]

Consequently, mulatto offspring were acknowledged more easily at a financial level than on an emotional one by their white fathers. In his will, Carothers, for instance, leaves a thousand dollars to Tomey's Turl who is concurrently his son and grandson, since leaving money *"was cheaper than saying My son to a nigger."*[23] Carothers' inherent rejection of his mulatto son is also accented by the fact that he gives the money "contemptuously, as he might cast off a hat or pair of shoes."[24] Since Tomey's Turl never asked for his inheritance, the claim devolves on his children by Tennie Beauchamp: Fonsiba, Lucas and James. The fact that Lucas is the only one who demands his inheritance and is motivated really by principle alone demonstrates Faulkner's point that, for the planter's black children and descendents, family love cannot generally be bartered for money. This refusal of a slave's inheritance is repeated again in "The Bear" when Thucydus Roskus refuses the land and money left him by Old Carothers.

In the Old South, money was often left to the Negro or mulatto concubine slaves or to mulatto offspring. In this case, Carothers leaves an inheritance to Eunice's husband, no doubt because he must feel, despite his callousness, some guilt and responsibility for the disintegration of Eunice's family. The fact that Tomey's offspring, with the exception of Lucas who stays and stubbornly defends his rights, either die or leave Yoknapatawpha County, is an indirect way in which the author maintains the dignity of the mulatto character by not allowing them to take part in the Southern system—a system which has, at best, allowed them to become only second-class citizens and family members. Faulkner clearly states, for example, that James Beauchamp leaves

Mississippi only because he wishes to remove himself from his familial and racial context:

> It was as though he had not only (as his sister was later to do) put running water between himself and the land of his mother's betrayal and his father's nameless birth, but he had interposed latitude and geography too, shaking from his feet forever the very dust of the land where his white ancestors could acknowledge or repudiate him from one day to another, according to his whim.[25]

Slaveowners who were either guilt-ridden or emotionally committed often provided for their concubine slaves and mulatto children in their wills. There was no guarantee of protection, however, because some states did not recognize that slaves could be legal heirs. In many wills no reference is made by the white man to his relationship to the slave; it is only by studying accompanying documents that the relationship to the slave woman or child can be discovered. Other slaves were kept in the white household to serve half brothers and sisters as privileged houseservants.

Theoretically, this connection gave to the mulatto child the advantages to be extracted from close association with the white parent and family. Elnora, in "There Was a Queen," who was probably also a slave, is the mulatto daughter of Colonel John Sartoris and the half sister and house servant of Bayard Sartoris. She also appears, although only as a house servant and not as a relative, in "All the Dead Pilots" and as a cook in *Sartoris* and *Flags in the Dust*. Elnora is given by her father, John, the privileged role of protectress in the house before he dies. Elnora, for example, thinking of Virginia du Pre says to herself: "I can take care of her," and continues "Because it's a Sartoris job. Cunnel knowed that when he died and tole me to take care of her. Tole me. Not no outsider from town."[26] This quotation gives evidence that, at least in the short story, Elnora was, in all probability, aware that she was part Sartoris. Clytemnestra, who is unquestionably originally a slave, is the daughter of Thomas Sutpen in *Absalom! Absalom!* and remains, even after his death, as a house servant. Sutpen's attitude toward Clytie is, by contrast to Sartoris', one of disdain and thorough indifference.

Finally, and again for emotional reasons, with priority given to them over the other slaves, the concubine slave women or slave progeny were often freed at the time of the master's death. The large number of mulattoes found among the free Negroes indicates that many planters freed their slaves or more specifically their concubine slaves and their mulatto offspring at the time of their deaths rather than condemn them to slavery or risk their being sold at the master's demise. In "The Bear," probably because of contrition towards Eunice, Old Carothers frees Thucydus Roskus and his parents, Roskus and Fibby; Eunice's husband; and her father and mother-in-law. Ironically, however, McCaslin does not free Tomey's Turl, his own child. The only logical explication for this seemingly irrational behavior is that Faulkner is trying to illustrate the very arbitrary nature with which the mulattoes are treated by their families.

Concubinage during the pre-Civil War period was not, however, limited to the planters and the slave women on the plantations. Miscegenation with concubines was a common practice in the cities among the white upper-class men and Negro women. By 1860, there were nearly a million free Negroes in the South. While only about ten percent of the slaves were mulattoes, as many as forty percent of the free Negroes were mulattoes.[27] In Charleston, in Mobile, and especially in New Orleans miscegenetive relations were so widespread that they began to take the form of a social institution, as described by Mr. Compson in *Absalom, Absalom!*:

> ... a situation in which probably all his contemporaries who could afford it were involved and which it would no more have occurred to him to mention to his bride or wife or to her family than he would have told them secrets of a fraternal organization.[28]

He continues that membership in this particular "fraternity" was "a situation which was as much a part of wealthy young New Orleansian's social and fashionable equipment as his dancing slippers."[29] Yet, despite the increasing sophistication and frequency of these relationships in the cities, historically, as well as in Faulkner's work, the result very often remains the same—the mulatto offspring is an alienated individual who belongs nowhere. In a certain sense, the mulatto slave progeny such as Tomey's Turl is able to accept his ambiguous social and family status much more easily than the evolved free Negroes such as Charles Bon or his son, Charles Etienne de Valery Bon, since the mulatto family member like Tomey's Turl tends to identify less with his white family than these more sophisticated mulattoes.

Charles Bon, son of Thomas Sutpen and a high mulatto daughter of a Haitian planter, is completely obsessed, for example, by a need for even the most minimal recognition from his father. Although in his Virginia interviews, the author claims that Bon's revenge is not personal revenge on his father, but vindication of his abandoned mother,[30] an examination of *Absalom, Absalom!* shows that Bon is also attempting to rectify the injustice done to him, personally, by his father. This is particularly well evidenced in the dramatic scene on the battlefield in *Absalom, Absalom!* where Bon tells Henry that he is going to marry Judith, despite Sutpen's opposition, since for the last four years Sutpen has refused him any recognition at all:

> *And he sent me word? He did not ask you to send me to him? No word to me, no word at all? That was all he had to do, now, today; four years ago or at anytime during the four years. That was all. He would not have needed to ask it, require it, of me. I would have offered it. I would have said, I will never see her again before he could have asked it of me. He did not have to do this, Henry. He didn't need to tell you I am a nigger to stop me. He could have stopped me without that, Henry.[31]*

Sutpen's unwillingness to recognize Charles Bon is the most egregious illustration in all of Faulkner's work of the mulatto rejected by a father. Yet, the author himself found this relationship typical of family relations generally in the South. He described the relationship between Sutpen and Bon as "a manifestation of general racism in the South," the epitome of "a constant general condition."[32] Sutpen's rejection of Bon results in the ultimate destruction of both his mulatto and white sons: Bon is killed by Henry, and Henry afterwards disappears and only returns home to the plantation to die. Olga Vickery perceptively states, apropos of *Absalom, Absalom!*: "The shadow of a Negro effectively separates brother from brother, son from father, lover from beloved."[33] In "Evangeline," the earlier short story version of *Absalom, Absalom!*, Henry kills Bon after he learns that he has married Judith, while in *Absalom, Absalom!*, he kills Bon before they marry. In both the short story and the novel the reason for Henry's killing Sutpen is the miscengenetic relationship rather than the incestuous one. This is simply expressed in *Absalom, Absalom!*: "So it's miscegenation, not the incest which you can't bear." [34] Henry's response of accepting incest before miscegenation is also not surprising when one considers even the serious legal penalties aforementioned, which are indicative of the Southerner's condemnation of the miscegenation between white and black men.

Charles Etienne de Saint Valery Bon, who is the son of Charles Bon with his octoroon mistress, is another example of a mulatto offspring who finds himself without roots and family. Years later Charles Etienne suddenly appears in Jefferson "with a face not old but without age, as if he had no childhood ... as if he had not been human born but instead created without agency of man or agony of woman and orphaned by no human agency." [35] This description of Charles Etienne, interestingly, resembles Faulkner's description of Charles Etienne's father whom he describes as " shadowy: a myth, a phantom something which they engendered and created whole themselves; some effluvium of Sutpen blood and character, as though as a man he did not exist at all." [36]

Charles Bon, furthermore, has

> for background the shadowy figure of a legal guardian rather than any parents—a personage who in the remote Mississippi of that time must have appeared almost phoenix-like, fullsprung from no childhood, born of no woman and impervious to time and, vanished, leaving no bones nor dust anywhere —[37]

> ... [he was] a mental and spiritual orphan whose fate it apparently was to exist in some limbo between where his corporeality was and his mentality and moral equipment desired to be—[38]

While Charles Bon is hurt by Thomas Sutpen's rejection, Charles Etienne suffers mainly from his father's absence since he is recognized by his father. When Charles Bon visits the mother, he, at least, bestows affection upon his son. Nor is there evidence that like Charles Bon, Charles Etienne is taught by his mother to dislike his father.

Yet, Charles Etienne still agonizes over both his orphaned state and his ambiguous racial identity. His emotional desolation is poignant when he stands despairingly near his father's grave in the cedar grove or later when he is orphaned in New Orleans and is brought back to the plantation by Clytie with whom he is unable to communicate since he cannot speak English. Similarly, his feelings of racial alienation are first awakened when Judith places him on a trundle bed beside herself and between Cytie who is sleeping on a pallet on the floor; she thereby reinforces the confusion of his identity:

> *You are not up here in this bed with me, where through no fault nor willinging of your own you should be, and you are not down here on the pallet floor with me, where through no fault nor willing of your own you must and will be, not through any fault or willing of our own who would not what we cannot.*[39]

Furthermore, he informs Grandfather Compson that he does not feel sure that Charles Bon is his father. Confronted with the problem of his personal identity and racial identity, Grandfather Compson can only propose that Charles Etienne leave and go to live among strangers where he can assume any identity he chooses. Yet, tragically, Compson at the same time realizes:"*Better that he were dead, better that he had never lived."* [40]

Even though Charles Etienne is distressed by his racial ambiguity, he is at the same time aware that his having one-sixteenth Negro blood requires him to identify more with his black aunt, Clytie, than with his white aunt, Judith, as suggested by the use of "we." He later reacts to the frustration of his mixed identity through violence, by attacking the Negroes involved in a dice game or picking fights with Negro stevedores and deckhands on steamboats or in city honky-tonks where they consider him to be white. In a similar way, he also fights with whites to whom he claims to be black. His systematic violence towards those who are alleged to be of the opposite color not only shows his racial confusion, frustration and obsession but also indicates his need to affirm an identity whether black or white and to belong at least to one group or the other. His marriage to a "coal black and ape-like woman"[41] may initially make one believe that he decides wholeheartedly to assume his black identity. However, the subsequent flinging of his marriage license in Judith's face and, more importantly, the fact that he "kennels" his wife to a slave cabin, as if she were an animal, and does not see her during the first year of marriage, again shows his ambivalence. Charles Etienne does not resent "his black blood so much as he denied the white." [42] He finally assumes a black identity not simply by default but mainly to make a statement in opposition to the racism of his whole family. In this way, like his father, he too revolts when he is not given the form of recognition that he deems part of his birthright.

Lastly, although Jim Bond, Charles Etienne's idiot son with his black wife, differs from his father and grandfather in that he is not the child of a high class mulatto woman, nor does he grow up in the sophisticated social atmosphere of New Orleans but instead at Sutpen's Hundred, he is very important on a symbolic level. Jim Bond is the epitome of a young man who is the *fin de race* and the paradigm of family disintegration. He is the symbol of the accursed result of the white men's abuse of the Negro woman; he is the black man's deserved revenge and Faulkner's indictment of white victimizers as best represented by Jim's great-grandfather, Thomas Sutpen.

Faulker's treatment of miscegenation and its negative consequences for family relationships, also involves the free quadroon women and their offspring in the major Southern cities. Arranged by their mothers, they sometimes became lifelong concubines to the white man. The duration of the relationship depending entirely on the white man's decision. Paid by him, they were in a sense the white man's free slaves and were obligated to devote themselves to their lord who bought them usually when they were around sixteen years old. Unable to marry these white men because of the miscegenation laws, yet beholden to them, the concubines were, as a result, prevented from forming other, more legitimate attachments with men of their own color should they desire to do so, unless, of course, they were released. Despite this tremendous limitation on their freedom, they were, not unlike the slave women, proud of the attention given them by upper-class men. In addition, these women often became very emotionally involved with their white squires to the point of bestowing upon them lifelong fidelity. In *Absalom, Absalom!*, they are referred to as

> the only true chaste women, not to say virgins, in America, and they remain true and faithful to the man and not merely until he dies or frees them, but until they die.[43]

Yet at the same time, a normal family life was completely ruled out for them and their children, except in the rare case when the white man lived exclusively with them.

The quadroon daughters, were presented to white society at affairs which resembled debutante balls. They were held weekly in the major Southern cities and the very high fee, at that time, of two dollars was required. The most famous of these balls was probably the one in New Orleans which took place during the pre-Civil War period in the Salle d'Orleans. Ironically, shortly after the Civil War the building became a convent to house Negro nuns and is presently a Hilton-like hotel.

The ball took place on Wednesday nights and its popularity was such that even the opera was obliged to close that night. The teenaged girls, elegantly attired in their Parisian finery, their clothes alone sometimes representing the mother's life savings, were escorted by their mothers who made a settlement for themselves and their daughters. The quadroon's value was determined by her attractiveness and by the number and prestigiousness of the other suitors she had had or might reasonably expect to have. If there was a problem of rivalry between the suitors, a duel was fought in order to determine who would buy her. These issues having been settled, the young gentlemen paid somewhere around two thousand dollars with which the quadroon could retire when the liaison terminated. He also installed her in a well furnished apartment. In *Absalom, Absalom!*, Faulkner describes this Southern system of concubinage:

> Creatures taken at childhood, culled and chosen and raised more carefully than any white girl, any nun, than any blooded mare even, by a person who gives them the unsleeping care and attention which no mother ever gives. For a price, of course, but a price offered and accepted or declined through a system more formal than any that white girls are sold under since they are more valuable as commodities than white girls, raised and trained to fulfill a woman's sole end and purpose; to love, to be beautiful, to direct; never to see a man's face hardly until brought to the ball and offered to and chosen by some man who in return, not can and not will but *must*, supply her with the surroundings proper in which to love and be beautiful and divert, and who must usually risk his life or at least his blood for the privilege.[44]

However, the author sympathizes with the quadroon whom he
describes as being

> the supreme apotheosis of chattelry, of human flesh bred of
> the two races for that sale—a corridor of doomed and tragic
> flower faces walled between the grim duenna row of old
> women and the elegant shapes of young men trim predatory
> and (at the moment) goatlike.[45]

He describes her as having a face like a "tragic magnolia." [46] and he
equally feels pity for her children whom he sympathizes with for
having slave status. Like Charles Etienne, who is a sixteenth black
rather than an eighth black, the octoroon children are described by the
author as being

> the child, the boy, sleeping in silk and lace to be sure yet
> complete chattel of him who, begetting him, owned him body
> and soul to sell (if he chose) like a calf or puppy or sheep.[47]

Although the octoroon or high mulatto child was certainly often
faced with insurmountable family and identity problems; it was very
unusual, barring financial difficulties, that he should be sold back into
slavery. Habitually, the octoroon girls did not become courtesans,
though Charles Bon's octoroon wife proves an exception. Instead, most
octoroons were sent to France or to the North where they could pass for
white. Although quadroon boys were sold into slavery or sent to work on
farms unless there was enough money to educate and send them abroad,
the octoroon boys, who were the offspring, almost inevitably, of
wealthy white Southern men, were educated and, like their sisters,
sent abroad. Although Charles Etienne is not actually sent abroad, he
is certainly raised by his mother as if he were a foreigner, speaking no
English when he moved to Sutpen's Hundred. Yet, Charles Bon's octoroon mistress and Charles Etienne, her son, like their historical counterparts, are well provided for financially.

In fact, the high mulatto concubines living in the lower South were
so well taken care of that laws were passed there, especially in
Louisiana, to limit the munificence of these more Latin and less puritanical whites toward their mulatto families. Being Catholic and
often of French or Spanish origin, these white men attached much less
stigma to concubinage. Although in Louisiana concubines and illegiti-

mates could not inherit under the law, this was usually circumvented by bequeathing the estate to some friend who had agreed to turn the property over to them. Finally, in Louisiana, an act of 1857 even prohibited the emancipation of mulatto children, as well as the inheritance of property.

Despite the fact that, like certain slaves, quadroons and octoroons, in particular, were well protected financially, they were still, though to a lesser degree, at the mercy of the white men as were their plantation sisters. Despite Charles Bon's mistress' stylish clothes, her parasols and her crystal bottles containing smelling salts and although Faulkner, admittedly for the first time, treats a mulatto woman with definite ridicule, she is still, like her quadroon sisters, the victim of the white men. In fact, when they became tired of their relationships with their octoroon mistresses, they often left them in order to marry white women of their own social class. Others maintained both a white and a Negro home and lived a double life which was sometimes discovered only after their deaths, as a consequence of careful examination of their wills. In any case, this form of concubinage was only available to the very wealthy Southerner and when discovered left both the white and the black family, particularly the former, jealous, uncertain and fragmented.

Considering the frequency of relations between white men and Negro women (Wendell Phillips spoke of the South as "one great brothel." [48]) it is interesting to cite the psychological reasons for miscegenation incisively offered by Sarah Patton Boyle in her work, *The Desegregated Heart*. Boyle explains the motivation for race mixture between the white men and the black women as follows:

> the lure of forbidden fruit, nostalgic memories of Negroes, economic pressure which drives Negro women to prostitution, greater secrecy because of segregated housing, and security against forced marriage.[49]

The "lure of the forbidden fruit" and the influence of nostalgic childhood memories is certainly exemplified in *Go Down, Moses* by Roth who is very attached to his surrogate mother, Molly, and who later finds a mulatto mistress as her substitute. Charles Bon is raised on a Haitian plantation and in New Orleans and later marries an octoroon. Charles Etienne is also raised in New Orleans and later by his mulatto half-sister, Clytemnestra, and afterwards marries a black woman. Both are examples of white men who, in all probability, were showered with affection and even breast-fed by their adoring mammies. Later, they were unable to extricate themselves from these maternal images and thus chose a woman who closely resembled their foster black mothers.

In the late nineteenth- and early twentieth-century South the white man's motivation for miscegeneration remained the same, and the double standard, completely advantageous to the white man, left him complete freedom of action. In some regions of the South, particularly those with a large Negro population, cohabitation of a white man with a Negro woman was considered a less serious breach of the racial code than illicit intercourse between a Negro man and a white woman. Even white prostitutes were not allowed to accept the business of black men. The double standard, which existed between the white man and both Negro and white women, also existed between the white man and the Negro man and is clearly shown by Jesus in "That Evening Sun" when he says: "I can't hang around white man's kitchen" and continues

> But white man can hang around mine. White man can come
> in my house, but I can't stop him. When white man want to
> come in my house, I ain't got no house. I can't stop him.[50]

W.E.B. Dubois in *Souls of Black Folk*, referring to both slavery and post-slavery, said that the white man had been responsible for the destruction of the Negro home: "the hereditary weight of a mass of corruption from white adulterers threaten[ed] almost the obliteration of the Negro home."[51] Unfortunately for the black man, the average Negress or mulatto was not insensitive to the attention of the white man and generally far preferred miscegenous relations with even a lower class and worthless white man to marriage with a black. The average mulatto of either sex considered union with a black degrading. In *Light in August*, for instance, the alleged mulatto Joe Christmas is already repulsed at fourteen by the Negro prostitute whom he beats after he finds himself "enclosed by the womanshenegro."[52]

While the frequency of relations between white men and Negro women has been uncontestable, the attraction between Negro men and white women has been controversial. Generally, however, miscegenetic

relations in the pre-Civil War period were infrequent. These relationships were usually prohibited not only by the laws regarding miscegenation and intermarriage but also by other laws and social taboos and
by severe punishment for their violation such as lynching, castration
and electrocution. In fact, Southern white men were fearful that having
deserted their white wives and left them like Penelope on their isolated pedestals, the black man, renown for his sexuality, could then
tempt them away from their lofty isolation. Wilbur Cash states that
fear of the black man's sexual potency resulted in the white man deliberately developing what was referred to as a "rape complex": the
white man projected the image of the Negro as a savage rapist in order
to soothe his guilt.[53] Norman Mailer suggests that the white man ra-
tionalizes his remorse with regard to his treatment of the black man by
convincing himself that, in reality, they have established among
themselves an equitable balance of power:

> The white man unconsciously feels that the balance had
> been kept, that the old arrangement was fair. The Negro had
> his sexual supremacy and the white had his white
> supremacy.[54]

The idealization of the white woman demeaned the black woman
in relationship to the black man and contributed negatively to the integrity of the black home. According to Calvin Hernton in *Sex and
Racism*, the black male pursued the white woman because of a feeling
of social deprivation. She was a status symbol who could reinforce his
sexual pride and serve as a form of vengeance on the woman of the civi-
lization which had reduced him to an inferior position.[55] Both Joe
Christmas, who in *Light in August* is apparently mulatto, and Charles
Bon in *Absalom, Absalom!* are definite illustrations of this psychology.
Both are social outcasts as a result of their families' rejection and are,
consequently, unable to belong anywhere. They both suffer from an ambiguous sexuality that manifests itself in Joe's case by his definite preference for male companionship, as well as by his hatred of women.
Charles Bon's sexuality is questionable as a result of his dandified
clothes and effeminate presence, but mainly through his homosexual
attachment to his half brother, Henry. Ironically, Faulkner seems to
need to compromise the sexuality of both these men in order to prevent

the consummation of even this act of assertion toward the white woman.

This theme of vengeance through the white woman is another element that is certainly observable, although indirectly, in the behavior of both Joe Christmas and Charles Bon. While Joe kills Joanna mainly because he resents her constant reminders of his supposed black identity, both Charles Bon's engagement and his marriage in "Evangeline" and *Absalom, Absalom!* represent his vengeance against his father, who refuses to recognize him because of his black blood. Hernton observes that the black man hates what he cannot have.[56] Christmas deeply hates Joanna, as becomes clear when, before having sex together, he tells her: "I'll show you! I'll show the bitch." [57] Charles also has a tremendous rancor for his father, and Judith is, by contrast, the vehicle through which he expresses it.

Finally, again as portrayed by Hernton, many white women who became involved in these relationships were latent or unconscious homosexuals.[58] Even though this is applicable to neither Judith nor to Elly, in the short story "Elly," it is an appropriate description of Joanna Burden who, until her relationship with Joe, was a middle-aged spinster whose masculinity is constantly alluded to and who is among Faulkner's most androgynous women. She is depicted as "manlike" [59] with "the mantrained muscles and the mantrained habit of thinking born of heritage and environment." [60] When Christmas has sexual relations with her, it was as if "he struggled physically with another man" [61] and he thinks to himself "'it was like I was the woman and she was the man.'" [62]

Not only are the relations between Negro men and white women important, but so are the sexual fantasies of white women involving black men. Unfulfilled by their white husbands, Southern women were frequently victims of sexual hysteria. John Dollard states that in a private correspondence Helene Deutsch, the psychiatrist, reported hysterical and strong masochistic fantasies among white female patients.[63] De Martino also reports among her white women patients dreams and fantasies of sexual intercourse with black men.[64]

In addition, black women who worked in white homes in the South have attested that the white mistress of the house was known to speak openly about her sexual frustrations and to show infinite curiosity with regard to the black woman's sexual experiences. A white woman in

Yoknapatawpha County, fantasizing about sexual relations with a black man is described in "Dry September," or in its earlier version, "Droath." [65] The story depicts another frustrated spinster, Minnie Cooper, who is "allegedly" assaulted, frightened or insulted by Will Mayes, a respected Negro watchman at the ice plant. The author makes it clear that Will Mayes' lynching is another manifestation of the unjust consequences which miscegenetic relations, in this case miscegenous fantasies, can bring upon the black man. The theme is also found in "Selvage" [66] and in its later and more developed version, "Elly," where fantasy becomes reality, and Elly kills her Louisiana mulatto lover, Paul de Montigny, and her grandmother in a car accident in order to prevent her grandmother from telling Elly's father about her miscegenous affair.

Finally, Hernton has also stated in *Sex and Racism* that women who become involved with black or mulatto men, besides having a homosexual side, also tend to have strong, domineering fathers,[67] such as Calvin Bundren or Elly's father. In "Mountain Victory," both Vatch and his father, exemplars of this overbearing white male, suspect the innocent Saucier Weddel of a miscegenous affair with their sister and daughter, respectively. Even though Weddel is part Indian and not black, and though he has no designs on the young girl, he and his slave are killed by Vatch and his father. Faulkner depicts the Southerner as prepared to defend the illusion of white womanhood and simultaneously reinforce his supremacy as a white male—whether the fantasy or the reality of her womanhood is being protected is a matter of little relevance. The consequent exploitation results not only in a weakening of the black man's self esteem but in the reinforcement of his debilitated position within the black family and within society in general. In short we see that Faulkner has once again sided strongly with the black or mulatto male whom he portrays as the arbitrary victim of white society.

The white man's most effective means of curbing relations between black men and white women was lynching: extra-legal mob action against a victim, customarily a Negro or mulatto, and usually with the justification of "protection of white women." [68] All of Faulkner's lynch victims or near-lynch victims are dark skinned with the exception of Lee Goodwin. In fact, by 1935 lynchings in the South exclusively involved Negroes. Lynching was not considered murder and lynchers went unpunished. The highest incidence of lynching was in Mississippi and Georgia and it occurred mainly in small towns, like Jefferson. When Faulkner was only eleven a murder similar to Joanna Burden's occurred and must have marked him. A white woman, named Mrs. Mattie McMillan, living like Joanna Burden outside of the town, had her throat cut from ear to ear by a Negro man using a razor. The main difference between the two murders was that Nelse Patton, Mrs. McMillan's Negro assaulter, was drunk. Patton was arrested and before he could be tried a mob of several hundred rushed to the jail and dug through the walls until they reached the cell. His ears were cut off, he was scalped, his testicles were cut off, and his body was dragged around the street. He was finally hung on a tree outside the courthouse.[69]

Issues of sex and/or racism were almost always involved in lynching, and this is demonstrated systematically throughout Faulkner's work: in the near lynching of Lucas Beauchamp in *Intruder in the Dust*, in the quasi-lynching of Joe Christmas in *Light in August*, or in the actual lynching of Rider in "Pantaloon in Black," of Will Mayes in "Dry September," or of Lee Goodwin in *Sanctuary*. Although Joe Christmas' mutilation and castration at the hands of Percy Grimm in *Light in August* is not technically a lynching, since there is no mob scene, it resembles one in every other way. Percy Grimm's attack on Christmas is particularly important not only because race and sex are involved, but because, exceptionally and significantly, religion is also involved. The lynching had now come to incorporate all the major Southern prejudices: race, sex and religion, each of which acts to undermine the Southerner, both white and black, and ultimately impairs his functioning within a familial context. Percy Grimm regards himself as the instrument of God, the pawn being moved by the Player, and speaks in the "clear and outraged" voice of "a young priest."[70] While castrating the dying Christmas, Grimm informs him, "Now you'll let white women alone, even in hell."[71] The union of race, sex, and religion is all the more embodied in Christmas' grandfather, Hines, who would also like to have lynched him and who sees himself as a part of God's "purpose and His vengeance,"[72] as his instrument to avenge the "bitchery and abomination"[73] which is considered to be associated with Christmas' existence.

Lynching was usually carried out by the lower classes as illustrated by Percy Grimm in a quasi-lynching scene in *Light in August*, the Birdsongs in "Pantaloon in Black," John McLendon in "Dry September" or Lee Goodwin in *Sanctuary*. The mutilation that often accompanied lynching is important in that it can be seen as an ironic manifestation of the white Southerner's guilt feelings for violating Negro women. It is also an act of defense against the Negro's presumed sexual superiority. Yet, Lillian Smith, who in *Killers of the Dream*, according to Nancy M. Tischler, views the "lynching ritual as a sort of Dixie version of the old Bacchic rites" [74] offers an alternative explanation: she believes that the Negro becomes the scapegoat for the white man's hate or a receptacle for his hidden sexual feelings.[75] As Gunnar Myrdal points out, lynching was more an expression of the Southern fear of Negro progress than of Negro crime.[76] Blacks were lynched and mutilated for looking at, speaking to, or whistling at white women, or unintentionally rubbing against them on the street. Lynching could also occur when Negroes or mulattoes were only suspected of sexual affairs which they had not even committed, as indicated by Will Mayes in "Dry September." Yet, when a woman was known to acquiesce to these sexual relations with a Negro or mulatto, as Joanna Burden is considered to have done, and provided that murder was not involved, the usual procedure was to waylay the couple, whip the Negro and force them both from town.

The outrage of lynching was addressed during World War I by a group of church women who formed the Association of Southern Women for the Prevention of Lynching. They took action against a series of violent lynchings of that period, maintaining that the Southern white women had not asked for protection against Negro men. That the white woman did not actually need protection against the black man was probably true. However, equally defensible, or at least understandable, is John Dollard's position concerning white women and Negro men presented in *Caste and Class in a Southern Town*: Dollard states quite perceptively that, despite the injustice of the racial taboos and punishments, if there was no chance of an attraction of significant importance on the part of the white women toward the Negroes, the white Southerner would never have gone to the excessive lengths he did to forbid these relationships.[77] Barring sexual attraction, these miscegenetic affairs were generally based on feelings of guilt as well, typified by Joanna Burden in *Light in August*, who had been indoctrinated since her youth in her father's Calvinism. Her giving herself to Christmas whom she considers to be her black "God-phallus" is certainly in part her way, at least subconsciously, of atoning for the guilt that she inherited from her father with respect to slavery and racism.

Even though lynchings involving sexual mutilation were still reported as late as 1965, as of the 1950s Southern violence had for the most part taken on a less fatal form; lynchings were replaced by house bombings, abductions and floggings. Yet, the existence of lynching at all, and particularly its acceptance by twentieth-century Southern society, shows to what degree the psycho-sexual male-female relations were unbalanced and why family relations inevitably suffered.

The critics, quite erroneously, seem rather systematically to consider Faulkner a racist with regard to his treatment of the mulatto and miscegenation. For them, Faulkner becomes a modern Wendell Phillips who, like other abolitionists, viewed miscegenation with extreme disgust. This is well illustrated by Charles I. Glicksberg, Maxwell Geismar, Melvin Seiden and Irving Howe. Charles Glicksberg in "William Faulkner and the Negro Problem" writes that

> No Faulkner novel is complete without its compounded plot of horror, seduction, illegitimate children, rape, incest, perversion, but overriding all these elements is the theme of Negro blood as a source of defilement, in the horror-haunted mind of Faulkner but also in the collective mind of the South.[78]

Maxwell Geismar continues:

> So we see, just as Faulkner was punishing the Northern women in *Light in August*, now he threatens the entire western hemisphere with the rape of the Negro. And what better images, after all, could the artist have found to express his discontent—the great hatred of the entire complex of modern northern industrial society—than the Negro and the Female? The emancipated Negro who to the Southern writer is the cause of the destruction of all he held dear. And now showing the Negro as Joe Christmas, as Jim Bond, as the inhuman criminal, the degenerate who will dominate the civilization which freed him, Faulkner proclaims at once his anger and his revenge upon those who have destroyed his home. What more appropriate symbol than the woman who to the Southern writer is the particular treasured image of the bygone, cavalier society that he is lamenting and lost in: the Southern Lady, elevated and sacrosanct, the central figure of

the southern age of chivalry, of those gallant agrarian knights
who, very much like Quixote, went forth in 1861 to perish in
combat with the dynamo.[79]

According to Geismar, Faulkner's use of miscegenation is additionally:

the last step in his sequence of discontent: Faulkner makes
the female with the Negro, the savage for whom the Southern
lady was sacrificed, and spawns out of his modern union the
colored degenerate who is reign supreme, the moronic em-
peror of the future.[80]

Melvin Seiden in "Faulkner's Ambiguous Negro" further examines what
he calls "Faulkner's lurid racist theme" in *Absalom, Absalom!*
Faulkner's treatment of Clytie, says Seiden, is "exactly what the liberal who suspects him of racism would expect," while Charles Bon is

a figure who seems to remain in Faulkner what he has always
been in popular fiction and cinema: the enemy within, the
alien who must destroy us all, the scourge who must be made
a victim.[81]

Finally, in Irving Howe's article, despite the fact that he too believes
that Faulkner feels menaced by the threat of miscegenation, he, at
least, sees that the author is not without pity for his coffee-colored
brother:

Mulattoes are living agents of the "threat" of miscegenation,
a "threat" which seems most to disturb Faulkner whenever
he is most sympathetic to the Negro. All rationalizations for
his prejudice having crumbled, there remains only an inherited fear of blood-mixture. The more Faulkner abandons the
"ideas" of the folk mind in relation to Negroes, the more does
he find himself struggling with the deeper phobias of the folk
mind. In two of the novels where miscegenation is a major
theme, *Light in August* and *Absalom, Absalom!* it arouses a
painfully twisted response.[82]

Faulkner is presented by the critics as condemning miscegenation.
As an emancipated Southerner, Faulkner would only fit the critics' description if a family member or a close friend becomes sexually involved
with a Negro or mulatto. Despite his relative acceptance of miscegen-

eration, the author places a large enough distance between himself, his close environment, and the black or mulatto, that the possibility of miscegenous relations occurring would seem remote, if not impossible. Since he views his black, if not his brown brothers, from an Olympian point of view, he is generally able to react spontaneously and with the compassion they deserve. Faulkner maintains very conservative, if not completely wrong, notions about miscegenetic relations causing sterility and about the degrees of black and white blood determining behavior. Contrary to the critics' assertions, he continues to be conflicted but, still for his time, liberal in his view of miscegenous relations. He will, however, simultaneously depict the mulatto, with little deviation from the mulatto archetypes and patterns, as the dark scapegoat of their families and white society.

Faulkner's beliefs regarding sterility are particularly relevant because they demonstrate to what extent even the most open-minded Southerner still remains, despite himself, a prisoner of his education and upbringing. In Sherwood Anderson's memoirs, Anderson quotes Faulkner as telling him quite seriously that the cross between the white man and Negro woman always resulted after the first crossing in sterility. He speaks of "the cross between the jack and the mare that produced the mule and [said] that, as between the white man and the Negro woman, it was just the same." [83]

Faulkner's attitudes toward sterility are probably best illustrated in "The Old People" and Sam Fathers whom he describes as follows:

> The old man past seventy whose grandfathers had owned the land and long before the white man ever saw it and who vanished from it now with all their kind, what blood they left behind them running now in another race and for a while even in bondage and now drawing toward the end of its alien and irrevocable course, barren, since Sam Fathers had no children.[84]

When Sam collapses after the death of Old Ben, he is described as "the wild man not even one generation from the woods, childless, kinless, peopleless." [85]

In the same way that Faulkner believes miscegenation between a white man and Negro woman results in sterility, he also contends that a mulatto is influenced positively by his white blood and negatively by his black blood. In one case, and according to the lawyer Gavin Stevens

in *Light in August,* Joe Christmas not only suffers from the psychological conflict common to those of mixed identity, but he is without any *li-
bre-arbitre* and is purely at the mercy of the blood battle within himself:

> Because the black blood drove him first to the Negro cabin.
> And then the white blood drove him out of there, as it was the
> black blood which snatched up the pistol and the white blood
> which would not let him fire it. And it was the white blood
> which sent him to the minister, which rising in him for the last
> and final time, sent him against all reason and all reality, into
> the embrace of a chimera, a blind faith in something read in
> a printed Book. Then I believe that the white blood deserted
> him for the moment. Just a second, a flicker, allowing the
> black to rise in its final moment and make him turn upon that
> on which he had postulated his hope of salvation. It was the
> black blood which swept him by his own desire beyond the
> aid of any man, swept him up into the ecstasy out of a black
> jungle where life has already ceased before the heart stops
> and death is desire and fulfillment. And then the black blood
> failed him again, as it must have in crises all his life. He did
> not kill the minister. He merely struck him with the pistol and
> ran on and crouched behind the table and defied the black
> blood for the last time, as he had been defying it for thirty
> years. He crouched behind that overturned table and let
> them shoot him to death, with that loaded and unfired pistol
> in his hand.[86]

Much later, in 1958, in his essay "A Word to Virginians" which
was an appeal to Virginia to lead the South in what Faulkner viewed
as the only pragmatic position in the integration crisis, he reiterates
his views of many years earlier regarding the influence of black and
white blood upon an individual. The author states the following:

> Perhaps the Negro is not yet capable of more than second-
> class citizenship. His tragedy may be that so far he is compe-
> tent for equality only in the ration of his white blood.[87]

Before examining the author's later depiction of miscegenation
and its consequences upon familial relations in the nineteenth- and
twentieth-century South, it is important to consider Faulkner's mulatto
portrayals in relation to the standard mulatto psychological

archetypes and patterns. One sees that Faulkner's mulattoes, though conforming to these psychological patterns, also suffer a particular form of family rejection which is not of negligible importance.

Everett V. Stonequist in *A Study of Personality and Cultural Conflict* compares the anomalous position of immigrants, Jews and "mulattoes"; he stresses the "profound, inner conflict" suffered by the latter group which, in this case, includes many who could "pass" as either white or black.[88] Charles H. Nolan's *The Negroes' Image in the South: The Anatomy of White Supremacy* and Winthrop D. Jordan's *White over Black: American Attitudes toward the Negros, 1550-1812* continue to stress the conflicts confronted by the mulatto or half-breed and add that he tends to be more violent, treacherous and suicidal.[89]

Stonequist's, Nolan's and Jordan's conviction that mulattos are troubled is systematically demonstrated by Joe Christmas, Charles Bon or Charles Etienne, or, in *Go Down, Moses*, by Lucas McCaslin or Sam Fathers. In each of these cases the anguish they experience is related to their ambiguous racial identity for which they have been cast out by their families. Because his grandfather, Hines, considers Christmas a bastard with black blood, initially he rejects him and places him in an orphanage where he becomes familyless. Joe, never certain of his identity, spends the remainder of his life attempting with great difficulty to develop one. Charles Bon, also rejected by his father because of his black blood, obsessively devotes himself to achieving paternal recognition. His son, Charles Etienne, is repudiated as an equal by his Aunt Judith. Having been made aware of his ambiguous racial identity, he attempts to resolve his conflict by denying his white identity through marriage with a black. Similarly, in "The Fire and the Hearth," even though Zack's behavior is condoned by the racial codes, he alienates his black cousin, Lucas, by keeping his wife for six months in the house. Lucas is not only a mulatto but also a McCaslin and, as a result of his discord with his wife, he attempts to shoot Zack because he believes that his cousin has taken sexual advantage of Molly. Lucas realizes that murder would have resulted in a lynching entailing a hanging, or a lynching where burning by coal oil is also involved:

> *I would have paid. I would have waited for the rope, even the coal oil. I would have paid. So I reckon I ain't got old Carother's blood for nothing, after all. Old Carothers, he thought, I needed him and he came and even spoke for me.*[90]

Lastly, Sam Fathers' conflict is best described in the following quotation where his discord should be interpreted purely on a psychological level:

> Not betrayed by the black blood and not wilfully betrayed by his mother, but betrayed by her all the same, who had bequeathed him not only the blood of slaves but even a little of the very blood which had enslaved it; himself his own battleground, the scene of his own vanquishment and the mausoleum of his defeat.[91]

Like many of Faulkner's other mulattoes, Sam is also alienated from his family because his father, Doom, sells him and his quadroon mother to Carothers McCaslin. Thus, because of his black blood, Sam is forced to grow up fatherless like Charles Bon or Joe Christmas. This additional mixture of Indian blood only reinforces and extends "the battleground" of his racial torment. Faulkner's depiction of the search for acceptance is a sympathetic and in that sense, a liberal view.

Nolan and Jordan's observation that the mulatto also tends to be violent, treacherous and suicidal is also found in Sterling Brown's archetypal tragic male mulatto. In Sterling Brown's *The Negro in American Fiction*, the author claims that there are two archetypal mulattoes: one male, one female. The first involves the male tragic mulatto who kills someone close to him and in turn dies. In this male or Cain myth, the "tragic" mulatto begins in isolation unable to identify with either the white or black groups. Since he cannot resolve this conflict he releases his frustration in the murder of a close family member such as a brother. His own violent death usually follows the murder and he is either killed in retribution or by suicide—if not, he finds himself an exile: homeless, wifeless and childless. While the tragic male archetype represents psychological fragmentation, the female archetype primarily involves social justice. The female tragic mulatto is not fraught with inner conflict but because of her black blood is faced with the difficulty of social acceptance when marriage is involved. Often, her forthcoming marriage results in the disclosure of racial mixture and is followed by her exile and death.[92]

Roth's mistress in "Delta Autumn" is an example of the less complex tragic female mulatto archetype. The problem of racial identity is the key motivating factor in Christmas' behavior. He kills Joanna, who replaces the brother figure in that she, in her own way, is certainly the person that Christmas is closest to. The suicide element is also present when Christmas courts his own lynching by going into Mottesville in broad daylight. By contrast, Charles Bon is more concerned with parental recognition than racial identification. Yet, he too fits the tragic male mulatto pattern, although by inversion: rather than killing his half-brother, Henry, Bon is killed by him. A suicidal element is still suggested in that he too sets himself up for his death. Likewise, although Lucas, in "The Fire and the Hearth," is not fragmented by his racial identity but rather by his male identity, he is only saved from his archetypal destiny by a misfire. He has every intention of killing his cousin Zack, the substitute brother-figure, and also seriously contemplates killing himself. Finally, in *Intruder in the Dust* one finds him "living alone in the house, solitary kinless." [93]

Sam Fathers like Joe Christmas is "the battleground" and "the mausoleum" of his fated identity conflict. Although he does not kill it, Sam Fathers hunts the bear, who is, at least in metaphorical terms, the brother figure, being the one who most resembles Sam. In the same way that Sam is isolated like "something looked upon after a long time in a preservative bath in a mausoleum" [94] the bear is also a lonely anachronism who has outlived his time:

> the old bear had earned a name, and through which ran not even a mortal beast but an anachronism indomitable and invincible out of an old dead time, a phantom, epitome and apotheosis of the old wild life which the little puny humans swarmed and hacked at in a fury of abhorence and fear like pygmies about the ankles of a drowsing elephant; the old bear, solitary, indomitable, and alone; widowered childless and absolved of mortality—old Priam reft of his old wife and outlived all his sons. [95]

Furthermore by hunting the bear, Sam, like Christmas, involves himself in a very self-destructive act. Sam is first wounded and then asks Boon to kill him; his death is marked by elements of attempted murder and suicide. On the one hand, he is partly killed by the bear while trying to destroy it, on the other, he is murdered by Boon. In each case, like Christmas and Bon, he has sought his own death.

Lastly, Roth's mistress is aware that her mixed blood will necessarily exclude her marriage to Roth, who is also her relative: " ' But not marriage,' Ike says, 'Not marriage. He didn't promise you that. Don't lie to me. He didn't have to.' " [96] She responds:

> No. He didn't have to. I didn't ask him to. I knew what I was doing. I knew that to begin with, long before honor I imagine he called it told him the time had come to tell me in so many words what his code I suppose he would call it would forbid him forever to do.[97]

When Roth no longer wants to see her, she must exile herself. So Faulkner's mulatto characters generally show many similarities to Brown's tragic mulatto archetype, the major elaboration being that not only male mulattoes but also female mulattoes must work out their destinies in relation to a family member, not just an outsider.

The critics have, for the most part, misinterpreted Faulkner's attitude toward miscegenation and the mulatto. The author's mulattoes, apart from family exploitation, remain generally faithful to the archetypes and patterns. Faulkner continues, as in his earlier portrayals, to link the problems of racial and family identity with solitude and rejection. Despite his attempt to evade it, he portrays the white Southerner as being overwhelmed by the initial guilt regarding slavery and victimization and its consequent effects on his mulatto brother.

Joe Christmas is undebatably the most complex example of a mulatto faced with the problem of racial identity. Charles Bon or Charles Etienne, is forced into family estrangement because of alleged black blood. Joe's problem, however, is more serious than Faulkner's other heroes in that he is uncertain whether he is black or white. This is indicated when Christmas is a very young boy at the orphanage and the Negro gardener tells him quite brutally: "You are worse than that [a nigger]. You don't know what you are. And more than that, you won't never know." [98] In the original manuscript, Faulkner describes Christmas as being black; in this version, Christmas reveals that he knew little about his parents, "Except that one of them was a nigger." [99] When Faulkner typed the line, he added the racial ambiguity: "Except that one of them was part nigger." [100] Faulkner, said of Joe Christmas that he is in "the most tragic condition that an individual can have—to not know who he was." [101] Since he is without family or identity, "his only salvation in order to live with himself is to repudiate mankind, to live outside the human race." [102] Alfred Kazin refers to him as "the most solitary character in American literature." [103]

While many critics indicate that a solution to his dilemma lies in an acceptance of his black identity, some even saying that he achieves this when he wears the Negro shoes, it is John Lewis Longley, Jr., who perceptively states that, contrary to what certain of the critics may feel, the author never really gives him this choice: he is classified as a white man.[104] Already when he is at the orphanage, the dietician says of Christmas: *"He will look just like a pea in a pan full of coffee beans."* [105] This prediction proves true in that Negroes always seem to view him as "whiteman" [106] or "whitefolks." [107] Yet Joe, like Charles Etienne and the other non-fictional mulattoes, despite the fact that he too looks like a "phantom, a spirit" [108] or that he is "a shadow," [109] desires, if possible, to assume his white identity. This is underlined by Christmas, himself, when he goes to the white section of town: "'That's all I wanted,' he thought. 'That don't seem like a whole lot to ask.'" [110] Christmas remembers how he, like Charles Etienne, had once tricked or teased white men into calling him Negro in order to fight them or beat them or be beaten by them. In like fashion he fought the Negro who called him white. As noted by Melvin Backman, Christmas hopes, through violence, to break out of his aloneness.[111] His other attempt at resolving his racial identity problem—and, again one notes his similarity to Charles Etienne—is to become involved with a woman who "resembled an ebony carving," [112] with whom he lives rather than marries, and through whom he hopes to achieve a black identity. Ultimately, Christmas' identity problem, is not only a problem for himself, but also, although to a more limited degree, for the others. The people of Mottesville are only reassured by what is definable, and thus have difficulty in accepting Christmas' racial ambiguity: "He never acted like either a nigger or a white man. That was it. That was what made folks so mad." [113]

The complexity of Christmas' racial problem is increased because elements of sex and religion are also intermeshed. Regarding sex, the hero has been confronted since childhood with negative experiences when sex and race are intertwined; thus, he is faced not only with the dilemma of racial identity but also with that of defining himself sexually. His first contact with sex is when he is spurned by the dietician as

a "nigger bastard," [114] when accidentally he discovers her making love
or when he refuses to accept the money she offers him. His second experience with sex is equally repellent to him and involves a Negro woman
in the shed. After he has sexual relations with her, he vomits. Afterwards, Bobbie, who is his first girlfriend, tells her friends that Joe is a
Negro after Joe has exposed her to Simon McEachern's denunciation of
her as a whore. His Negro identity is also associated with sex when
Joanna is excited erotically by the fact that Joe is part Negro; she
wildly screams out "Negro! Negro! Negro!" [115] Joe's sexual identity is
again connected to his racial identity at the time of his lynching. It is
not surprising then that our hero becomes a complete misogynist and is
reassured only by a male presence where he can, at least temporarily,
suspend his sexuality, that force which inevitably seems to aggravate
his racial ambiguity. When fighting with other males he is solaced,
for example, by the absence of the female.

> Then it was male he smelled, they smelled; somewhere be-
> neath it in the She scuttling, screaming. They trampled and
> swayed, striking at whatever hand or body touched, until they
> all went down in a mass, he underneath. Yet he still struggled,
> fighting, weeping. There was no She at all now. They just
> fought; it was if a wind had blown among them, hard and
> clean.[116]

Joe later continues that:

> Perhaps he was thinking then how he and the man could al-
> ways count upon one another, depend upon one another; that
> it was the woman who was unpredictable.[117]

Joe's problems of sexual and racial identity are also accentuated by
religion. Melvin Backman accurately notes that Christmas as a child is
already "the victim of his grandfather's pathological religion of
white supremacy." [118] As he grows up, Simon McEachern, his adopted
father, teaches Joe to correlate sex and sin. As an adult, Christmas, who
is already the victim of his sexual and racial identity, is unable to accept the added religious dimension that acts to underline his black
identity. Consequently, when Joanna, the white object of his sexuality,
asks him to pray with her, he reacts by killing her. Finally, the lynch-

ing scene again demonstrates the inseparable association of sex, race and religion as forces in Christmas' search for identity.

Christmas is a unique example in Faulkner's work of an alleged mulatto so overcome by racial problems that his family problems become peripheral. The only similar example, although to a lesser degree, is Sam Fathers. Like Christmas, Sam is alienated from his family and becomes preoccupied with the more extended identity problems related to race, rather than the interpersonal ones stemming from interfamily relationships. Yet, while Christmas is confronted primarily with the enigma of his identity, Sam deals with the problem of being in a world where the Indians no longer exist; he is a racial solitary. Even in the post-Civil War period Sam would have found himself in Mississippi without any Indian compatriots. Although scattered Chickasaw families were still moving to Indian territory as late as 1850, by 1839 almost all of the Indians were out of the country. In fact, the United States Bureau of the Census report for 1860 claims that at the beginning of the Civil War, there were no Indians living in Faulkner's territory, Lafayette county.[119]

Yet, Sam is faced with a second problem that is common to Joe Christmas as well as to the author's other mulattoes. Sam identifies with his Indian blood, not his black blood, in the same way the others are proud of their white blood rather than their black blood. Actually, the number of Indians of mixed blood, like Sam, was large during the later part of the nineteenth century. The Indian Commission received 24,635 applications for registration from Indians east of the Mississippi, of which only 2,335 were accepted.[120] Dabney concludes that of the thousands of rejected applicants, most must have been largely of mixed blood.[121] Sam, like other literary and historical mulattoes, is forced to accept the lower status of Negro. Like these others, he must cope with his mixed identity and the isolation it entails:

> *And he was glad, he told himself. He was old. He had no children, no people, none of his blood anywhere above earth that he would ever meet again. And even if he were to, he could not have touched it, spoken to it, because for seventy years now he had had to be a negro. It was almost over now and he was glad.*[122]

Despite the crippling effect of racial prejudice, Faulkner also shows that the mulatto may still take great pride in the cultural heritage of the lighter family member, whether Indian or white, with whom he identifies. Yet, simultaneously the presence of this family member can at times be an additional source of alienation. Faulkner stresses that these familiar relationships tend generally to be unilateral and the mulatto is, in any case, almost inevitably a prisoner of his destiny. Finally, it is only during periods of tremendous hardship that the barriers between the mulatto and his family are transcended.

Despite the ambivalence felt by the mulatto, both Sam Fathers in "The Old People" and Jobacker in "The Bear" take pride in their Indian parents. While Sam is "still the son of that Chickasaw chief and the negroes knew it," [123] Boon "who on occasion resented with his hard and furious fists the imitation of one single drop of alien blood," usually after whiskey, "affirmed with the same fists and the same fury that his father had been the full-blood Chickasaw and even a chief and that even his mother had been the only half-white." [124]

Not aware of McCaslin's incest, Lucas in "Fire and the Hearth" and again in *Intruder in the Dust* is possibly the mulatto who shows the most visible family esteem. In "Fire and the Hearth," he tells Zack quite simply "I'm a nigger" and continues "But I'm a man too. I'm more than just a man. The same thing made my pappy that made your grandmaw," [125] and proceeds to tell Zack that he is coming to take Molly back. Before taking revenge on Zack for his alleged sexual relations with Molly, he refers to himself as "Old Carothers." [126] His revenge, as previously stated, is strongly linked to his idolization of his white family. In the later novel, *Intruder in the Dust*, Lucas continues the adulation of his white family, as exemplified by his encounter with the young men at the saw mill to whom he haughtily announces: "I ain't a Edmonds. I don't belong to these new folks. I belongs to the old lot. I'm a McCaslin." [127] In *Intruder in the Dust* Lucas also carries with great self-satisfaction the heavy gold watch chain, the gold toothpick and the worn beaver hat belonging to his grandfather. Despite his glorification of Old Carothers, when he is directly confronted by a white relative such as Zack, he becomes much more self-conscious, and his cousin acts as a mirror reflecting his racial alienation:

> I am not looking at a face older than mine and which has
> seen and winnowed more, but a man most of whose blood

was pure ten thousand years when my own anonymous be-ginnings became mixed enough to produce me.[128]

The veneration shown by Lucas with regard to his white family, in general, and his grandfather specifically, is also seen in Elnora in "There Was a Queen" and Clytemnestra in *Absalom, Absalom!*. Both Elnora and Clytie devote themselves to their white families. While Elnora takes charge of the entire Sartoris household, Clytemnestra is equally the backbone of Sutpen's Hundred. Each also has a certain superciliousness in connection to her white family. Elnora, makes the distinction between Narcissa and Virginia Du Pre. She insists that the young woman "won't never be a Sartoris woman," [129] because she lacks the quality of a woman of Virginia Du Pre's caliber. She further elaborates on the nature of that quality which, as a Sartoris, she understands instinctively. She explains that "Born Sartoris or born quality of any kind ain't *is*, it's *does*." [130]

In a like manner Clytie considers herself a member of the Sutpen family. Her snobbishness is, however, more acute. This can probably be best understood by the fact that Clytemnestra is never given the recognition by Thomas Sutpen that John Sartoris gives his mulatto daughter. Sutpen favors his white children on his return from the war. Instead of the kisses he gives Judith, he barely acknowledges his mulatto daughter; his only comment to her is "Well, Clytie." [131] Clytie, herself, rendered insecure by her father, needs to affirm her family status, which she does by asserting her relative social power over Negroes or poor whites—those who by the Southern social codes are her inferiors. When she finds Charles Etienne playing with a Negro boy, she becomes very angry with her nephew and curses the Negro boy out of sight. Likewise, she bars the kitchen door to Wash and tells him very emphatically that, "You ain't never crossed this door while Colonel was here and you ain't going to cross it now." [132]

Faulkner shows that the mulatto, whether Indian or white, is a prisoner of his destiny. For example, Sam, the author insists, "He was born in the cage and has been in it all his life; he knows nothing else." [133] Faulkner views Joe Christmas in much the same way:

It had been a paved street, where going should be fast. It had made a circle and he is still inside of it. Though during the last seven days he has had no paved street, yet he has trav-

elled further than in all the thirty years before. And yet he is
still inside the circle.[134]

The only means for a mulatto to escape his racial imprisonment
and its subsequent family complexities and prejudice is in circumstances
where society and the white family are committed to priorities other
than racial prejudice. In *Absalom, Absalom!*, because of poverty after
the Civil War, Rosa notes that racial and, more specifically, family
barriers have been broken down:

> We grew and tended and harvested with our own hands the
> food we ate, made and worked that garden just as we cooked
> and ate the food which came out of it: with no distinction
> among the three of us of age or color but just as to who could
> build this fire or stir this pot or weed this bed ... It was as
> though we were one being, interchangeable and indiscrimi-
> nate, which kept that garden growing ... [135]

Faulkner's treatment of miscegenation and of the widespread psychological exploitation of the mulatto progeny in the Southern society
need to be examined in relation to the key theme of the white Southerner's guilt. Both the enlightened Southerner and Faulkner feel the
same culpability and responsibility with regard to the Southern past.
Faulkner believes, like Calvin Bundren in *Light in August*, that the
white Southerner is the recipient of "the curse which God put on the
whole race" and he furthermore describes the black race as:

> doomed and cursed to be forever and ever a part of the white
> race's doom and curse for its sins. Remember that. His doom
> and his curse. Forever and ever. Mine. Your mother's. Yours,
> even though you are a child.[136]

The same guilt that Calvin Bundren perceives is transposed onto family
relations and developed in *Absalom, Absalom!* in relationship to Sutpen's mulatto daughter, Clytie.

Clytemnestra, unlike her Greek counterpart in the *Orestia*, seeks
neither revenge nor passive vengeance. Instead, she dedicates her life
entirely to her white relatives and to her father's plantation, Sutpen's
Hundred. But according to Rosa Coldfield, who in this novel is representative of the guilt ridden Southerner and white relative, her dis-

tant mulatto relative's behavior does not stem from gratitude. In Rosa's opinion, Clytie refuses her freedom and remains on the plantation, in order to serve as witness and passive avenger of the old world, like her ancient namesake. Rosa describes Clytie as "already there, rock-like and firm and antedating time and house and doom." [137] Rosa continues to allude to "her sphinx face," [138] implying that Clytemnestra knows the historical verity. She concludes that Clytie declines her freedom in order to avenge slavery: "to be that from which its purpose had been to emancipate her, she deliberately remained to represent the threatful portent of the old." [139] Although referred to as Ruby, Clytemnestra's role of witness and passive avenger is even more clearly delineated in "Evangeline" when, after the house is set on fire, one is told that Ruby

> came through and she leaned for a moment in the window, her hands on the burning ledge, looking no bigger than a doll, as impervious as an effigy of bronze, serene, dynamic, musing in the foreground of Holocaust.[140]

The guilt that the white family member is obliged to assume is also suggested when he is touched physically by the mulatto. The white individual is repulsed by the mulatto because the mulatto kin (in this case, Clytie and Charles Etienne) serve as living reminders to the lighter family members of racial sin and guilt. Their touch is thus equated with verity and this truth is the reality that the white Southerner chooses to avoid. Rosa Coldfield in *Absalom, Absalom!* claims the following:

> *Because there is something in the touch of flesh with flesh which abrogates, cuts sharp and straight across the clarions intricate channels of decorous ordering, which enemies as well as lovers know because it makes them both—touch and touch of that which is the citadel of the central I—Am's private own: not spirit, the liquorish and ungirdled mind is anyone's to take in any darkened hallway of this earthly tenement. But let flesh touch with flesh, and watch the fall of all the eggshell shibboleth of caste and color too.[141]*

The repulsion that Rosa experiences when touched by Clytie is similar to the aversion of Judith when she comes in physical contact with her nephew, Charles Etienne. Charles Etienne is:

aware of the woman on the bed whose every look and action
toward him, whose every touch of the capable hand seemed
at the moment of touching his body to lose all warmth and
become imbued with the cold implacable antipathy.[142]

Despite the mulatto's very fragile and weakened position,
Faulkner tries at all times to maintain his hero's dignity. When Lucas
attempts to kill Zack in "Fire and the Hearth," the author has the
cousin admit that despite the racial codes, Zack has taken advantage
of the situation: " ' I tell you! Don't ask too much of me!' *I was wrong,*
the white man thought. *I have gone too far.*" [143] This same anguish,
reminiscent of her slave relatives, makes Roth's mistress want to deny
the money he offers her as a substitute for love. Yet, regardless of the
author's desire to have his characters transcend their racial and familiar circumstances they remain, almost without fail, their victim. Furthermore, Faulkner demonstrates that comingled with the white man's
culpability is self-hatred, even when this occurs on a subconscious level.
The white Southerner's self-abasement is usually directed as rancor
toward the mulatto or Negro, who thus becomes the white man's scapegoat. The malevolence directed against the white man's darker brother
evolves into abhorrence of others as well as into greater self-hatred
and he, like Sam Fathers, becomes "contemptuous . . . of all blood black,
white, yellow or red, including his own." [144]

Faulkner's overwhelming preoccupation with miscegenation and
the mulatto's plight comes to an abrupt halt with the publication of
Requiem for a Nun in 1951. This is also true with regard to Faulkner's
other novels published during the 1950s. In *The Fable, The Town* and
The Mansion there is no reference to miscegenation and the mulatto. At
this time Faulkner had reached a much more tranquil phase in his own
family life, and this is reflected by the absence of this theme in his
work. With the publication of *The Reivers,* however, the mulatto
reappears in the form of Ned McCaslin and Boon Hogganbeck, but this
time the mulatto family member is a totally integrated and contented
individual; he is no longer fragmented by his racial and family identity.

In Faulkner's last novel, *The Reivers,* the white family, contrary
to Uncle Buddy in "Was," is no longer gambling over a mulatto half
brother, but instead is betting on more conventional stakes such as cars

and horses. Ned McCaslin, the Priests' coachman and mulatto relative, though not given equal family status by Faulkner because of his own Southern ambivalence, is nevertheless treated by the family with particular respect because he is one of their kin. Mrs. Priest refers to him as "Uncle Ned" and insists that her four sons do likewise since he is what she describes as their "family skeleton." [145] Ned, like Lucas McCaslin, is also proud of his white ancestry:

> that his mother had been the natural daughter of old Lucius
> Quintus Carothers himself and a Negro slave; never did Ned
> let any of us forget that he, along with Cousin Isaac, was an
> actual grandson to old time-honored Lancaster where we
> moiling Edmondses and Priests, even though three of us—
> you, me and my grandfather—were named for him, were di-
> minishing connections and hangers-on.[146]

In fact, when Ned needs to give himself strength, not unlike the way Lucas repeats Old Carothers' name in "Fire and the Hearth," he repeats his name *"Ned William McCaslin"* [147] in order to affirm his family identity. Meanwhile Boon is no longer an example of the tragic-mulatto vanishing-Indian myth.[148] While in *Go Down, Moses*, Boon is as childless as Sam or Isaac, in *The Reivers* he marries and becomes the proud father of a son. Boon is at last the contented mulatto Indian who is integrated on a social, racial and familial level: " —Jefferson, McCaslin, DeSpain, Compson—were not just home but fathers and mothers both." [149] Lastly, the integration of both Ned McCaslin and Boon Hogganbeck into the white family and society shows that the author has evolved since his work of the fifties and is now able to incorporate, although with restrictions, even the mulatto into his familial and societal environment. Faulkner's increasingly optimistic vision once again coincides with his more stable home environment.

The critics judgment is that Faulkner is threatened by his mulatto brothers. Yet, close evaluation of his work over time shows instead that he is sympathetic to the mulatto. As an enlightened Southerner and tortured Puritan, he even takes his responsibility in the South's collective guilt. Miscegenous relations in both the Old and the New South destroyed both the white and black home. The misogyny that Faulkner feels toward the Southern white woman, the remorse evoked by his Southern puritanical conscience for his black, and especially mulatto, brothers cause him to be concerned with the dissolution of the black and mulatto homes resulting from these interracial sexual relations, rather than with the white families. He exposes the black and the mulatto as the scapegoats of Southern society, a subject which is explored by Olga Vickery in "Southern, White, and Elect." [150] The black and, particularly, the mulattoes and their families are undermined by the double standard established by the white Southerner. This leaves the mulatto without an identity, an isolated prisoner of his mixed heritage. Throughout the major part of his work Faulkner shows the futility of their plight. Although his work of the 1950s and 1960s shows a definite evolution, and in spite of the fact that the mulatto's position within the context of the white family is certainly improved by the time of his last novel, *The Reivers*, color still bars the mulatto from an equal position with his white kin.

CHAPTER 7

The Black Family and the Foster Family

Faulkner's treatment of the Negro family, both slave and free, is understood most clearly in its socio-historical framework and as a function of the author's liberal but still limited and ambivalent attitude as a Southerner. Although Faulkner, whom James Baldwin not unjustly referred to as the "Squire of Oxford," [1] empathizes with the Negro and portrays him realistically in his familial context, the Negro is relegated, however sympathetically, and almost without exception, to slavery or to the rural middle class. Faulkner's black families, whether the Strothers of *Sartoris, The Unvanquished* and "There Was a Queen;" the Gibsons of *The Sound and the Fury*; the Beauchamps in *Go Down, Moses;* or even the Sanders in *Intruder in the Dust,* are all tightly knit groups that offer unremitting support to their white employers. They are frequently stronger psychologically than those they must serve. The duality of the two races is resolved only in *The Reivers,* in which the Priests and Parshams become symbolically interchangeable—but not because Faulkner's political views have become more liberal. On the contrary, in his own life he has become the contented, conservative grandfather who is consequently less preoccupied with racial problems and appears now to have transcended them.

In order to realistically examine Faulkner's Negro families, one must first understand the author's racial position within its Southern context. Faulkner was a product of Mississippi, certainly among the most conservative of the Southern states. Immediately following the Civil War, Mississippi was the first Southern state to enact the Black

Codes. These laws forbade any Negro to vote, to keep firearms, or to "make insulting gestures," and stipulated that any Negro over eighteen who was without employment could be declared a vagrant, fined fifty dollars, and turned over to any "master or mistress." [2] This open bigotry came to mark contemporary Mississippi. Not until 1964, for example, did the federal courts force integration in the schools, and not until 1969 were a large number of Negroes attending schools with whites. Even then five-sixths of black school children were still in all black schools; complete integration of the schools went into effect only in 1970.[3] The University of Mississippi during the 1970's had only about three hundred black undergraduates and law students out of an enrollment of eight thousand.[4]

It is not surprising then that William Faulkner, a strong proponent of equality, was considered by many of his fellow Mississippians a "nigger lover," [5] or that even his own family never agreed with what they considered to be his "liberal" view.[6] Faulkner likened the racial problem to a "cancer" [7] and considered it "an outrageous, an anomalous condition that simply cannot continue." [8] He believed that "for peaceful coexistence all must be one thing, either all first-class citizens or all second-class citizens, either all people or all horses, either all cats or all dogs." [9] To "live anywhere in the world of A.D. 1955 and to be against equality because of race or color is like living in Alaska and being against snow." [10] Although Faulkner would agree with Robert Penn Warren that "race prejudice . . . ain't our hate; it's the hate hung on us by the old folks dead and gone," [11] and that the South is a prisoner of its own history, the Mississippian would also agree with Gavin Stevens when he tells Chick Mallison in *Intruder in the Dust* that Southerners must assume responsibility for this injustice: "I only say that injustice is ours, the South's. We must expiate and abolish it ourselves, alone and without help." [12]

Faulkner finds that the root of racial prejudice and injustice is economic and that the Southerner is mainly desirous of maintaining the status quo and limiting Negro advancement for economic reasons. The author, like any other liberal Southerner, is not without guilt with regard to his Southern heritage. It is this feeling which makes him regularly portray Negro families as more laudable than their white patrons:

He's [the black man] calmer, wiser, more stable than the white man. To have put up with this situation so long with so little violence shows a sort of greatness. With a little more social, economic, and educational equality the Negro will often be the landlord and the white man will be working for him.[13]

Even though the writer, like Quentin Compson, understands the subtlety and complexity of the Negro's predicament—conscious that "a nigger is not a person as much as a form of behavior,"[14] aware that the Negro is in some sense the white man's projection and, consequently, dependent on the white's perception of his identity—it can be argued that Faulkner defended his black brother more avidly prior to 1955 than after it. His early advocacy can be seen in letters to the *Memphis Commercial Appeal* in which he attacked the injustices suffered by Negroes in Southern courts or ardently criticized the segregated school system.[15]

Though he was still a believer in equality and integration, statements made in Japan in 1955 show that the author had begun to qualify his position, now stressing that equality for the Negro must be a gradual process.[16] The Nagano Conference marks the beginning of Faulkner's very definite stand as a Southerner,[17] anticipating the interview with Russel Warren Howe in which he maintained that as long as there was a middle road he would stay on it, "but if it came to fighting, I'd fight for Mississippi against the United States."[18] Despite the fact that the author later retracted this statement on the basis that he had been drinking, his more conservative Southern side makes one question to what degree his loyalties were not really deeply and primarily to the white South first. Furthermore, in the Howe interview, as well as in the 1956 essays in *Life* and *Ebony* magazines,[19] Faulkner states his opposition to compulsory integration and urges a "go slow" policy in devising the civil rights programs. It was also in 1956 that, for the first time, Faulkner's attitudes were attacked by both liberals and Negroes, their position best summarized by James Baldwin's criticism of a "middle-road" policy.[20]

This conservative trend continues into 1957, when Faulkner expresses relief that the Eisenhower administration's Civil Rights Bill was not passed. In 1958, while still evincing a desire for equality, Faulkner declared himself emphatically against racial assimilation as a solution to the problem of integration. Initially a fervent supporter of the National Association for the Advancement of Colored People (NAACP), by 1960 he deems the organization too liberal for the needs of black Southerners. Faulkner here is best described as having become a tired and "retired" liberal who, in spite of second thoughts, feels a deep bond with the black man, whom he recognizes as being an integral part of his life and heritage.

Given the complexity of Faulkner's racial position, it is easier to understand the ambivalence with which he views slavery and, specifically, the slave family. Darwin T. Turner in his article "Faulkner and Slavery" draws the perspicacious conclusion that while Faulkner is certainly a strong opponent of slavery in theory, he seems not to have seen the system as deleterious to the slave in practice.[21] This observation is sustained throughout the author's work with the exception of *Go Down, Moses* in which, although the damage done to a slave family is only alluded to, it is still significant. Eunice is a slave girl pregnant with Carothers McCaslin's child when she marries Thucydides, another slave. McCaslin also impregnates their daughter Tomasina, and when Eunice learns of her daughter's pregnancy on Christmas day, she drowns herself. Historically, sexual relations between masters and slave women are believed to have occurred frequently. Although incest coupled with miscegenation was certainly not frequent, it was probably more common than might be imagined.

Faulkner constantly criticizes the evils of slavery until the publication of *Intruder in the Dust* in 1948, when he no longer concerns himself with the problem. In "The Bear," for example, the author says that slavery was "founded on injustice and erected by ruthless rapacity and carried on even yet with at times downright savagery."[22] Nevertheless, Faulkner gives no depiction in his work of the physical brutality, of the whippings and brandings to which black slaves were subjected. Instead, in "Was," Tomey's Turl, the slave half brother of Buck and Buddy, repeatedly runs away to visit Tennie, a female slave whom he loves. This captured fugitive becomes part of a burlesque game of escape and capture with his half brother, Buck, rather than a victim of the intolerable injustices of slavery.

The author's basically contradictory attitude toward slavery is also illustrated by the way his characters behave once given their freedom. With the exception of Loosh in *The Unvanquished*, who is disparagingly conveyed as a rebellious black and who claims "I don't belong to John Sartoris now; I belong to me and God," [23] freed slaves choose to remain with their masters. This choice is exemplified in *Go Down, Moses* by Rocius and Phoebe, a husband and wife who are slaves of Old Carothers and who are freed upon his death in 1837 yet refuse to leave; or by Percival Brownlee, a slave incapable of work who, when Theophilus McCaslin tries to free him, refuses. In *The Unvanquished* other examples of slaves who want to retain the status quo are Louvinia and Joby, who despite the war's end wish to remain with the Sartoris family, just as Caroline Barr and Ned Barnett, who belonged to the Falkners prior to the Civil War, also chose to remain with them. As with the majority of Faulkner's characters, for Ned Barnett the Emancipation Proclamation changed nothing; he insisted that it "never took effect as far as he was concerned . . . that he never was freed because he just refused to be freed." [24]

The most striking illustration of a slave's emotional attachment and devotion to his master is probably Pomp's attitude toward Hightower's grandfather in *Light in August*. Following his master's death, it is rumored that Pomp is inconsolable and has consequently disappeared from the bivouac. Like Rider in "Pantaloon in Black," Pomp cares so deeply that he is incapable of accepting the death which confronts him: " 'No suh,' " he would say. " ' Not Marse Gail, Not him. Dey wouldn't *dare* to kill a Hightower. Dey wouldn't *dare*. Dey got 'im hid somewhar.' " [25]

Theoretically at least, Faulkner understands slavery as "the curse" which plagues the South. Rosa Coldfield feels that there is a "fatality and curse on the South" as well as on her own family, as though some ancestor of hers "had elected to establish his descent in a land primed for fatality and already cursed with it." [26] It is this same fatality which alters the relationship between Roth Edmonds and his "foster brother" Henry Beauchamp: "The old course of his fathers, the old haughty ancestral pride based not on any value but on accident of geography, stemmed not from courage and honor but from wrong and shame." [27] In "The Bear," Ike sees the plantation system as anathematized and cries to Fonsiba's husband, "Don't you see? This whole land, the whole South is cursed, and all of us who derive from it, whom it ever suckled, white and black both, be under the curse?" [28]

When asked about the recurrent theme of "the curse of the South" in his fiction, Faulkner replied that, "the curse is slavery, which is an intolerable condition. No man shall be enslaved and the South has got to work the curse out." [29] Faulkner, like Joanna Burden, is incapable of self-absolution; through his heroine, he even shows his fear of potential retribution on the part of the Negro:

> I thought of all the children coming forever and ever into the world, white, with the black shadow already falling upon them before they drew breath. And I seemed to see the black shadow in the shape of the cross. And it seemed like the white babies were struggling, even though they drew breath to escape from the shadow that was not only upon them but beneath them too, flung out like their arms were flung out, as if nailed to the cross. I saw all the little babies that would ever be in the world, the ones not even born—a long line of them with their arms spread, on their black crosses. [30]

It is instructive to consider slavery and the slave family in their socio-historical context because the family patterns that the Negroes were forced to establish during bondage were those which set the precedent for later black family patterns. Ironically, the slave family was to have a greater influence on nineteenth- and twentieth-century urban black Southern families than on their rural counterparts. On the other hand, the free Negro families bore a closer resemblance to the rural black Southern families of which the Faulknerian families were part.

Generally, slave masters wanted to keep slave families together because it was definitely to their advantage not to incite their slaves to revolt. In the late antebellum period several states even moved to forbid the division of mother and child; however, Louisiana seems to have been the only state successful in achieving this end. As late as 1855 there was already a petition, for example, before the North Carolina Legislature requesting

> that the parental relation . . . be acknowledged and protected . . . ; and that the separation of parents from their young children, say of twelve years and under, be strictly forbidden, under heavy pains and penalties. [31]

Despite the efforts made to protect the Southern slave family, the slave family in Latin America was much better protected because its members, as decreed by the Catholic Church, could not be separated.

Herbert Gutman points out that in the United States only one in four slave couples reported long marriages.[32] The slave wedding itself varied from a primitive ritual of jumping over a broomstick to a serious ceremony conducted by a white minister. When the slave families were not separated, the women tended to have children with the same mate, and these marriages were in fact solidified by the arrival of children. Weddings followed most prenuptial slave pregnancies, as it was important for the slave woman to have a husband before the child's birth. Fidelity was expected of slave men and women, providing of course there was no interference from white masters.

Although the emotional basis of such unions may be difficult to determine, Thomas Jefferson in his *Notes on Virginia*, after careful examination of his own slaves, deduced that they are amorous, but incapable of love.[33] The Virginian's conclusion may have been based to a large extent on his inherent prejudices as a Southerner. In *The Unvanquished* the two slave couples, Louvinia and Joby and their son, Loosh, and his wife, Philadelphy, seem to be couples whose marriages have a solid emotional basis. The solidity of the marriage of Louvinia and Joby is shown not only by their harmony, but by the unity of attitude that they manifest in discouraging their son's liberalism. When Loosh tells them that the North is going to free the blacks, Joby tells him to be quiet, and Louvinia hits him. Furthermore, when Loosh has left with the family silver, Louvinia tells Granny Millard to "tell them niggers to send Loosh to you, and you tell him to get that chest and them mules, and then you whup him!"[34] In the younger couple, Philadelphy, contrary to Jefferson's beliefs, shows a deep sense of love for her husband, as demonstrated by the fact that she follows him off the plantation despite her realization that freedom for them is synonymous with drowning "in homemade Jordan."[35] Profound affection in a slave couple is illustrated by Cinthy's relationship to her husband, Pomp, in *Light in August*. Since she cares for him with intense emotion, Cinthy is unable to believe the rumor of his death and waits endlessly for his return.

The slave couple was not patriarchal because the male had no economic leverage. On the contrary, like the later urban black family, the slave family was matriarchal because the woman for numerous reasons was in the advantaged position. Although she was primarily important as a breeder, she was also generally more valued than the male slave because her usefulness lasted longer. When she was no longer prized as a breeder or houseslave, she could always serve as a cook or mammy to white children or other slave children. The nature of black-white relations bestowed preferential attention onto the slave woman for other reasons as well. Hildreth asserted this point in 1854, when she wrote the following passage about the slave woman:

> Among the slaves, a woman, apart from mere natural bash-fulness, has no inducement to be chaste; she has many in-ducements the other way. Her person is her only means of purchasing favors, indulgences, presents. To be favorite of the master or one of his sons, of the overseer, or even of a driver, is an object of desire, and a situation of dignity. It is as much esteemed among the slaves as an advantageous mar-riage would be among the free . . . [36]

While the female slave was capable of raising herself to a privileged relationship with white men, the slave man remained "Tennie's Jim" without any identity of his own. Furthermore, if children were to be sold, the younger ones remained, in general, with the mother rather than with the father. Finally, slaveowners very often reinforced the primary position of the woman by installing her with the children in a cabin and distributing food to her, thereby undermining the father's control over his family.

Traditionally, the slave mother has been unjustly represented as being devoted solely to her white wards and showing complete indif-ference to her own progeny. The preferential treatment shown to her white charges was attributed to the fact that she spent more time with them, while her neglect of her own young was explained by the fact that she associated them with the pain of pregnancy and childbirth. Even if a slave mother devoted herself to the white children, this did not indicate, of course, that she did not also care deeply for her own family, as shown by Eunice and Louvinia.

By contrast, consider the dynamics of the free Negro family which was more like a white family in the sense that it, too, was patriarchal. Ironically, the free Negro male wielded even more power as a husband than the corresponding white male, but in contrast to the slave mother, the free Negress had no power and was often purchased by her spouse from slavery along with her children. Even though the marriages of free Negroes were generally quite stable and their family patterns usu-ally resembled those of the whites, there is evidence that if the relationship was troubled the husband tended to sell the wife back into slavery.

Before discussing Faulkner's twentieth-century black families, one ought to examine more closely his portrait of the Negro generally, which not surprisingly often reflects the complexity and ambivalence in his position on race and slavery. Many critics take issue with this viewpoint, consider Faulkner's character portrayals individualistic, realistic, and sympathetic, and with few exceptions ignore their complexity. Charles Nilon asserts that "perhaps the most distinctive thing about Faulkner's creation of Negro characters is his destruction of the Negro stereotype . . . Faulkner's characters are individuals." [37] Hugh Gloster would agree with Nilon, and, though he declares that Faulkner's depiction tends to be pessimistic, he says of the author that he has an "enlightened approach to the representation of the Negro character" and that "he views Southern society with a steady eye, portraying both races without the traditional preconceptions." [38] Irving Howe, also, sees Faulkner's Negroes as depicted with imagination and at the same time with an empathetic and realistic attitude:

> No other American novelist has watched the Negroes so carefully and patiently; none other has listened with such fidelity to the nuances of their speech and recorded them with such skill; none other has exposed his imagination so freely, to discover, at whatever pain or discomfort, their meaning for American life.[39]

An especially significant appreciation of the intricacy of Faulkner's attitude is that made by Ralph Ellison who considers that Faulkner has, in fact, not rejected the Negro stereotype but has instead incorporated it and later transcended it:

> Faulkner's attitude is mixed. Taking his cue from the Southern mentality in which the Negro is often dissociated into a malignant stereotype (the bad nigger) on the one hand and a benign stereotype (the good nigger) on the other, most often Faulkner presents characters embodying both . . . As for the Negro minority, he [Faulkner] has been more willing perhaps than any other artist to start with the stereotype, accept it as true, and then seek out the human truth which it hides.[40]

Although Faulkner does transcend the traditional stereotypes of good and bad "niggers," his Negro, with few exceptions, is not given a very distinctive identity. It is probably Edmond Volpe who comes closest to perceiving the problem with the greatest incisiveness when he says that "chief Negro characters [of Faulkner's fiction] are delineated with skill and respect for their individuality and character, but most of the other hundred or so Negroes are renditions of traditional Negro stereotypes." [41] One must qualify even Volpe's statement by adding that major Negro characters such as Nancy Mannigoe or Joe Christmas tend to be depicted as larger than life and, though certainly not stereotyped, tend for this reason not to be realistic. This distortion can probably be explained by Faulkner's difficulty in conceiving a Negro in a situation demanding a more intricate response than the simplistic one expected from a devoted domestic such as Ned Barnett or Caroline Barr, whom Faulkner had always known. Janet Pieper, whose position most closely resembles Volpe's, astutely likens Faulkner's Negroes to Henry James' "moveable backdrop." [42] For James,

> each of these persons is but wheels to the coach; neither belongs to the body of the vehicle, or is for a moment accommodated with a seat inside. There the subject alone is ensconced, in the form of its "hero and heroine," and of the privileged high officials, say, who ride with the king and queen. They run beside the coach "for all they are worth," they may cling to it till they are out of breath (as poor Miss Stackpole all so vividly does), but neither, all the while, so much as gets her foot on the step, neither ceases for a moment to tread the dusty road. [43]

Most of Faulkner's Negro characters are not only stereotypes but exist mainly as a function of the role in which they serve the white people surrounding them, specifically the families for which they work.

Faulkner's Yoknapatawpha County is populated by more blacks than whites; there are 9,313 blacks versus 6,298 whites, [44] though black people identified by a family name or a first name are limited to 160 out of over 1200. [45] The author's black characters are almost inevitably middle class, according at least to the class divisions established within black society. The exception is E.E. Peebles, Joanna Bundren's Memphis lawyer, who is probably the only upper-class black in Faulkner's work. Hortense Powdermaker in *After Freedom: A Cultural*

Study of the Deep South has classified Negro professional people of Faulkner's period—teachers, lawyers, education officials, doctors—as all belonging to the upper class. Otherwise, the upper class consisted also of Negro businessmen, landowners, and employers. The black middle-class was comprised of sharecroppers, renters, domestic servants and even manual laborers. This class included a few shopkeepers and most of the ministers. Those belonging to the lower class not only were poorer, but generally had no source of steady employment and depended on occasional odd jobs, relief, or charity.[46]

In Faulkner's work, black characters are usually domestically employed; they are typically cooks, nurses, carriage drivers, or stable employees. Otherwise, they tend to be janitors, porters, or livestock tenders. Among the minor characters there are also a band leader and two ministers: Brother Bedenberry, leader of the revival meeting in *Light in August,* and Reverend Stegog, the St. Louis preacher in *The Sound and the Fury* at Dilsey Gibson's church on Easter Sunday.

Interestingly, the majority of female servants are referred to only by their first names, names such as Callie, Chlory, Cinthy, Dicey, Leonora, Euphronia (Frony), Quester (also called Paralee), Leonara, Louvinia, Mandy, Philadelphia ('Philadelphy'), Pinkie, Sister Rachel, Rosie, Roxanne, and Thisbe. The even more numerous male servants, coachmen, janitors, body servants, and field hands are also referred to only by first names like Abe, Ash, Clefus, Ephriam, Ephum, Grover, Hump, Houston, Isham, Isom, Jake, Fingus, Job, Joby, John Henry, John Paul, Jonas, Jubal, Ludus, Marengo (Ringo), Mose, Oliver, Pomp, Samson, Secretary, Simon, Tobe, Top, and Versh. Many of these characters do not even have last names, unless they adopt the last name of the white people for whom they work, as the Beauchamps do.

Notwithstanding the fact that the number of black doctors, lawyers, teachers, businessmen and landowners do not constitute a majority, those belonging to the South's black upper-class are still very much in existence and growing. Although in Faulkner's time talented Negroes, because of opportunity, tended to go North, there remained in the South many more, proportionally, than the select few who appear in the author's work. Horace Judson explains this phenomenon by Faulkner's limited contact with the diverse strata of black society:

> Faulkner did not know everything about the South ... at least about the new South. He knew few Negroes well, and no

civil rights leaders at all, except in briefest acquaintance. He
never understood (or anyway portrayed) the urban and educated Negroes that have been the spearhead of the civil
rights fight.[47]

Judson is right in that Faulkner was mainly in contact with the
middle-class Negroes of Oxford or the rural Negroes serving his family. Even though Faulkner sent Norfleet, the son of his Negro laundress,
to college in Atlanta[48] and also knew affluent Negroes like Rob Boles,
who owned a shoe-repair shop and considerable property in Lafayette
County,[49] it is revealing that Faulkner makes no allusion to this
group. Faulkner's silence implies that, despite his liberal theories,
when confronted with any Negro of equivalent social standing, the author reflected his own education and experience as a Southerner and
proved incapable, regardless of the sympathy he might feel, of accepting him as a peer. The limitations of Faulkner's black characteriza-
tions extend most significantly to his black families. Since the author
really can accept only the black middle and lower class with which he
has been familiar since childhood and to which he feels socially superior, the Negro families depicted in his work do not overstep the bounds
of this rural middle class.

From a sociological standpoint, however, it is the urban middle
class that has drawn the most attention. Traditionally, historians and
sociologists have taken the stand that the urban black family as described by Hortense Powdermaker is a "maternal family." [50] The theory
of "black matriarchy" was first conceived in 1939 by Franklin E. Frazier, who concluded that the black female dominated the black male
because of his historically weak economic position. Frazier relied on
data which showed a higher incidence of female-headed households
in which the husband was more often present among blacks than in corresponding white households.[51] Other researchers such as Kenneth
Clark or Lee Rainwater have echoed this finding.[52] The thesis was
probably most vehemently supported by Daniel Patrick Moynihan,
who claimed in 1965 that female-dominated and thus dysfunctional
households lay at the center of widespread family disorganization and
pathology in lower-income black communities.[53]

Although revisionist specialists of the 1970's and 1980's, such as
Jerold Heiss, Arnold H. Taylor, and Herbert Gutman have written to re-
fute this theory, it is currently controversial. According to John Heiss in

The Case of the Black Family: A Sociological Inquiry, despite the fact that the dynamics of black and white family life are not identical, there are many similarities. The families are particularly comparable when related by age of marriage and family size. Heiss refutes the earlier theories that black families are more matriarchal than white ones.[54] Arnold H. Taylor contends in *Travail and Triumph; Black Life and Culture in the South since the Civil War* that in the lower-class black family the role of the man as the principal bread-winner conforms to national and regional patterns. He adds that the overwhelming majority of single-parent families among blacks which are headed by a woman results from widowhood, desertion, divorce, or unmarried motherhood, widowhood accounting for most of the single-parent families among the black Southerners.[55]

Finally, Herbert Gutman states in *The Black Family in Slavery and Freedom, 1750-1925* that most rural and urban Southern blacks in 1880 lived in husband- or father-present households and subfamilies, even though there was a large enough percentage of father-absent households and subfamilies to deserve special attention. Gutman considers, however, that many historians and sociologists exaggerate their significance and too often describe the lower-class black Southern family as a maternal family. He believes that such matriarchal households and families are more common in an urban than a rural environment, but should not be considered an urban phenomenon. He agrees with Taylor that many such families are headed by widows. When younger women head households, it can often be attributed to the fact that there is a larger surplus of adult black women of all ages in Southern cities than in rural areas. Gutman concludes, however, that most Southern black women head neither households nor subfamilies, and that while black women under thirty live with parents rather than head households, the majority of elderly black women remain with their husbands or married children.[56]

Nevertheless, prior to these revisionist viewpoints, in Faulkner's time, as in that of slavery, the woman's domestic primacy could still be explained in great part by her utility as well as by her relationship with the white male. Negro women were, also, much better educated than Negro men: more Negro women went to college, and six percent of Negro women were professionals, versus only one percent or slightly more for the males.[57] Negro women often were paid more and could find employment as domestics, while the men had much more difficulty finding work. Additionally, as it was the black woman who held a position of importance in the kitchen or in the nursery, it was also she who did business with the white man. Finally, the Negro woman exercised a considerable power of seduction over the white male, and sexual relations were fairly frequent.

Although the entrance of the male black worker into industry has strengthened his position, the economic discrimination he long suffered has generally had deleterious consequences on his homelife unknown in the slave family and which have led to much family instability. It has contributed to crime, illegitimacy, drug addiction, homosexuality and the high school drop-out rate. Furthermore, desertion is higher among black urban Negroes of the middle and, particularly, lower class than for any other race and is the most frequently cited reason for divorce. This pattern of instability is discussed by sociologists in relation to the urban black family. Though comparatively infrequent, such patterns do occur in Faulkner's work, and their transference to Yoknapatawpha County, though limited, is probably proof of the author's awareness of their prevalence in the cities.

In Faulkner's work, for example, even though Samuel Worsham Beauchamp, the grandson of Molly and Lucas Beauchamp, goes to Joliet, Illinois, a Northern city where he is executed for murder, the other black characters commit their crimes in rural Yoknapatawpha. The husband of Lucas and Molly's unnamed daughter is sent to the state penitentiary for manslaughter; Elnora's husband, Caspey, in "There Was A Queen" is imprisoned for stealing; and, most important, Nancy Mannigoe, a prostitute and dope addict, is executed in *Requiem for a Nun* for the murder of the youngest Stevens' child. Finally, both the Beauchamps' daughter and Nancy are victims of desertion.

Apart from the woman's superiority, another family pattern formed during slavery consisted of extensive time and emotional energy given by the black female to the white children of the slave-holding family. During the era of slavery the black woman was known to devote to her own children the same affection, but such was apparently not the case after the Civil War in the urban black family. In the lower and middle classes the mother's so-called neglect of her own children can in great part be explained by the fact that the Negro woman worked very hard and was employed outside her own home. The other reason which is generally adduced to explain the "indifference" of the black urban mother toward her children is the one given by the earlier sociologists regarding the slave mother: that the black woman associated her own children with the burdens of pregnancy, childbirth, and childcare. Beth Day in *Sexual Life between Blacks and Whites* notes that black children greatly resented the amount of time their mothers spent with white children, as well as her treating her own with much greater severity than she did her white charges.[58] Powdermaker emphasizes that black middle-class mothers were very ambitious for their children,[59] which makes their stern discipline understandable. Equally understandable, young Negroes rebelled, anxious to be free from both work and parental control.

At the same time, despite the negative aspects of child-bearing, there were certain positive factors that ought not be overlooked. Motherhood, for example, was respected in the Negro community, seen as necessary in order for the black female to fulfill her role as a woman. Furthermore, having a child was also facilitated by the attitude toward illegitimate children, at least in the middle and lower classes. While upper-class Negroes had very rigid codes regarding sex and marriage, middle- and lower-class marriages were much more of the common law type and therefore quite flexible in their moral code. According to Gunnar Myrdal, there was about eight times as much illegitimacy among blacks as among native whites and sixteen times as much illegitimacy as among foreign-born whites.[60] In addition, children were viewed as a type of economic asset in the sense that they were considered a source of old-age insurance. Furthermore, this laissez-faire attitude toward children born out of wedlock can be seen as a hangover from slave times when children could be taken away and women forced to bear children from couplings they neither desired nor assented to. Thus, these children were seen as more of a communal, rather than simply a personal, type of family responsibility. Finally, the black urban family's great elasticity allowed the grandmother to act as family head during the mother's frequent absences, a practice which provided the children with the surrogate mother they needed.

The relations in the rural, black Southern middle-class family were, by contrast, much more balanced. There, family patterns more closely resembled those of the free Negro family prior to the Civil War, or those of the white family, in that the family structure tended to be patriarchal. The father was present as in Faulkner's families and worked close to his home, and the mother was also generally at home. In Yoknapatawpha County, in fact, a black family often seems to live with the people who employ them. Each constitutes a close family unit in which children are brought up with close supervision and taught their parents' work.

In Faulkner's earlier novels, the Gibsons, the Strothers, and the Beauchamps are among the most developed of the author's black families and provide good examples of the dynamics of the black rural family. Dilsey and Roskus in *The Sound and the Fury* are a happily married couple with a closely knit family. The fire burning at the home of their son T.P., with Roskus sitting back against it, is symbolic of their family harmony. Family continuity is important to the Gibsons, and T.P. has been trained by his father to replace him. Dilsey tells Roskus, for example, "Versh is working and Frony married off your hands and T.P. getting big enough to take your place when rheumatism finish getting you." [61] T.P. also takes care of the milking when his father is too disabled by rheumatism. The behavior and attitudes of the younger generation are carefully overseen by the elders. When Luster, Dilsey's and Roskus' grandson, mistreats Benjy, his Uncle Versh immediately admonishes him and warns him that he will inform Dilsey: "Aint you taking biggity. I bet you better not let your grandmammy hear you talking like that." [62] When Luster is again unkind to Benjy, Dilsey protects the idiot, hits Luster, and tells Versh. Not only is Luster punished directly, but the chastisement is reinforced by other family members; the power of the older, male family member is regularly acknowledged.

Negro standards of discipline are, in fact, seen in Faulkner's work as early as *Soldiers' Pay*. While Cecily defies her father and refuses to visit Donald Mahon, her apparent fiancé, Loosh, the young Negro, obeys his grandmother Callie immediately and goes to speak to the dying man, taking his hand warmly in his own. In the later novel, Luster has a mildly sadistic side, resembling Jason, but while Mrs. Compson reinforces Jason's unpleasant behavior, Dilsey does all that is possible to curb it in Luster. Values are of the utmost importance in the Gibson family, as distinct from the Compsons where they are almost nonexistent. When Frony, Dilsey's and Roskus' daughter, worries about the gossip involved in bringing the idiot to church, Dilsey immediately reproaches her. Dilsey also, at all times, makes a conscious effort to keep her family together; for example, when she reproaches Roskus for his superstitiousness, which she sees as dividing the family: "Your bad luck talk got them notions into Versh. That ought to satisfy you." [63] Family unity is also illustrated when Frony, who has married a Pullman porter and moved to St. Louis, moves back to Memphis to make a home for Dilsey, who would not move any further. The Gibson family, indeed, like the other black families before *The Reivers*, acts as a foil to the disintegration occurring within the corresponding white family. The Gibsons act in counterpoint to the declining House of Compson.

The Strother family, that in *Flags in the Dust* and *Sartoris* is an extension of Louvinia and Joby's family in *The Unvanquished*, is another example of family compatibility. Euphony Strother, wife of Simon and mother of Elnora and Caspey in *Flags in the Dust* and *Sartoris*, remains very much in the background. In these works, Faulkner concentrates on vertical family relationships which, as in *Soldiers' Pay* and *The Sound and the Fury*, are not limited to those between parent and child but extend to uncles and grandparents. When Isom seems overly impressed with his Uncle Caspey's liberal notions about the war and black freedom, it is his grandfather Simon who emphatically tells Isom:

> "I kep' tellin' you dem new-fangled war notions of yo'n wa'n't gwine ter work on dis place," [and tells him] "And you better thank de good Lawd fer makin' yo' haid hard ez hit is. You go'n git dat mare, and save dat nigger freedom talk fer townfolks: What us niggers want ter be free fer, anyhow?"[64]

Furthermore, when Simon and Bayard find Isom recklessly driving the car, Isom is given the strap by Simon. Even Caspey, who is himself rebellious, assumes his nephew's discipline and tries, for example, to prevent his smoking when they are out hunting. Here again, the black family acts in contrast to the white family by whom they are employed: unlike Isom, young Bayard, the white grandson, is completely impervious to the little discipline which his family attempts to impose. The contrast between black and white is especially sharp when, on Christmas day, Bayard drops in on a Negro family. He and they are "two opposed concepts antipathetic by race, blood, nature and environment, touching for a moment and fused within the illusion of a contradiction." [65] Within their home, Bayard senses security, and briefly he is capable, for once, of feeling the peace and tranquillity radiated by the family's fire warming its black home in Yoknapatawpha:

> The stale, airtight room dulled him; the warmth was insidious to his bones wearied and stiff after the chill night. The negroes moved about the room, the woman busy at the hearth with her cooking, the pickaninnies with their frugal and sorry gewgaws and filthy candy. Bayard . . . dozed the morning away . . . with peaceful detachment.[66]

The black family presented here is well defined by Melvin Backman in his article "Sickness and Primitivism." He describes the Negro family in Faulkner's work as "an integral unit . . . drawing strength from the very struggle to fulfill the basic physical needs of life, and maintaining despite a meager existence a generosity and cheerfulness of outlook." [67]

The Beauchamps in *Go Down, Moses* provide another illustration of the strong love felt within the black family. The chief relationships among Negroes in this work are the marital one between Molly and her husband Lucas and, on a more sophisticated level, the relationship between Molly and her grandson, Samuel Worsham Beauchamp. The Beauchamps' marriage (as implied by the chapter title, "Fire on the Hearth") is, at least initially, a very close one. The chapter's title refers specifically to the fire Lucas lights on their wedding day and which, significantly, is still burning. The strength of their marriage is demonstrated by the fact that it withstands Zack's removal of Molly as well as Lucas' nightly escapades with his beloved money-finding machine. After six months, when Zack does not send back his Molly, Lucas breaks the racial codes and is prepared to risk both Zack's and his own life to see that she is returned. Later, after Roth warns Lucas that his marriage is in jeopardy because of his money hunts, Lucas immediately renounces his quest and affectionately brings to Molly a little sack of the stick candy that she loves as a peace offering.

Though the relationship between the Beauchamps and their children is not well developed, the one between Molly and her grandson is psychic and profound. Molly, who is closer to her primitive roots than the any of the whites, reacts to her blood feelings. Before her grandson is executed, through pure telepathy she realizes that he is dying and walks seventeen miles into Jefferson to ask for help. Her instinct is reminiscent of Cass Edmonds' comment to Ike about Sam Fathers: "When he was born all his blood on both sides, except the little white part, knew things that had been tamed out of our blood so long that we have forgotten them." [68]

The Beauchamps, as do the Gibsons and the Strothers, act in sharp contrast to the white McCaslins' sterility and lack of emotion and family involvement. As Lionel Trilling notes, there is a dearth of white male-female relationships in *Go Down, Moses*. [69] Uncle Buck and Uncle Buddy, "who should have been a woman to begin with," [70] live in a section "where ladies were so damn seldom thank God that a man could ride for days in a straight line without having to dodge a single one." [71] Uncle Buck marries Sophonisba Beauchamp after she has played the active role in their courtship. Buck marries her late in life and has his first and only son at age sixty-eight. Uncle Ike is a childless widower who, anyway, wishes "the woods would be his mistress and his wife." [72] At the end, Edmonds and Zack are left widowers, and Roth is forty-three and unmarried.

In "Pantaloon in Black," although Rider and his wife, Mannie, do not constitute a family unit like the Gibsons, the Strothers and the Beauchamps, as a couple they exhibit the intense emotion Faulkner depicts within the black family. Like Lucas, Rider builds a fire on his wedding day which is likewise still burning. When Mannie dies, Rider helps dig her grave in order to expedite her burial, attempting to minimize the agony he feels. Rider is so grief-stricken at Mannie's death that he cannot sleep, so he walks the country roads at night or gets drunk in order to sleep. His inability to accept her death is poignantly shown in the scene in which he draws two chairs to the table at mealtime and talks to her as if she were still present. This incident parallels the behavior of Hightower's black nurse, Cinthy, in *Light in August*, awaiting her dead husband's return. Rider's reaction to his wife's death is also a strong contrast to the total indifference shown by the deputy's wife toward the deputy. Rider's chagrin is referred to in *Requiem for a Nun* and is again used as a contrast, in this case to Temple's emotional indifference to her child's death. In the final analysis, one cannot but agree with Michael Millgate when he speaks of the "intensity and longevity of family loyalty and love in which the Negroes of the novel show themselves to be much the superiors of their white relatives and neighbors." [73]

Most of the strength of the black, rural middle-class family, as well as the fortitude of the blacks as a whole, can be understood by examining the black church. Frank S. Loescher aptly remarks that if one were to write a history of white Protestantism's relations with Negroes, "the balance sheet would be heavily on the debit side." [74] In the years after the Civil War not only were the churches among the first to institutionalize second-class citizenship for Negroes, but also the white churches were among the first Southern institutions also to segregate.

The Negroes were most attracted to the Baptist Church because of its decentralized and democratic structure and because of the ebullience and immediacy of its religious services. By the end of the nineteenth century the Baptists claimed more black members than all the other denominations combined, followed by the Methodists, who, like the Baptists, wanted to maintain their black membership. However, in each case the denomination's Negro members were unwilling to accept inferior status and so formed their own churches. Ironically, Negroes themselves sometimes segregated their own churches. The Colored Methodist Episcopal Church, as described by Charles E. Wynes, at the time of its foundation specified that no white person could become a member; when one later solicited admission in, he was rejected.[75]

After World War I the Protestant Church did become more progressive. It reproved lynchings and brutality and during the Depression even supported equal opportunity. Furthermore, World War II marked the recognition of racial discrimination in economics, politics and civil affairs. After World War II, also, it was recognized that segregation in employment, in education, in housing and in the church was at the heart of the Negro-white housing conflict. However, churches in the South still remained very segregated except in areas where there were very few Negroes, in which instance integration tended to occur.

As early as *Soldiers' Pay* the role of religion in the black community is strongly contrasted with that in the white. Reverend Mahon's or even Faulkner's ambiguous "God of Circumstance" [76] acts in contrast to the personal and immediate New Testament God of the Negro race, who took "the white man's word as readily as it took his remote God and made a personal Father of Him." [77] Dilsey, in *The Sound and the Fury*, places her faith in a New Testament philosophy, a vision of life that stresses "de resurrection en de light" rather than "de darkness en de death." [78] In Faulkner's first novel, the black church is already portrayed as absorbing the black man's sorrows and giving dignity to his pain. Gilligan and Mahon see "the shabby church become beautiful with mellow longing, passionate and sad." [79] One is reminded of the mellow, passionless song of the unnamed cook in *Soldiers' Pay,* or later in *Sartoris* and *Flags in the Dust* of Elnora "crooning one of her mellow endless songs" [80] she "crooned mellowly as she labored; her voice became rich and plaintful and sad along the sunny reaches of the air." [81]

Grace Holt observes that a primary function of the church was to nourish and maintain the souls of black folks by equating them with the essence of humaneness; consequently, the black church became the institution that promoted "self-worth and dignity, a variable identity," and "help in overcoming fear." [82] It focused on the trials and tribulations of the black man's present life without concerning itself with the intangibility of an afterlife. This emphasis is implied in *The Sound and the Fury* when an anonymous churchgoer responds to Frony's statement that "Mammy aint feelin well dis mawnin" by telling her, "Dat's too bad. But Rev'un Shegog' 'll cure dat. He'll give her de comfort en de unburden." [83] The church also reflected compassion, as when Dilsey brings Benjy to the Negro church and an old woman reacts by saying, "Tell um de good Lawd don't keer whether he smart er not. Don't nobody but poor white trash keer dat." [84] Because the lives of its participants were arduous and uncertain, the black religion, according to Benjamin E. Mays, was based on a God "able to help . . . bridge the chasm existing between the actual and the ideal." [85]

Religion was crucial in keeping the black family, especially the rural black family, together. Three generations of the Gibson family attend the Easter Service together. The black church provided them with the faith they needed to cope with the strife involved in their daily lives. Their religious optimism is probably best portrayed by Nancy, who tells Temple to "Believe." [86] She also adds:

> He don't tell you not to sin, He just asks you not to. And he dont tell you to suffer. But He gives you the chance. He gives you the best He can think of, that you are capable of doing. And He will save you.[87]

The interaction of the blacks within their own families was paralleled only by the relationship of black domestics and the children of the white families they worked for. In this pattern Faulkner's work echoes historical fact. Almost inevitably, it was the mother or mammy figure, or sometimes the black retainer, who acted as a protectress or protector of the white family. Infrequently the roles were reversed, and it was the white family that was beckoned to take care of their surrogate black kin as in the case of Molly in *Go Down, Moses* or Simon in *Flags in the Dust* and *Sartoris*.

This protecting black family member is a personage very familiar to Faulkner as both Caroline Barr and Ned Barnett had been members of his own family since slavery times. Caroline Barr, to whom he dedicated *Go Down, Moses*, is described by the author as one who was "born in slavery and who gave to my family a fidelity without stint or calculation of recompense and to my childhood an immeasurable devotion and love." [88] At her funeral service at Rowan Oak his home, he spoke of the devotion and love she had given him and his family and the security with which she had invested his childhood. Following Caroline's death, the author wrote that he had "little of heart or time either for work [since the] funeral." [89] Callie, the unnamed mammy in *Soldiers' Pay*; Paralee, Rachel and Eunice in *Flags in the Dust* and *Sartoris*; Dilsey, Molly, and even Cinthy, in a somewhat different way, are all based partly on Caroline Barr, and all show an equal sense of devotion to the white families for whom they work. The major difference between Caroline Barr and her fictional counterparts was only, as Malcolm Cowley points out, that Caroline Barr had more spunk and less humility than her fictional sisters.[90] Joseph Blotner adds that Caroline had "a salty vocabulary and a taste for men." [91]

The Faulkner family felt a similar attachment to Ned Barnett. On the first Christmas following Ned's death, Estelle and William Faulkner spent the holiday crying, after having discovered in his cedar chest a birthday cake Estelle had baked for him four years before, parts of the Old Colonel's Confederate uniform, as well as cast-off items from other Faulkner family members, all of which he had saved as precious. Uncle Ned, like the other black surrogate family members, was buried in a cemetery adjacent to the Faulkners'.

Given Faulkner's intimacy with his own black surrogate family members, he shows a tendency to idealize such relationships when they are transposed to his work. His characters and their family relationships, though very much drawn from reality, tend to stereotyping;

they are drawn from a limited frame of reference whose perimeters Faulkner, as a Southerner, does not wish to extend.

The mammy figure, protectress of her surrogate white children, is seen as early as *Soldiers' Pay*. Here Callie, who shares the cherished Caroline Barr's nickname, shows maternal devotion to Donald Mahon when, dying, he returns from war. Not only does she see to it that Loosh treats him kindly, but Callie, who has replaced Donald's deceased mother, also tells him, "Lawd, de white folks done ru'nt you, but nummine yo' mammy gwine look after her baby." [92] This maternal attitude is again seen in the novel when the nameless cook, whom Thadious M. Davis describes as an "embryonic Dilsey," [93] also gives comfort, this time to a young boy experiencing the trauma of loss and grief:

> He mounted the steps and entered wanting his mother—But of course, she had not got back from—He found himself running suddenly through the hall toward a voice raising in comforting, crooning song. Here was a friend mountainous in blue calico, her elephantine thighs undulating gracious as the wake of a ferry boat as she moved between table and stove.
>
> She broke off her mellow, passionless song, exclaiming: "Bless yo' heart, honey, what is it?"
>
> But he did not know. He only clung to her comforting, voluminous skirt in a quest of uncontrollable sorrow, while she wiped biscuit dough from her hands on a towel. Then she picked him up and sat upon a stiff-backed chair, rocking back and forth and holding him against her balloon-like breast until his fit of weeping shuddered away.[94]

Paralee Sander in *Intruder in the Dust* is another example of the black mammy figure. Although not a particularly developed character, Paralee, like the rest of Faulkner's black maternal figures, cares deeply for her surrogate son, Charles Mallison. She shows similar feelings for her son, Alex, and is unlike Southern urban black mothers, who allegedly cared almost exclusively for their white charges. The warm family atmosphere created by Paralee is still appreciated by Charles Mallison at age sixteen:

> He and Alex Sander played in the bad weather when they were little and Paralee would cook whole meals for them halfway between two meals at the house and he and Alex

Sander would eat then together, the food tasting, the same to each.[95]

The warm atmosphere in Paralee's home is reminiscent of Paralee's father, Ephraim, as Charles remembers him sitting in front of the fire.

Rachel, the Mitchells' cook, is another of Faulkner's black characters who is not particularly individualized but who shows concern for her surrogate white daughter, Little Belle, and even for Little Belle's father, Harry. Rachel, presumptuously though justly, advises Harry to beat Belle in order to end Belle's mistreatment of both her daughter and her husband.

Eunice, the Benbows' cook, also is not well developed as a character, but she remains in the mammy tradition. When Narcissa comes home, for example, Eunice shows concern for her mistress's foster son and tells her that she feeds Horace as best she can, but that, despite her chocolate pies, he needs his sister back.

Dilsey is certainly one of the most important examples of the black, surrogate mother figure. Cleanth Brooks believes that Dilsey, compared to the Compsons, "affirms the ideal of wholeness in a family which shows in every other member splintering and disintegration." [96] Melvin Backman concurs with Brooks and says that she is "the enduring rock in the splintered and rotting house of Compson." [97] Even young Luster is capable of making the distinction between his family and the Compsons. Luster says, "Dese is funny folks. Glad I ain't none of em." [98] Faulkner, himself, says of his black heroine: "Dilsey the Negro woman, she was a good human being. That she held the family together not for the hope of reward, but just because it was the decent and proper thing to do." [99]

Dilsey's role as surrogate mother serves to protect the Compson children from harmful parental influence: from their father's pessimism and their mother's self-absorbed hypochondria. The extent of Dilsey's responsibilities is best expressed by Dilsey herself when she asks the following question regarding little Quentin: "Who else gwine raise her 'cep me? Aint I raised eve'y one of y' all?" [100] Although Jason reacts to Dilsey with characteristic cynicism, Dilsey has become the one responsible for the family; fortunately, contrary to Jason's distorted perspective, she successfully manages to "run the whole family," [101] being the Compson children's only oasis in the emotional desert in which they exist. Only Jason complains:

> That's the trouble with nigger servants, when they've been
> with you for a long time they get so full of self-importance
> that they're not worth a damn. Think they run the whole fam-
> ily.[102]

Jason is himself the most destructive force in the household, more
pernicious even than his parents. He is certainly the most negative personality among the younger Compsons, and much of Dilsey's energy is
devoted to attempts to control Jason or to act as a buffer between him
and the younger family members, white or black. His poison is best illustrated by his cruelty toward young Quentin. After completely alien-
ating her from her mother, after stealing from her, he also decides to
beat her. Dilsey shields Quentin from her uncle by stepping in front of
her and comforts Quentin by telling her, "I ain't gwine let him tech
you." [103] She tells Jason to hit her, Dilsey, instead. Jason's behavior toward Luster is similar, but it is gratuitously even more diabolic. Jason
drops the passes to the minstrel show into the fire purely for the perverse pleasure of watching Luster's disappointment. Dilsey again reproaches Jason for his behavior. Jason sadistically chooses his victims
among those he considers weaker; in this case, they are parentless or
black. Yet, with equal devotion, Dilsey takes their defense.

Besides protecting the children from Jason's deviltry, another of
Dilsey's major functions is to take care of Benjy, on whom she showers
affection. Not only does she take him to her church on Easter Sunday,
among many other acts of kindness, but she also makes him a birthday
cake using her own money. The love bestowed on the Compson children
by Dilsey and her family is deeply felt by the sensitive Quentin. Coming back on the train from Cambridge, he realizes that he misses
"Roskus and Dilsey and them" and feels nostalgia for the race that
"protects them it loves out of all reason." [104] On the last day of his life,
Uncle Lou, the possum hunter, and Dilsey provide Quentin with his
only memories of childhood security and love.

Molly in *Go Down, Moses* is another example of the black surrogate
mother who, like Callie in *Soldier's Pay*, replaces the mothering of the
dead white mother. Roth says that Molly is the one who

> had raised him, fed him from her own breast as she was actu-
> ally doing her own child, who had surrounded him always with

> care for his physical body and for his spirit too, teaching him
> his manners, behavior—to be gentle with his inferiors,
> honourable with his equals, generous to the weak and con-
> siderate of the aged, courteous, truthful and brave to all—
> who had given him, motherless, without stint of expectation of
> reward that constant and abiding devotion and love which
> existed nowhere else in the world for him.[105]

The love Molly gives him, like Caroline Barr's to Faulkner, is purely
spontaneous and without calculation. When Roth is older, he still visits with her once a month and brings her a tin of tobacco and a small
sack of the soft cheap candy she loves. Most importantly, he protects
her against Lucas' obsession with the money-hunting machine and
warns Lucas that, if this caprice engenders a divorce, Molly must be entitled to half the house and half the crop.

   While growing up Roth saw more of Lucas than of his own father.
However, toward Lucas as well as Butch (Samuel Worsham
Beauchamp) he is much more distant than he is toward Molly. He does
not like the fact that Lucas does not call him "Sir," and Roth immediately sends Butch away after he breaks into the commissary. Roth's reactions can in great part be explained by the essential role that the
black woman alone played in the development of the young Southern
boy. Lillian Smith, for example, sees the attachment to the black surrogate mother as so fundamental that it can cause the Southerner to turn
away "from all women, shunning them white and black," [106] and to
spend "his real feelings on men and his hours in companionship with
them." [107] This might be explained by the fact that the white man
could feel subconsciously a dependent prisoner to his mammy as well as
conflicted by the social attitudes about these relationships prevailing
at the time. This observation is certainly applicable to Roth, who has
dropped his mulatto mistress and who is still unmarried in his early
forties.

   Cinthy is a final example of Faulkner's black surrogate mothers.
She, too, resembles Caroline Barr in the sense that like Faulkner's
nurse, who was unable to read and write, Cinthy remembers many stories about the Civil War which she passes on to the Hightowers.
Cinthy is also an interesting illustration of the Negro adopting the
white man's myths and using them to glamorize the past. Ironically, a

black thus becomes the greatest propagator of the white family's myths:

> with the phantom the child . . . talked about the ghost. They never tired: the child with rapt, wide, half dread and half delight, and the old woman with musing and savage sorrow and pride. But this to the child has just peaceful shuddering of delight. He found no terror in the knowledge that his grandfather on the contrary had killed men by the hundreds as he was told and believed.108

In fact Hightower's grandfather was a Civil War officer-hero only in fantasy and was supposed to have been shot very unheroically during a raid on a chicken house. Yet, because of its magnetism, Hightower himself accepts the veracity of the myth of his grandfather:

> Now this is what Cinthy told me. And I believe. I know, It's too fine to doubt. It's too fine, too simple, ever to have invented by white thinking. A negro might have invented it. And if Cinthy did, I still believe. Because even fact cannot stand with it. 109

However, it is precisely the tenacity with which Hightower guards these fantasies that impairs his functioning in the present. Cinthy is really the only example in Faulkner's work of a mammy figure who, in spite of herself, has an adverse effect on her white protégé.

Of course, the most notable exception is Nancy Mannigoe who, in *Requiem for a Nun*, is probably the author's most controversial black figure. Like Cinthy, Nancy Mannigoe is well-meaning, which is why the author, Temple Drake and, with few exceptions, the critics have given her their support. Faulkner portrays Nancy as the true nun—not Temple—and says of her that she is destined to "the tragic life of a prostitute which she had to follow simply because she was . . . just doomed and damned by circumstances to that life." 110 Even Temple praises Nancy directly, saying:

> You have always been so good to my children and to me—my husband too—all of us—trying to hold us together in a household, a family, that anybody should have known all the

time couldn't possibly hold together? even in decency, let
alone in happiness?[111]

Albert Camus sees her as "murderous and saintly at the same time," [112]
and says that, according to Faulkner, "she becomes also the saint, the
singular nun who unexpectedly confers the dignity of a cloister on the
brothels and prisons in which she lived." [113] Most of the American critics would agree with Camus for taking a positive stand on her behalf.

Nancy, alias "nigger-dope-fiend whore," [114] is certainly not "de
cradle-rocking black mammy" [115] seen generally in the South and particularly in Faulkner's novels. She is surely more ambiguous than the
conventional mammy figure, but like the others, despite her seeming
lack of rationality, she is in her unique way, self-abnegating and
devoted to the Stevens family.

While the black mammy figure is of utmost importance as a symbolic member of the white family, the black retainer has a similar position. Despite the fact that he is less significant, the black retainer is
still consequential. Though both are very much part of the white family, the major difference which separates them is that the mammy is
generally a protectress of the children while the black retainer is a
projection or a mirror of the adults. For example, Simon is undoubtedly
the most notable of Faulkner's black retainers, and he is certainly modeled on Ned Barnett, a former slave to Faulkner's great-grandfather,
and one who greatly admired his old master. Uncle Ned believed in a
traditional and ceremonious life and, modeling himself after the Old
Colonel, he wore high-crowned hats, frock coats and silk ties. Like the
real-life Ned, Simon takes the top hat and duster, Old Bayard's cigar
and whip, and condescendingly declares that the automobile "is all
right for pleasure and excitement, but fer de genu-wine gen'lmun tone,
dey aint but one thing: dat's hosses." [116] His family pride, which bor-
ders on arrogance, also manifests itself when he takes Miss Jenny to a
card party and pompously tells another black driver, "Don't block off
no Sartoris' ca'iage, black boy," [117] he continues, "Block off de common-
ality, if you wants, but don't invoke no equipage waitin' on Cunnel er
Miss Jenny. Dey won't stan fer it." [118] The pride felt by the black man
through association with his white family is well expressed by Simon,
one of five generations serving the Sartorises, when he smugly announces that the "Sartorises set de quality in dis country."

Simon's attachment to John Sartoris is so great that he seems incapable of accepting his death. While working in the stables or in the flower beds, Simon can be heard speaking quite calmly with John Sartoris' ghost. Because of Simon's habit, John Sartoris in turn becomes very much a part of the universe of his grandson, Isom.

Roskus is another black servant who has an impact on the family he works for. However, Roskus, being married to Dilsey, is quite overshadowed by her and consequently never achieves the importance of Simon. Roskus makes his greatest impression on Quentin, who misses him when he is at the university. On the day preceding his death, Quentin leaves an outfit of clothing with a letter to Deacon, the negro factotum of Southern students at Harvard. Deacon reminds him of his cherished Roskus: "I saw Roskus watching me from behind all his white folks' claptrap of uniforms and politics and Harvard manner, different, secret, inarticulate and sad." [119]

Finally, Uncle Job in "Smoke" and Tobe in "A Rose for Emily" are examples of minor characters in Faulkner's work who illustrate the devotion of the black male servant. For seventeen years, Uncle Job sits all day outside the judge's office and states that "I looked after him like I promised Mistis," [120] his tears expressing his feelings at the time of the judge's death. In much the same way, Tobe is completely devoted to Miss Emily Grierson and sacrifices his life to her narrow universe until her death, when he leaves her home irrevocably.

Although most of Faulkner's black mammies or retainers behave quite selflessly, sometimes they, too, expect a certain reciprocity. This expectation is evident in both Molly and Simon. Molly is actually disappointed by the surrogate white son to whom she devotes herself. When Roth, for instance, catches Butch breaking into the commissary, he immediately orders him off the property. Since Butch is forced to leave home and goes to Illinois, where he kills a Chicago policeman, in Molly's mind Roth becomes indirectly responsible for the murder. "Roth Edmonds sold my Benjamin. Sold him in Egypt. Pharaoh got him—." [121] Edmond Volpe feels that, in fact, Molly equates the death of her grandson with the enslavement of her race. [122]

Simon (who, by contrast, resembles a court jester and is much more clever and calculating than Molly) is certainly less sentimental than Molly and manages to achieve his ends. When Simon uses the church funds he is holding to subsidize his girlfriend, he pressures Old Bayard to replace them on the grounds that it would cause the Sartoris family great embarrassment to have him in jail. The episode closely resembles the real-life Uncle Ned, who, with a similar ruse, would come to Faulkner each year in the late summer and ask him for money, telling him, "Master, I ain't gonna live to see my crop. Give me the money to go home to Ripley and die." [123] Each year, Faulkner would comply.

Apart from the surrogate mother and the black-retainer relationships, other black/white relationships are quite similar and equally important in Faulkner's work and in the South. The parallels of life and art are particularly evident in foster brother relationships and foster sister relationships and especially in the former. Faulkner himself had experienced such a relationship:

> I grew up with Negro children, my foster mother was a Negro woman, I slept in her bed and the Negro children and I slept in the same bed together. To me they were no different than anyone else. I noticed that with my own children. It's only when the child becomes a middle-aged man and becomes a part of the economy that the latent quality appears.[124]

Although Faulkner also states that "the whole trouble between black and white is not in anything racial or (ethnic)," [125] in his early works a close look at the response of the young white heroes in front of their black playmates shows the problem quite differently. Faulkner's white heroes draw color barriers when they are still young boys, for example, between Roth Edmonds and Henry Beauchamp in *Go Down Moses,* or Bayard Sartoris and Ringo Strothers in *Unvanquished.* In *Go Down Moses,* Zack strongly separates himself from his foster brother, Lucas—though later in life and not for economic reasons. Finally, in *Intruder in the Dust,* despite the fact that Charles Mallison never really removes himself from his foster brother, Alex Sander, he is still subject to racial prejudice.

The author's fiction seems inconsistent with the belief he voiced, but one can bridge this paradox, at least to some degree, by understanding that the race consciousness that his heroes instinctively feel at a young age has its roots according to Faulkner in the white man's desire to retain his economic superiority. Nevertheless, in his work, Faulkner portrays this as a uniquely racial problem whose roots are social. Roth Edmonds and Henry Beauchamp (foster brothers), for example, have a very congenial relationship until Roth becomes seven years old and feels reflexively his father's racial prejudice:

> Even before he was out of infancy, the two houses had become interchangeable: himself and his foster brother sleeping on the same pallet in the white man's house or in the same bed in the negro's and eating of the same food at the same table in either, actually preferring the negro house, the hearth on which even in summer a little fire always burned centering the life into it to his own.126

When Roth refuses to allow Henry to share his bed with him, it is ironically the white brother, not Henry, who actually becomes the victim of racial prejudice. While Henry goes fast to sleep, Roth lies "in a rigid fury of the grief he could not explain, the shame he would not admit." 127 They do not hunt together that morning, they never sleep in the same room again, and they never again eat at the same table. When, a month later, Roth, obviously feeling ambivalent about the situation, tries to have dinner at Molly's with Henry, it is too late: "So he entered his heritage. He ate its bitter fruit."128

The relationship between Henry and Roth, is completely analogous to the one between Bayard and Ringo in *Unvanquished*:

> Ringo and I had been born in the same month and had both fed at the same breast and had slept together and eaten together for so long that Ringo called Granny "Granny" just like I did, until maybe he wasn't a nigger any more and maybe I wasn't a white boy any more.129

Bayard's father even reinforced their relationship to Ringo's advantage by insisting that the black boy was slightly smarter that his own son: "Father always said that Ringo was a little smarter than I was, but that didn't count with us, any more that the difference in the colour of our skins counted." 130 This claim proves to be only empty rhetoric because, like all Southern foster white and black brothers, Bayard is to find himself on "the bed itself, Ringo on the pallet beside it." 131 Furthermore, after they leave the Yankee camp with twelve chests of silver, the mules, and the Negroes, Ringo takes command and responds to the Yankee lieutenant who questions them about the mules.

It is also Ringo who understands the complexity of Ab Snopes, whom Granny is forced to deal with, and it is the black boy who is first aware that Ab sold out.   Again, in the church scene, it is Ringo who has kept Granny's accounts in the ledger and who reads out the names of the people whom Mrs. Millard has helped with loans and mules. Yet because of the same racial prejudice, it is this clever black boy who cannot sit with the family but, instead, must remain in the galley set apart for the former slaves.

The relationship shared between Zack and Lucas during their youth is parallel to those just discussed:

> They had fished and hunted together, they had learned to swim in the same water, they had eaten at the same table in the white boy's kitchen and in the cabin of the negro's mother; they had slept under the same blanket before a fire in the woods.[132]

However, despite these close brotherly ties, Zack unscrupulously takes Molly from Lucas because the racial code permits it.

Finally, in *Intruder in the Dust*, although economic considerations are not involved and although now there is no immediate problem between Charles Mallison and his foster black brother, Alex Sander, the racial prejudice to which Chick is susceptible is illustrated by his constant use of the word "nigger." Also important is his inability, at least until his initiation, to accept Lucas as a man and not just as a "nigger." Charles had wished that "he would just be a nigger first, just one second, one little infinitesimal second." [133]

Concerning the childhood relationship between the Southern white boy and this black brother, Irving Howe concludes that the white Southerner deeply misses a time of lost innocence which the Negro's presence alone recalls to him:

> The white man is repeatedly tempted by a memory playing on the rim of consciousness: a memory of boyhood, when he could live with his Ringo or Henry Beauchamp—his Nigger Jim or Queequeg—and not yet wince under the needle of self-consciousness. The memory—or a longing in the guise of memory?—can be downed by the will and blunted by convention, but it is too lovely and in some final sense too real to

be discarded entirely. Beneath the pretense to superiority, the white man reaches for what is true: the time when man reaches for what is true: the time when he could compare bits of knowledge about locomotives with Ringo, share food with Henry Beauchamp, not in equality or out of it—for the mere knowledge of either is a poison—but in chaste companionship. This is what the white man has lost forever and forever; and the Negro need not remind him of it, he need only walk past him on the street.[134]

The childhood related in McDonald's *Life in Old Virginia,* carefully describes the complicity between young black and white children in the pre-Civil War South:

The children play together on terms of great equality and if the white child gives a blow, he is apt to have it returned with interest. At the tables you will find the white children rising from them, with their little hands full of the best of everything to carry to the nurses or playmates, and I have often known them to deny themselves for the sake of their favorites.[135]

He observes that this relationship is continued in adulthood:

When the young master (or mistress) is installed into his full rights of property, he finds around him no alien hirelings, ready to quit his service upon the slightest provocation, but attached and faithful friends, known to him from his infancy, and willing to share his fortunes.[136]

In Faulkner's works, Roth and Lucas are illustrative of the antithetical foster brother relationship described by McDonald. A positive relationship in later years does develop, however, between Molly and Miss Worsham, her foster sister in *Go Down, Moses.* In this case, it is really Eunice Habersham (as this sister is referred to in *Intruder in the Dust*), who helps her black sister rather than the reverse. Molly and Eunice Habersham grow up in much the same way as Faulkner's foster brothers:

... old Molly, Lucas' wife, who had been the daughter of one of old Doctor Habersham's, Miss Habersham's grandfather's

> slaves, she and Miss Habersham the same age, born in the
> same week and both suckled at Molly's mother's breast and
> grown up together almost inextricably like sisters, like twins,
> sleeping in the same room, the white girl in the bed, the Ne-
> gro girl on a cot at the foot of it almost until Molly and Lucas
> married ...137

Miss Worsham states that "Molly and I were born in the same month.
We grew up together as sisters would." [138] Belle Worsham is also the
godmother of Molly's first child, and it is she who saves Lucas from being lynched. Most important, when Molly's grandson, Samuel
Beauchamp, is executed, Miss Worsham empathizes with Molly as
would a sister and considers Samuel's conviction "our grief," [139] con-
tributing all her savings to the funeral expenses. Thus, Faulkner's work
generally reflects the relationships existing between blacks and whites
who are bonded usually and everlastingly from childhood.

In conclusion, the black family in *The Reivers*, can best be examined apart from the rest of Faulkner's opus. Although it treats many of
the same themes as the author's earlier works, Faulkner's last novel
shows the black family in total harmony with the white family and
consequently no longer as a foil. The black family is still associated
with a domestic fireside, in this case in Uncle Parsham's bedroom,
where "even in May there was a smolder of fire on the hearth." [140] The
loving atmosphere particular to the black home is also present in *The
Reivers*:

> Lycurgus mother, Uncle Parsham's daughter, was cooking
> dinner now; the kitchen smelled of the boiling vegetables.
> But she had kept my breakfast warm-fried sidemeat, grits,
> hot biscuits and butter milk or sweet milk or coffee; she un-
> tied my riding glove from my hand so I could eat, a little sur-
> prised that I had never tasted coffee since Lycurgus had
> been having it on Sunday morning since he was two years old.
> And I thought I was just hungry until I went to sleep right
> there in the pallet until Lycurgus half dragged, half carried
> me to his bed in the lean-to.141

This time, however, such a congenial home life is shared equally by
the white family.

Religion remains important for the black family, but in *The Reivers* it is no longer seen as a necessary refuge in order to escape the brutality of the white world; on the contrary, religion is shown playing a positive and comparable role in both black and white families. We can see this parity when Uncle Parsham begins to say grace and is compared by Lucius to his own Grandfather Priest:

> "Bow your head," and we did so and he said grace, briefly, courteously but with dignity, without abasement or cringing: one man of decency and intelligence to another: notifying Heaven that we were about to eat and thanking it for the privilege, but at the same time reminding It that It had some help too; that if someone named Hood or Briggins (so that was Lycurgus' and his mother's name) hadn't sweated some, the acknowledgement would have graced mainly empty dishes, and said Amen and unfolded his napkin and struck the corner in his collar exactly as Grandfather did, and we ate.142

In this scene Faulkner has created a domestic triangle which includes the two family members whom he particularly cherished as a young boy: the mother and the grandfather. In *The Reivers* the young black boy, Lycurgus, has his mother, Mary, and his grandfather, Uncle Parsham. Significantly, Mary no longer replaces Lucius' mother, but now only assists her since the Priests are a balanced family with a constructive and healthy family life themselves. Most importantly, the color barrier between the two races is no longer evident. Unlike the situation for other "foster brothers," who are habitually separated in Faulkner's work, Lucius is no longer subject to the social problems of racial condescension of earlier heroes.

While as late as *Intruder in the Dust* Chick Mallison is preoccupied with Lucas' inability to accept his Negro identity, in *The Reivers* the young hero shows the same respect for Uncle Parsham that he does for his grandfather, and he considers the black man "the aristocrat for us all and judge of us all." 143 When Uncle Parsham suggests that Lucius take Lycurgus' bed and Lycurgus use a pallet on the floor, Lucius (again unlike the earlier heroes) states that he prefers to sleep with Uncle Parsham as he does with his own grandfather. Lucius, also, recoils from the word "nigger" since both his father and grandfather have taught

him "that no gentleman ever referred to anyone by his race or religion." [144] Again differing from the earlier heroes, Lucius is obedient to
his grandfather Priest in the same way that Lycurgus is to Uncle Parsham. Lucius does, however, disobey Aunt Callie, his adored mammy,
who (like Mary) now aids rather than replaces the white family. Yet,
unlike Jason, who prides himself on his unruliness, Lucius is remorseful
that he has broken his promise to help Aunt Callie to look after the
other children.

The black retainer is also reintroduced as a character type in this
last novel, but now he plays a completely constructive role in the life of
the young white boy. Ned McCaslin, coachman for the Priests, feels responsible for Lucius, and when he realizes that he can no longer take
care of the young boy, he carefully replaces himself with Uncle Parsham, who teaches Lucius how to drive the mule cart while simultaneously teaching him both human psychology and respect:

> But a mule is gentleman too, and when you act courteous and
> respectful to him without trying to buy him or scare him, he'll
> act courteous and respectful back to you—as long as you
> don't overstep him.[145]

As with his other family themes, Faulkner's treatment of the
black family shows a definite transformation by the time of the last
novel, *The Reivers*, when many of his own family problems are, at least
to some degree, resolved by the birth of his grandchildren. He seems to
now regard life, generally, and racial problems, specifically, with a
greater sense of detachment. Nevertheless, when considering the great
body of his work, one cannot avoid being aware of Faulkner's haunting
preoccupation with the guilt he assumes as a liberal Southerner, both
the guilt that he inherits historically and that which he experiences
contemporaneously, in relation to blacks. The complexity of Faulkner's
racial feelings is seen through his treatment of the black family and
the foster black family within his work. These feelings are marked by
a fundamental ambivalence because Faulkner instinctively feels sensitivity for and empathy with his black families, but at the same time
he creates boundaries around them, leaving them in the servant postion
so that under all circumstances they retain the distance necessary not to
threaten his superiority as a Southern white.

Final Thoughts

Despite the fact that Faulkner does not deliberately intend to recreate, biographically or sociologically, his own or the South's intra- and interfamily relations, this process occurs nonetheless in his work. The author's fictional world is necessarily the natural offspring of his own experience and background. Yet Faulkner's portrayal of the family is a negative and exaggerated view of interfamily relations in the South, with the exception of the miscegenetive ones and the inter-relationships within the black family.

Since he tends to identify less directly with the family relations involving the mulatto and the black, he is often more objective. However, ridden with guilt, Faulkner is apt to depict the mulatto family member almost always as the victim of his white family and of society at large. Motivated again by culpability, Faulkner presents the black rural family as an harmonious family unit which acts as a counterpoint to the degenerate white family that employs them. Thus, during his early and middle work, though he gives a prejudicial image of husband-wife, parent-child and incestuous relations within the white family, by contrast, within the mulatto and black family, his portrait is more realistic because he is sufficiently removed not to project his own demons and yet aware and remorseful enough to expose these relationships honestly.

The distortion in family relationships to which Faulkner's work is subject during his early and middle period is one that he shares with his Southern literary contemporaries. All of the other Southern authors, whether Robert Penn Warren, Thomas Wolfe, Katherine Anne

Porter, Caroline Gordon, James Agee, Carson McCullers, Erskine Caldwell, William Styron, or Flannery O'Connor, represent the family as problematical to the individual. Although the exaggerated sensitivity of the artist makes him acutely susceptible to suffering relationships, there is certainly truth in the anguishing divisions that these authors describe as arising between family members. Yet, as Faulkner makes clear in his work beginning in the late forties with *Intruder in the Dust,* the family cannot be regarded solely as a negative force but can act equally as the Southerner's major source of solace and support. Ultimately, Faulkner's depiction of the family moves from one of complete condemnation to one of near eulogy. Throughout Faulkner's work as the reader encounters the family in all its facets, its dominant feature is its stature. It is potentially a fundamental source of support if the individual does not allow himself to be overpowered or incarcerated by it.

Faulkner's families, as well as the families in general in the South, must be understood after examining the philosophical and socio-historical context from which they emerge. Yoknapatawpha, Faulkner's mythical kingdom, is the fictional counterpart of Oxford, Mississippi and the surrounding area. Yoknapatawpha is symbolic of the South and its inhabitants must also confront a changing society. The traditional Southerner like Faulkner and many of his protagonists is totally nostalgic for the pre-Civil War South. He is a temporal outcast—for him "what is past is perfect."[1] He resembles the older women in *Intruder in the Dust* who were:

> still spinsters and widows waiting even seventy-five years
> laters for the slow telegraph to bring them news of Tennessee
> and Virginia and Pennsylvania battles."[2]

Like his fellow Southerners of the upper class, the author and many of his heroes have difficulty in coming to terms with the mercantile wasteland represented by the Snopeses. This traditional Southerner wishes to escape from the empty materialism and moral vacuity of the New South. He finds himself within a familial prison where he is often besieged by many of the problems besetting the South generally, among them guilt, isolation, rejection and ambivalence. The Southerner is strongly motivated by the instinct for self preservation and he often feels, though it is usually an illusion, that it is only in the dialogue with a family member that he can avoid self-destruction.

Since the Civil War, the South often regarded itself as accursed as a consequence of its collective responsibility for slavery and injustice. In *Absalom, Absalom!* Rosa Coldfield implies that the South and even the Southern family is condemned to a Calvinistic hell. She speaks of her family

> as though there were a fatality and curse on our family and God Himself were seeing to it that it was performed and discharged to the last drop and dreg. Yes, fatality and curse on the South and on our family as though because some ancestor of ours had elected to establish his (descent) in a land primed for fatality and already cursed with it, even if it had not rather been our family, our father's progenitors, who had incurred the curse long years before and had been cursed by Heaven, into establishing itself in the land and the time already cursed ... [3]

The Southerner, frustrated and lost, attempts through discourse with his family to reconstruct his identity. Southerners as typified by the Sartorises, McCaslins, Compsons, or even the Sutpens, who rise in social rank, are inevitably in Faulkner's major work, also the victims of their families' ultimate decline. They belong, comments William Stadiem, to the "Old families (who) never die. They just fade away,"[4] thus leaving the Southerner with a sense of personal and familial impotence.

The many difficulties besetting the South frequently appear first at the level of interpersonal familial relationships. The family is itself a mirror for Southern society. Faulkner's puritan South is fraught with frustration, violence, guilt and determinism, all a direct result of the Calvinism preponderant in this region. Faulkner's uprooted and materialistic Dixie is marked by questions of identity, rejection, alienation, narcissism and ambivalence. These issues, found at the level of interpersonal family relationships, reflect the Southerner's fragmentation in the wake of the Civil War.

The South, notes Howard Zinn, is uncontestably separate from other parts of the country. It's distinctiveness is clarified in Zinn's *The Southern Mystique:*

> Deep-set in the Southern mystique is the notion that the
> South is more than just "different," that it is distinct from the
> rest of the nation—a sport, a freak, an explicable variant from
> the national norm. The South, so it goes, does more than
> *speak* differently; it *thinks* differently.[5]

The South is considered more provincial, conservative, fundamentalist,
nativist, violent, conformist, militarist, and xenophobic than other
parts of the country. The South is also the area in which the family is
and has always been the central institution second only to the church.
The obsession with genealogy continues to be so great that Florence King
even remembers, as she states in *Southern Ladies and Gentlemen,* a
friend of her grandmother's who managed to claim direct descent from
God.[6] It is not surprising that the South is the only area in America
where children of either sex frequently carry their mother's maiden
name. Richmond psychiatrist, Dr. Latham, diagnosed insanity in the
South as being "a family tree under every bush."[7]

Besides the family, the Southerner is marked by his region's religion. The guilt fundamental to the Protestant South is well described by
Wilbur Cash in *The Mind of the South:*

> The world he knew, the hot sting of the sun in his blood, the
> sidelong glance of the all-complaisant Negro woman—all
> these impelled him irresistibily to joy. But even as he danced,
> and even though he had sloughed off all formal religion, his
> thoughts were with the piper and his fee.[8]

Although both the family and the church remained extremely influential in the post-Civil War South, neither were as unconditionally accepted as before.

Familial relations beginning in this period were re-evaluated.
The paternal system supported by the Protestant religion favored the
Pauline doctrine of male domination and white supremacy with both
the Negro and the female relegated to second class citizenship. With
the advent of the Civil War, both the Negro and the female began to
assert themselves as the white man's role of both master and male became weaker. In the antebellum South, the white upper-class male
conveniently structured the chivalric code to his double standard. The
white woman was elevated and isolated on her lofty pedestal by her
beloved squire who, meanwhile, indulged himself in frequent trysts

with slaves or, in some cases, established a second home with an octoroon mistress. A woman's identity was wholly dependent on a male, while a man's identity was dependent on his profession.

The white man's position has continued to weaken since the era of the Civil War. The Southern woman as late as Faulkner's time was still subject to a certain Manichæan judgment according to which she was classified as either mother or prostitute. Considering Faulkner's puritanism and reticence about sex, it is understandable that these two poles represent a kind of security; in neither case is a mature sexual relationship demanded. The author exposes himself as a misogynist of the first order, which is partially a consequence of his puritan background but also a result of his upbringing.

Faulkner is heavily influenced by his family, and many of his themes come directly from those family experiences. The fundamental issue of his misogyny is readily understood when one takes into consideration his obsessive and unhealthily close relationship with his mother. His inability to cut the umbilical cord with an overpowering mother to a great extent accounts for the emasculating female who populates his work. Likewise, Faulkner's father is projected onto the ineffectual male, typified by Mr. Compson, who is representative of the end of his line. The South, as well as Faulkner's Yoknapatawpha, is also inhabited by men who, like their female counterparts, are authoritarian and egocentric. These potent male figures also have their archetypes in the Falkner family, as exemplified by Faulkner's grandfather and particularly his great-grandfather. Discord in marriage is a problem with which the author is directly familiar in his own marriage and in that of his parents—both fraught with strife. The sibling rivalry existent in his work reflects his competitive relationship with his brother, John. The psychologically incestuous relationship, particularly between mother and son, is a fictional rendering of Maud's relationship not only with William, but also with her other sons. Faulkner's portrayal of the black and mulatto family also has its parallels in the author's own family: his grandfather is alleged to have had a mulatto daughter. Finally, the complete dependence of the whites on their black families is a relationship with which the author was directly involved, given the close bond with his black retainer, Ned Barnett, or his mammy, Caroline Barr.

With the exception of the parent-child relationships which begin to evolve positively as early as 1942, at the time of the publication of *Go Down, Moses* and the creation of the Mallison family in *Intruder in the Dust*, Faulkner's treatment of the family begins to undergo a positive metamorphosis. Simultaneously, Faulkner's own life undergoes a constructive transformation, both professionally and personally. Faulkner was practically out of print until Malcolm Cowley published *The Portable Faulkner* in 1946. Four years later, Faulkner was awarded the Nobel Prize for Literature. Until that time, he had been largely rejected, even in Oxford. As described by his step-granddaughter, Victoria Black, he was viewed in his hometown as "a drunk, he was a scapegoat; he was a bad man."[9] Even though he was suddenly "IT"[10] according to Vicki, when he received the Nobel Prize, years later and despite his fame, Faulkner had still not entirely outlived his earlier reputation. When his niece, Dean, started teaching Faulkner's work at the local high school in Oxford, one of the teachers still could not comprehend why Dean would want to teach that "dirty old man who stood on the corner with his fly open."[11]

Despite certain reservations from a very limited audience in Oxford, Faulkner by 1950 had found total reprieve from his earlier anonymity. His personal life had undergone constructive changes. His wife stopped drinking and, to his delight, he acquired a series of grandchildren. The author during this period came to project his familial happiness into his work just as previously he had projected his difficulties.

By the time of his last novel, *The Reivers*, the Priests had supplanted the Sartorises and the Compsons, the earlier, decadent incarnations of the Falkners. With the exception of Faulkner's unresolved conflict with his father, preventing his creation of an affirmative, potent father or husband figure, the parent-child relations and the marital relations in the Priest family reflect a healthy, stable home life. Simultaneously, the problematic incestuous relationships are no longer being replaced by substitute and surrogate incest as they were in the Mallison family but have been totally removed. The mulatto family member embodied by Ned McCaslin is now accepted, not rejected, by his white family despite the subordinate position he is given by them. The Parshams are no longer the foils of the Priests but instead are comparable family units that incorporate the positive qualities of the Southern family.

In the final analysis, Faulkner's later work generally shows a very different facet of the South than his early work. Initially, the region's decline is elucidated by him through the degeneration of its families as they attempt to survive in their puritan context. At the time of his later work, his own fulfillment on a familial level allows him to transcend these conflicts without ever being able fully to overcome the fact that he is his father's son as well as the ambivalent heir of the South's heritage.

NOTES

PREFACE

1. Donald M. Kartiganer, "Quentin Compson and Faulkner's Drama of the Generations," *Critical Essays on William Faulkner: The Compson Family*, ed. Arthur F. Kinney (Boston: Hall, 1982) 381.
2. Malcolm A. Franklin, *Bitterweeds: Life with William Faulkner at Rowan Oak* (Irving: Society for the Study of Traditional Culture, 1977) 59.
3. Gloria Franklin, telephone conversation, May 20, 1977.
4. Lamar Stevens, personal interview, May 19, 1977.
5. William Faulkner, *Absalom, Absalom!* (Middlesex: Penquin, 1975) 25.
6. Faulkner, *Absalom* 25.
7. Ibid.
8. Robert Penn Warren, "William Faulkner," *William Faulkner: Three Decades of Criticism*, ed. Frederick J. Hoffman and Olga W. Vickery (New York: Harcourt, 1963) 111-12.

CHAPTER 1

1. Maurice Edgar Coindreau, "William Faulkner," *La Nouvelle Revue Française* 36 (juin 1931): 926.
2. Phil Stone, Preface, *The Marble Faun and A Green Bough*, by William Faulkner (New York: Random House, 1965) 7.
3. Richard Gray, *Writing in the South: Ideas of an American Region* (Cambridge: Cambridge University Press, 1986) 171.
4. Faulkner, *Absalom* 214.
5. Faulkner, *Intruder* 62.
6. William Faulkner, "The Bear," *Go Down, Moses* (New York: Vintage, 1973) 193.
7. William Faulkner, Introduction, *The Sound and the Fury: A Faulkner Miscellany*, Edited by James B. Meriwether (Jackson: University Press of Mississippi, 1974) 157.
8. Thomas Wolfe, *Look Homeward, Angel: A Story of a Buried Life* (New York: Scribner's, 1957) 158.
9. Wolfe, Ibid. 172.
10. Wilbur Cash, *The Mind of the South* (New York: Vintage, 1969) 13.

11. Jean-Paul Sartre, "A propos de *Le Bruit et la Fureur:* La Temporalité chez Faulkner," *Situation I* (Paris: Gallimard, 1947) 72, 73.
12. Jean Pouillon, "Temps et Destinée chez Faulkner," *Temps et Roman* (Paris: Gallimard, 1946) 241.
13. Pouillon 246.
14. James B. Meriwether and Michael Millgate, eds., *Lion in the Garden: Interviews with William Faulkner, 1926-1962.* (New York: Random, 1968) 255.
15. Frederick L. Gwynn and Joseph Blotner, eds. *Faulkner in the University: Class Conferences at the University of Virginia, 1957-58* (New York: Vintage, 1965) 84.
16. Meriwether, *Lion* 70.
17. William Faulkner, *Requiem for a Nun* (New York: Random, 1968) 80.
18. Faulkner, *Intruder* 187.
19. Faulkner, *Absalom 9.*
20. Ibid.
21. Andrew Nelson Lytle, " The Working Novelist and the Mythmaking Process, "*Daedalus* 87 (Spring 1959): 330.
22. William Faulkner, *Sanctuary* (New York: Vintage, 1958) 258.
23. Dwight Dorough, *The Bible Belt Mystique* (Philadelphia: Westminster, 1974) 196.
24. Gwynn, *Class Conferences* 94.
25. Elvy E. Callaway, *The Other Side of the South* (Chicago: Ryerson, 1934) 66.
26. William Faulkner, *Mosquitoes* (New York: Liveright, 1955) 112.
27. Peter Swiggart, *The Art of Faulkner's Novels* (Austin: University of Texas, 1970) 133.
28. William Faulkner, *Light in August* (Middlesex: Penguin, 1985) 276.
29. Gwynn, *Class Conferences* 173.
30. Lillian Smith, *Killers of the Dream* (New York: Norton, 1961) 32.
31. Joseph H. Fichter and George L. Maddox, "Religion in the South, Old and New," *The South in Continuity and Change,* Edited by John McKinney and Edgar T. Thompson (Durham: Duke University Press, 1965) 362.
32. William Faulkner, *The Town* (New York: Vintage, 1961) 307.
33. Charles P. Roland, *The Improbable Era: The South since World War II* (Lexington: University of Kentucky Press, 1976) 119.
34. Alwyn Berland, *"Light in August* : The Calvinism of William Faulkner," *Modern Fiction Studies* 8 (Summer 1962): 167.
35. George Santayana, *Winds of Doctrine* (N. Y.: Scribner,1931) 167.
36. Faulkner, "William Faulkner: An Interview" 70.
37. William Faulkner, *Soldiers' Pay* (Middlesex: Penguin, 1976).
38. Faulkner, *Requiem* 237.
39. Meriwether, *Lion* 70.
40. William Faulkner, *A Fable* (New York: Vintage, 1978) 152.
41. John Shelton Reed, *The Enduring South* (Lexington: Heath, 1972) 57.
42. Wilbur Cash, *The Mind of the South* (N. Y.: Vintage, 1969) 136.

43. Ibid. 58.
44. Faulkner, *Light* 211.
45. William Faulkner, Letter to Maurice E. Coindreau, April 14, 1932, *Selected Letters of William Faulkner*, Edited by Joseph Blotner (New York: Random, 1977) 63-64.
46. Ann M. Springer, "Die Jüngsten" - John dos Passos, Ernest Hemingway, William Faulkner, Thomas Wolfe, *The Americaqn Novel in Germany: A Study of the Critical Reception of Eight American Novelists between the Two World Wars* (Hamburg: Cram, de Gryter, 1960) 86.
47. Gwynn, *Class Conferences* 38.
48. Faulkner, "The Bear" 258.
49. William Faulkner, *Flags in the Dust* (New York: Vintage, 1974) 314. William Faulkner, *Sartoris* (New York: Signet, 1964) 226.
50. Clarence Hugh Holman, "The Dark, Ruined Helen of His Blood: Thomas Wolfe and the South." *The Roots of Southern Writing: Essays on the Literature of the American South.* (Athens University of Georgia Press, 1972) 131.
51. Faulkner, Introduction, *The Sound* 157.
52. Thomas Wolfe, *You, Can't Go Home Again* (New York: Harper, 1940) 393.
53. William Faulkner, *The Wild Palms* (Middlesex: Penguin, 1970) 173.
54. William Faulkner, *The Sound and the Fury* (Middlesex: Penguin, 1971) 73.
55. Arthur Calhoun, *A Social History of the American Family* 3 vols. (New York: Barnes, 1960) 1: 241.
56. Francis Simkins, *A History of the South* (N. Y.: Knopf, 1953) 388.
57. Ibid. 389.
58. Eugene D. Genovese, *Roll, Jordan Roll: The World the Slaves Made* (New York: Vintage, 1976) 73-75, 133-49.
59. Hodding Carter, *Where Main Street Meets the River* (New York: Holt, 1953) 10.
60. Richard King, *A Southern Renaissance: The Cultural Awakening of the American South, 1930-1955* (New York: Oxford University Press, 1980) 27.
61. William Stadiem, *A Class by Themselves: The Untold Story of the Great Southern Families,* (New York: Crown, 1980) 263.
62. Clement Eaton, *The Mind of the South* (Baton Rouge: Louisiana State University Press, 1964) 241.
63. Eugene D. Genovese, *Roll, Jordan, Roll: The World the Slaves Made* (New York Vintage, 1976) 74.
64. Bruce Mazlish and Edwin Diamond, *Jimmy Carter; Interpretive Biography* (New York: Simon, 1979) 19.
65. Ibid. 19.
66. Mary Boykin Chesnut, *A Diary from Dixie* (New York: Appleton, 1906) 122-23.
67. Wolfe, *Look* 440.
68. Wolfe, *The Hills Beyond* (Garden City: Sun, 1943) 227.

69. Katherine Ann Porter, "Old Mortality," *Pale Horse, Pale Rider: Three Short Novels* (New York: NAL, 1962) 57.
70. Katherine Ann Porter, "The Downward Path to Wisdom," *The Leaning Tower* (New York: NAL, 1969) 76.
71. Robert Penn Warren, *All the King's Men* (New York: Bantam, 1974) 35.
72. Eudora Welty, *Delta Wedding* (New York:Harcourt, 1946) 84.
73. Thomas Nelson Page, *Red Rock: A Chronicle of Reconstruction* (New York: Scribner's, 1898) 76.
74. Faulkner, *Requiem* 39.
75. Frederick J. Hoffman, *William Faulkner* (New York: Twayne, 1961) 78.
76. Faulkner, "The Bear", 256.
77. Stadiem, *Class by Themselves*, 3.
78. Ibid. 2.
79. Cash, *Mind of the South*, 42.
80. Cleanth Brooks, *William Faulkner: Toward Yoknapatawpha and Beyond* (New Haven: Yale University Press, 1978) 334.
81. Joe Carl Bruice, "The Rise and the Fall of Aristocratic Families in Yoknapatawpha County," Ph.D. diss. East Texas State University, 1970, 137.
82. William Faulkner, *The Mansion* (New York: Vintage, 1965) 87.

CHAPTER 2

1. Blotner, *Faulkner: A Biography* 197.
2. William Blotner, *Faulkner: A Biography* 2 vols. (New York: Random House, 1976) 1: 811.
3. Malcolm Cowley, ed. *The Faulkner-Cowley File: Letters and Memories, 1944-1962 New York: Viking, 1967)* 66.
4. Faulkner, *Flags* 427. and Faulkner, *Sartoris* 298.
5. Faulkner, *Flags*5. Faulkner, *Sartoris* 19.
6. Faulkner, *Flags* 432-3. Faulkner, *Sartoris* 302.
7. Edmond L. Volpe, *A Reader's Guide to William Faulkner.* (New York: Farrar, 1976) 68.
8. Volpe 68.
9. Olga W. Vickery, *The Novels of William Faulkner,* (Baton Rouge: Louisiana State University Press, 1964) 19.
10. Faulkner, *Light* 48.
11. Faulkner, *Light* 49-50.
12. Faulkner, *Flags* 6. Faulkner, *Sartoris* 35.
13. Faulkner, *Flags* 360.
14. Faulkner, *Sartoris* 252.
15. Faulkner, *Flags* 323. Faulkner, *Sartoris* 234.

16. Faulkner, *Flags* 409. Faulkner, *Sartoris* 234.
17. Dorothy Tuck, *Apollo Handbook of Faulkner* (New York: Crowell, 1964) 233.
18. Robert Coughlan, *The Private World of William Faulkner* (New York: Cooper, 1972) 38.
19. Minnie Ruth Little, personal interview, May 16, 1977.
20. Jill Faulkner Summers, telephone conversation, July 18, 1977.
21. Malcolm A. Franklin, personal interview, Sept. 15, 1977.
22. Gloria Franklin, telephone conversation, May 15, 1977.
23. William Faulkner, "Sepulture South: Gaslight," *Uncollected Stories of William Faulkner*, Edited by Joseph Blotner (New York: Random, 1981) 455.
24. Ernest Jones, *Papers on Psycho Analysis* (Boston: Beacon, 1948) 412.
25. Jones, 407.
26. Ibid., 409.
27. Ibid.,
28. Ibid., 410.
29. Cowley, *The Faulkner-Cowley File*, 66.
30. John Faulkner, *My Brother Bill: An Affectionate Reminiscence* (New York: Trident,1963) 123.
31. Cowley, *The Faulkner-Cowley File*, 66.
32. Annie Brierre, "Faulkner Parle," *Les Nouvelles Littéraires* 43 (6 Oct. 1955): 6.
33. Blotner, *Faulkner: A Biography* 1:92.
34. Ibid. 2:1057.
35. Ibid. 2:1069.
36. Phil Stone, "William Faulkner, The Man and His Work," *Oxford Magazine*, Copies 1,2,3 (1934): 4.
37. Blotne, *Faulkner: A Biography* 124.
38. Gloria Franklin, telephone conversation, May 15, 1977.
39. Blotner, *Faulkner: A Biography* 117-18.
40. Ibid. 118.
41. Ibid. 1:768.
42. Ibid. 1:768
43. Sue Falkner, personal interview, May 16, 1977.
44. Blotner, *Faulkner: A Biography* 276.
45. Ibid. 295.
46. Ibid. 276.
47. Ibid. 323.
48. Ernest Jones, *The Life and Work of Sigmund Freud*, Edited by Lionel Trilling and Steven Marcus. (New York: Basic, 1961) 5.
49. Murry C. Falkner, *The Falkners of Mississippi: a Memoir* (Baton Rouge: Louisiana State University Press, 1967) 192.
50. Blotner, *Faulkner: A Biography* 1: 658.
51. Faulkner, *Early* 115.

52. Faulkner, *Mosquitoes* 250.
53. Ibid. 210.
54. Ibid. 228.
55. Blotner, *Faulkner: A Biography* 559.
56. Ibid. 2:1374.
57. Walter Toman, *Family Constellation* (N. Y.: Springer, 1961) 24.
58. Ibid. 24.
59. Dean Faulkner Wells, personal interview, May 17, 1977.
60. Blotner, *Faulkner: A Biography* 518.
61. Joan Williams, *The Wintering* (New York: Harcourt, 1971) 101,131-32.
62. Blotner, *Faulkner: A Biography* 2: 1184.
63. Ibid. 359.
64. Ibid.
65. Meta Carpenter Wilde and Orin Borsten, *A Loving Gentleman.* (New York: Simon, 1976) 137.
66. Blotner, *Faulkner: A Biography* 30.
67. Ibid. 679.
68. Sue Falkner, personal interview, May 16, 1977.
69. David Minter, *William Faulkner: His Life and Work* (Baltimore: John Hopkins University Press, 1980) 15.
70. Blotner, *Faulkner: A Biography* 16.
71. Ibid. 16.
72. Ibid. 1: 306.
73. William Faulkner, *Vision of Spring* (Austin: University of Texas Press, 1984) 67.
74. Faulkner, *Vision* 75.
75. Blotner, *Faulkner: A Biography* 205.
76. Dr. Richard McCool, telephone conversation, May 17, 1977.
77. Marion Hall, personal interview, May 19, 1977.
78. Williams, *The Wintering* 101.
79. Margaret Brown, personal interview, May 14, 1977.
80. Ann Abadie, ed., *William Faulkner: A Life on Paper* (Jackson: University Press of Mississippi, 1980) 68.
81. Wilde, *A Loving Gentleman*, 52.
82. Malcolm A. Franklin, personal interview, Sept. 15, 1977.
83. Emily Stone, personal interview, May 13, 1977.
84. Ibid.
85. Faulkner, *Absalom* 90.
86. Malcolm A. Franklin, personal interview, Sept. 15, 1977.
87. Ibid.
88. Blotner, *Faulkner: A Biography* 2: 1327.
89. Ibid. 459.
90. Williams, *The Wintering* 233.
91. Smith, *Killers* 133.

92. Wilde *A Loving Gentleman*, 75.
93. Minter, *William Faulkner*, 162.
94. Margaret Brown, personal interview, May 14, 1977.
95. Gloria Franklin, personal interview, May 15, 1977.
96. Meta Carpenter Wilde, personal interview, July 17, 1977.
97. Wilde *A Loving Gentleman*, 311-12.
98. Faulkner, "The Bear" 326.
99. William Faulkner, letter to Malcolm Cowley, Sept. 20, 1945, *Selected Letters of William Faulkner*, Edited by Joseph Blotner (New York: Random, 1977) 203.
100. Rose Roland, personal interview, May 20, 1977.
101. Murry C. Falkner, *The Faulkners of Mississippi: A Memoir* (Baton Rouge: Louisiana State University Press, 1967) 11.
102. Ibid. 12.
103. Cornell Franklin, telephone conversation, May 22, 1977.
104. Malcolm A. Franklin, *Bitterweeds: Life with William Faulkner at Rowan Oak.* (Irving: Society for the Study of Traditional Culture, 1977) 97.
105. H. Edward Richardson, *William Faulkner: The Journey to Self-Discovery* (Colombia: University of Missouri Press, 1969) 34.
106. Emily Stone, personal interview, May 13, 1977.
107. William Faulkner, "And Now What's To Do." *A Faulkner Miscellany*, Edited by James B. Meriwether. (Jackson: University Press of Mississippi, 1974) 147.
108. Faulkner, "*And*" 147.
109. Blotner, *Faulkner: A Biography* 1:118.
110. Jelliffe, Robert A. ed. *Faulkner at Nagano.* (Tokyo: Kenkyusha, 1956) 104.
111. Blotner, *Faulkner: A Biography* 217.
112. Faulkner, *The Sound* 97.
113. Blotner, *Faulkner: A Biography* 520.
114. William Faulkner, "Appendix: The Compsons," *The Portable Faulkner*, Edited by Malcolm Cowley (N. Y.: Viking, 1967) 708.
115. Gwynn, *Class Conferences* 3.
116. Robert Coughlan, *The Private World of William Faulkner* (New York: Cooper, 1972) 48.
117. Blotner, *Faulkner: A Biography* 102.
118. Kenneth E. Richardson, *Force and Faith in the Novels of Faul-kner* (Hague: Mouton, 1967) 46.
119. Blotner, *Faulkner: A Biography* 123.
120. Ibid. 204.
121. Ibid. 2:1182.
122. Ibid. 2: 1181.
123. Ibid. 562.
124. Ibid. 2:1439.
125. Ibid. 2:1344.

126. Ibid. 2:1467.
127. Emily Stone, personal interview, May 13, 1977.
128. Blotner, *Faulkner: A Biography* 1:405-6.
129. Ibid. 1:415.
130. Ibid. 1:415.
131. Ibid. 1:416.
132. Meriwether, *Essays* 10.
133. Blotner, *Faulkner: A Biography* 416.
134. Ibid. 500.
135. James B., Meriwether, and Michael Millgate, eds. *Lion in the Garden: Interviews with William Faulkner 1926-1962.* (New York: Random House, 1968) 120.
136. Blotner, *Faulkner: A Biography* 1:430.
137. Faulkner, *Mosquitoes* 241.
138. Ibid. 242.
139. Ibid. 243.
140. William Faulkner, Dedication, *Sartoris,* by Faulkner (New York: Signet, 1964)
141. Blotner, *Faulkner: A Biography* 485.
142. Ibid. 2: 1357.
143. Jelliffe, *Faulkner at Nagano* 54.
144. Jill Faulkner Summers, telephone conversation, July 18, 1977.
145. Blotner, *Faulkner: A Biography* 2:1228.
146. Ibid. 506.
147. Cornell Franklin, telephone conversation, May 22, 1978.
148. Abadie, *A Life on Paper* 67.
149. Blotner, *Faulkner: A Biography* 480-81.
150. Ibid. 481.
151. Ibid. 2: 1169.
152. Jeanne Franklin, personal interview, Oct. 8, 1978.
153. Blotner, *Faulkner: A Biography* 2:1474.
154. Ibid. 705.
155. Ibid. 2:1510.
156. Jill Faulkner Summers, telephone conversation, July 18, 1977.
157. Dean Faulkner Wells, personal interview, May 17, 1977.
158. Victoria Fielden Black, personal interview, May 19, 1977.
159. Gloria Franklin, personal interview, May 15, 1977; Jean Stein, personal interview, Oct. 6, 1977.
160. Jeanne Franklin, personal interview, Oct. 8, 1977.
161. Dean Faulkner Wells, personal interview, May 17, 1977.
162. Arthur Guyton, personal interview, May 18, 1977.
163. James M. Faulkner, personal interview, May 17, 1977.
164. Malcolm A. Franklin, personal interview, Sept. 15, 1977.
165. Ashton Holly, telephone conversation, May 20, 1977.

166   Jeanne Franklin, personal interview, Oct. 8, 1978.
167. Jeanne Franklin, personal interview, Oct. 8, 1978.
168. Arthur Guyton, personal interview, May 18, 1977.
169. Franklin, Dedication, *Bitterweeds*.
170. Charles Nelson and David Goforth, *Our Neighbor, William1Faulkner* (Chicago: Adams, 1977) 38.
171. Franklin, *Bitterweeds* 99.
172. Blotner, *Faulkner: A Biography* 2:1057.
173. Dean Faulkner Wells, "A Biographical Study. Dean Swift Faulkner," M. A. thesis, University of Mississippi, 1975, 165.
174. Faulkner, *Flags* 48–49. Faulkner, *Sartoris* 54.
175. Faulkner, *Flags* 330. Faulkner, *Sartoris* 240.
176. Faulkner, *Flags* 359. Faulkner, *Sartoris* 10.
177. Faulkner, *Flags* 359. Faulkner, *Sartoris* 251.
178. Walter M. Brylowski, *Faulkner's Olympian Laugh: Myth in the Novels* (Detroit: Wayne State University Press, 1968) 55.
179. Blotner, *Faulkner: A Biography* 356.
180. Dean Faulkner Wells, "A Biographical Study. Dean Swift Faulkner." Master's Thesis: University of Mississippi, 1975) 185.
181. Ibid. 184.
182. Ibid. 184.
183. Wilde, *A Loving Gentleman* 33.
184. Dean Faulkner Wells, personal interview, May 17, 1977.
185. Erik Erikson, "Reflections on the American Identity," *Childhood and Society*, 2nd edition by (New York: Norton, 1950) 267.
186   Lucille Faulkner, personal interview, May 16, 1977.
187. Blotner, *Faulkner: A Biography* 246.
188. Lucille Faulkner, personal interview, May 16, 1977.
189. Blotner, *Faulkner: A Biography* 246.
190. Toman, *Family Constellation* 24.
191. Sue Falkner, personal interview, May 20, 1977.
192. Linda Welshimer Wagner, et al. "Faulkner and Women," *The South and Faulkner's Yoknapatawpha: The Actual and the Apocrypal*, Edited by Evans Harrington and Ann J. Abadie (Jackson: University Press of Mississippi, 1977) 150.
193. Abadie, *A Life on Paper* 105.
194. Jill Faulkner Summers, telephone conversation, July 18, 1977.
195. Malcolm A. Franklin, personal interview, Sept. 15, 1977.
196. Irving Malin, *William Faulkner: An Interpretation* (New York: Gordian, 1972) 96.
197. Blotner, *Faulkner: A Biography* 614.
198. James M. Faulkner, personal interview, May 20, 1977.
199. William Faulkner, "Hair," *The Penguin Collected Stories of William Faulkner* (Middlesex: Penguin, 1985) 133.

200. Wells, "A Biographical Study" 135.
201. James M. Faulkner, personal interview, May 20, 1977.
202. Blotner, *Faulkner: A Biography* 98.
203. William Faulkner, dedication, *The Wishing Tree*, by Faulkner (New York: Random, 1950) n.p.
204. Blotner, *Faulkner: A Biography* 197-98.
205. Ibid. 380.
206. Malcolm A. Franklin, personal interview, Sept. 15, 1977.
207. Lewis Dollarhide, personal interview, May 20, 1977.
208. Ibid.
209. Victoria Fielden Black, personal interview, May 19, 1977.
210. Blotner, *Faulkner: A Biography* 449.
211. Wilde, *A Loving Gentleman* 77.
212. Ibid. 98.
213. Abadie *A Life on Paper* 103.
214. Blotner, *Faulkner: A Biography* 2:1484.
215. Williams, *The Wintering* 117-18.
216. Joan Williams, personal interview, Oct. 7, 1978.
217. Williams, *The Wintering* 117-18.
218. Joan Williams, personal interview, Oct. 7, 1978.
219. Blotner, *Faulkner: A Biography* 516.
220. Ibid. 579.
221. Blotner, *Faulkner: A Biography* 2:1484.
222. Joan Williams, personal interview, Oct. 7 1978.
223. Blotner, *Faulkner: A Biography* 512.
224. Blotner, *Faulkner: A Biography* 522.
225. William Faulkner, letter to Joan Williams, Jan. 13, 1950, *Selected Letters of William Faulkner*, Edited by Joseph Blotner (New York: Random House, 1977) 297.
226. Blotner, *Faulkner: A Biography* 689.
227. Jean Stein, personal interview, Oct. 6, 1977.
228. Ibid.
229. Ibid.
230. Lourie Strickland Allen, "Colonel William C. Falkner: Writer of Romance and Realism," Ph.D. dissertation, University of Alabama, 1972, 209.
231. Blotner, *Faulkner: A Biography* 671.

CHAPTER 3

1. Ann Firor Scott, *The Southern Lady; From Pedestal to Politics 1830-1930* (Chicago: University Press of Chicago, 1970) 13.

2. Arthur Calhoun, *A Social History of the American Family*, 3 vols. (New York: Barnes, 1960) 2:274.

3. Noël Polk, ed.,*William Faulkner: Sanctuary: The Original Text*. (New York, Random House, 1981) 51.

4. Faulkner, *Flags* 121. Faulkner, *Sartoris* 103.

5. Keith F. McKean, "Southern Patriarch: A Portrait." *Virginia Quarterly Review* 36 (Summer 1960) 378.

6. Louise Blackwell, " Faulkner and the Womenfolk", *Kansas Magazine* 1967: 75.

7. Ellen Douglas, "Faulkner's Women," *A Cosmos of My Own*, ed. Doreen Fowler and Ann J. Abadie (Jackson: University Press of Mississippi, 1981) 162-64.

8. Faulkner, *The Wild* 60.

9. Faulkner, *Intruder* 231.

10. Faulkner, *The Town* 227.

11. William Faulkner, *As I Lay Dying* (N. Y.: Vintage, 1957) 162.

12. Gwynn, *Class Conferences* 114.

13. Faulkner, *Flags* 285. Faulkner, *Sartoris* 210.

14. Faulkner, *Flags* 401.

15. William Faulkner, "Elly," *The Penguin Collected Stories of William Faulkner* (Middlesex: Penguin, 1985) 213.

16. Faulkner, "Elly" 213.

17. William Faulkner, *The Unvanquished* (Middlesex: Penguin, 1975) 132.

18. Ibid. 132.

19. Faulkner, *Absalom* 198.

20. Ibid. 56.

21. Ibid. 62.

22. Ibid. 11.

23. Ibid. 13.

24. Ibid. 217.

25. Ibid. 89.

26. Thomas Nelson Page, *Social Life in Old Virginia* (New York: Scribner's, 1897) 38-42.

27. Mary Chesnut, *A Diary from Dixie* (Boston: Houghton, 1961) 486.

28. Ibid. 49.

29. Ibid. 49.

30. Angelina Emily Grimké, *Letters to Catherine E. Beecher* (Boston: Knapp, 1838) 116.

31. Susan Dabney Smedes, *Memorials of a Southern Planter* (Baltimore: Cushings, 1887) 179.

32. Calhoun, *Original Text* 2: 323.

33. Gunnar Myrdal, *An American Dilemma* (N. Y.: Harper, 1962) 591.

34. Lillian Smith, *Killers of the Dream*. (New York: Norton, 1961) 153.

35. Ibid. 123, 124, 122,

36. Wilbur Cash, *The Mind of the South* (New York: Vintage, 1960) 86.
37. Carl Rowan, *South of Freedom* (New York: Knopf, 1952) 226.
38. Calhoun, *Original Text* 2: 275.
39. Howard Odum, *The Way of the South* (New York: Mac Millan, 1947) 77,138.
40. Sarah Moore Grimké, *Letters on the Equality of the Sexes and the Condition of Women, Addressed to Mary S. Parker* (Boston: Knapp, 1838) 47-55.
41. Gwynn, *Class Conferences* 254.
42. Faulkner, *Mosquitoes* 252.
43. Faulkner, *Soldiers' Pay* 184.
44. Faulkner, *Absalom* 78.
45. Ibid. 79.
46. Ibid. 80.
47. Ibid. 159.
48. Ibid. 165.
49. Ibid. 165.
50. Ibid. 170.
51. Ibid. 149.
52. Scott, *The Southern Lady* 137.
53. Ibid. 137.
54. Elizabeth M. Kerr, "The Women of Yoknapatawpha," *The University of Mississippi Studies in English* 15 (1978): 85.
55. Ethel M. Smith, *Towards Equal Rights for Men and Women* (Washington: National League of Women Voters, 1929) 14-17.
56. Ibid. 14.
57. The United States Women's Bureau. *The Legal Status of Women in the United States* (Washington: National League of Women Voters, 1945) 3.
58. Smith, *Towards* 17.
59. The U.S. Women's Bureau 5.
60. Ibid. 5.
61. Ibid. 5.
62. Ibid. 5.
63. Ibid. 7.
64. Ibid. 10.
65. Ibid. 11.
66. Ibid. 12.
67. Kerr, "Women of Yoknapatawpha" 92.
68. Faulkner, *Requiem* 118.
69. Ibid. 147.
70. Faulkner, "Elly" 211.
71. Jelliffe, *Faulkner at Nagano* 66-67.
72. Ibid. 24.
73. Joseph Blotner, "William Faulkner: Seminar", *The University of Mississippi Studies in English* 14 (1977): 64.

74. Gwynn, *Class Conferences* 74.
75. Blotner, "William Faulkner" 69.
76. Blotner, *Faulkner: A Biography* 294.
77. Meriwether, *Lion* 58.
78. William Faulkner, "Delta Autumn," *Go Down, Moses* (New York: Vintage, 1973) 352.
79. Faulkner, *Mosquitoes* 112.
80. Faulkner, *Sanctuary* 180.
81. Faulkner, *Intruder* 70.
82. Faulkner, *Absalom* 255.
83. Faulkner, *Mosquitoes* 320.
84. Faulkner, *The Wild* 83.
85. Shelby Foote, "It's Worth a Grown Man's Time," *Kite-Flying and Other Irrational Acts: Conversations with Twelve Southern Writers,* Edited by John Carr (Baton Rouge: Louisiana State University Press, 1972) 19.
86. Faulkner, "And" 146.
87. Ibid. 147.
88. William Faulkner, "Nympholepsy," *A Faulkner Miscellany* (Jackson: University of Mississippi, 1974) 153.
89. William Faulkner, *The Hamlet* (New York: Vintage, 1964) 119.
90. Ibid. 115.
91. Ibid. 130.
92. Ibid. 97.
93. Ibid. 99.
94. Ibid. 121.
95. Faulkner, "Nympholepsy" 153.
96. Faulkner, *The Sound* 118.
97. Faulkner, *Light* 143.
98. Gloria Franklin, telephone conversation, May 15, 1977.
99. Faulkner, *The Wild* 118.
100. Faulkner, *Mosquitoes* 221.
101. Faulkner, *The Wild* 99.
102. Ibid. 99.
103. Faulkner, *The Sound* 75.
104. Faulkner, *Mosquitoes* 320.
105. Faulkner, *Flags* 209. Faulkner, *Sartoris* 161.
106. Faulkner, *Mosquitoes* 305.
107. Faulkner, "Hair" 133.
108. Faulkner, *Light* 96.
109. Faulkner, *The Sound* 90.
110. Faulkner, *Light* 238.
111. Polk, *Original Text* 282.
112. Elizabeth Kerr, "William Faulkner and the Southern Concept of Woman," *Mississippi Quarterly* 15 (Winter 1962): 14.

113. Kerr, "Women of Yoknapatawpha" 98.
114. Ibid. 100.
115. Ibid. 100.
116. Sally R. Page, *Faulkner's Women: Characterization and Meaning* (Deland: Everett, 1972) 139-74.
117. Page, *Faulkner's Women* 1-42.
118. Ibid. 45-71.
119. Ibid. 93-135.
120. Ibid. 134.
121. Irving Malin, *William Faulkner: An Interpretation.* (New York: Gordian, 1972) 96.
122. Ibid. 95.
123. Leslie Fiedler, *Love and Death in the American Novel* (New York: Criterion, 1970) 309.
124. Ibid. 285.
125. Cleanth Brooks, *William Faulkner: The Yoknapatawpha Country.* (New Haven: Yale, 1963) 130.
126. Kenneth E. Richardson, *Force and Faith in the Novels of Faulkner. (Hague: Mouton, 1967)* 65.
127. Samuel A. Yorks, "Faulkner's Women: The Peril of Mankind," *Arizona Quarterly* 17 (Summer 1961): 119-20.
128. Ilse Dusoir Lind, "Faulkner's Women," *The Maker and the Myth: Faulkner and Yoknapatawpha,1977*, Edited by Evans Harrington and Ann J. Abadie (Jackson: University Press of Mississippi, 1978) 94.
129. Thomas Lorch, "Thomas Sutpen and the Female Principle," *Mississippi Quarterly* 20 (Winter 1967): 42.
130. Karl E. Zink, "Faulkner's Garden: Women and the Immemorial Earth," *Modern Fiction Studies* 2 (Autumn 1956): 139-49.
131. Albert J. Guerard, *The Triumph of the Novel* (New York: Oxford University Press, 1976) 109-10.
132. Ibid. 110.
133. Richard King, *A Southern Renaissance: The Cultural Awakening of the American South 1930-1955* (New York: Oxford, 1980) 80.
134. David Miller, "Faulkner's Women" *Modern Fiction Studies* 13 (Spring 1967): 3.
135. Jelliffe, *Faulkner at Nagano* 24-25.
136. Fiedler, *Love* 284.
137. Page, *Faulkner's Women* 182.
138. Ruel E. Foster, "Social Order and Disorder in Faulkner's Fiction," *Approach* No. 55 (Spring 1965): 26.
139. Irving Howe, *William Faulkner: A Critical Study.* (Chicago: University of Chicago Press, 1975) 141.
140. Ibid. 141.
141. Faulkner, *Mosquitoes* 26.

142. Lind, "Faulkner's Women" 102.
143. Ibid. 102.
144. Malin, *Faulkner: An Interpretation* 95-96.
145. Maxwell Geismar, "William Faulkner: The Negro and the Female," *Writers in Crisis: The American Novel between Two Wars* (Boston: Houghton, 1942) 147.
146. Ibid. 164.
147. Barbara Giles, "The South of William Faulkner," *Masses and Mainstream* Feb. 1950: 37.
148. Malcolm Cowley ed. Introduction, *The Portable Faulkner* (New York: Viking, 1966)
149. Ilse Dusoir Lind, "The Design and Meaning of *Absalom, Absalom!,*" *William Faulkner: Three Decades of Criticism,* Edited by Frederick J. Hoffman and Olga Vickery (New York: Harcourt, 1963) 293.
150. Polk, *Original Text* 66.
151. Faulkner, *Absalom* 312.
152. Faulkner, *Soldiers'* 153.
153. Ibid. 37.
154. Faulkner, *Flags* 158-59.
155. Ibid. 338.
156. Faulkner, *Light* 361.
157. William Faulkner, "Zilphia Gant," *Uncollected Stories of Wil-liam Faulkner,* Edited by Joseph Blotner (New York: Random House, 1981) 380.
158. Faulkner, *Absalom* 56.
159. Faulkner, *Flags* 287. Faulkner, *Sartoris* 212.
160. Faulkner, *The Hamlet* 206.
161. Ibid. 207.
162. Faulkner, *The Wild* 61.
163. Ibid. 95.
164. Faulkner, *As* 164.
165. Ibid. 105.
166. Faulkner, *Light* 125.
167. Ibid. 126.
168. Ibid. 49-50.
169. Ibid. 239.
170. Ibid. 285.
171. Ibid. 281.
172. Ibid. 277.
173. Ibid. 98.
174. Ibid. 355.
175. Faulkner, *Requiem* 147.
176. Gwynn, *Class Conferences* 121.
177. James Agee and Walker Evans, *Let Us Praise Famous Men* (New York: Ballantine, 1974) 331.

178. Shields McIlwaine, *The Southern Poor White from Lubberland to Tobacco Road* (Noman: University of Oklahoma P, 1939) 274.
179. Merrel Macquire Skaggs, *The Folk of Southern Fiction* (Athens: University of Georgia Press, 1972) 66. Sylvia Jenkins Cook, *From Tobacco Road to Route 66, The Southern Poor White in Fiction* (Chapel Hill: University of North Carolina Press, 1972) 5.
180. Herbert Weaver, *Mississippi Farmers 1850-1960* (Gloucester: Smith, 1968) 37. W. H. Peck, *The McDonalds; or the Ashes of Southern Homes: A Tale of Sherman's March* (New York: Met. Record Office, 1867) 114.
181. Jean Rouberol, *L'Esprit du Sud dans l'oeuvre de Faulkner* (Paris: Didier, 1982) 233.
182. Margaret Jarman Hagood, *Mothers of the South: Portraiture of the White Tenant Farm Woman* (New York: Greenwood, 1939) 158-59.
183. William Faulkner, "Adolescence," *Uncollected Stories of William Faulkner*, Edited by Joseph Blotner (New York: Random House, 1981) 467.
184. Faulkner, *As* 29.
185. Faulkner, *Light* 14.
186. Melvin Backman, *Faulkner: The Major Years* (Bloomington: Indiana University Press, 1966) 157.
187. William Faulkner, "Wash," *The Penguin Collected Stories of William Faulkner* (Middlesex: Penguin, 1985) 538.
188. Faulkner, *The Mansion* 256.
189. Faulkner, *The Reivers* 46-47.
190. Ibid. 111.
191. Leslie A. Fiedler, "The Last of William Faulkner," *The Manchester Guardian* 28 Sept. 1962: 6.
192. Edmond L. Volpe, *A Reader's Guide to William Faulkner.* (New York: Farrar, 1976) 147.
193. Kerr, "Women of Yoknapatawpha" 90.
194. Faulkner, *The Reivers* 44.
195. Linda Welshimer Wagner, et al. "Faulkner and Women." *The South and Faulkner's Yoknapatawpha: The Actual and the Apocryphal* (Jackson: University Press of Mississippi, 1977) 150.
196. Blotner, *Faulkner: A Biography* 2: 295.

CHAPTER 4

1. D. R. Hundley, esq., *Social Relations in Our Southern States* (New York: Pierce, 1860) 98-99.
2. Burleigh B. Gardner, et al., *Deep South: A Social Anthropogical Study of Caste and Class.* (Chicago: University Press of Chicago, 1965) 133.

3. Margaret Jarman Hagood, *Mothers of the South: Portraiture of the White Tenant Farm Woman.* (New York: Greenwood, 1939) 125.

4. Faulkner, *As I Lay Dying* 168.

5. Burleigh B. Gardner et al. *Deep South: A Social Anthropological Study of Caste and Class* (Chicago: University of Chicago Press, 1965) 124.

6. André Bleikasten, "Fathers in Faulkner," *The Fictional Father: Lacanian Readings of the Text.* Edited by Robert Con Davis (Amherst: University of Massachusetts, 1981) 142.

7. Bleikasten, "Fathers" 115.

8. Faulkner, *Soldiers'* 191.

9. Faulkner, "Appendix:" 719.

10. Faulkner, *As I Lay Dying,* 202.

11. William Faulkner, *Pylon* (New York: Random, 1962) 20.

12. Albert J. Devlin, "Parent-Child Relationships in the Works of William Faulkner," Ph.D thesis, University of Kansas, 1970,48.

13. Faulkner, " The Bear" 308.

14. Bleikasten, "Fathers" 117.

15. Faulkner, *Light* 357.

16. Ruth Shonle Cavan, *The Family* (New York: Crowell, 1948) 443.

17. Faulkner, *As* 246.

18. Cleanth Brooks, *William Faulkner: The Yoknapatawpha Country* (New Haven: Yale, 1963) 227.

19. Faulkner, *Absalom* 115.

20. Ibid. 145.

21. Ibid. 6.

22. Ibid. 49.

23. Faulkner, *Light* 355.

24. Ibid. 282.

25. William Van O'Connor, *The Tangled Fire.* (New York: Gordian Press, 1968) 75-76.

26. Faulkner, *Light* 114.

27. Glenn Sanstrom, "Identity Diffusion: Joe Christmas and Quentin Compson," *American Quarterly* 19 (Summer 1967): 221.

28. Faulkner, *Light* 182.

29. Ibid. 190.

30. Faulkner, *The Sound* 159.

31. Faulkner, *As* 161.

32. Jones, *Papers on Psycho-Analysis.* (Boston: Beacon, 1948) 411.

33. Ibid. 411.

34. Faulkner, *Light* 215.

35. Thomas E. Connolly "Fate and the 'Agony of Will': Determinism in Some Works of William Faulkner" *Essays on Determinism in American Literature* (Kent: Kent State University Press, 1964) 37.

36. Albert Devlin, "Parent-Child Relationships in the Works of William Faulkner" Ph. D Thesis, University of Kansas 2.
37. Gardner, *Study of Caste and Class* 94.
38. Joan Williams, "In Defense of Caroline Compson," *Critical Essays on William Faulkner: The Compson Family*, Edited by Arthur F. Kinney (Boston: Hall, 1982) 405.
39. Brooks, *William Faulkner: The* 333-34.
40. Walter M. Brylowski, Faulkner's Olympian Laugh: Myth in the Novels. (Detroit: Wayne State University Press, 1968) 67.
41. Faulkner, *The Sound* 89.
42. Ibid. 121.
43. Ibid. 157.
44. John K. Simon, "What Are You Laughing at, Darl? Madness and Humor in *As I Lay Dying*," *College English* 25 (Nov. 1963): 108.
45. William Handy, "*As I Lay Dying*: Faulkner's Inner Reporter," *Kenyon Review* 21(Summer 1959): 447.
46. Faulkner, *As I Lay Dying*, 76.
47. Ibid. 164.
48. Ibid. 164.
49. Faulkner, *The Wild* 37-39.
50. George L. Friend, "Levels of Maturity: The Theme of Striving in the Novels of William Faulkner," Ph.D Univ. of Illinois, 1964, 83.
51. Gwynn, *Class Conferences* 36.
52. Faulkner, *The Town* 346.
53. Keith McKean, "Southern Patriarch: A Portrait" *Virginia Quarterly Review*, 36 (Summer 1960) 377.
54. Florence King, *Confessions of a Failed Southern Lady* (Marek: St. Martin's, 1985) 10.
55. Florence King, *Southern Ladies and Gentlemen* (New York: Bantam, 1976) 186.
56. Faulkner, *The Unvanquished* 11.
57. Stuart A. Queen, et al., *The Family in Various Cultures* (New York: Lippincott, 1952) 39.
58. Faulkner, *Sanctuary* 53.
59. Ibid. 282.
60. Brylowski 102.
61. Faulkner, *Sanctuary* 118.
62. Lawrence S. Kubie, M.D., "William Faulkner's *Sanctuary*." *Faulkner: A Collection of Critical Essays*. ed. Robert Penn Warren (Englewood Cliffs: Prentice, 1966) 137-46.
63. Gwynn, *Class Conferences* 185.
64. William Faulkner, "A Rose for Emily," *The Penguin Collected Stories of William Faulkner* (Middlesex: Penguin, 1985) 123.

65. Irving Malin, *William Faulkner: An Interpretation.* (New York: Gordian, 1972) 37.
66. Faulkner, *Sanctuary* 50.
67. Faulkner, *The Unvanquished* 154.
68. Faulkner, *Sartoris* 18.
69. Melvin Backman, *Faulkner* , The Major Years. (Blooming: Indiana University Press, 1966) 8.
70. Ibid. 8,9.
71. Brooks, *Yoknapatawpha Country* 107, 111.
72. Faulkner, *Flags* 360-61. Faulkner, *Sartoris* 252.
73. Faulkner, *Flags* 377. Faulkner, *Sartoris* 264.
74. Faulkner, *Flags* 263. Faulkner, *Sartoris* 254.
75. Devlin, "Parent-Child Relationships" 137.
76. Faulkner, *The Wild* 5-6.
77. Faulkner, *The Wild* 25.
78. Brylowski, *Faulkner's Olympian Laugh* 153-54.
79. William Faulkner, "The Old People," *Go Down, Moses* (New York: Vintage, 1973) 170.
80. Faulkner, " The Bear," 326.
81. Faulkner, " The Old" 174.
82. Faulkner, " The Bear" 297.
83. Ibid., 297.
84. Gwynn, *Class Conferences* 5.
85. Michael Millgate, *The Achievement of William Faulkner* (New York: Vintage, 1966) 207.
86. Faulkner, " The Bear" 300.
87. Ibid. 300.
88. Faulkner, "Delta" 351.
89. Gwynn, *Class Conferences* 246.
90. William Faulkner, "The Fire and the Hearth," *Go Down, Moses* (New York: Vintage, 1973) 109.
91. Faulkner, "Delta" 345.
92. William Faulkner, "Race at Morning," *Uncollected Stories of William Faulkner,* Edited by Joseph Blotner (New York: Random House, 1981) 309.
93. William Faulkner, "Two Soldiers," *The Penguin Collected Stories of William Faulkner* (Middlesex: Penguin, 1985) 87.
94. William Faulkner, "Shall Not Perish," *The Penguin Collected Stories of William Faulkner* (Middlesex: Penguin, 1985) 109.
95. Faulkner, "Shall" 111.
96. Faulkner, *The Mansion* 321.
97. Ibid.
98. Ibid. 218-19.
99. Faulkner, *William Faulkner: The* 206.

100. Faulkner, *The Town* 3.
101. Faulkner, *Intruder* 198-99.
102. Ibid.
103. Faulkner, *The Mansion* 353.
104. Ibid. 353.
105. Lillian Smith, *Killers of the Dream. (New York: Norton, 1961)* 153.
106. Delvin, "Parent-Child Relationships" 36.
107. Faulkner, *Intruder* 121.
108. Ibid. 34.
109. Ibid. 121.
110. William Faulkner, *A Fable* (New York: Vintage, 1978) 299-300.
111. Blotner, *Faulkner: A Biography* 2:1366.
112. Faulkner, *A Fable* 294.
113. Faulkner, *The Town* 40.
114. Faulkner, *The Town* 143.
115. Faulkner, *The Mansion* 87.
116. Erik Erikson, "Reflections on the American Identity." *Childhood and Society* (New York: Norton, 1950) 271.
117. Faulkner, *The Reivers* 301.
118. Ibid. 302.
119. Ibid. 50-51.
120. Ibid. 66.
121. Ibid. 118.
122. Ibid. 47.
123. Elizabeth M. Kerr, *The Reivers*: The Golden Book of Yokna-patawpha County," *Modern Fiction Studies* 13 (Spring 1967):103-4

CHAPTER 5

1. Richard King, *Southern Renaisssance: The Cultural Awakening of the American South* 1930-1955. (New York: Oxford University Press, 1980) A 27.
2. Paul Conner, "Patriarchy: Old and New," *American Quarterly* 17.1 (Spring 1965): 13.
3. Andrew Lytle, "The Working Novelist and Mythmaking Process." *Daedalus 88* (Spring 1959) 331.
4. Faulkner, *Absalom* 82.
5. Lytle, "Working Novelist,"331.
6. Ibid.
7. Ibid.
8. Ibid.
9. Ibid.

10. David Lester, "Incest," *Journal of Sex Research* 8.4 (Nov 1972): 269.
11. Ibid.
12. Samuel G. Kling, *Sexual Behavior and the Law* (New York: Geis, 1965) 163.
13. Ibid. 168-69.
14. Ibid.
15. Sanford H. Kadish, ed., *Encyclopedia of Crime and Justice*, 4 vols. (New York: Free Press, 1983) 3:881-82.
16. Ibid. 882.
17. Ibid. 882.
18 Ibid. 882.
19. Faulkner, *Absalom* 282.
20. David Webster Cory, *Violation of Taboo; Incest in Great Literature of the Past and the Present* (New York: Julien, 1963) 12.
21. Herbert Maisch, *Incest* (New York: Stein, 1972) 15.
22. Ibid. 14.
23. Ibid. 15.
24. Carvel Collins, "The Interior Monologues of *The Sound and the Fury*," *Psychoanalysis and American Fiction*, ed. Irving Malin (New York: Dutton, 1965) 238.
25. Otto Rank, *Daz-Inzest-Motiv in Dichtung und Sage* (Vienna: Deuticke, 1912) 443-65.
26. Samuel Kirson Weinberg, *Incest Behavior* (New York: Citadel, 1963) 73.
27. Ibid. 81.
28. Ibid.
29. Noël Polk, ed. *William Faulkner: Sanctuary, The Original Text.* (New York: Random House, 1981) 39.
30. Faulkner, *Flags* 170. Faulkner, *Sartoris* 139.
31. Faulkner, *Flags* 188. Faulkner, *Sartoris* 152.
32. Faulkner, *Sartoris* 149.
33. Faulkner, *Flags* 283.
34. Polk, *Sanctuary, Original Text* 16.
35. Faulkner, *Flags* 285. Faulkner, *Sartoris* 210.
36. Polk, *Sanctuary, Original Text* 64.
37. Julien Bigras, et al. "En deçà et au delà de l'inceste chez l'ado-lescente," *Canadian Psychiatric Association Journal* 11.3 (1966): 189-90.
38. Jones, *Papers on Psycho-Analysis.* (Boston: Beacon, 1948) 323.
39. Samuel Kirsen Weinberg, *Incest Behavior.* (New York: Citadel, 1963) 268-69.
40. Edmond L. Volpe, *A Reader's Guide to William Faulkner.* (New York: Farrar, 1976) 144.
41. Polk, *Sancturary, Original Text* 38.
42. Maurice Edgar Coindreau, préface, *Le bruit et la fureur*, by William Faulkner (Paris: Gallimard, 1987) 7.

43. Gwynn, Class Conferences 6.
44. Faulkner, introduction, *The Sound* 59.
45. Polk, *Sancturary, Original Text* 27.
46. Faulkner, "Adolescence" 471.
47. Faulkner, *Absalom* 82.
48. Faulkner, *Absalom* 99.
49. Bryan Strong, "Toward a History of the Experimental Family: Sex and Incest in the Nineteenth-Century Family," *Journal of Marriage and the Family* 35.3 (Aug.1973): 461.
50. Ibid. 461.
51. Weinberg, *Incest Behavior* 85.
52. Blotner, *Faulkner: A Biography* 652.
53. Faulkner, *The Sound* 96-97.
54. Ibid. 220.
55. Ibid.
56. Faulkner, *As I Lay Dying* 15.
57. Olga W. Vickery, *The Novels of William Faulkner.* (Baton Rouge: Louisiana State University Press, 1964) 68.
58. Faulkner, *The Sound* 85.
59. Hans H. Skei, *William Faulkner: The Novelist as a Short Story Writer: A Study of William Faulkner's Short Fiction* (Oslo: Universitetsforlaget, 1985) 119.
60. Ibid. 119.
61. William Faulkner, "The Brooch," *The Penguin Collected Stories of William Faulkner* (Middlesex: Penguin, 1985) 660.
62. Polk, *Sanctuary, Original Text* 17-18.
63. Ibid. 18.
64. Ibid. 59.
65. Ibid. 77.
66. Michael Millgate, *The Achievement of William Faulkner.* (New York: Vintage, 1966) 85.
67. Polk, *Sanctuary, Original Text* 143.
68. Ibid. 40.
69. Faulkner, *The Hamlet* 114.
70. Ibid. 101.
71. Ibid. 143.
72. Walter M. Brylowski, Faulkner's Olympian Laugh: Myth in the Novel. (Detroit: Wayne State Universtiy Press, 1968) 140.
73. Vickery, *The Novels of William Faulkner.* 37.
74. Faulkner, "Appendix" 709-10.
75. Faulkner, *The Sound* 75.
76. Ira L. Reiss, *The Family System in America* (New York: Holt, 1971) 367.
77. Ibid.
78. Ibid.

79. Masters, R. E. L. *Patterns of Incest* (N. Y.: Julian, 1963) 267-68.
80. William Faulkner, "The Portrait of Elmer." *Uncollected Stories of William Faulkner*, Edited by Joseph Blotner (New York: Vintage, 1981) 637.
81. Faulkner, "The Portrait" 616.
82. Ibid. 610.
83. Faulkner, *The Unvanquished* 151.
84. Ibid. 154.
85. Faulkner, *Pylon* 49.
86. Faulkner, "Adolescence" 461.
87. Faulkner, *The Wild* 30.
88. Ibid. 30.
89. Ibid. 31.
90. Ibid. 11.
91. Faulkner, *Mosquitoes* 24.
92. Cleanth Brooks, *William Faulkner: Toward Yoknapatawpha and Beyond.* *(New Haven: Yale University Press, 1978)* 124.
93. Faulkner, *The Sound* 118.
94. Ibid. 135.
95. Ibid. 159.
96. Faulkner, *As I Lay Dying* 243-44.
97. Faulkner, *The Sound* 122.
98. Ibid. 134.
99. Carl G. Jung, *Psychology and Alchemy*, translated by R. F. Hull (New York: Pantheon, 1953) 29.
100. Carl G. Jung, *The Archetypes and the Collective Unconscious*, translated by R. F. C. Hull (London: Koutledge,1959) 284-85.
101. Otto Rank, *Beyond Psychology* (New York: Dover, 1958) 71-72.
102. John T. Irwin, *Doubling and Incest: Repetition and Revenge: A Speculative Reading of Faulkner* (Baltimore: John Hopkins University Press, 1975) 37.
103. Lawrence E. Bowling "Faulkner and the Theme of Innocence," *Kenyon Review* 20 (Summer 1958): 471.
104. Irwin, *Doubling and Incest* 46.
105. Faulkner, *The Sound* 75.
106. Ibid. 138.
107. Ibid. 102.
108. Peter Swiggart, *The Art of Faulkner's Novels.* (Austin: University of Texas Press, 1962) 92.
109. Faulkner, *The Sound* 104.
110. Ibid. 114.
111. Lawrance R. Thompson, "Mirror Analogues in *The Sound and the Fury*," *William Faulkner: Three Decades of Criticism*, Edited by Frederick J. Hoffman and Olga W. Vickery (New York: Harcourt, 1963) 212.
112. Millgate, *Achievement of Faulkner* 119.

113. Backman, *Faulkner* 42.
114. Volpe, *A Reader's Guide* 143. Brooks, *Yoknapatawpha Country* 129.
115. Faulkner, *Sanctuary* 162.
116. Polk, *Sanctuary, Original Text* 15.
117. Ibid. 143.
118. Ibid. 255.
119. Faulkner, *Sanctuary* 162-163.
120. Polk, *Sanctuary, Original Text* 60.
121. Faulkner, *The Unvanquished* 161.
122. William E. Walker, "*The Unvanquished*: The Restoration of Tradition," *Reality and Myth: Essays in American Literature in Memory of Richard Croom Beatty,* Edited by William E. Walker and Robert L. Walker (Nashville: Vanderbilt Univ. P. 1964) 290.
123. Faulkner, *The Unvanquished* 157.
124. Irwin, *Doubling and Incest* 58.
125. Faulkner, *Absalom* 88.
126. Ibid. 79.
127. Faulkner, "Appendix" 710.
128. Faulkner, *The Sound* 108.
129. George Marion O'Donnell, "Faulkner's Mythology." *William Faulkner: Three Decades of Criticism.* Edited by Frederick J. Hoffman and Olga Vickery. (New York: Harcourt, 1963) 86.
130. Faulkner, *As I Lay Dying* 15.
131. Faulkner, *The Sound* 76.
132. Faulkner, "Appendix" 710.
133. Faulkner, *Absalom* 267.
134. Faulkner, *The Sound* 160.
135. Millgate, *Achievement of William Faulkner* 96.
136. Faulkner, *The Sound* 107.
137. Ibid. 107.
138. Malin, *William Faulkner: An Interpretation* 17.
139. Faulkner, *Absalom* 287.
140. Faulkner, *Sanctuary* 214.
141. Ibid. 215.
142. Ibid. 216.
143. Irwin, *Doubling and Incest* 41.
144. Faulkner, *The Unvanquished* 163.
145. William Healy, et al., *Structure and Meaning of Psychoanalysis as Related to Personality and Behavior* (N. Y.: Knopf, 1931) 396.
146. Carl G. Jung, *Psychology of the Unconscious* (New York: Dodd, 1916) 390.
147. David Williams, *Faulkner's Women; The Myth and the Muse* (Montreal: McGill University Press, 1977) 85.
148. Faulkner, *The Sound* 158.

149. John Earl Bassett, "Family Conflict in *The Sound and the Fury*," *Critical Essays on William Faulkner: The Compson Family*, ed. Arthur F. Kinney (Boston: Hall, 1982) 421.
150. Faulkner, "Appendix" 711.
151. André Bleikasten, *Parcours de Faulkner* (Paris: Ophyrs, 1982) 122.
152. Faulkner, *As I Lay Dying* 97.
153. Ibid. 156.
154. Faulkner, *The Unvanquished* 164.
155. Ibid. 164.
156. Faulkner, *The Town* 45.
157. Ibid. 302.
158. Ibid. 57.
159. Ibid. 89.
160. Ibid. 36.
161. Millgate, *Achievement of William Faulkner* 247.
162. Faulkner, *The Town* 135-36.
163. Faulkner, *The Mansion* 423.
164. Brooks, *Yoknapatawpha Country* 196.
165. Cleanth Brooks, "Gavin Stevens and the Chivalric Tradition," *The University of Mississippi Studies in English* 15 (1978): 29.
166. John Lewis Longley, Jr., *The Tragic Mask: A Study of Faul-kner's Heroes* (Chapel Hill: Univ. of North Carolina Press, 1963) 49. James Gray Watson, *The Snopes Dilemma: Faulkner's Trilogy* (Coral Gables: Univ. of Miami Press, 1968) 81.
167. Volpe, *Reader's Guide to Faulkner* 326.
168. Faulkner, *The Town* 50.
169. Faulkner, *The Sound* 88.
170. Faulkner, *The Town* 76.
171. Ibid. 208-9.
172. Faulkner, *The Mansion* 216.
173. Cleanth Brooks, "Gavin Stevens and the Chivalric Tradition." *The University of Mississippi Studies in English*, 15 (1978): 28.
174. Faulkner, *The Mansion* 238.
175. Gwynn, Class Conferences 141.
176. Warren Beck, *Man in Motion: Faulkner's Trilogy* (Madison: University of Wisconsin Press, 1961)103.

CHAPTER 6

1. Robert F. Winch, et al., eds., *Selected Studies in Marriage and the Family*, rev. ed. (New York: Holt, 1962) 496.

2. John T. Irwin, *Doubling and Incest: Repetition and Revenge: A Speculative Reading of Faulkner.* (Baltimore: John's Hopkins University Press, 1975) 93.

3. George Elliott Howard, *A History of Matrimonial Institutions Chiefly in England and the United States* 3 vols. (New York: Humanities, 1964) 2:440.

4. Faulkner, *Absalom* 95.

5. Robert R. Bell, *Marriage and Family Interaction* (Homewood: Dorsey, 1963) 219.

6. Robert J. Sickels, *Race, Marriage and the Law* (Albuquerque: University of New Mexico Press, 1972) 71.

7. Ibid. 68.

8. Frederick Gwynn and Joseph Blotner, eds., *Faulkner in the University: Class Conferences at the University of Virginia 1957-58* (New York: Vintage, 1965) 227.

9. Faulkner, "Delta" 361.

10. Robert A. Jelliffe ed., *Faulkner at Nagano* (Tokyo: Kenkynsha, 1956) 166.

11. Russel Warren Howe, "A Talk with Faulkner," *The Reporter* 14 (Mar. 22, 1959): 19.

12. Norman Mailer, *Advertisements for Myself* (New York: Putnam's, 1959) 332.

13. Joseph Blotner, *Faulkner: A Biography.* 2 vols. (New York: Random House, 1984) 2:1675.

14. James Hugo Johnston, *Race Relations in Virginia and Miscegenation in the South 1776-1860* (Amherst: University of Massachusetts Press, 1970) 172-73.

15. Lillian Smith, *Killers of the Dream.* (New York: Norton, 1961) 121.

16. Faulkner, *Absalom* 42.

17. Ibid. 84.

18. Ibid. 10.

19. Kenneth M. Stampp, *The Peculiar Institution: Slavery in the Antebellum South* (New York: Vintage, 1956) 356.

20. Beth Day, *Sexual Life between Blacks and Whites* (London: Collins, 1974) 54.

21. Day, *Sexual Life* 104.

22. Faulkner, *Absalom* 50.

23. Ibid. 90

24. Frederick Douglass, *My Bondage and My Freedom* (New York: Arno, 1968) 59.

25. Faulkner, "The Bear" 269-70.

26. Ibid. 269.

27. Faulkner, "The Fire" 105.

28. William Faulkner, "There Was A Queen," *The Penguin Collected Stories of William Faulkner* (Middlesex: Penguin, 1985) 728.

29. John Hope Franklin, *From Slavery to Freedom: A History of Negro Americans* (New York: Vintage, 1969) 205.
30. Faulkner, *Absalom* 76.
31. Ibid. 83.
32. Gwynn, *Class Conferences* 93.
33. Ibid. 294.
34. Gwynn, *Class Conferences* 94.
35. Olga W. Vickery, *The Novels of William Faulkner.* (Baton Rouge: Louisiana State University Press, 1964) 98.
36. Faulkner, *Absalom* 294.
37. Ibid. 161.
38. Ibid. 85-86.
39. Ibid. 61.
40. Ibid. 102.
41. Ibid. 163.
42. Ibid. 169
43. Ibid.
44. Ibid. 170-71.
45. Ibid. 97.
46. Ibid. 96-97.
47. Ibid. 92.
48. Ibid. 94.
49. Ibid. 94.
50. Wendell Phillips, "Philosophy of the Abolition Movement," *Speeches, Lectures, and Letters* (Boston: Lee, 1870) 108.
51. Sarah Patton Boyle, *The Desegregated Heart* (New York: Morrow, 1962) 161.
52. William Faulkner, "The Evening Sun," *The Penguin Collected Stories of William Faulkner* (Middlesex: Penguin, 1985) 292.
53. William E. B. Dubois, *Souls of Black Folk* (Chicago: McClurg, 1903) 9.
54. Faulkner, *Light* 119.
55. Wilbur J. Cash, *The Mind of the South* (N. Y.: Vintage, 1960) 117.
56. Blotner, *Faulkner: A Biography* 2:1675.
57. Calvin C. Herton, *Sex and Racism* (London: Deutsch, 1969) 13.
58. Ibid. 65.
59. Faulkner, *Light* 177.
60. Herton, *Sex and Racism* 142.
61. Faulkner, *Light* 194.
62. Ibid. 176.
63. Ibid. 177.
64. Ibid. 177
65. Day, *Sexual Life* 108.
66. Ibid.
67. Blotner, Faulkner: *A Biography* 1: 646.

68. Blotner, Faulkner: 1: 604.
69. Hernton, *Sex and Racism* 51.
70. Day, *Sexual Life* 79.
71. John B. Cullen and Floyd C. Watkins, "Joe Christmas and Nelse Patton" *Old Times in the Faulkner Country* (Baton Rouge: Louisiana State University Press, 1975) 94-98. Blotner, *Faulkner: A Biography* 32.
72. Faulkner, *Light* 349.
73. Ibid. 349.
74. Ibid. 288.
75. Ibid. 272.
76. Nancy M. Tischler, *Black Masks: Negro Characters in Modern Southern Fiction:* (University Park: Pennsylvania State University Press, 1969) 108.
77. Lillian Smith, *Killers of the Dream* (New York: Norton, 1961) 145.
78. Gunnar Myrdal, *An American Dilemma* (New York: Harper, 1962) 563.
79. John Dollard, *Caste and Class in a Southern Town* (New York: Doubleday, 1957) 166-67.
80. Charles I. Glicksberg, "William Faulkner and the Negro Problem," 10 (June 1949): 156.
81. Maxwell Geismar, "William Faulkner: The Negro and The Female" *Writer's in Crisis: The American Novel Between Two Wars* (Boston: Houghton, 1942) 179-80.
82. Ibid. 180.
83. Melvin Seiden, "Faulkner's Ambiguous Negro," *Massachusetts Review* 4 (Summer 1963): 485.
84. Irving Howe, *William Faulkner: A Critical Study* (Chicago: University of Chicago Press, 1975) 128.
85. Sherwood Anderson, *Sherwood Anderson's Memoirs* (New York: Harcourt, 1942) 474.
86. Faulkner, "The Old" 165.
87. Faulkner, "The Bear" 246.
88. Faulkner, *Light* 337-38.
89. Blotner, *Faulkner: A Biography* 649.
90. Fay E. Beauchamp, "William Faulkner's Use of the Tragic Mulatto Myth," Ph. D dissertation University of Pennsylvannia, 1974, 25.
91. Ibid. 5.
92. Faulkner, "The Fire" 58.
93. Faulkner, "The Old" 168.
94. Beauchamp 6-7.
95. Faulkner, *Intruder* 24.
96. William Faulkner, "A Justice," *The Penguin Collected Stories of William Faulkner* (Middlesex: Penguin, 1985) 360.
97. Faulkner, "The Bear" 193-94.
98. Faulkner, "Delta" 358.
99. Ibid. 358.

100. Faulkner, *Light* 288.
101. Blotner, *Faulkner: A Biography* 1: 763.
102. Ibid.
103. Gwynn, *Class Conferences* 118.
104. Ibid. 118.
105. Alfred Kazin, "The Stillness of *Light in August. William Faul-kner: Three Decades of Criticism*," Edited by Frederick Hoffman and Olga Vickery (New York: Harcourt, 1963) 253.
106. John Lewis Longley Jr., *The Tragic Mask: A Study of Faulkner's Heroes* (Chapel Hill: University of North Carolina Press, 1963) 74.
107. Faulkner, *Light* 99.
108. Ibid. 90.
109. Ibid. 90
110. Ibid. 87.
111. Faulkner, *Absalom* 91.
112. Faulkner, *Light* 249.
113. Melvin Backman, *Faulkner: The Major Years* (Bloomington: Indiana University Press, 1966) 74.
114. Faulkner, *Light* 170.
115. Ibid. 263.
116. Ibid. 94.
117. Ibid. 195.
118. Ibid. 119.
119. Ibid. 121
120. Backman, *The Major Years* 72.
121. Lewis M. Dabney, "Faulkner, the Red, and the Black," *Columbia Forum* 1.2 (Spring 1972) 52.
122. Ibid. 53.
123. Ibid. 53.
124. Faulkner, "The Old" 164.
125. Ibid. 170.
126. Faulkner, "The Bear" 227.
127. Faulkner, "The Fire" 47.
128. Ibid. 54.
129. Faulkner, *Intruder* 20.
130. Faulkner, "The Fire" 71.
131. Faulkner, "There" 730.
132. Ibid. 752.
133. Faulkner, *Absalom* 156.
134. Ibid. 232.
135. Faulkner, "The Old" 167.
136. Faulkner, *Light* 255.
137. Faulkner, *Absalom* 128.
138. Faulkner, *Light* 190.

139. Faulkner, *Absalom* 113.
140. Ibid. 112.
141. Faulkner, *Absalom* 129.
142. William Faulkner, "Evangeline," *Uncollected Stories of William Faulkner,* Edited by Joseph Blotner (New York: Random House, 1981) 607.
143. Faulkner, *Absalom* 115.
144. Ibid. 163.
145. Faulkner, "The Fire" 58.
146. Ibid. 118.
147. Ibid. 30.
148. Ibid. 31.
149. Ibid. 265.
150. Richard Slotkin, *Regeneration Through Violence: The Mythology of the American Frontier 1600-1860* (Middletown: Wesleyan University Press, 1973) 356-57.
151. Faulkner, *The Reivers* 45-46.
152. Vickery, *Novels of Faulkner* 116.

CHAPTER 7

1. James Baldwin, "Faulkner and Desegregation," *Partisan Review* 32 (Fall 1956): 568.
2. Neal R. Pierce, *The Deep South States of America* (New York: Norton, 1974) 168.
3. Ibid. 176.
4. Ibid. 178-79.
5. Carter Hodding, "Faulkner and His Folk," *Princeton University Library Chronicle* 18 (Spring 1957): 106.
6. John Faulkner, letter, *Memphis Commercial Appeal* 3 Avr. 1955, Sec. 5: 3.
7. James B. Meriwether and Michael Millgate, eds. *Lion in the Garden: Interviews with Willian Faulkner, 1926-1962* (New York: Random House, 1968) 114.
8. Frederick L. Gwynn and Joseph Blotner, eds. *Faulkner in the University: Class Conferences at the University of Virginia, 1957-1958* (New York: Vintage, 1965) 162.
9. Ibid. 209-10.
10. James B. Meriwether ed. *Essays Speeches and Public Letters* (New York: Random House, 1965) 146.
11. Robert Penn Warren, *Segregation: The Inner Conflict of the South* (New York: Random House, 1956) 62.
12. Faulkner, *Intruder* 202.

13. Meriwether, *Lion* 263-64.
14. Faulkner, *The Sound* 82.
15. Charles D. Peavy, *Go Slow Now: Faulkner and the Race Question* (Eugene: University of Oregon, 1971) 84.
16. Robert A. Jelliffe, ed. *Faulkner at Nagaro* (Tokyo: Keykyusha, 1956) 5.
17. Ibid. 185.
18. Russel Warren Howe, "A Talk with Faulkner," *The Reporter* 22 Mar. 1956: 19.
19. Peavy, *Go Slow Now* 85.
20. Baldwin, "Faulkner and Desegregation" 570.
21. Darwin T. Turner, "Faulkner and Slavery," *The South and Faulkner's Yoknapatawpha: The Actual and the Aprocryphal*, ed. Evans Harrington and Ann J. Abadie (Jackson: University Press of Mississippi, 1977) 65-66.
22. Faulkner, "The Bear" 227.
23. Faulkner, *The Unvanquished* 229.
24. Blotner, *Faulkner: A Biography* 1: 51.
25. Faulkner, *Light* 16.
26. Faulkner, *Absalom* 91
27. Faulkner, "The Fire" 111.
28. Faulkner, "The Bear" 278.
29. Gwynn, *Class Conferences* 79.
30. Faulkner, *Light* 190-91.
31. Leslie H. Owens, *This Species of Property: Slave Life and Culture in the Old South* (New York: Oxford University Press, 1976) 192.
32. Herbert G. Gutman, *The Black Family in Slavery and Freedom* (New York: Vintage, 1976) 15.
33. Thomas Jefferson, *Notes on the State of Virginia* (New York: Harper, 1964) 139.
34. Faulkner, *The Unvanquished* 57.
35. Ibid. *The Unvanquished* 72.
36. Arthur Calhoun, *A Social History of the American Family*, 3 vols. (New York: Barnes, 1960) 2: 293.
37. Charles H. Nilon, *Faulkner and the Negro* (New York: Citadel, 1965) 110.
38. Hugh Gloster, *Negro Voices in American Fiction* (Chapel Hill: University of North Carolina Press, 1948) 201-02.
39. Irving Howe, *William Faulkner: A Critical Study* (Chicago: University of Chicago Press, 1975) 134.
40. Ralph Ellison, "Twentieth-Century Fiction and the Black Mask of Humanity," *Shadow and the Act* (New York: Random House, 1964) 58-59.
41. Edmond L. Volpe, *A Reader's Guide to William Faulkner* (New York: Farrar, 1976) 17.
42. Janet Leah S. Pieper, "Black Characters in Faulkner's Fiction," diss. Univ. of Nebraska, 1976, 29.
43. Henry James, *The Art of the Novel* (New York: Scribner's, 1934) 54-5.

44. Harry Runyan, *A Faulkner Glossary* (New York: Citadel, 1966) 285.
45. Ibid. 11-182.
46. Hortense Powdermaker, *After Freedom: A Cultural Study of the Deep South* (New York: Russell, 1966) 65-68.
47. Horace Judson, "The Curse and the Hope," *Time* 84 (July 17, 1964): 48.
48. Malcolm Franklin, *Bitterweeds: Life with William Faulkner at Rowan Oak* (Irving: Society for the Study of Traditional Culture, 1977) 121.
49. Blotner, *Faulkner: A Biography* 490.
50. Powdermaker, *After Freedom* 145-46.
51. Walter B. Allen, "The Search for Applicable Theories of Black Family Life," *Journal of Marriage and Family* 40.1 (Feb.1978) 119.
52. Ibid. 119.
53. Ibid. 119.
54. Jerold Heiss, *The Case of the Black Family: A Sociological Inquiry* (New York: Colombia University Press, 1975) 133.
55. Arnold H. Taylor, *Travail and Triumph: Black Life and Culture in the South since the Civil War* (Westport: Greenwood, 1976) 170-71.
56. Herbert G. Gutman, *The Black Family in Slavery and Freedom* (New York: Vintage, 1976) 444.
57. C. Eric Lincoln, "The Absent Father Haunts the Negro Family," *The Contemporary American Family*, Edited by William J. Goode (Chicago: Quadrangle, 1971) 161.
58. Beth Day, *Sexual life between Blacks and Whites* (London: Collins, 1974) 129.
59. Powdermaker, *After Freedom* 211.
60. Gunnar Myrdal, *An American Dilemma* (New York: Harper, 1962) 933.
61. Faulkner, *The Sound* 33.
62. Ibid. 22.
63. Ibid. 35.
64. Faulkner, *Flags* 87. Faulkner, *Sartoris* 81.
65. Faulkner, *Flags* 393. Faulkner, *Sartoris* 227. "two opposed concepts antipathetic by race, blood, nature and environment, touching for a moment and fused with the illusion."
66. Faulkner, *Flags* 393. Faulkner, *Sartoris* 227.
67. Melvin Backman, "Sickness and Primitivism: A Dominant Pattern in William Faulkner's Work," *Accent* 14 (Winter 1954): 63.
68. Faulkner, "The Old" 167.
69. Lionel Trilling, "The McCaslins of Mississippi," rev. of *Go Down, Moses*, *The Nation* 30 May 1942: 63.
70. Faulkner, "The Bear" 272.
71. Faulkner, "Was" 7.
72. Faulkner, "The Bear" 326.
73. Michael Millgate, *The Achievement of William Faulkner* (New York: Vintage 1966) 205-06.

74. Frank S. Loescher, *The Protestant Church and the Negro: A Pattern of Segregation* (New York: Association, 1948) 117.
75. Wynes, Charles E., ed., *The Negro Church and the South* (University: University of Alabama Press, 1965) 246.
76. Faulkner, *Soldiers'* 266.
77. Ibid. 266.
78. Faulkner, *The Sound* 263.
79. Faulkner, *Soldiers'* 266.
80. Faulkner, *Flags* 240. Faulkner, *Sartoris* 179.
81. Faulkner, *Flags* 240. Faulkner, *Sartoris* 179.
82. Grace Sims Holt, "Stylin' outta the Black Pulpit," *Rappin' and Stylin' Out: Communication in Urban Black America*, ed. Thomas Kockman (Urbana: University of Illinois Press, 1972) 189.
83. Faulkner, *The Sound* 259.
84. Ibid. 258.
85. Benjamin E. Mays, *The Negroes' God as Reflected in His Literature* (Boston: Chapman, 1958) 255.
86. Faulkner, *Requiem* 243.
87. Faulkner, *Requiem* 238.
88. William Faulkner, dedication, *Go Down, Moses*, by Faulkner (New York: Signet, 1964) n.p.
89. Faulkner, William, letter to Robert K. Haas, Feb. 5, 1940, *Selected Letters of William Faulkner* ed. Joseph Blotner (New York: Random House, 1977) 117.
90. Malcolm Cowley, "Dilsey and the Compsons," University of Mississippi's Faulkner and Yoknapatawpha Conference, Oxford, Aug. 16, 1974.
91. Blotner, *Faulkner: A Biography* 219.
92. Faulkner, *Soldiers'* 141.
93. Thadious M. Davis, *Faulkner's Negro: Art and the Southern Context* (Baton Rouge: Louisiana State University Press,1983) 57.
94. Faulkner, *Soldiers'* 249.
95. Faulkner, *Intruder* 13.
96. Cleanth Brooks, "Faulkner's Vision of Good and Evil," *The Hidden God* (New Haven: Yale University Press, 1963) 22-23.
97. Melvin Backman, *Faulkner The Major Years* (Bloomington: Indiana University Press, 1966) 32.
98. Faulkner, *The Sound* 245.
99. Gwynn, *Class Conferences* 85.
100. Faulkner, *The Sound* 178.
101. Ibid. 186.
102. Ibid. 186.
103. Ibid. 168.
104. Ibid. 82.
105. Ibid. 83.

106. Faulkner, "The Fire" 117.
107. Lillian Smith, *Killers of the Dream* (New York: Norton, 1961) 113.
108. Faulkner, *Light* 358.
109. Ibid. 363-64.
110. Gwynn, *Class Conferences* 196.
111. Faulkner, *Requiem* 163.
112. Albert Camus, Préface, *Requiem pour une nonne, par William Faulkner* (Paris: Gallimard, 1957) xii.
113. Ibid. xiv.
114. Faulkner, *Requiem* 136.
115. Ibid. 136.
116. Faulkner, *Flags* 259. Faulkner, *Sartoris* 191.
117. Faulkner, *Flags* 26. Faulkner, *Sartoris* 37.
118. Faulkner, *Flags* 121. Faulkner, *Sartoris* 104.
119. Faulkner, *The Sound* 93.
120. William Faulkner, "Smoke," *Knight's Gambit* (New York: Vintage, 1978) 31.
121. William Faulkner, "Go Down, Moses," *Go Down, Moses* (New York: Vintage, 1973) 371.
122. Volpe, *Reader's Guide* 169.
123. Blotner, *Faulkner: A Biography* 398-99.
124. Jelliffe, *Faulkner at Nagano* 169.
125. Ibid. 77.
126. Faulkner, "The Fire" 110.
127. Ibid. 112.
128. Ibid. 114.
129. Faulkner, *The Unvanquished* 90.
130. Ibid. 58.
131. Ibid. 16.
132. Faulkner, "The Fire" 55.
133. Faulkner, *Intruder* 23.
134. Howe, *Faulkner: A Critical Study* 118-19.
135. Calhoun, *Social History of the American Family* 2: 289.
136. Ibid. 289.
137. Faulkner, *Intruder* 85-86.
138. Ibid. 281.
139. Ibid. 286.
140. Faulkner, *The Reivers* 250.
141. Ibid. 171.
142. Ibid. 247.
143. Ibid. 176.
144. Ibid. 143.
145. Ibid. 245.

NOTES FOR FINAL THOUGHTS

1. Florence King, *Southern Ladies and Gentlemen.* New York: Bantam, 1976) 4.
2. Faulkner, *Intruder* 116.
3. Faulkner, *Absalom* 16.
4. William Stadiem, *A Class by Themselves: The Untold Story of the Great Southern Families.* (New York: Crown, 1980) 256.
5. Howard Zinn, *The Southern Mystique* (New York: Simon, 1972) 12.
6. King, *Southern* 27.
7. Ibid. 12.
8. Wilbur Cash, *The Mind of the South.* (New York: Vintage, 1960) 56.
9. Victoria Black, et al., "William Faulkner of Oxford: Panel Discussion," *The University of Mississippi Studies in English* 15 (1978): 201.
10. Ibid.
11. Mary Elisabeth Gwin, personal interview, May 15, 1977. ß

BIBLIOGRAPHY

Faulkner: Fiction

Faulkner, William. *A Fable*. New York: Vintage, 1978.
___ *Absalom, Absalom!*. Middlesex: Penguin, 1975.
___ *As I Lay Dying*. New York: Vintage, 1957.
___ *Early Prose and Poetry*. Edited by Carvel Collins. Boston: Little, 1962.
___ *Flags in the Dust*. New York : Vintage, 1974.
___ *Go Down, Moses*. New York: Vintage, 1973.
___ *Intruder in the Dust*. Middlesex: Penguin, 1975.
___ *Knight's Gambit*. New York: Vintage, 1978.
___ *Light in August*. Middlesex: Penguin, 1985.
___ *Marionettes*. Oxford: Yoknapatawpha, 1975.
___ *Mosquitoes*. New York: Boni, 1955.
___ *Pylon*. New York: Random House, 1962.
___ *Requiem for a Nun*. New York: Random House, 1975.
___ *The Portable Faulkner*. Edited by Malcolm Cowley. New York: Viking, 1967.
___ *The Reivers*. New York: Vintage, 1962.
___ *The Sound and the Fury*. Middlesex: Penguin, 1971.
___ *Sanctuary*. New York: Vintage, 1958.
___ *Sartoris*. New York: Signet, 1964.
___ *Soldiers' Pay*. Middlesex: Penguin, 1976.
___ *The Hamlet*. New York: Vintage, 1964.
___ *The Mansion*. New York: Vintage, 1965.
___ *The Marble Faun and A Green Bough*. New York: Random House, 1965.
___ *The Penguin Collected Stories of William Faulkner*. Middlesex: Penguin, 1985.
___ *The Town*. New York: Vintage, 1961.
___ *The Unvanquished*. Middlesex: Penguin, 1975.
___ *The Wild Palms*. Middlesex: Penguin, 1970.
___ *The Wishing Tree*. New York: Random House, 1950.
___ *Uncollected Stories of William Faulkner*. Edited by Joseph Blotner. New York: Random House, 1981.
___ *Vision of Spring*. Austin: University of Texas Press, 1984.

Faulkner: Interviews, letters, diverse

Blotner, Joseph, ed. *Selected Letters of William Faulkner*. New York: Random House, 1977.

Cowley, Malcolm, ed. *The Faulkner - Cowley File: Letters and Memories, 1944-1962*. New York: Viking, 1967.

Fant, Joseph L., and Robert Ashley, eds. *Faulkner at West Point*. New York: Random House, 1964.

Faulkner, William and William P. Spratling. *Sherwood Anderson and Other Famous Creoles*. New Orleans: Pelican, 1926.

Gwynn, Frederick L., and Joseph Blotner, eds. *Faulkner in the University: Class Conferences at the University of Virginia 1957-1958*. New York: Vintage, 1965.

Jelliffe, Robert A., ed. *Faulkner at Nagano*. Tokyo: Kenkyusha, 1956.

James B. Meriwether, ed. *A Faulkner Miscellany*. Jackson: University Press of Mississippi, 1974.

_____ *Essays, Speeches and Public Letters*. New York: Random House, 1965.

Meriwether, James B., and Michael Millgate, eds. *Lion in the Garden: Interviews with William Faulkner 1926-1962*. New York: Random House, 1968.

Mohrt, Michel, comp. *William Faulkner. Jefferson Mississippi*. Paris: Club, 1956.

Personal Interviews

Black, Victoria Fielden. Personal Interview, May 19, 1977.

Brown, Margaret. Personal Interview, May 14, 1977.

Dollarhide, Lewis. Personal Interview, May 20, 1977.

Falkner, Sue. Personal Interview, May 20, 1977.

Faulkner, James M. Personal Interview, May 20, 1977.

Faulkner, Lucille. Personal Interview, May 16, 1977.

Franklin, Jeanne. Personal Interview, Oct. 8, 1978.

Franklin, Malcolm A. Personal Interview, Sept. 15, 1977.

Guyton, Arthur. Personal Interview, May 18, 1977.

Gwin, Mary Elizabeth. Personal Interview, May 15, 1977.

Hall, Marion. Personal Interview, May 19, 1977.

Little, Minnie Ruth. Personal Interview, May 16, 1977.

Roland, Rose. Personal Interview, May 20, 1977.

Stein, Jean. Personal Interview, Oct. 8, 1978.

Stone, Emily. Personal Interview, May 13, 1977.

Stevens, Lamar. Personal Interview, May 19, 1977.

Wells, Dean Faulkner. Personal Interview, May 17, 1977.

Wilde, Meta Carpenter. Personal Interview, July 17, 1977.

Williams, Joan. Personal Interview, Oct 7, 1978.

Telephone Interviews

Franklin, Cornell. Telephone conversation, May 22, 1978.
Franklin, Gloria. Telephone conversation, May 15, 1977.
Holly, Ashton. Telephone conversation, May 20, 1977.
McCool, Dr. Richard. Telephone conversation, May 18, 1977.
Summers, Jill Faulkner. Telephone conversation, July 18, 1977.

Lectures

Cowley, Malcolm. "Dilsey and the Compsons." University of Mississippi's Faulkner and Yoknapatawpha Lecture. Oxford, August 16, 1974.

Books

Abadie, Ann, ed. *William Faulkner; A Life on Paper.* Jackson: University Press of Mississippi, 1980.
Backman, Melvin. *Faulkner: The Major Years.* Bloomington: Indiana University Press, 1966.
Beck, Warren. *Man in Motion: Faulkner's Trilogy.* Madison: University of Wisconsin Press, 1961.
Bleikasten, André. *Parcours de Faulkner.* Paris: Ophyrs, 1982.
Bleikasten, André, et. al. *William Faulkner: As I Lay Dying, Light in August.* Paris: Colin, 1970.
Blotner, Joseph. *Faulkner: A Biography.* 2 vols. New York: Random House, 1976.
_____ *Faulkner: A Biography.* New York: Random House, 1984.
Brooks, Cleanth. *William Faulkner: The Yoknapatawpha Country.* New Haven: Yale University Press, 1963.
_____ *William Faulkner: Toward Yoknapatawpha and Beyond.* New Haven: Yale University Press, 1978.
Brown, Calvin S. *A Glossary of Faulkner's South.* New Haven: Yale University Press, 1976.
Brylowski, Walter M. *Faulkner's Olympian Laugh: Myth in the Novels.* Detroit: Wayne State University Press, 1968.
Coughlan, Robert. *The Private World of William Faulkner.* New York: Cooper, 1972.
Cullen, John B. *Old Times in the Faulkner Country.* Baton Rouge: Louisiana State University Press, 1975.
Dabney, Lewis M. *The Indians of Yoknapatawpha: A Study of Literature and History.* Baton Rouge: Louisiana University Press, 1974.
Dasher, Thomas E. *William Faulkner's Characters: An Index to the Published and Unpublished Fiction.* New York: Garland, 1981.
Dain, Martin J. *Faulkner's County: Yoknapatawpha.* New York: Random House, 1964.

Davis, Thadious M. *Faulkner's Negro: Art and the Southern Context.* Baton Rouge: Louisiana State University Press, 1983.

Douglas, Harold J., and Robert Daniel. *Religious Perspectives in Faulkner's Fiction.* Edited by J. R. Barth. Notre Dame: Notre Dame University Press, 1972.

Everett, Walter K. *Faulkner's Art and Characters.* Woodbury: Barrons, 1969.

Falkner, Murry C. *The Falkners of Mississippi: A Memoir.* Baton Rouge: Louisiana State University Press,1967.

Faulkner, John. *My Brother Bill: An Affectionate Reminiscence.* New York: Trident, 1963.

Fowler, Doreen, and Ann J. Abadie, eds. *Faulkner and Women: Faulkner and Yoknapatawpha, 1985.* Jackson: University Press of Mississippi, 1986.

Franklin, Malcolm A. *Bitterweeds: Life with William Faulkner at Rowan Oak.* Irving: Society for the Study of Traditional Culture, 1977.

Hall, Constance Hill. *Incest in Faulkner: A Metaphor for the Fall.* Ann Arbor: University of Michigan, 1986.

Hoffman, Frederick J. *The Art of Southern Fiction: A Study of Some Modern Novelists.* Carbonale: Southern Illinois University Press, 1967.

Hoffman, Frederick J. *William Faulkner.* New York: Twayne, 1961.

Howe, Irving. *William Faulkner: A Critical Study.* Chicago: University of Chicago Press, 1975.

Guerard, Albert Joseph. *The Triumph of the Novel: Dickens, Dostoevsky, Faulkner.* New York: Oxford University Press, 1976.

Irwin, John T. *Doubling and Incest: Repetition and Revenge: A Speculative Reading of Faulkner.* Baltimore: John Hopkins University Press, 1975.

Jehlen, Myra. *Class and Character in Faulkner's South.* New York: Colombia University Press, 1975.

Jenkins, Lee Clinton. *Faulkner and Black-White Relations: A Psychoanalytic Approach.* New York: Colombia University Press, 1981.

Judson, Harry. *A Faulkner Glossary.* New York: Citadel, 1966.

Kerr, Elizabeth M. *Yoknapatawpha: Faulkner's Little Postage Stamp of Native Soil.* New York: Fordam University Press, 1969.

Longley, John Lewis, Jr. *The Tragic Mask: A Study of Faulkner's Heroes.* Chapel Hill: University of North Carolina Press, 1963.

Malin, Irving. *William Faulkner: An Interpretation.* New York: Gordian, 1972.

Millgate, Michael. *The Achievement of William Faulkner.* New York: Vintage, 1966.

Minter, David. *William Faulkner: His Life and Work.* Baltimore: John Hopkins University Press, 1980.

Nathan, Monique. *Faulkner par lui-même.* Paris: Seuil, 1963.

Nelson, Charles, and David Goforth. *Our Neighbor, William Faulkner.* Chicago: Adams, 1977.

Nilon, Charles H. *Faulkner and the Negro.* New York: Citadel, 1965.

O'Connor, William Van. *The Tangled Fire.* New York: Gordian, 1968.

Oates, Stephen B. *William Faulkner: The Man and the Artist.* New York: Harper, 1987.

Page, Sally K. *Faulkner's Women: Characterization and Meaning*. Deland: Everett, 1972.

Peavy, Charles D. *Go Slow Now: Faulkner and the Race Question*. Eugene: University of Oregon, 1971.

Peters, Erskine. *The Yoknapatawpha World and Black Being*. Darby: Norwood, 1963.

Polk, Noel, ed. *William Faulkner: Sanctuary: The Original Text*. New York: Random House, 1981.

Raimbault, René Noel. *William Faulkner*. Paris: Seuil, 1963.

Richardson, H. Edward. *William Faulkner: The Journey to Self-Discovery*. Columbia: University of Missouri Press, 1969.

Richardson, Kenneth E. *Force and Faith in the Novels of Faulkner*. Hague: Mouton, 1967.

Rouberol, Jean. *L'Esprit du Sud dans l'oeuvre de Faulkner*. Paris: Didier, 1982.

Runyan, Harry. *A Faulkner Glossary*. New York: Citadel, 1966.

Ruppersburg, Hugh M. *Voice and Eye in Faulkner's Fiction*. Athens: University of Georgia Press, 1983.

Seyppel, Joachim. *William Faulkner*. New York: Ungar, 1971.

Skei, Hans H. *William Faulkner: The Novelist as a Short Story Writer: A Study of William Faulkner's Short Fiction*. Oslo: Universitetsforlaget, 1985.

Swiggart, Peter. *The Art of Faulkner's Novels*. Austin: University of Texas, 1970.

Tuck, Dorothy. *Apollo Handbook of Faulkner*. New York: Crowell, 1964.

Vickery, Olga W. *The Novels of William Faulkner*. Baton Rouge: Louisiana State University Press, 1964.

Volpe, Edmond L. *A Reader's Guide to William Faulkner*. New York: Farrar, 1976.

Waggoner, Hyatt H. *William Faulkner: From Jefferson to the World*. Lexington: University of Kentucky Press, 1959.

Wasson, Ben. *Count No' Count: Flashbacks to Faulkner*. Jackson: University Press of Mississippi, 1983.

Watson, James Gray. *The Snopes Dilemma: Faulkner's Trilogy*. Coral Gables: University of Miami Press, 1968.

Webb, James W., and A. Wigfall Green, eds. *William Faulkner of Oxford*. Baton Rouge: Louisiana State University Press, 1965.

Wilde, Meta Carpenter, and Orin Borsten. *A Loving Gentleman*. New York: Simon, 1976.

Williams, David. *Faulkner's Women; The Myth and the Muse*. Montreal: McGill University Press, 1977.

Williams, Joan. *The Wintering*. New York: Harcourt, 1971.

Woodworth, Stanley. *William Faulkner en France: 1931-1952*. Paris: Minard, 1959.

Faulkner: Articles, Chapters from Edited Books

Adamowski, Thomas H. "Dombey and Son and Sutpen and Son." *Studies in the Novel* 4·3 (Fall 1972): 378-79.

_____ "Children of the Idea: Heroes and Family Romances in *Absalom, Absalom!*." *Mosaic* 10 (Fall 1976): 115-31.

Adams, Percy G. "The Franco-American Faulkner." *Tennessee Studies in Literature* 5 (1960): 1-13.

Adams, Richard P. "Faulkner and the Myth of the South." *Mississippi Quarterly* 14 (Summer 1961): 131-37.

Aiken, Conrad. "William Faulkner: The Novel as Form." *Atlantic Monthly* 164 (Nov. 1939): 650-54.

Alexander, Margaret Walker. "Faulkner and Race." *The Maker and the Myth: Faulkner and Yoknapatawpha, 1977.* Edited by Evans Harrington and Ann J. Abadie. Jackson: University Press of Mississippi, 1978. 105-21.

Allen, Walter, et. al. "The Worldwide Influence of William Faulkner: Reports from Six Capitals." *New York Times Book Review* 15 Nov. 1959: 52-53.

Angell, Leslie E. "The Umbilical Cord Symbol As Unifying Theme in *Absalom, Absalom!*." *Massachusetts Studies in English* (Fall 1968): 106-10.

Asselineau, Roger. "William Faulkner, Moraliste Puritain." *Configuration critique de William Faulkner, Revue des Lettres Modernes* 40-42 (Hiver 1958-59): 231-50.

Backman, Melvin. "Sickness and Primitivism: A dominant Pattern in William Faulkner's Work." *Accent* 14 (Winter 1954): 61-73.

_____ "The Wilderness and the Negro in Faulkner's 'The Bear'" *PMLA* 76 (Dec. 1961): 595-600.

Baldwin, James. "Faulkner and Desegregation." *Partisan Review* 32 (Fall 1956): 568-73.

Barthe, J. Robert. "Faulkner and the Calvinist Tradition." *Thought* 39 (Mar. 1964): 100-20.

Basset, John Earl. "Family Conflict in *The Sound and the Fury.*" *Critical Essays on William Faulkner: The Compson Family.* Edited by Arthur F. Kinney. Boston: Hall, 1982. 408-23.

Beach, Joseph Warren. "William Faulkner: The Haunted South." *American Fiction 1920-1940.* New York: Macmillan, 1942. 123-43.

Beck, Warren. "Faulkner and the South." *Antioch Review* 1 (Spring 1941): 82-94.

Behrens, Ralph. "Collapse of Dynasty: The Thematic Center of *Absalom, Absalom!*." *PMLA* 89 (Jan. 1974): 24-33.

Bellman, Samuel I. "Two-Part Harmony: Domestic Relations and Social Vision in the Modern Novel." *California English Journal* 3 (Winter 1967): 31-41.

Berland, Alwyn. "*Light in August*: The Calvinism of William Faulkner." *Modern Fiction Studies* 8 (Summer 1962): 159-70.

Black, Victoria, et. al. "William Faulkner of Oxford: Panel Discussion." *The University of Mississippi Studies in English* 15 (1978): 187-203.

Blackwell, Louise. "Faulkner and the Womenfolk." *Kansas Magazine* 1967: 73-77.

Bleikasten, André. "Fathers in Faulkner." *The Fictional Father: Lacanian Readings of the Text*. Edited by Robert Con Davis. Amherst: University of Massachusetts Press, 1981. 115-46.

_____ "Les maîtres fantômes: paternité et filiation dans les romans de Faulkner." *Revue Française d'Etudes Américaines* 8 (Oct. 1979): 157-81.

Blotner, Joseph. "As I Lay, Dying: Christian Lore and Irony." *Twentieth Century Literature* 3 (Apr. 1957): 14-19.

_____ "The Falkners and the Fictional Families." *Georgia Review* 30·3 (Fall 1976): 572-92.

_____ "William Faulkner: Seminar." *The University of Mississippi Studies in English* 14 (1977): 63-78.

Bowling, Lawrence E. "Faulkner and the Theme of Innocence." *Kenyon Review* 20 (Summer 1958): 466-87.

Bradford, Melvin E. "Brother, Son, and Heir: The Structural Focus of Faulkner's *Absalom, Absalom!.*" *Sewanee Review* 78·1 (Jan.-Mar. 1970): 76-98.

_____ "Faulkner among the Puritans." *Sewanee Review* 72 (Jan.-Mar. 1964): 146-50.

_____ "Faulkner, James Baldwin, and the South." *Georgia Review* 20 (Winter 1966): 431-43.

_____ "That Other Patriarchy: Observations on Faulkner's 'A Justice.'" *Modern Age* 18 (Summer 1974): 266-71.

Brierre, Annie. "Faulkner Parle." *Les Nouvelles Littéraires* 43 (6 Oct. 1955): 6.

Brooks, Cleanth. "Faulkner's Vision of Good and Evil." *The Hidden God*. New Haven: Yale University Press, 1963. 23-43.

_____ "Gavin Stevens and the Chivalric Tradition." *The University of Mississippi Studies in English* 15 (1978): 19-32.

_____ "The British Reception of Faulkner's Work." *William Faulkner: Prevailing Verities and World Literature*. Edited by W. T. Zyla and Wendell M. Aycock. Lubbock: Texas Tech University Press, 1973. 41-55.

Broughton, Panthea Reid. "An Interview with Meta Carpenter Wilde." *The Southern Review* 18 (Oct. 1982): 776-801.

Burroughs, Franklin G., Jr. "God the Father and Motherless Children: *Light in August.*" *Twentieth Century Literature* 19 (July 1973): 189-202.

Burrows, Robert N. "Institutional Christianity as Reflected in the Works of William Faulkner." *Mississippi Quarterly* 14 (Summer 1961): 138-47.

Butor, Michel. "Les Relations de Parenté dans 'L'Ours' de William Faulkner." *Les Lettres Nouvelles* 4 (mai-juin 1956): 734-45.

Callen, Shirley. "Planter and Poor White in *Absalom, Absalom!.* 'Wash,' and The Mind of the South." *South Central Bulletin* 23 (1963): 24-36.

Camus, Albert. Préface. *Requiem pour une nonne*. Par William Faulkner. Paris: Gallimard, 1957. ix-xiv.

Cantwell, Robert. "The Faulkners: Recollections of a Gifted Family." *New World Writing* 2nd Mentor Selection (1952): 300-15.

Ciancio, Ralph A. "Faulkner's Existentialist Affinities." *Studies in Faulkner.* Carnegie Series in English, No. 6. Pittsburgh: Carnegie Institute of Technology, 1961. 70-91.

Coindreau, Maurice Edgar. Préface. *Le Bruit et la Fureur.* Par William Faulkner. Paris: Gallimard, 1987. 7-17.

_____ Préface. *Lumière d'août.* Par William Faulkner. Paris: Gallimard, 1935. 5-16.

_____ "Un an après sa mort Faulkner reste méconnu aux Etats-Unis." *Arts* du 10 au 23 juillet 1963: 3.

_____ "William Faulkner." *La Nouvelle Revue Française* 36 (juin 1931): 926-30.

_____ *William Faulkner in France, Yale French Studies* No. 10 (1953): 85-91.

Collins, Carvel. "A Conscious Literary Use of Freud?." *Literature and Psychology* 3 (June 1953): 2-4.

_____ "Miss Quentin's Paternity Again." *Texas Studies in Literature and Language* 2 (Autumn 1960): 253-60.

_____ "The Interior Monologues of *The Sound and the Fury.*" *Psychoanalysis and American Fiction.* Edited by Irving Malin. New York: Dutton, 1965. 223-43.

_____ "The Pairing of *The Sound and the Fury* and *As I Lay Dying.* Princeton *University Library Chronicle* 18 (Spring 1957): 114-23.

Connolly, Thomas E. "Fate and the 'Agony of Will': Determinism in Some Works of William Faulkner." *Essays on Determinism in American Literature.* Edited by Sidney J. Krause. Kent: Kent State University Press, 1964. 36-52.

Cowley, Malcolm. Introduction. *The Portable Faulkner.* Edited by Malcolm Cowley. By William Faulkner. New York: Viking, 1966. vii-xxxiii.

_____ "William Faulkner's Legend of the South." *Sewanee Review* 53 (Summer 1945): 343-61.

Cullen, John B., and Floyd C. Watkins. "Joe Christmas and Nelse Patton." *Old Times in the Faulkner Country.* Baton Rouge: Louisiana State University Press, 1975. 94-98.

Dabney, Lewis M. "Faulkner, the Red, and the Black." *Columbia Forum* 1·2 (Spring 1972): 52-54.

Daniel, Bradford. "Faulkner on Race." *Ramparts* 2 (Winter 1963): 43-49.

_____ "William Faulkner and the Southern Guest for Freedom." *Black, White and Gray: Twenty-one Points of View on the Race Question.* Edited by Bradford Daniel. New York: Sheed, 1964. 291-308.

Dauner, Louise. "Quentin and the Walking Shadow: The Dilemma of Nature and Culture." *Arizona Quarterly* 21 (Summer 1965): 159-71.

Davenport, F. Garvin. "William Faulkner." *The Myth of Southern History: Historical Consciousness in Twentieth-Century Southern Literature.* Nashville: Vanderbilt University Press, 1970. 82-130.

Douglas, Ellen. "Faulkner's Women." *A Cosmos of My Own: Faulkner and Yoknapatawpha, 1980.* Edited by Doreen Fowler and Ann J. Abadie. Jackson: University Press of Mississippi, 1981.

Douglas, Harold J., and Robert Daniel. "Faulkner and the Puritanism of the South." *Tennessee Studies in Literature* 2 (1957): 1-13.

Edmonds, Irene C. "Faulkner and the Black Shadow." *Southern Renascence: The Literature of the Modern South.* Edited by Louis D. Rubin, Jr. and Robert D. Jacobs. Baltimore: John Hopkins University Press, 1953. 192-206.

Emmanuel, Pierre. "Faulkner and the Sense of Sin." *Harvard Avocate* 135 (Nov. 1951): 20.

Faulkner, John. Letter. *Memphis Commercial Appeal* April 3, 1955, sec. 5: 3.

Ferris, William R., Jr. "William Faulkner and Phil Stone: An Interview with Emily Stone." *South Atlantic Quarterly* 68 (Autumn 1969): 536-42.

Fiedler, Leslie A. "The Last of William Faulkner." *The Manchester Guardian* 28 Sept. 1962: 6.

Fischer, Marvin. "The World of Faulkner's Children." *University of Kansas City Review* 27 (Autumn 1960): 13-18.

Foote, Shelby. "Faulkner's Depiction of the Planter Aristocracy." *The South and Faulkner's Yoknapatawpha: The Actual and the Apocrypal.* Edited by Evans Harrington and Ann J. Abadie. Jackson: University Press of Mississippi, 1977. 40-61.

Foster, Ruel E. "Social Order and Disorder in Faulkner's Fiction." *Approach* No. 55 (Spring 1965): 20-28.

Gallagher, Susan. "To Love and to Honor: Brothers and Sisters in Faulkner's Yoknapatawpha County." *Essays in Literature* 7:2 (Fall 1980): 213-24.

Geismar, Maxwell. "William Faulkner: The Negro and the Female." *Writers in Crisis: The American Novels between Two Wars.* Boston: Houghton, 1942. 143-83.

Giles, Barbara. "The South of William Faulkner." *Masses and Mainstream* Feb. 1950: 26-40.

Glicksberg, Charles I. "William Faulkner and the Negro Problem." *Phylon* 10 (Spring 1949): 153-60.

Godden, Richard. "William Faulkner, Addie Bundren, and Language." *The University of Mississippi Studies in English* 15 (1978): 101-23.

Guerard, Albert J. "Forbidden Games (III): Faulkner's Misogyny." *The Triumph of the Novel: Dickens, Dostoevsky, Faulkner.* New York: Oxford University Press, 1976. 109-35.

_____ "The Misogynous Vision as High Art: Faulkner's *Sanctuary.*" *Southern Review* 12 (Apr. 1976): 215-31.

Hamilton, Edith. "Sorcerer or Slave?" *Saturday Review* July 12, 1952: 8-10.

Handy, William. "*As I Lay Dying*: Faulkner's Inner Reporter." *Kenyon Review* 21 (Summer 1959): 437-51.

Hardwick, Elizabeth. "Faulkner and the South Today." *Partisan Review* (Oct. 1948): 1130-35.

Heimer, Jackson W. "Faulkner's Misogynous Novel: *Light in August.*" *Ball State University Forum* 14 (Summer 1973): 11-15.

Hodding, Carter. "Faulkner and His Folk." *Princeton University Library Chronicle* 18 (Spring 1957): 95-107.

Hoffman, Frederick. " An Introduction." *William Faulkner: Three Decades of Criticism.* Edited by Frederick J. Hoffman and Olga Vickery. New York: Harcourt, 1963. 1-50.

Howe, Russell Warren. "A Talk with Faulkner." *The Reporter* March 22, 1956: 18-20.

Howell, Elmo. "A Note on Faulkner's Negro Characters." *Mississippi Quarterly* 15 (Winter 1962): 21-26.

_____ "A Note on Faulkner's Presbyterian Novel." *Papers on Language and Literature* 2 (Spring 1966): 182-87.

_____ "Faulkner's Wash Jones and the Southern Poor White." *Ball State University Forum* 8·1 (Winter 1967): 8-12.

_____ "William Faulkner's Southern Baptists." *Arizona Quarterly* 23 (Autumn 1967): 220-26.

Irwin, John T. "The Dead Father in Faulkner." *The Fictional Father: Lacanian Readings of the Text.* Edited by Robert Con Davis. Amherst: University of Massachusetts Press, 1981. 146-68.

Jacobs, Robert D. "William Faulkner: The Passion and the Penance." *South: Modern Southern Literature in its Cultural Setting.* Edited by Louis D. Rubin, Jr. and Robert D. Jacobs. Garden City: Dolphin, 1961.142-76.

Jafford, Paul. "Le double aspect de l'oeuvre de Faulkner." *Critique* 9 (juin 1953): 496-507.

Jaloux, Edmond. "Sartoris, par William Faulkner, translated by R. N. Raimbault et H. Degore (*Nouvelle Revue Française.*)" *Les Nouvelles Littéraires* Sept. 17, 1938: 4.

Judson, Horace. "The Curse and the Hope." *Time* 84 (July 17 1964): 44-48.

Juin, Hubert. "L'Univers clos de William Faulkner." *Esprit* 24 (Nov. 1956): 704-15.

Kartiganer, Donald M. "Quentin Compson and Faulkner's Drama of the Generations." *Critical Essays on William Faulkner: The Compson Family.* Edited by Arthur F. Kinney. Boston: Hall, 1982. 381-401.

Kazin, Alfred. "Faulkner: The Rhetoric and the Agony." *On Native Grounds.* New York: Reynal, 1942. 453-70.

Kazin, Alfred. "The Stillness of *Light in August.*" *William Faulkner: Three Decades of Criticism.* Edited by Frederick Hoffman and Olga Vickery. New York: Harcourt, 1963. 247-65.

Kerr, Elizabeth M. "*The Reivers*: The Golden Book of Yoknapatawpha Country." *Modern Fiction Studies* 13 (Spring 1967): 95-113.

_____ "The Women of Yoknapatawpha." *The University of Mississippi Studies in English* 15 (1978): 83-100.

_____ "William Faulkner and the Southern Concept of Woman." *Mississippi Quarterly* 15 (Winter 1962): 1-16.

Kinney, Arthur F. "Topmost in the Pattern: Family Structure in Faulkner Studies." *New Directions in Faulkner and Yoknapatawpha, 1983.* Jackson: University Press of Mississippi,1984.

Kubie, Lawrence S., M. D. "William Faulkner's *Sanctuary*." *Faulkner: A Collection of Critical Essays*. Edited by Robert Penn Warren. Englewood Cliffs: Prentice, 1966.137-46.

Landor, Mikhail. "Faulkner in the Solviet Union." *Solviet Criticism of American Literature in the Sixties: An Anthology*. Edited and trans.lated by Carl R. Proffer. Ann Arbor: Ardis, 1972. 173-82.

Lensing, George S. "The Metaphor of Family in *Absalom, Absalom!*." *Southern Review* No. 1 (Jan. 1975): 99-117.

Lewis, Wyndam. "William Faulkner: The Moralist with the Corn-Cob." *Men Without Art*. New York: Russell, 1964. 42-64.

Lind, Ilse Dusoir. "Faulkner's Women." *The Maker and the Myth: Faulkner and Yoknapatawpha, 1977*. Edited by Evans Harrington and Ann J. Abadie. Jackson: University Press of Mississippi, 1978. 89-104.

_____ "The Calvinistic Burden of *Light in August*. *New England Quarterly* 30 (Sept. 1957): 307-29.

_____ "The Design and Meaning of *Absalom, Absalom!*." *William Faulkner: Three Decades of Criticism*. Edited by Frederick J. Hoffman and Olga W. Vickery. New York: Harcourt, 1963. 278-304.

Longley, John L., Jr. "'Who Never Had a Sister': A reading of *The Sound and the Fury*." *Mosaic* 7·1 (Fall 1973): 35-53.

Lorch, Thomas. "Thomas Sutpen and the Female Principle." *Mississippi Quarterly* 20 (Winter 1967): 38-42.

Malraux, André. Préface. *Sanctuaire*. Par William Faulkner. Paris: Gallimard. 1972. 7-11.

Marshall, Sarah L. "Fathers and Sons in *Absalom, Absalom!*." *The University of Mississippi Studies in English* 8 (1967): 19-29.

Materassi, Mario. "Faulkner Criticism in Italy." *Italian Quarterly* 15 (Summer 1971): 47-85.

McHaney, Thomas L. "Watching for the Dixie Limited: Faulkner's Impact upon the Creative Writer." *Fifty Years of Yoknapatawpha: Faulkner and Yoknapatawpha, 1979*. Edited by Doreen Fowler and Ann J. Abadie. Jackson: University Press of Mississippi, 1980. 226-47.

_____ "The Elmer Papers: Faulkner's Comic Portrait of the Artist." *Mississippi Quarterly* 26 (Summer 1973): 281-311.

_____ "Robinson Jeffers 'Tamar' and *The Sound and the Fury*." *Mississippi Quarterly* 22 (Summer 1969): 261-63.

Miller, David. "Faulkner's Women." *Modern Fiction Studies* 13 (Spring 1967): 3-11.

Miner, Ward L. "The Southern White-Negro Problem through the Lens of Faulkner's Fiction." *Journal of Human Relations*, 14 (Fourth Quarter 1966): 507-17.

Nores, Dominique. "Contre un Théâtre d'effraction: A propos de *Requiem pour une nonne*." *Revue Théâtrale* 36 (1958): 46-52.

O'Connor, William Van. "Faulkner's Legend of the Old South." *Western Humanities Review* 7 (Fall 1953): 293-30.

_____ "Protestantism in Yoknapatawpha County." *Southern Renascence*. Edited by Louis Rubin, Jr. and Robert D. Jacobs. Baltimore: John Hopkins University Press, 153-69.

O'Donnell, George Marion. "Faulkner's Mythology." *William Faulkner: Three Decades of Criticism*. Edited by Frederick J. Hoffman and Olga W. Vickery. New York: Harcourt, 1963. 82-93.

Peavy, Charles D. "'Did You Ever Have a Sister?' Holden, Quentin, and Sexual Innocence." *Florida Quarterly* 1.3 (1968): 82-95.

_____ "'If I'd Just Had a Mother': Faulkner's Quentin Compson." *Literature and Psychology* 23.3 (1973): 114-21.

Pouillon, Jean. "Temps et Destinée chez Faulkner." *Temps et Roman*. Paris: Gallimard, 1946. 238-60.

Richardson, H. Edward. "Faulkner, Anderson, and Their Tall Tale. *American Literature* 34 (May 1962): 287-91.

Roberts, James L. " The Individual and the Family: Faulkner's *As I Lay Dying*." *Arizona Quarterly* 16 (Spring 1979): 26-38.

Rollins, Ronald G. "Ike McCaslin and Chick Mallison: Faulkner's Emerging Southern Hero." *West Virginia University Philological Papers* 14 (Oct. 1963): 74-79.

Sabiston, Elizabeth. "Women, Blacks, and Thomas Sutpen's Mythopoeic Drive in *Absalom, Absalom!. Modernist Studies: Literature and Culture, 1920-1940* 1·3 (1974): 15-26.

Sanstrom, Glenn. "Identity Diffusion: Joe Christmas and Quentin Compson." *American Quarterly* 19 (Summer 1967): 207-23.

Sartre, Jean-Paul. "A Propos de *Le Bruit et la Fureur:* La Temporalité chez Faulkner." *Situation I*. Paris: Gallimard, 1947. 70-81.

_____ "Sartoris, par W. Faulkner, traduction de N. R. Raimbault et H. Delgove (Edition de la N. R. F.)." *La Nouvelle Revue Française* 50 (fév. 1938): 323-28.

Seiden, Melvin. "Faulkner's Ambiguous Negro." *Massachusetts Review* 4 (Summer 1963): 675-90.

Shaw, Joe C. "Sociological Aspects of Faulkner's Writing." *Mississippi Quarterly* 14 (Summer 1961): 148-152.

Simon, John K. "What Are You Laughing At, Darl? Madness and Humor in *As I Lay Dying*." *College English* 25 (Nov. 1963): 104-10.

Slabey, Robert M. "Joe Christmas, Faulkner's Marginal Man." 21 (Fall 1960): 266-77.

_____ "Quentin Compson's 'Lost Childhood.'" *Studies in Short Fiction* 1 (Spring 1964): 173-83.

Springer, Ann M. "Die Jüngsten"—John Dos Passos, Ernest Hemingway, William Faulkner, Thomas Wolfe." *The American Novel in Germany: A Study of the Critical Reception of Eight American Novelists between the Two World Wars*. Hamburg: Cram, de Gruyter, 1960. 75-95.

Stewart, Randall. "Hawthorne and Faulkner." *College English* 17 (Feb. 1956): 258-62.

Stone, Phil. Préface. *The Marble Faun and A Green Bough.* By William Faulkner. New York: Random, 1965. 6-8.

_____ "William Faulkner, The Man and His Work." *Oxford Magazine.* Copies 1,2,3 (1934): 4.

Taylor, Nancy Dew. "The Dramatic Productions of *Requiem for a Nun.*" *Mississippi Quarterly* 20 (Summer 1967): 123-34.

Taylor, Walter F., Jr. "Faulkner's Curse." *Arizona Quarterly* 28 (Winter 1972): 333-38.

_____ "Let My People Go: The White Man's Heritage in *Go Down, Moses.*" *South Atlantic Quarterly* 58 (Winter 1959): 20-32.

_____ Jr. "The Freedman in *Go Down, Moses*: Historical Fact and Imaginative Failure." *Ball State University Forum* 8 (Winter 1967): 3-7.

Tazewell, William L. "Faulkner and the Negro Stereotype." *Norfolk Virginian-Pilot* 9 July 1962: 4.

Thompson, Lawrance R. "Mirror Analogues in *The Sound and the Fury.*" *William Faulkner: Three Decades of Criticism.* Edited by Frederick J. Hoffman and Olga W. Vickery. New York: Harcourt, 1963. 211-25.

Trilling, Lionel. "The McCaslins of Mississippi," rev. of *Go Down , Moses. The Nation* May 30, 1942: 632-33.

Turner, Arlin. "William Faulkner, Southern Novelist." *Mississippi Quarterly* 14 (Summer 1961): 117-30.

Turner, Darwin T. "Faulkner and Slavery." *The South and Faulkner's Yoknapatawpha: The Actual and the Aprocyphal.* Edited by Evans Harrington and Ann J. Abadie. Jackson: University Press of Mississippi, 1977. 62-85.

Vinson, Audrey L. "Miscegenation and Its Meaning in *Go Down, Moses.*" *College Language Association Journal* 14 (Dec. 1970): 143-55.

Wagner, Linda Welshimer, et al. "Faulkner and Women." *The South and Faulkner's Yoknapatawpha: The Actual and the Aprocyphal.* Edited by Evans Harrington and Ann J. Abadie. Jackson: University Press of Mississippi, 1977. 147-51.

Walker, William E. "*The Unvanquished:* The Restoration of Tradition." *Reality and Myth: Essays in American Literature in Memory of Richard Croom Beatty.* Edited by William E. Walker and Robert L. Walker. Nashville: Vanderbilt University Press, 1964. 275-97.

Warren, Robert Penn. "Faulkner: The South and the Negro." *Southern Review* 1 (July 1965): 501-29.

Warren, Robert Penn. "William Faulkner." *William Faulkner: Three Decades of Criticism.* Edited by Frederick J. Hoffman and Olga W. Vickery. New York: Harcourt, 1963. 109-24.

Wilde, Meta Doherty. "An Unpublished Chapter from A Loving Gentleman." *Mississippi Quarterly* 30.3 (Summer 1977): 449-60.

Williams, Joan. "In Defense of Caroline Compson." *Critical Essays on William Faulkner: The Compson Family*. Edited by Arthur F. Kinney. Boston: Hall, 1982. 402-07.

Yorks, Samuel A. "Faulkner's Women: The Peril of Mankind." *Arizona Quarterly* 17 (Summer 1961): 119-29.

Zink, Karl E. "Faulkner's Garden: Women and the Immemorial Earth." *Modern Fiction Studies* 2 (Autumn 1956): 139-49.

University Studies on Faulkner

Allen, Lourie Strickland. "Colonel William C. Falkner: Writer of Romance and Realism." Ph.D. diss. University of Alabama, 1972.

Beauchamp, Fay E. "William Faulkner's Use of the Tragic Mulatto Myth." Ph.D. diss. University of Pennsylvania, 1974.

Bowlin, Karla J. "The Brother and Sister Theme in Post-Romantic Fiction." Ph.D. diss. Auburn University, 1973.

Bruice, Joe Carl. "The Rise and the Fall of Aristocratic Families in Yoknapatawpha County." Ph.D. diss. East Texas State University, 1970.

Clark, William Bedford. "The Serpent of Lust in the Southern Garden: The Theme of Miscegenation in Cable, Twain, Faulkner, and Warren." Ph.D. diss. Louisiana State University and Agricultural and Mechanical College, 1973.

Coale, Samuel C. V. "The Role of the South in the Fiction of William Faulkner, Carson McCullers, Flannery O'Connor, and William Styron." Ph.D. diss. Brown University, 1970.

Devlin, Albert J. "Parent-Child Relationships in the Works of William Faulkner." Ph.D. diss. University of Kansas, 1970.

Friend, George L. "Levels of Maturity: The Theme of Striving in the Novels of William Faulkner." Ph.D. diss. University of Illinois, 1964.

Gresham, Jewell H. "The Fatal Illusions: Self, Sex, Race and Religion in William Faulkner's World." Ph.D. diss. Colombia University, 1970.

Makuck, Peter Landers. "Faulkner Studies in France: 1953-1969." Ph.D. diss. Kent State University, 1971.

Pieper, Janet Leah S. "Black Characters in Faulkner's Fiction." Ph.D. diss. University of Nebraska, 1976.

Shelton, Frank Wilsey. "The Family in the Novels of Wharton, Faulkner, Cather, Lewis, and Dreiser." Ph.D. diss. University of North Carolina, 1971.

Steinberg, Aaron. "Faulkner and the Negro." Ph.D. diss. New York University, 1966.

Taylor, Walter F. Jr. "The Roles of the Negro in William Faulkner's Fiction." Ph.D. diss. Emory University, 1964.

Waters, Maureen Ann. "The Role of Women in Faulkner's Yoknapatawpha." Ph.D. diss. Colombia University, 1975.

Master's Theses

Newman, Jules." The Religion of William Faulkner: An Inquiry into the Calvinist Mind." Thèse de Maîtrise. Columbia University, 1953.

Wells, Dean Faulkner. "A Biographical Study. Dean Swift. Faulkner." Thèse de Maîtrise. University of Mississippi, 1975.

Bibliography on Faulkner

Basset, John. *William Faulkner: An Annotated Checklist of Criticism.* New York: Lewis, 1972.

Bassett, John Earl. *Faulkner: An Annotated Checklist of Recent Criticism.* Kent: Kent State Univerfsity Press, 1983.

Hayashi, Tetsumaro. *William Faulkner: Research Opportunities and Dissertation Abstracts.* London: McFarland, 1962.

Ricks, Beatrice. *William Faulkner: A Bibliography of Secondary Works.* Metuchen: Scarecrow, 1981.

General Bibliography

Agee, James, and Walter Evans. *Let Us Now Praise Famous Men.* New York: Ballantine, 1974.

____ *A Death in the Family.* New York: Bantam, 1972.

____ *The Morning Watch.* New York: Ballantine, 1969.

Allen, Walter B. "The Search for Applicable Theories of Black Family Life." *Journal of Marriage and Family Life* 1 (Feb. 1978): 117-29.

Anderson, Sherwood. *Dark Laughter.* New York: Boni, 1925.

Anderson, Sherwood. *Sherwood Anderson's Memoirs.* New York: Harcourt, 1942.

Bailey, Kenneth K. *Southern White Protestantism in the Twentieth Century.* New York: Harper, 1964.

Bell, Robert R. *Marriage and Family Interaction.* Homewood: Dorsey, 1963.

Berlin, Ira. *Slaves Without Masters: The Free Negro in the Antebellum South.* New York: Vintage, 1976.

Bigras, Julien, et al. "En decà et au dela de l'inceste chez l'adolescente." *Canadian Psychiatric Association Journal* 11·3 (1966): 189-204.

Boyle, Sarah Patton. *The Desegregated Heart.* New York: Morrow, 1962.

Bradbury, John M. *Renaissance in the South: A Critical History of the Literature, 1920-1960.* Chapel Hill: University of North Carolina Press, 1963.

Brodin, Pierre. *Les écrivains de l'entre-deux guerres.* Paris: Horizons, 1946.

Brown, Sterling. *Negro Poetry and Drama and the Negro in American Fiction.* New York: Atheneum, 1969.

Calhoun, Arthur. *A Social History of the American Family.* 3 vols. New York: Barnes, 1960.

Callaway, Elvy E. *The Other Side of the South.* Chicago: Ryerson, 1934.

Capote, Truman. *The Grass Harp and the Tree of Night.* New York: Signet, 1951.

Carter, Hodding. *Where Main Street Meets the River.* New York: Holt, 1953.

Cash, Wilbur. *The Mind of the South.* New York: Vintage, 1960.

Cavan, Ruth Shonle. *The Family.* New York: Crowell, 1948.

Chadburn, James Harmon. *Lynching and the Law.* Chapel Hill: University of North Carolina Press, 1933.

Chesnut, Mary Boykin. *A Diary from Dixie.* New York: Houghton, 1961.

Cole, William Earle, and Roy Leonard Cox. *Southern Citizenship Problems.* Chattanouga: Harlow, 1960.

Conner, Paul. "Patriarchy: Old and New." *American Quarterly* 17·1 (Spring 1965): 48-62.

Cook, Sylvia Jenkins. *From Tobacco Road to Route 66, The Southern Poor White in Fiction.* Chapel Hill: University of North Carolina Press, 1972.

Cory, David Webster. *Violation of Taboo: Incest in the Great Literature of the Past and Present.* New York: Julien, 1963.

Couch, W. T., ed. *Culture in the South.* Chapel Hill: North Carolina University Press, 1934. 205-07, 386-87.

Cox, Earnest Sevier. *The South's Part in Mongrelizing the Nation.* Richmond: White America Soc., 1926.

Cowley, Malcolm. "American Novelists in French Eyes." *The Atlantic Monthly* 178 (Aug. 1946): 113-18.

Crowe, John Ransom. "Modern with the Southern Accent." *Virginia Quarterly Review* 2 (April 1935): 184-200.

Dabbs, James McBride. *Haunted by God.* Richmond: Knox, 1972.

Day, Beth. *Sexual Life between Blacks and Whites.* London: Collins, 1974.

Dollard, John. *Caste and Class in a Southern Town.* New York: Doubleday, 1957.

Dorough, C. Dwight. *The Bible Belt Mystique.* Philadelphia: Westminster, 1974.

Douglass, Frederick. *My Bondage and My Freedom.* New York: Arno, 1968.

Dubois, William E. B. *Souls of Black Folk.* Chicago: McClurg, 1903.

Eaton, Clement. *The Mind of the South.* Baton Rouge: Louisiana State University Press, 1964.

Elliott, Charles. *Sinfulness of American Slavery.* 2 vols. New York: Negro University Press, 1968.

Ellison, Ralph. "Twentieth-Century Fiction and the Black Mask of Humanity." *Shadow and Act.* Random House, 1964. 24-44.

Erikson, Erik. "*Reflections on the American Identity.*" *Childhood and Society.* New York: Norton, 1950. 244-83.

Fichter, Joseph H., and George L. Maddox. "Religion in the South, Old and New." *The South in Continuity and Change.* Edited by John McKinney and Edgar T. Thompson. Durham: Duke University Press, 1965. 359-83.

Fiedler, Leslie A. *Love and Death in the American Novel.* New York: Criterion, 1970.

Foote, Shelby. Entrevue. *Mississippi Writers Talking.* Edited by John Griffin Jones. Jackson: University Press of Mississippi, 1983. 37-92.

____ "It's Worth a Grown Man's Time." *Kite-Flying and Other Irrational Acts: Conversations with Twelve Southern Writers.* Edited by John Carr. Baton Rouge: Louisiana State University Press, 1972. 3-33.

Franklin, John Hope. *From Slavery to Freedom: A History of Negro Americans.* New York: Vintage, 1969.

Frazier, Edward Franklin. *The Negro Family in the United States.* Chicago: University of Chicago Press, 1939.

Gardner, Burleigh B., et. al. *Deep South: A Social Anthropological Study of Caste and Class.* Chicago: University of Chicago Press, 1965.

Genovese, Eugene D. *Roll, Jordan Roll: The World the Slaves Made.* New York: Vintage, 1976.

Gide, André. *Journal 1889-1939.* Paris: Gallimard, 1941.

Glasgow, Ellen. *The Woman Within.* New York: Harcourt, 1964.

Gloster, Hugh. *Negro Voices in American Fiction.* Chapel Hill: University of North Carolina Press, 1948.

Golden, Joseph. "Social Control of Negro-White Intermarriage." *Social Forces* 36 (1958): 267-69.

Goodsell, William. *The American Slave Code.* New York: Gray, 1853.

Gordon, Caroline. *None Shall Look Back.* New York: Scribner's, 1937.

____ *Penhally.* New York: Scribners, 1937.

Gray, Richard. *Writing in the South: Ideas of an American Region.* Cambridge: Cambridge University Press, 1986.

Grimké, Angelina Emily. *Letters to Catherine E. Beecher.* Boston: Knapp, 1838.

Grimké, Sarah Moore. *Letters on the Equality of the Sexes and the Condition of Women, Addressed to Mary S. Parker.* Boston: Knapp, 1838.

Guerard, Albert J. *The Triumph of the Novel.* New York: Oxford University Press, 1976.

Gutman, Herbert G. *The Black Family in Slavery and Freedom.* New York: Vintage, 1976.

Hagood, Margaret Jarman. *Mothers of the South: Portraiture of the White Tenant Farm Woman.* New York: Greenwood, 1939.

Harss, Luis, and Barbara Dohmann. *Into the Mainstream: Conversations with Latin-American Writers.* New York: Harper, 1967.

Healy, William, et. al. *Structure and Meaning of Psychoanalysis as Related to Personality and Behavior.* New York: Knopf, 1931.

Heiss, Jerold. *The Case of the Black Family: a sociological inquiry.* New York: Columbia University Press, 1975.

Hemingway, Ernest. *The Torrents of Spring: a Romantic Novel in Honor of the Passing of a Great Race.* New York: Scribner's, 1926.

Hernton, Calvin C. *Sex and Racism.* London: Deustch, 1969.

Hill, Samuel S. Jr., and Robert G. Torbet. *Baptists North and South.* Chicago: Judson, 1964.

Hill, Samuel S. Jr., et. al. *Religion and the Solid South.* Nashville: Abingdon, 1972.

Hill, Samuel S. Jr., *Southern Churches in Crisis.* New York: Holt, 1966.

Himelhoch, Jerome, and Sylvia Fleis Fava, eds. *Sexual Behavior in American Society.* New York: Norton, 1955.

Holman, Clarence Hugh. "The Dark, Ruined Helen of His Blood: Thomas Wolfe and the South." *The Roots of Southern Writing: Essays on the Literature of the American South.* Athens: University of Georgia Press, 1972. 118-33.

Holt, Grace Sims. "Stylin' outta the Black Pulpit." *Rappin' and Stylin' Out: Communication in Urban Black America.* Edited by Thomas Kockman. Urbana: University of Illinois Press, 1972. 189-204.

Hopkins, Charles Howard. *The Rise of the Social Gospel in American Protestantism 1865-1915.* New Haven: Yale University Press, 1940.

Howard, George Elliott. *A History of Matrimonial Institutions.* 3 vols. New York: Humanities, 1964.

Hudson, Winthrop S. *American Protestantism.* Chicago: University of Chicago Press, 1972.

Hundley, D. R., esq. *Social Relations in Our Southern States.* New York: Pierce, 1860.

Inge, M. Thomas "Contemporary American Literature in Spain." *Tennessee Studies in Literature* 16 (1971): 155-67.

James, Henry. *The Art of the Novel.* New York: Scribner's, 1934.

Jefferson, Thomas. *Notes on the Slave State of Virginia.* New York: Harper, 1964.

Johnston, James Hugo. *Miscegenation in the Ante-Bellum South.* New York: AMS, 1972.

_____ *Race Relations in Virginia and Miscegenation in the South 1776-1860.* Amherst: University of Massachusetts Press, 1970.

Jones, Ernest. *Papers on Psycho-Analysis.* Boston: Beacon, 1948.

Jones, Ernest. *The Life and Work of Sigmund Freud.* Edited by Lionel Trilling and Steven Marcus. New York: Basic, 1961.

Jordan, Winthrop D. *White over Black: American Attitudes toward the Negro, 1550-1812.* Chapel Hill: University of Carolina Press, 1968.

Jung, Carl G. *Psychology and Alchemy.* Translated by R. F. Hull. New York: Pantheon, 1953.

_____ *Psychology of the Unconscious; a study of the transformations and symbolisms of the libido, a contribution to the history of the evolution of thought.* New York: Dodd, 1949.

_____ *The Archetypes and the Collective Unconscious.* Translated by R. F. C. Hull. London: Koutledge, 1959.

Kadish, Sanford H., ed. *Enclopedia of Crime and Justice.* 4 vols. New York: Free, 1983.

Kendrick, Benjamin Burks, and Alex Mathews Arnet. *The South Looks at Its Past.* Chapel Hill: University of North Carolina Press, 1935.

King, Florence. *Confessions of a Failed Southern Lady*. Marek: St. Martin's, 1985.

____ *Southern Ladies and Gentlemen*. New York: Bantam, 1976.

King, Richard. *A Southern Renaissance: The Cultural Awakening of the American South 1930-1955*. New York: Oxford University Press, 1980.

Kling, Samuel G. *Sexual Behavior and the Law*. New York: Geis, 1965.

Lester, David. *The Journal of Sex Research* 8·4 (Nov. 1972): 268-85.

Lewis, W. David, and B. Eugene Greissman, eds. *The Southern Mystique: Technology and Human Values in a Changing Region*. University: University of Alabama Press, 1977.

Lincoln, C. Eric. "The Absent Father Haunts the Negro Family." *The Contemporary American Family*. Edited by William J. Goode. Chicago: Quadrangle, 1971. 155-63.

Loescher, Frank S. *The Protestant Church and the Negro: A Pattern of Segregation*. New York: Association, 1948.

Lytle, Andrew. "The Working Novelist and Mythmaking Process." *Daedalus* 88 (Spring 1959): 326-38.

McCullers, Carson. *Reflections in a Golden Eye*. New York: Bantam, 1971.

____ *The Member of the Wedding*. Middlesex: Penguin, 1961.

McGill, Ralph. *The South and the Southerner*. Boston: Little, Brown and Company, 1963.

McIlwaine, Shields. *The Southerner Poor White from Lubberland to Tobacco Road*. Norman: University of Oklahoma Press, 1939.

McKean, Keith F. "Southern Patriarch: A Portrait." *Virginia Quarterly Review* 36 (Summer 1960): 376-89.

Mailer, Norman. *Advertisements for Myself*. New York: Putnam, 1959.

Maisch, Herbert. *Incest*. New York: Stein, 1972.

Masters, R. E. L. *Patterns of Incest*. New York: Julien, 1963.

Mathews, Donald G. *Religion in the Old South*. Chicago: University of Chicago Press, 1977.

Mayes, Benjamin E. *The Negroes' God as Reflected in His Literature*. Boston: Chapman, 1958.

Mazlish, Bruce, and Edwin Diamond. *Jimmy Carter; Interpretive Biography*. New York: Simon, 1979.

Myrdal, Gunnar. *An American Dilemma*. New York: Harper, 1962.

Nolan, Claude H. *The Negro's Image in the South: The Anatomy of White Supremacy*. Lexington: University of Kentucky Press, 1967.

O'Connor, Flannery. "The Grotesque in Southern Fiction." *Mystery and Manners*. London: Faber, 1969. 36-50.

____ *The Violent Bear It Away*. New York: NAL, 1961.

____ *Wise Blood*. New York: Farrar, 1962.

Odum, Howard. *The Way of the South*. New York: MacMillan, 1947.

Ogburn, William Fielding. "Ideologies of the South in Transition." *In Search of the Regional Balance*. Edited by Howard Odum and Katherine Jocher. Chapel Hill: University of North Carolina Press, 1945. 92-100.

Osterweis, Rollin G. *Romanticism and Nationalism in the Old South.* Baton Rouge: Louisiana State University Press, 1949.

Owens, Leslie H. *This Species of Property: Slave Life and Culture in the Old South.* New York: Oxford University Press, 1976.

Page, Thomas Nelson. *Red Rock: A Chronicle of Reconstruction.* New York: Scribner's, 1898.

____ *Social Life in Old Virginia.* New York: Scribner's, 1897.

Peck, W. H. *The M'Donalds; or The Ashes of Southern Homes: A Tale of Sherman's March.* New York: Met. Record Office, 1867.

Percy, William Alexander. *Lanterns on the Levee: Recollections of a Planter's Son.* New York: Knopf, 1941.

Phillips, Wendel. "Philosophy of the Abolition Movement." *Speeches, Lectures, and Letters.* Boston: Lee, 1870. 98-153.

Pierce, Neal R. *The Deep South States of America.* New York: Norton, 1974.

Porter, Katherine Ann. *Pale Horse, Pale Rider: Three Short Novels.* New York: NAL, 1962.

Porter, Katherine Ann. *The Leaning Tower.* New York: NAL, 1969.

Posey, Walter Brownlow. *Religious Strife on the Southern Frontier.* Baton Rouge: Louisiana State University Press, 1965.

____ *The Baptist Church in the Lower Mississippi Valley 1776-1845.* Lexington: University of Kentucky Press, 1957.

Powdermaker, Hortense. *After Freedom; A Cultural Study in the Deep South.* New York: Russell, 1966.

Queen, Stuart, A., et al. *The Family in Various Cultures.* New York: Lippincott, 1952.

Rank, Otto. *Beyond Psychology.* New York: Dover, 1958.

____ *Daz - Inzest - Motiv in Dichtung und Sage.* Vienna: Deuticke, 1972.

Ransom, John Crowe. "Modern with the Southern Accent." *Virginia Quarterly Review* 2 (Apr. 1935): 184-200.

Reed, John Shelton. *The Enduring South.* Lexington: Heath, 1972.

Reiss, Ira L. *The Family System in America.* New York: Holt, 1971.

Reuter, Edward B. *The Mulatto in the United States.* New York: Negro University Press, 1918.

____ *Race Mixture: Studies in Intermarriage and Miscegenation.* New York: Negro University Press, 1969.

Robbe-Grillet, Alain. *Pour un nouveau roman.* Paris: Gallimard, 1963.

Rogers, Katherine M. *The Troublesome Helpmate: A History of Misogyny in Literature.* Seattle: University of Washington Press, 1966.

Roland, Charles P. *The Improbable Era: The South since World War II.* Lexington: University of Kentucky Press, 1976.

Rowan, Carl. *South of Freedom.* New York: Knopf, 1952.

Rubin, Louis D., Jr. "The Image of the South." *The Lasting South: Fourteen Southerners Look at Their Home.* Edited by Louis D. Rubin, Jr. and J. J. Kilpatrick. Chicago: Renery, 1957. 1-15.

____ "The South and the Faraway Country."*Virginia Quarterly Review* 38 (Spring 1962): 444-59.

Rubin, Morton. *Plantation Country.* Chapel Hill: University of North Carolina Press, 1951.

Santiago, Luciano P. R. *The Children of Oedipus: Brother-Sister Incest in Psychiatry, Literature, History and Mythology.* New York: Libra, 1973.

Santayana, George. *Winds of Doctrine.* New York: Scribner's, 1931.

Saxton, Lloyd. *The Individual, Marriage and the Family.* Belmont: Wadsworth, 1977.

Schultz, Christian. *Travels on an Inland Voyage through the States of New York, Pennsylvania, Virginia, Ohio, Kentucky, and Tennessee, and through the Territories of Indiana, Louisiana, Mississippi, and New Orleans, Performed in the Years 1807 and 1808.* 2 vols. New York: Riley, 1810.

Scott, Ann Firor. *The Southern Lady: From Pedestal to Politics 1830-1930.* Chicago: University of Chicago Press, 1970.

Sickels, Robert J. *Race, Marriage and the Law.* Albuquerque: University of New Mexico Press, 1972.

Silver, James W. *The Closed Society.* New York: Harcourt, 1964.

Simkins, Francis Butler. *A History of the South.* New York: Knopf, 1953.

Skaggs, Merrel Macquire. *The Folk of Southern Fiction.* Athens: University of Georgia Press, 1972.

Slotkin, Richard. *Regeneration through Violence: The Mythology of the American Frontier 1600-1860.* Middletown: Wesleyan University Press, 1973.

Smedes, Susan Dabney. *Memorials of a Southern Planter.* Baltimore: Cushings, 1887.

Smith, Ethel M. *Toward Equal Rights for Men and Women.* Washington: Com. on Legal Status of Women, Nat. League of Women Voters, 1929.

Smith, Lillian. *Killers of the Dream.* New York: Norton, 1961.

Smith, Maxwell. "A Visit of Giono." *Books Abroad* 33 (Winter 1959): 23-26.

Stadiem, William. *A Class by Themselves: The Untold Story of the Great Southern Families.* New York: Crown, 1980.

Stampp, Kenneth M. *The Peculiar Institution: Slavery in the Ante-Bellum South.* New York: Vintage, 1956.

Starke, Catherine. *Black Portraiture in American Fiction: Stock Characters, Archetypes, and Individuals.* New York: Basic, 1971.

Stonequist, Everett V. *The Marginal Man: A Study in Personality and Cultural Conflict.* New York: Russell, 1937.

Strong, Bryan. "Toward a History of the Experimental Family: Sex and Incest in the Nineteenth-Century Family." *The Journal of Marriage and the Family* 35·3 (Aug. 1973): 457-66.

Styron, William. *Lie Down in Darkness.* Indianapolis: Bobbs, 1951.

Styron, William. *Set This House on Fire.* New York: Signet, 1961.

Sydnor, Charles Sackett. *Slavery in Mississippi.* New York: Appleton, 1933.

Tate, Allen. "The New Provincialism." *Essays of Four Decades.* London: Oxford University Press, 1968. 535-46.

Taylor, Arnold H. *Travail and Triumph: Black Life and Culture in the South since the Civil War.* Westport: Greenwood, 1976.

The United States Women's Bureau. *The Legal Status of Women in the United States.* Washington: Nat. League of Women's Voters, 1945.

Thompson, Edgar T. *Plantation Societies, Race Relations, and the South: The Regimentation of Populations.* Durham: Duke University Press, 1975.

Tinker, Edward Larocque. *Creole City: Its Past and Its People.* New York: Longmans, 1953.

Tischler, Nancy M. *Black Masks: Negro Characters in Modern Southern Fiction.* University Park: Pennsylvania State University Press, 1969.

Toman, Walter. *Family Constellation.* New York: Springer, 1961.

Tower, Philo, Rev. *Slavery Unmasked.* Rochester: Advertiser, 1856.

Woodward, Comer Vann . *The Burden of Southern History.* Baton Rouge: Louisiana State University Press, 1960.

Warren, Robert Penn. *All the King's Men.* New York: Bantam, 1974.

_____ *At Heaven's Gate.* New York: Harcourt, 1943.

_____ *Band of Angels.* New York: Random House, 1955.

_____ *Night Rider.* Boston: Houghton, 1939.

_____ *Segregation: The Inner Conflict of the South.* New York: Random House, 1956.

_____ "T. S. Stribling: a Paragraph in the History of Critical Realism." *American Review* 2 (Nov. 1933 - Mar. 1934): 483-86.

Weatherby, W. J. *Love in the Shadows.* New York: Stein, 1966.

Weaver, Herbert. *Mississippi Farmers 1850-1960.* Gloucester: Smith, 1968.

Weinberg, Samuel Kirson. *Incest Behavior.* New York: Citadel, 1963.

Welty, Eudora. *Delta Wedding.* New York: Harcourt, 1946.

_____ *The Bride of Innisfallen and Other Stories.* New York: Harcourt, 1955.

_____ *The Robber Bridegroom.* New York: Atheneum, 1963.

_____ Entrevue. *Mississippi Writers Talking.* Edited by John Griffin Jones. Jackson: University of Mississippi Press, 1983. 3-35.

Wharton, Vernon Lane. *The Negro in Mississippi 1865-1890.* New York: Harper, 1965.

White, Deborah Gray. *Ar'n't I a Woman?: Female Slaves in the Plantation in the South.* New York: Norton, 1985.

White, Ellington. "The View from the Window." *The Lasting South: Fourteen Southerners Look at Their Home.* Edited by Louis D. Rubin, Jr. and J. J. Kilpatrick. Chicago: Renery, 1957. 163-70.

Winch, Robert F., et al., eds. *Selected Studies in Marriage.* Rev. ed. New York: Holt, 1962.

Wolfe, Thomas. *Look Homeward, Angel: A Story of a Buried Life.* New York: Scribner's, 1957.

_____ *The Hills Beyond.* Garden City: Sun, 1943.

_____ *The Story of a Novel.* New York: Scribner's, 1964.

_____ *You, Can't Go Home Again.* New York: Harper, 1940.

Woofter, T. J. "Southern Children and the Family Security." *In Search of the Regional Balance of America.*" Edited by Howard W. Odum and Katherine Jocher. Chapel Hill: University of North Carolina Press, 1945. 124-33.

Wynes, Charles E., ed. *The Negro Church and the South.* University: University of Alabama Press, 1965.

Zinn, Howard. *The Southern Mystique.* New York: Simon, 1972.